Data Analysis and Related Applications 5

Big Data, Artificial Intelligence and Data Analysis Set

coordinated by
Jacques Janssen

Volume 13

Data Analysis and Related Applications 5

Models, Methods and Techniques

Edited by

Yiannis Dimotikalis
Christos H. Skiadas

iSTE

WILEY

First published 2025 in Great Britain and the United States by ISTE Ltd and John Wiley & Sons, Inc.

ISTE Ltd
27-37 St George's Road
London SW19 4EU
UK

www.iste.co.uk

John Wiley & Sons, Inc.
111 River Street
Hoboken, NJ 07030
USA

www.wiley.com

Library of Congress Control Number: 2025938439

British Library Cataloguing-in-Publication Data
A CIP record for this book is available from the British Library
ISBN 978-1-83669-041-2

The manufacturer's authorized representative according to the EU General Product Safety Regulation is Wiley-VCH GmbH, Boschstr. 12, 69469 Weinheim, Germany, e-mail: Product_Safety@wiley.com.

Contents

1

Modeling/Forecasting Patient Recruitment in Multicenter Clinical Trials Using Time-dependent Models

Clinical trials in the modern era are characterized by their complexity and high costs and usually involve hundreds/thousands of patients to be recruited across multiple clinical centers in many countries, as typically it is required to achieve a rather large sample size to prove the efficiency of a particular drug.

As the imperative to enroll vast numbers of patients across multiple clinical centers has become a major challenge, an accurate forecasting of patient recruitment is one of the key factors for the operational success of clinical trials. A classic Poisson-gamma (PG) recruitment model assumes time-homogeneous recruitment rates. However, there can be potential time-trends in the recruitment driven by various factors, for example, seasonal changes and exhaustion of patients on particular treatments in some centers. Recently, a few authors have considered some extensions of the PG model to time-dependent rates under some particular assumptions. In this chapter, a natural generalization of the original PG model to a PG model with non-homogeneous time-dependent rates is introduced. Some tests on homogeneity of the rates (non-parametric using a Poisson model and parametric using a PG model) are considered. The techniques for modeling and simulation of the recruitment using time-dependent model are discussed; for re-projection of the remaining recruitment, it is proposed to use a moving window and re-estimating parameters at every interim time. The results are supported by simulation of some artificial data sets.

1.1. Introduction

Contemporary late-phase clinical trials involve hundreds or even thousands of patients that need to be recruited across multiple clinical centers in many countries,

Chapter written by Volodymyr ANISIMOV and Lucas OLIVER.

For a color version of all figures in this chapter, see www.iste.co.uk/ dimotikalis/data5.zip as typically it is required to achieve a rather large sample size to prove the efficiency of a particular drug. Citing Ken Getz, director, Tufts Center for Study of Drug Development, USA, patient recruitment and retention are among the greatest challenges that the clinical research enterprise faces today, and they are a major cause of drug development delays.

To address these challenges, novel approaches and predictive analytic techniques are required for efficient data analysis, monitoring and decision-making.

Let us consider typical multicenter clinical trials used in the pharmaceutical industry where the patients are recruited by many clinical centers in different countries and then randomized to different treatments.

Using Poisson models for modeling patient recruitment in clinical trials is a well-accepted approach. Several papers use Poisson processes in different clinical centers with fixed recruitment rates (Carter et al. (2005); Senn (1997, 1998)).

However, in real trials, different centers typically have different capacity and productivity, and the recruitment rates vary. To model this variation, Anisimov and Fedorov (2007) introduced a Poisson-gamma (PG) model, where the patient arrival is modeled using Poisson processes with some rates and the variation in rates in different centers is modeled using a gamma distribution.

This model can be described in the framework of the empirical Bayesian approach where the prior distribution of the rates is a gamma distribution with parameters that are evaluated either using historical data or data provided by study investigators. In Anisimov and Fedorov (2007), a maximum likelihood technique was proposed for estimating the parameters of the rates and the Bayesian technique for adjusting the posterior distribution of the rates at any interim time using recruitment data in the individual centers. Various applications to real trials are considered in Anisimov and Fedorov (2007), Anisimov et al. (2007) and Anisimov (2011a).

This technique was developed further to account for random delays and the closure of clinical centers (Anisimov (2011a, 2020)) and for modeling events in event-driven trials (oncology) (Anisimov (2011b, 2020); Anisimov et al. (2022)).

Note that independently, Gajewski et al. (2008) later considered a similar approach to modeling recruitment as a Poisson process with gamma distributed rate, however their model is applicable to only one clinical center.

The PG model was also used in Mijoule et al. (2012) to consider some extensions related to other distributions of the recruitment rates and sensitivity analysis, in Minois et al. (2017) to evaluate the duration of recruitment process when historical trials are available, and in Bakhshi et al. (2013) for the evaluation of parameters of a PG model using meta-analytic techniques for historic trials. A survey on using mixed Poisson models is provided in Anisimov (2016).

It is also worth mentioning the recent investigations devoted to centralized statistical monitoring and forecasting recruitment performance and also forecasting patient recruitment under various restrictions and creating an optimal cost-efficient recruitment design (Anisimov and Austin (2020, 2022, 2023); Anisimov (2023)).

There are also other approaches to recruitment modeling described in the literature; however, they mainly deal with the analysis of the global recruitment and therefore have some limitations. These approaches typically require rather large number of centes and patients and cannot be applied to predicting recruitment on center/country level (see survey papers by Barnard et al. (2010), Heitjan et al. (2015) and Gkioni et al. (2019)).

Currently, the originally developed PG model (Anisimov and Fedorov (2007); Anisimov (2011a)) has gained world-wide recognition and in some recent papers is now called "one of the most popular techniques" and an "industry-standard" model.

This model assumes that patient recruitment rates do not change over time. However, in real trials there can be some time-trends, seasonable changes, and recruitment can change in some countries over time due to different reasons, for example, a slowdown in recruitment near the end of a trial.

Therefore, to capture these situations, in some recent papers (Lan et al. (2019); Best et al. (2022); Perperoglou et al. (2023); Turchetta et al. (2023); Urbas et al. (2022)), the standard PG model was extended to the cases where the recruitment rates can be time dependent.

Lan et al. (2019) proposed a non-homogeneous Poisson process model that allows for staggered center activation and heterogeneity within centers modeled by a gamma distribution and assuming that after a period of steady recruitment, the center mean recruitment rate gradually declines as a negative exponential with some coefficient. They calculated the posterior distribution and considered some applications to real trials. Urbas et al. (2022) proposed a more general time-dependent PG model that allows for a wider range of recruitment rate functions. The model is fitted using a maximum likelihood approach and is used to select the best model among a set of candidate models. Perperoglou et al. (2023) compared the performance of the standard PG model to two time-dependent models: the models proposed in Lan et al. (2019) and Urbas et al. (2022). The study found that the time-dependent models outperformed the PG model in terms of prediction accuracy, especially in trials with time-varying recruitment rates. Best et al. (2022) considered a standard PG model as the starting point and developed a more flexible version that introduces variation in rates over time as a function of COVID-19-dependent covariates, which is implemented in a fully

Bayesian probabilistic framework. Turchetta et al. (2023) proposed a time-dependent PG model allowing recruitment rates to vary over time through B-splines that is fitted using a Bayesian approach. The model was evaluated in a simulation study and found to perform well in a variety of scenarios.

All five papers above contribute to the advancement of recruitment modeling in multicenter clinical trials by extending the standard time-homogeneous PG model to accommodate time-dependent recruitment rates.

The flexibility of the original PG model allows a rather natural extension to model time-dependent rates on the center level. However, the main question here is: What type of time-dependence to use, especially, how to detect the change time-point of the behavior of the rates, and how to test this dependence in real trials? Thus, the choice of a suitable time-dependent model is trial specific.

In this chapter, the authors consider a natural generalization of a PG model to a time-dependent model using a general framework of a standard PG model, which is similar to the way considered in Urbas et al. (2022). The basic methodology of using a PG model with time-dependent rates is developed by the first author in Anisimov (2024). This chapter extends some results of Anisimov (2024); in particular, a new PG criterion is investigated for testing the recruitment rates for homogeneity. In Anisimov (2024), a novel analytic methodology is also proposed for modeling/forecasting patient recruitment using the recent results in Anisimov and Austin (2020) about a PG approximation of the sums of PG processes in different centers that can be applied to modeling recruitment even in not so large countries/regions, which is also described in this chapter for completeness of presentation.

Note that this analytic methodology is not reflected in the five papers mentioned above but is crucial, as the country process under general assumptions is not a PG process and also for a small number of centers a normal approximation in general cannot be applied. Therefore, for using analytic tools for modeling/forecasting patient recruitment on different levels instead of Monte Carlo simulation, we need to develop some analytic approximations of country processes for time-dependent models similar to Anisimov and Austin (2020), as well.

The first author also proposes a fast algorithm of simulation of the time-dependent model in R using discrete event simulation (section 1.3.2) that is used in applications, and has developed a non-parametric criterion using Poisson assumptions for testing the recruitment rates for time dependence (section 1.4.1) that is considered in Anisimov (2024), as well.

The new parametric criterion for testing rates for time-dependence using assumptions of a PG model (section 1.4.3) is analyzed by the second author who has also run many simulated scenarios using the Monte Carlo technique to test the applicability of a non-homogeneous PG model and compare with using a classic one. These results are briefly discussed in section 1.5.

1.2. Poisson-gamma model with time-dependent rates

Consider a multicenter clinical trial, which is designed to recruit n patients by N clinical centers. A standard PG model (Anisimov and Fedorov (2007); Anisimov (2011a)) assumes that the recruitment rates in different centers are modeled as independent gamma distributed random variables with some parameters that do not depend on time. Thus, the recruitment process in any interval where the center is active follows a time-homogeneous mixed Poisson process with gamma distributed rate (PG process).

First consider some definitions: denote by $\Pi(a)$ a Poisson random variable with parameter a, and by $\Pi_a(t)$ an ordinary homogeneous Poisson process with rate a. This means, for any $t > 0$:

$$\mathbf{P}(\Pi_a(t) = k) = e^{-at}\frac{(at)^k}{k!}, \quad k = 0, 1, ...$$

Also denote by $\mathrm{Ga}(\alpha, \beta)$ a gamma distributed variable with parameters (α, β) (shape and rate) and probability density function:

$$f(x, \alpha, \beta) = \frac{e^{-\beta x}\beta^{\alpha}x^{\alpha-1}}{\Gamma(\alpha)}, \quad x > 0, \qquad [1.1]$$

where $\Gamma(\alpha) = \int_0^{\infty} e^{-x}x^{\alpha-1}dx$ is a gamma function.

1.2.1. *The case of homogeneous rates*

Consider first the basic definitions used in a standard PG model. Let $\Pi_\lambda(t)$ be a doubly stochastic Poisson process where $\lambda = \mathrm{Ga}(\alpha, \beta)$. According to terminology in Bernardo and Smith (2004), this is a PG process with parameters (t, α, β). We denote it as $\mathrm{PG}(t, \alpha, \beta)$ to reflect the dependence on (α, β). Then for any $k = 0, 1, ..,$:

$$\mathbf{P}(\mathrm{PG}(t, \alpha, \beta) = k) = \frac{\Gamma(\alpha + k)}{k!\,\Gamma(\alpha)}\,\frac{t^k\beta^{\alpha}}{(\beta + t)^{\alpha+k}}. \qquad [1.2]$$

For $t = 1$, $\Pi_\lambda(1)$ has the same distribution as $\Pi(\lambda)$, which is a PG variable with parameters (α, β). For this case, we omit $t = 1$ and use the notation $\mathrm{PG}(\alpha, \beta)$ instead of $\mathrm{PG}(1, \alpha, \beta)$.

Note that $\Pi_\lambda(t)$ has a negative binomial distribution and for any $\alpha > 0, \beta > 0$, $t > 0$, the following relation is true: for any $k = 0, 1, ..$:

$$\mathbf{P}(\mathrm{PG}(t, \alpha, \beta) = k) = \mathbf{P}(\mathrm{Nb}(\alpha, \beta/(\beta + t)) = k) \quad [1.3]$$

where $\mathrm{Nb}(\alpha, p)$ denotes a random variable that has a negative binomial distribution with size α and probability p:

$$\mathbf{P}(\mathrm{Nb}(\alpha, p) = k) = \frac{\Gamma(\alpha + k)}{k!\,\Gamma(\alpha)} p^\alpha (1-p)^k, \ k = 0, 1, ..$$

This relation is useful in calculations of a PG distribution using R, as there are standard functions pnbinom() and dnbinom().

Now consider modeling recruitment. We denote by $n_i(t)$ the recruitment process in center i (the number of patients recruited in time interval $[0, t]$), and by $n(I_j, t)$ the recruitment process in some region with the set I_j of N_j clinical centers. Also denote by u_i the date of initiation of center i.

Assume that the recruitment process in center i during an active recruitment stage follows a homogeneous PG process with rate λ_i, which has a gamma distribution with parameters (α_i, β_i). Then the mean rate m_i and the variance s_i^2 are calculated as $m_i = \alpha_i/\beta_i$, $s_i^2 = \alpha_i/\beta_i^2$. Correspondingly, the instantaneous rate at time t is $\lambda_i(t) = \lambda_i \chi(u_i < t)$, where $\chi(A)$ is the indicator function of the event A.

Consider a more convenient representation via a cumulative rate. We denote $x(t, u) = \max(0, t - u)$ (the duration of active recruitment at time t for a center activated at time u). So, if center i is active at time $t > u_i$, then $x(t, u_i) = t - u_i$.

Then the cumulative rate of the process $n_i(t)$ is $\Lambda_i(t, u_i) = \lambda_i x(t, u_i)$. This means, if $\lambda_i = \mathrm{Ga}(\alpha_i, \beta_i)$, $n_i(t)$ is a PG process with parameters $(x(t, u_i), \alpha_i, \beta_i)$, and the distribution of $n_i(t)$ can be calculated using [1.2], where in the right-hand side we should use $x(t, u_i)$ instead of t, and parameters (α_i, β_i).

Correspondingly, for any region with a subset of centers I_j, the recruitment process $n(I_j, t)$ in this region as a sum of the recruitment processes in the centers from this region is a non-homogeneous Poisson process with the instantaneous rate $\lambda(I_j, t) = \sum_{i \in I_j} \lambda_i(t)$ and, in distribution, $n(I_j, t) = \Pi(\Lambda(I_j, t))$, where the region cumulative rate has the form:

$$\Lambda(I_j, t) = \sum_{i \in I_j} \Lambda_i(t, u_i).$$

Note that in general a sum of gamma distributed variables with different parameters does not have a gamma distribution; therefore, in general, the process $n(I_j, t)$ is not a PG process. The technique for the approximation of $n(I_j, t)$ by a PG process was developed in Anisimov and Austin (2020).

1.3. Non-homogeneous PG model

Now consider an extension of the PG model to time-dependent rates.

Assume that the recruitment rates can proportionally change over time according to some non-negative function $r(t), t \geq 0$.

A realistic type of dependence can be a piece-wise linear dependence: linear increase in some initial interval, then a constant rate in some larger interval in the middle of recruitment, and then linear decrease in the last interval closer to the end of recruitment. Another opportunity can be an exponential decay starting from 1 until some proportion, for example, 50%, at the end of recruitment.

Of course, the main question can arise – how to define the form of function $r(t)$. However, this question is for separate investigation, and potentially the form of function $r(t)$ can be chosen using similar historic trials, or monitoring the data for the current study and using some extrapolations of the rate dependence up to the interim point for the remaining interval.

Assume also for simplicity that the function $r(t)$ is the same for all centers, which means that time-dependence is defined only by the duration of the recruitment in the trial. However, in general, this assumption can be relaxed and we can assume different time dependence in different regions, though regional type dependence would be harder to extract from historic trials.

Therefore, a non-homogeneous PG model can be defined as follows (Anisimov (2024)).

Assume that if a center i is active at time t, then the recruitment rate has the form

$$\lambda_i r(t) \qquad [1.4]$$

where λ_i is some baseline rate, which has a gamma distribution with parameters (α_i, β_i), and $r(t)$ is some non-negative function.

Then, if a center i is initiated at time u_i, the instantaneous rate at time t is $\lambda_i(t) = \lambda_i r(t)\chi(u_i < t)$.

Define the cumulative proportional change in the rate for center i in the interval $[a,b]$ as:

$$R_i(a,b,u_i) = \int_a^b r(x)\chi(u_i < x)\mathrm{d}x$$

In particular, if there is no change in time, $r(x) \equiv 1$, and $R_i(a,b,u_i)$ is just a duration of recruitment window in the interval $[a,b]$.

The cumulative rate for center i in the interval $[a,b]$ is $\Lambda_i(a,b,u_i) = \lambda_i R_i(a,b,u_i)$. Correspondingly, the recruitment process $n_i(t)$ in interval $[0,t]$ is again a doubly stochastic PG process with cumulative rate $\Lambda_i(0,t,u_i)$. Then:

$$\mathbf{E}[\Lambda_i(0,t,u_i)] = m_i R_i(0,t,u_i), \mathbf{Var}[\Lambda_i(0,t,u_i)] = s_i^2 R_i^2(0,t,u_i)$$

Consider now the recruitment process in some country s with the set of centers I_s. Then a country process:

$$n(I_s,t) = \sum_{i\in I_s} n_i(t)$$

has a cumulative rate

$$\Lambda(I_s,t) = \sum_{i\in I_s} \Lambda_i(0,t,u_i)$$

Note that $n(I_s,t)$ is a mixed Poisson process but in general not a PG process.

We denote the mean and variance of $\Lambda(I_s,t)$ as:

$$\begin{aligned} E(I_s,t) &= \sum_{i\in I_s} m_i R_i(0,t,u_i), \\ S^2(I_s,t) &= \sum_{i\in I_s} s_i^2 R_i^2(0,t,u_i) \end{aligned} \quad [1.5]$$

Assuming that $S^2(I_s,t) > 0$, let us introduce the variables:

$$A(I_s,t) = E^2(I_s,t)/S^2(I_s,t), B(I_s,t) = E(I_s,t)/S^2(I_s,t) \quad [1.6]$$

The following statement is an extension of the result in Anisimov and Austin (2020) to the case where the rates are gamma distributed with different parameters.

LEMMA 1.1.– *The distribution of $n(I_s, t)$ can be well approximated by the distribution of a PG random variable $PG(A(I_s, t), B(I_s, t))$.*

In Anisimov and Austin (2020), it is shown using numerical calculations that this approximation provides a very good fit even for a small number of centers, $N = 2, 3$, and with the larger number of centers the difference between the exact and approximative distributions is decreasing to a negligible value around 10^{-4} or less.

This result can be used to create the approximate values of the mean and predictive bounds for the recruitment process $n(I_s, t)$ at any time point t.

Indeed, by definition:

$$\mathbf{E}[n(I_s, t)] = E(I_s, t) \qquad [1.7]$$

and P-confidence predictive bounds can be calculated using a quantile function of the negative binomial distribution:

```
qnbinom(P,size=M2/S2,prob=M/(M+S2))
```

where at time t we set $M = E(I_s, t)$, $S2 = S^2(I_s, t)$.

To create predictions for the global recruitment, we just need to use in relation [1.5] the sum by all active centers.

This technique allows us to create analytically the predictions of the recruitment process $n(I_s, t)$ over time with mean and predictive bounds assuming that the type of time dependence, function $r(t)$, is known.

1.3.1. *Estimation at the interim stage*

The technique for estimating parameters using interim data may depend on the form of time dependence.

Using an assumption of a standard PG model (Anisimov and Fedorov (2007); Anisimov (2011a)), where it is assumed that the parameters (α_i, β_i) of the rates are the same for all centers, and also assuming that the function $r(t)$ is known, for estimating parameters (α, β) we can use the same maximum likelihood technique developed in Anisimov and Fedorov (2007) and Anisimov (2011a) where in calculations of the likelihood we need to use the values $R_i(0, t, u_i)$ instead of recruitment windows v_i. The posterior distribution of the rates can be calculated similar as in Anisimov and Fedorov (2007) and Anisimov (2011a).

If the function $r(t)$ depends on some additional parameters, then the technique of estimation will depend on the form of the function $r(t)$. In this case, we can write a likelihood expression similar to that in Anisimov and Fedorov (2007) and Anisimov (2011a) and use $2 + d$ optimization, where d is the number of parameters used in the definition of the function $r(t)$.

Note that for time-dependent models, to closely capture the dependence on time, it can be recommended to use a moving window including data only for the last several months. The choice of the length of the window is trial specific, but as a general recommendation, the number of centers and the number of patients recruited during this window should be large enough to apply a maximum likelihood technique in the framework of a PG model. In applications to late-stage clinical trials, the length of the window can be chosen as 2, 3 and 4 months.

1.3.2. *Simulation of non-homogeneous PG model*

In general, it is preferable to use an analytic technique described in section 1.3, lemma 1.1. However, there can be different restrictions on the recruitment, or it can be required to evaluate different metrics related to recruitment performance. For example, to evaluate the probability that the recruitment process will fall into some region, say, within 20% bounds from the predicted mean during a particular number of months, and it is hard to develop the analytic relations for these situations. Therefore, in these cases, Monte Carlo simulation can be the most appropriate way. In addition, simulation can also serve as a useful tool to verify different analytic approaches.

Here, we describe the technique of simulation, which is based on the discrete event simulation approach and used directly in applications.

1.3.2.1. *Algorithm of simulation using R*

Consider a trial with N centers. Assume that for a center i, the time of initiation is u_i. We denote $vecu = (u_1, .., u_N)$.

Consider also a given interval of simulation, $[0, T]$, which should be large enough to ensure that for nearly all simulated trajectories, the stopping point will be reached. T can be evaluated as the upper predictive bound of the recruitment time using some analytic expressions, similar to Anisimov (2011a).

Define the vectors of parameters:

$veca = (\alpha_1, .., \alpha_N)$, $vecb = (\beta_1, .., \beta_N)$.

1) Create a sequence $vecR = r(1 : T)$ using function $r(t)$.

2) Generate a vector of gamma distributed rates in centers:

$vecla$ = rgamma(N, shape = $veca$, rate = $vecb$)

3) Define an output matrix for one run:

$outmat$ = matrix(nrow = N, ncol = T)

4) Use a loop by the number of centers N:

- For a center i, create the vector

$veclaik = vecla[i]*vecR$

of the rates in center i for each day.

- Update this vector by setting

$veclaik[k] = 0$ for $k \leq vecu[i]$

- Simulate the numbers of enrolled patients in each day $k, k = 1, .., T$ using vector of rates and Poisson distribution:

$vecptsday$ = rpois(T, $veclaik$)

- Use cumsum($vecptsday$) to generate a cumulative number of patients in center i over time;

- Save $outmat[i,]$ = cumsum($vecptsday$).

Now as the output in one simulation run, we get a matrix $outmat$ of the simulated trajectories of the recruitment in each center.

Depending on the purpose, we can use matrix calculations to calculate country or global trajectories and calculate different characteristics, for example, time to reach a total sample size and time to reach country targets.

By repeating this step many times, say, 10^4 simulation runs, we can calculate different summary statistics.

This technique works quite fast. To calculate the trajectories of the mean, median and predictive bounds for the global recruitment over time using 10^4 runs, it takes seconds for $N \leq 100$. For these cases, the predictions using analytic expressions or simulation practically coincide.

1.4. Testing the recruitment rates for homogeneity

Consider a trial with N centers initiated at different times $\{u_i, i = 1, .., N\}$ and consider during the recruitment period two disjoint intervals $[a, b]$ and $[c, d]$ (in months) where $a < b < c < d$. Define the observed number of patients in each interval $n[a, b]$ and $n[c, d]$ and denote the total number of patients $n[a, b, c, d] = n[a, b] + n[c, d]$.

For a given center, define the duration of the active recruitment window in the interval $[y, z]$ if the center is initiated at time u as the following function:

$$u(y, z, u) = \begin{cases} z - y & \text{if } u < y \\ u - y & \text{if } y \leq u < z \\ 0 & \text{if } u \geq z \end{cases} \qquad [1.8]$$

We denote by $U[a, b]$ and $U[c, d]$ the total durations of recruitment windows in each interval, which means:

$$U[a, b] = \sum_i u(a, b, u_i); \; U[c, d] = \sum_i u(c, d, u_i)$$

and put $U[a, b, c, d] = U[a, b] + U[c, d]$.

1.4.1. *Poisson-type test*

Let us propose a non-parametric test using Poisson assumptions. Consider testing the hypothesis:

$\boldsymbol{H}_0$: The mean recruitment rates in both intervals are the same.

Assume here a Poisson recruitment model.

LEMMA 1.2.– *Given the total number of patients $n([a, b, c, d])$ and hypothesis $\boldsymbol{H}_0$, the number of patients $n([a, b])$ has a binomial distribution $Bin(n([a, b, c, d]), p(a, b))$ where:*

$$p(a, b) = \frac{U[a, b]}{U[a, b, c, d]}$$

PROOF.– Under our assumptions, the number of patients $n([a, b])$ recruited in interval $[a, b]$ and the number of patients $n([c, d])$ recruited in the remaining interval $[c, d]$ are independent Poisson random variables with rates $mU[a, b]$ and $mU[c, d]$). Therefore, the proof follows from the known fact for Poisson variables. Indeed, consider two independent Poisson variables $\Pi(a_1)$ and $\Pi(a_2)$ with parameters a_1 and a_2. Then the conditional distribution of $\Pi(a_1)$, given that $\Pi(a_1) + \Pi(a_2) = n$, is a binomial distribution $\mathrm{Bin}(n, p)$ with $p = \frac{a_1}{a_1 + a_2}$.

1.4.2. *Criterion for testing hypothesis H_0*

Define two p-values:

Upper p-value:

$$P_{Upp}(a,b,c,d) = \mathbf{P}(\text{Bin}(n([a,b,c,d]), p(a,b)) \geq n([a,b])) \quad [1.9]$$

Low p-value:

$$P_{Low}(a,b,c,d) = \mathbf{P}(\text{Bin}(n([a,b,c,d]), p(a,b)) \leq n([a,b])) \quad [1.10]$$

Consider some small critical level, say, $\delta = 0.1$. Then:

1) if $P_{Upp}(a,b,c,d) \leq \delta$, with high probability the number of patients $n([a,b])$ is unusually large and it is likely that the mean recruitment rate in interval $[a,b]$ is larger compared to interval $[c,d]$;

2) otherwise, the mean rate in interval $[a,b]$ is smaller.

Correspondingly, we can detect intervals where the hypothesis $\boldsymbol{H_0}$ is not true. This allows us to detect the intervals with rather high or rather low recruitment rates.

Note that this criterion is non-parametric as it does not include the rate m, which is beneficial.

The proposed approach is exact, it does not require estimation of the parameters, and can be used for any number of centers and any number of recruited patients in any intervals.

As the next stage, we are coming to the following question: How many centers do we need to detect a particular proportional difference in rates with a given confidence?

1.4.2.1. *Dependence of p-values on the number of centers*

To analyze the dependence of p-values defined in [1.9] and [1.10] based on the number of centers for time-dependent model, consider a special case.

Assume that the intervals have the lengths L_1 and L_2 with the number of centers N_1 and N_2 that are active during each interval.

Suppose that the rates for each center in each interval are the same and equal to m_1 and m_2, respectively. Let us analyze the dependence of P_{Upp} on m_j, N_j and L_j. This will allow us to evaluate the number of centers needed for testing a particular difference in the rates m_1, m_2.

The number of recruited patients n_j in each interval j ($j = 1$ corresponds to $[a, b]$, $j = 2$ corresponds to $[c, d]$) is a Poisson random variable, $\pi_j = \Pi(m_j N_j L_j)$, and the expression for the upper P-value can be written as:

$$P_{Upp} = \mathbf{P}(X \geq 0) \qquad [1.11]$$

where $X = \text{Bin}(\pi_1 + \pi_2, p) - \pi_1, p = N_1 L_1/(N_1 L_1 + N_2 L_2)$.

Then, using a formula of total variance, after some algebra:

$$\mathbf{E}[X] = \frac{N_1 L_1 N_2 L_2}{N_1 L_1 + N_2 L_2}(m_2 - m_1), \mathbf{Var}[X] = \frac{N_1 L_1 N_2 L_2}{N_1 L_1 + N_2 L_2}(m_1 + m_2) \qquad [1.12]$$

As these expressions are rather large when $N_1 L_1$ and $N_2 L_2$ are large, we can use for X a normal approximation and get the relation:

$$P_{Upp} \approx \mathbf{P}\left(Z \leq \sqrt{\frac{N_1 L_1 N_2 L_2}{N_1 L_1 + N_2 L_2}} \frac{m_2 - m_1}{\sqrt{m_1 + m_2}}\right) \qquad [1.13]$$

where $Z = N(0, 1)$ is a standard normal variable. Then the relation $P_{Upp} = \delta$ can be approximated by the relation:

$$\sqrt{\frac{N_1 L_1 N_2 L_2}{N_1 L_1 + N_2 L_2}} \frac{m_2 - m_1}{\sqrt{m_1 + m_2}} = z_\delta \qquad [1.14]$$

where z_δ is a δ-quantile of a standard normal distribution.

In particular, if $N_1 = N_2 = N$, $L_1 = L_2 = L$ and $m_2 = q m_1$ for $q \in (0, 1)$:

$$N = \frac{2 z_\delta^2}{m_1 L} \cdot \frac{1 + q}{(1 - q)^2} \qquad [1.15]$$

Thus, $N = O(1/(1 - q)^2)$, and to detect small differences in rates requires many clinical centers, or we need to increase the duration of the interval L.

Consider a numerical example. Let us put $\delta = 0.1$, $m_1 = 0.04$ patients per center per day, $L = 90$ (days) and $q \in (0.5, 0.9]$. Figure 1.1 shows how many centers are required to detect the proportion in the rates q with confidence level 90% ($P_{Upp} \leq 0.1$). If q is closer to 1, the number of centers is growing as $1/(1 - q)^2$.

In Figure 1.1, analytic results based on the normal approximation are shown by a blue line and the exact results obtained by simulation by a red one. Note that both curves nearly coincide. That means, for evaluating the performance of Poisson criterion we can use analytic results based on the simple relation [1.15].

The power of a Poisson test can also be evaluated using Monte Carlo simulation. It is interesting to note that while using every value of proportion q for the number of centers calculated in Figure 1.1, simulation shows that the power varies in the range 0.7–0.73. Correspondingly, to get a larger power, for example, 80%, the number of centers should be increased. This part requires more detailed analysis and can be considered in the future research.

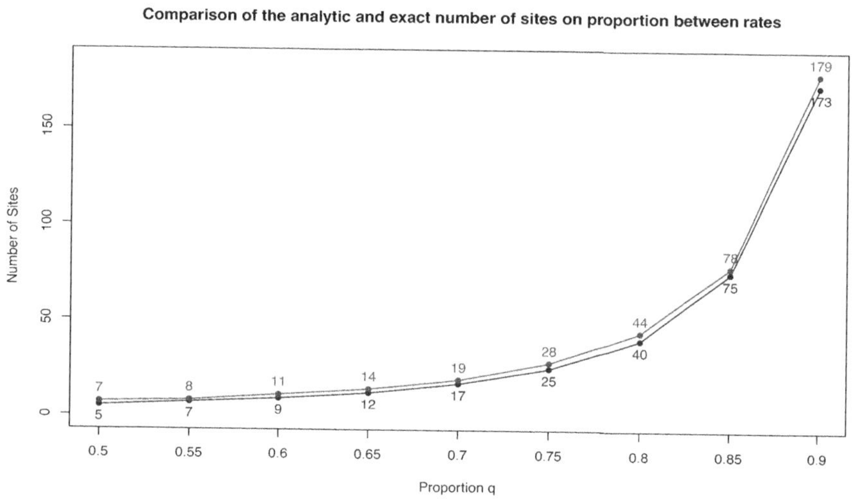

Figure 1.1. *Dependence of the number of centers N on the proportion q in the rates. Analytic results are shown by the blue line and simulation results by the red one*

1.4.3. *Poisson-gamma test*

We consider an approach for testing the hypothesis H_0 that parameters (α, β) are the same for two disjoint intervals $[a, b]$ and $[c, d]$ for a PG model. We assume there is possibly a different number of centers in these intervals.

Consider combining data in both intervals. Then, parameters (α, β) are estimated using these data with a standard ML technique. In each interval, using estimated parameters $(\hat{\alpha}, \hat{\beta})$ and active recruitment windows, we can create the predictive PG distribution.

Suppose we have some schedule of center initiations for N centers given by $U = (u_1, \ldots, u_N)$. Then we have N_1 centers active in interval $[a, b]$, and N_2 centers active in interval $[c, d]$ (not necessarily $N_1 = N_2$). For each interval, say, $[a, b]$, define the duration of the active recruitment window for center i using [1.8], as $v_i = u(a, b, u_i)$, and correspondingly for interval $[c, d]$.

We denote the pools of active centers as J_1 and J_2 for intervals $j = 1, 2$, $[a, b]$ and $[c, d]$, respectively. Then in interval j, we have the data (k_i, v_i), the number of patients enrolled and the center's active recruitment window.

Now, for every center, we combine data from intervals $j = 1, 2$ to get data $(k_i, v_i), i \in J_1 \cup J_2$, the total number of patients and total active recruitment window, which is the sum of windows on both intervals (for simplicity keep the same notation k_i, v_i for the total patients and sum of windows).

We can use these data to estimate the parameters of a PG model, for example, using ML technique and numerical optimization (assuming we have a suitable amount of data). For data of N centers, $\{(k_i, v_i), i = 1, \ldots, N\}$, the log-likelihood $\mathcal{L}(\alpha, \beta)$ has the form (Anisimov and Fedorov (2007); Anisimov (2011a)):

$$\sum_{i=1}^{N} [\ln \Gamma(\alpha + k_i) + \alpha \ln \beta - \ln \Gamma(\alpha) - (\alpha + k_i) \ln(\beta + v_i) + k_i \ln v_i - \ln(k_i!)]$$

Now, given estimated parameters $(\hat{\alpha}, \hat{\beta})$ using the union of the intervals, we denote $m = \hat{\alpha}/\hat{\beta}$, $s^2 = \hat{\alpha}/\hat{\beta}^2$.

In interval j with a pool of active centers J_j, we consider the country mean and variance of the cumulative rate. So we have:

$$E(J_j) = m \sum_{i \in J_j} v_i, \quad S^2(J_j) = s^2 \sum_{i \in J_j} v_i^2$$

Let us introduce the variables $A(J_j) = E^2(J_j)/S^2(J_j)$, $B(J_j) = E(J_j)/S^2(J_j)$. In Anisimov and Austin (2020), it was proved that the number of enrolled patients n_j in interval j can be approximated by a PG variable $\text{PG}(A(J_j), B(J_j))$ with parameters $(A(J_j), B(J_j))$, where $\text{PG}(A, B)$ is a mixed Poisson variable with the rate $\text{Ga}(A, B)$. Now we can define the upper and lower p-values in interval j as:

$$\begin{aligned} P_{Upp}(J_j) &= \mathbf{P}(\text{PG}(A(J_j), B(J_j)) \geq n_j) \\ P_{Low}(J_j) &= \mathbf{P}(\text{PG}(A(J_j), B(J_j)) \leq n_j) \end{aligned} \qquad [1.16]$$

where $n_j = \sum_{i \in J_j} k_i$ is the total number of patients recruited in the pool of centers J_j in corresponding interval j.

To calculate these values, we can use the cumulative probability function of a negative binomial distribution in R via the relation:

$$\mathbf{P}(\text{PG}(A(J_j), B(J_j)) \leq k) =$$

$$\text{pnbinom}\left(k, \text{size} = \frac{E^2(J_j)}{S^2(J_j)}, \text{prob} = \frac{E(J_j)}{E(J_j) + S^2(J_j)}\right)$$

1.4.3.1. *Some analytic considerations*

To analyze the dependence on the number of centers, consider a particular case when all centers are active during the whole intervals. Define by L_1 and L_2 the durations of intervals. Then $E(J_j) = mN_jL_j$, $S^2(J_j) = s^2N_jL_j^2$, so $A(J_j) = \frac{m^2}{s^2}N_j$, $B(J_j) = \frac{m}{s^2L_j}$, and:

$$\begin{aligned} P_{Upp}(J_j) &= \mathbf{P}\left(\text{PG}\left(\frac{m^2}{s^2}N_j, \frac{m}{s^2L_j}\right) \geq n_j\right) \\ P_{Low}(J_j) &= \mathbf{P}\left(\text{PG}\left(\frac{m^2}{s^2}N_j, \frac{m}{s^2L_j}\right) \leq n_j\right) \end{aligned} \quad [1.17]$$

Now consider the behavior of values in [1.17] when hypothesis H_0 is not true. That means we may have different parameters of a PG model (m_j, s_j^2) in different intervals. Note that the parameters (m, s^2) in the relations above are estimated using data in the union of intervals assuming H_0. Now, as $\mathbf{E}[\Pi_\lambda(t)] = \mathbf{E}[\lambda]t$, using the method of moments estimates, approximately:

$$m \approx \frac{n_1 + n_2}{N_1L_1 + N_2L_2} = \frac{n_1}{N_1L_1}\frac{N_1L_1}{N_1L_1 + N_2L_2} + \frac{n_2}{N_2L_2}\frac{N_2L_2}{N_1L_1 + N_2L_2} \quad [1.18]$$

Note that n_j is a PG variable with parameters (A_j, B_j), where $A_j = \frac{m_j^2}{s_j^2}N_j$, $B_j = \frac{m_j}{s_j^2L_j}$ and $\mathbf{E}[n_j] = m_jN_jL_j$. Then, $m_j \approx \frac{n_j}{N_jL_j}$, and from [1.18]:

$$m \approx m_1\frac{N_1L_1}{N_1L_1 + N_2L_2} + m_2\frac{N_2L_2}{N_1L_1 + N_2L_2} \quad [1.19]$$

So, if $m_1 > m_2$, then the estimated value m using a union of intervals satisfies the relation $m_1 > m > m_2$.

However, under H_0, $\mathbf{E}[\mathrm{PG}(A(J_j), B(J_j))] = mN_jL_j$. Thus, if $j = 1$ in [1.17] for P_{Upp}, using the means of the left- and right-hand side parts under the sign of probability we have:

$$\mathbf{E}[\mathrm{PG}(A(J_1), B(J_1))] = mN_1L_1 < \mathbf{E}[n_1] = m_1N_1L_1.$$

Thus, as $N_1 \to \infty$,$N_2 \to \infty$, the right-hand side has a higher order of tendency to ∞, thus, $P_{Upp} \to 0$, and we can use this criterion to detect the case when $m_1 > m_2$.

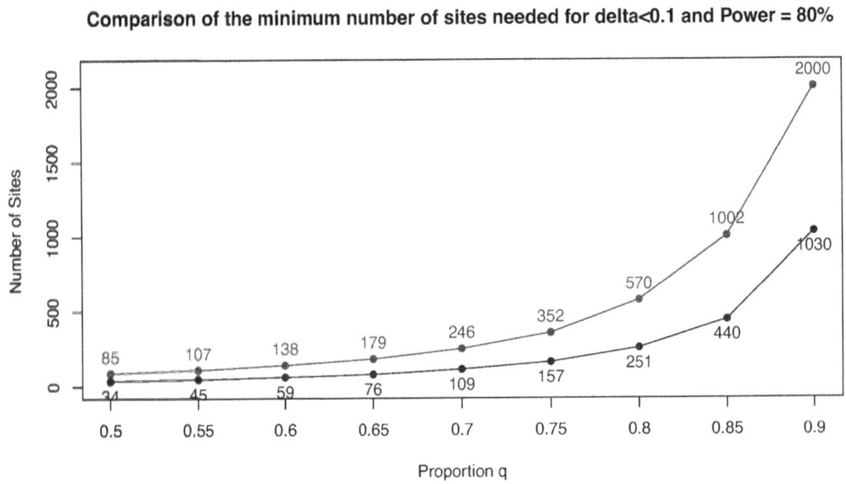

Figure 1.2. *Dependence of the number of centers N on the proportion q in the rates evaluated by using simulation. Minimal N to reach $P_{Upp} \leq 0.1$ is shown in blue and to reach the Power = 80% in red*

1.4.3.2. *Simulation using PG test*

We can again consider a simplified scenario of two intervals of equal length $L = 90$, with centers active for the whole intervals, and $N_1 = N_2 = N$. Consider also $\delta = 0.1$, rate in interval 1 as $m_1 = 0.04$ and proportion q with rate $m_2 = qm_1$ in interval 2. Using Monte Carlo simulation, we can evaluate the minimal number of centers N needed to detect the change in the rate with confidence 90% ($P_{Upp} \leq 0.1$). We can also look at the minimal number such that the power of the test is $\geq 80\%$. Figure 1.2 shows the results obtained by simulation using 10^4 runs.

As this test involves estimating parameters, it can be oriented to trials with quite a large number of centers and patients recruited. The properties of this test can be evaluated using Monte Carlo simulation. Correspondingly, to detect the proportional difference in the mean rates, more centers are required compared to the Poisson test.

Note that the Poisson test is more conservative as the random variation in the number of recruited patients is larger for a PG model. Therefore, it can be the case that the Poisson test shows time-dependence, but in reality this is just explained by random fluctuations. Therefore, in this case, it is recommended to apply a PG test as the next step. However, if the Poisson test does not show time-dependence, there is no need to use a PG test in addition.

1.5. Implementations

To verify how the technique for modeling and forecasting non-homogeneous patient recruitment in clinical trials is working, different case studies were considered using artificial data and exhaustive Monte Carlo simulation.

At the initial stage when we only have planned rates and some schedule of center initiation, a few specific forms of function $r(t)$ including piece-wise linear dependence and exponential decay over time were considered. Recruitment was simulated using the technique proposed in section 1.3.2 and prediction of the recruitment was created using the analytic technique proposed in section 1.3. The results show a perfect coincidence of the analytically calculated mean and predictive bounds with the results of simulation even for not so large number of clinical centers.

At the interim stage, first it is recommended to test the recruitment rates on time-dependence using two previous time-intervals and the developed Poisson and PG criteria. If the tests do not show any time-dependence, for predicting future recruitment we can use a standard PG model and the techniques developed in Anisimov (2011a).

However, if the tests show time-dependence, there can be different options. One way can be to use a window of the most recent data, for example, 3 months, and create predictions using the same technique as in Anisimov (2011a). In this case, the recruitment rates will use only the latest 3 months of data and will be adjusted to the time-trend by repeating this procedure at every interim time in the future. Results from simulation show that when rates change monotonically, this approach is an improvement over the techniques in Anisimov (2011a).

Another more advanced opportunity can be to assume some particular time-dependence, say, linear or exponential function $r(t)$. Then, we can estimate the parameters of the rates and the function $r(t)$ using data in the moving window and maximum likelihood technique, and then use these parameters for predicting future recruitment using the analytic technique proposed in section 1.3.

The results of simulation of several scenarios show that if the rate changes steadily over time (linear or exponential increase/decrease), both approaches show improved results compared to using a standard PG model, where the second approach also outperforms the first one.

1.6. Acknowledgment

The authors would like to express their sincere gratitude to Matt Austin, David Edwards, Behzad Beheshti and the whole Data Science Team at the Center for Design & Analysis, Amgen for the constant and useful discussions on forecasting patient recruitment in multicenter clinical trials.

1.7. References

Anisimov, V. (2011a). Statistical modeling of clinical trials (recruitment and randomization). *Communications in Statistics – Theory and Methods*, 40(19–20), 3684–3699.

Anisimov, V. (2011b). Predictive event modelling in multicentre clinical trials with waiting time to response. *Pharmaceutical Statistics*, 10(6), 517–522.

Anisimov, V. (2016). Discussion on the paper "Real-time prediction of clinical trial enrollment and event counts: A review" by D.F. Heitjan et al. *Contemporary Clinical Trials*, 40, 7–10.

Anisimov, V. (2020). Modern analytic techniques for predictive modelling of clinical trial operations. In *Quantitative Methods in Pharmaceutical Research and Development: Concepts and Applications*, Marchenko, O. and Katenka, N. (eds). Springer, New York.

Anisimov, V. (2023). An analytic methodology for forecasting patient enrolment performance in multicentre clinical trials. In *ICoMS '23: Proceedings of the 2023 6th International Conference on Mathematics and Statistics*, 14–16 July, Leipzig. ACM, New York.

Anisimov, V. (2024). Modelling/forecasting patient recruitment in clinical trials using Poisson-gamma model with time-dependent rates. In *ICoMS '24: Proceedings of the 2024 7th International Conference on Mathematics and Statistics*, 23–25 June, Amarante. ACM, New York.

Anisimov, V. and Austin, M. (2020). Centralized statistical monitoring of clinical trial enrollment performance. *Communications in Statistics – Case Studies and Data Analysis*, 6(4), 392–410.

Anisimov, V. and Austin, M. (2022). Modeling restricted enrollment and optimal cost-efficient design in multicenter clinical trials. *arXiv*. doi: 10.48550/arXiv.2212.12930.

Anisimov, V. and Austin, M. (2023). Forecasting and optimizing patient enrolment in clinical trials under various restrictions. In *Stochastic Processes, Statistical Methods, and Engineering Mathematics*. Springer, New York.

Anisimov, V. and Fedorov, V. (2007). Modelling, prediction and adaptive adjustment of recruitment in multicentre trials. *Statistics in Medicine*, 26(27), 4958–4975.

Anisimov, V., Downing, D., Fedorov, V. (2007). Recruitment in multicentre trials: Prediction and adjustment. In *mODa 8 – Advances in Model-Oriented Design and Analysis*. Springer, New York.

Anisimov, V., Gormley, S., Baverstock, R., Kineza, C. (2022). Predicting event counts in event-driven clinical trials accounting for cure and ongoing recruitment. In *Data Analysis and Related Applications 2: Multivariate, Health and Demographic Data Analysis*, Zafeiris, K.N., Skiadas, C.H., Dimotikalis, Y., Karagrigoriou, A., Karagrigoriou-Vonta, C. (eds). ISTE Ltd, London and John Wiley & Sons, New York.

Bakhshi, A., Senn, S., Phillips, A. (2013). Some issues in predicting patient recruitment in multi-centre clinical trials. *Statistics in Medicine*, 32(30), 5458–5468.

Barnard, K.D., Dent, L., Cook, A. (2010). A systematic review of models to predict recruitment to multicentre clinical trials. *BMC Medical Research Methodology*, 10, 63.

Bernardo, J.M. and Smith, A.F.M. (2004). *Bayesian Theory*. John Wiley & Sons, Hoboken, NJ.

Best, N., Perevozskaya, I., Lunn, D., Archer, G., Euesden, J., Fillmore, C., Sherina, V., Thompson, D., Zwierzyna, M. (2022). Predicting the COVID-19 pandemic impact on clinical trial recruitment. *Statistics in Biopharmaceutical Research*, 14(1), 67–79.

Carter, R.E., Sonne, S.C., Brady, K.T. (2005). Practical considerations for estimating clinical trial accrual periods: Application to a multi-center effectiveness study. *BMC Medical Research Methodology*, 5, 11–15.

Gajewski, B.J., Simon, S.D., Carlson, S.E. (2008). Predicting accrual in clinical trials with Bayesian posterior predictive distributions. *Statistics in Medicine*, 27, 2328–2340.

Gkioni, E., Riusd, R., Dodda, S., Gamblea, C. (2019). A systematic review describes models for recruitment prediction at the design stage of a clinical trial. *Journal of Clinical Epidemiology*, 115, 141–149.

Heitjan, D.F., Ge, Z., Ying, G.S. (2015). Real-time prediction of clinical trial enrollment and event counts: A review. *Contemporary Clinical Trials*, 45(Part A), 26–33.

Lan, Y., Tang, G., Heitjan, D.F. (2019). Statistical modeling and prediction of clinical trial recruitment. *Statistics in Medicine*, 38(6), 945–955.

Mijoule, G., Savy, S., Savy, N. (2012). Models for patients' recruitment in clinical trials and sensitivity analysis. *Statistics in Medicine*, 31(16), 1655–1674.

Minois, M.N., Lauwers-Cances, V., Savy, S., Attal, M., Andrieua, S., Anisimov, V., Savy, N. (2017). Using Poisson-gamma model to evaluate the duration of recruitment process when historical trials are available. *Statistics in Medicine*, 36(23), 3605–3620.

Perperoglou, A., Zhang, Y., Kipourou, D.-K. (2023). Modeling time-varying recruitment rates in multicenter clinical trials. *Biometrical Journal*, 65(6), 1–12.

Senn, S. (1997). *Statistical Issues in Drug Development*. Wiley, Chichester.

Senn, S. (1998). Some controversies in planning and analysis multi-center trials. *Statistics in Medicine*, 17, 1753–1756.

Turchetta, A., Savy, N., Stephens, D.A., Moodie, E.E.M., Klein, M.B. (2023). A time-dependent Poisson-Gamma model for recruitment forecasting in multicenter studies. *Statistics in Medicine*, 42, 4193–4206.

Urbas, S., Sherlock, C., Metcalfe, P. (2022). Interim recruitment prediction for multi-center clinical trials. *Biostatistics*, 85–506.

2

Forecasting the Next Megacycle of the Economy

The year 2024 has been the most important year of this century since it marked the beginning of new changes that shook the world. Never before has the world seen such a rapid pace of change. The next economic megacycle of the economy began in 2024. During the stagnation that will follow in the next 28 years, 2024–2052, humanity will discover and apply new technologies that, when widely disseminated into every business and every household, will lead to a new mega cycle of economic growth throughout the years 2052–2080. New technologies such as artificial intelligence (AI), 3D printing, new materials technologies, biotechnology and quantum computing will transform economies and societies in the coming decades. Some of these new technologies will enable the widespread deployment and integration into the global production infrastructure of the cheap, clean and inexhaustible fuel for nuclear fusion that will emerge in the 2040s, which, in turn, will surpass oil, which had been the dominant cheap source during the 1940–1968 upward cycle, and surpassed cheap coal from 1884 to 1912. New technologies increase productivity. The innovations thus far have increased our muscle strength. New innovations in AI will massively increase intellectual capabilities and increase productivity. With cheap energy and productivity growth, there will be growth in states and decent survival of households and businesses until the end of the next economic cycle in 2080.

2.1. Introduction

History is often misperceived as the study of the past, a collection of events, dates and personalities. However, a deeper understanding reveals that history is not simply a retrospective narrative, but the study of dynamic processes; of change itself. The fundamental purpose of historical analysis is to observe how systems evolve; how societies, economies, and technologies transform over time; and, critically, to identify the mechanisms behind these transformations. As we face the

Chapter written by George S. ATSALAKIS and Ioanna ATSALAKI.

most rapid and profound changes ever experienced, the study of these mechanisms has never been more important (Lo 2021). In 2024, we stand at the crossroads of such a transformative period, poised at the end of a global economic megacycle and on the dawn of a new one. Historical change, whether in political systems, economies, or technologies, does not occur in isolation. It is driven by a complex interplay of forces: economic innovations, technological breakthroughs, social shifts and geopolitical realignments. Understanding the broader patterns that govern historical shifts allows us to interpret our current moment in time and anticipate future developments. What we are witnessing today is not merely the continuation of established trends but also the exponential acceleration of change, particularly in the realms of technology and the global economy. Historically, moments of significant transition have often been precipitated by technological innovation. The Industrial Revolution, for example, fundamentally transformed not only the economy but also the very structure of society, altering the relationships among labor, capital and production. Similarly, the digital revolution of the late 20th century reshaped industries, created new markets and redefined communication and information exchange. Today, in 2024, we are at the precipice of yet another revolution, one driven by AI, automation, quantum computing and renewable energy technologies. These developments are not isolated but are deeply interconnected with the global economic system (Modis 2017; Ben-Ishai et al. 2024).

2.2. 2024: the end of an economic megacycle

The concept of economic megacycles refers to long-term patterns of expansion and contraction in the global economy. These cycles, often spanning several decades, are marked by phases of growth, saturation, crisis and realignment. Since the end of World War II, we have witnessed several such cycles, each characterized by their own distinct features: the postwar boom, the rise of globalization in the late 20th century and the technological surge brought about by the digital revolution. However, the megacycle we are currently in – one dominated by low interest rates, high debt and unprecedented central bank intervention – appears to be reaching its conclusion (Reinhart et al. 2016).

The year 2024 marks a critical juncture. The global economy is grappling with the aftermath of the Covid-19 pandemic, inflationary pressures, increasing geopolitical tensions and the growing realization that existing economic structures are unsustainable in the long term. The economic paradigms that have defined the past 30 years – globalization, free trade and monetary policy – are being questioned. In many ways, 2024 represents the tipping point, where the existing global economic system will undergo a radical transformation, potentially giving rise to new models of economic governance, monetary policy and trade relations (Hung 2022).

2.3. The role of technology in shaping the future

Technology, perhaps more than any other factor, is poised to be the primary driver of this next phase of global economic development. Innovations in AI and machine learning are revolutionizing industries, automating tasks previously thought impossible and fundamentally changing the nature of work itself. The economic consequences of this technological shift are profound. As automation becomes more widespread, traditional labor markets are being disrupted, necessitating new models of education, workforce development and income distribution (Furman and Seamans 2019).

Moreover, the energy sector is undergoing a massive transformation. The global shift toward renewable energy sources, such as solar and wind power, marked a significant departure from the fossil fuel-based economies of the past. This shift is not merely a technological one but also a geopolitical realignment, as countries that have historically dominated the energy market face new competition from nations investing heavily in renewables. This energy revolution will redefine global trade patterns, economic dependencies and geopolitical alliances (Smith Stegen 2018).

2.4. The economic consequences of the new cycle

The end of the current financial megacycle signals the need for a rethinking of economic policies. As the global economy becomes increasingly interconnected through technology, the potential for innovation-driven growth is immense. However, this new cycle will also present challenges. Rising inequality, driven by the uneven distribution of technological advancements, could exacerbate social and political tensions. Governments will need to adapt by implementing policies that ensure inclusive growth and address the needs of displaced workers in industries disrupted by technology.

Additionally, the international financial system may experience significant reforms. Central banks, which have been instrumental in stabilizing economies through unconventional monetary policies, may need to reconsider their approaches in light of inflationary pressures and unsustainable debt levels. Digital currencies, blockchain technology and decentralized finance (DeFi) platforms are also emerging as potential game changers in the way that global transactions are conducted, challenging the hegemony of traditional financial institutions (Dafermos 2024).

As we enter 2024, it becomes evident that this year marks a critical moment in the evolution of the global economy and technological landscape. The convergence of multiple forces – economic, technological and geopolitical – signals the end of the old order and the beginning of a new order. The way we manage these transitions will determine the trajectory of the coming decades. This moment requires not only an understanding of the past but also an appreciation of the mechanisms that drive historical change.

The challenges we face are immense, but so are the opportunities. Just as previous eras of technological and economic transformation have ushered in new periods of growth and prosperity, the changes occurring in 2024 could pave the way for a more resilient, equitable and innovative global economy. However, achieving this requires careful stewardship, informed by a deep understanding of historical change and the mechanisms that shape it (Henderson 2021).

2.4.1. *Presenting past megacycles*

The historical patterns of global energy consumption and economic growth have often followed nonlinear trends. One such pattern, as illustrated in Figure 2.1, deviates from the traditional logistic growth model and presents a hypothetical oscillation spanning 56-year cycles. These "megacycles" are divided into two distinct phases: a 28-year period of stagnation or recession, followed by a 28-year phase of growth. The dynamics within each phase are closely tied to technological revolutions, shifts in energy sources and transformative changes in transport infrastructure, all of which leave a lasting imprint on economic productivity (Modis 2017).

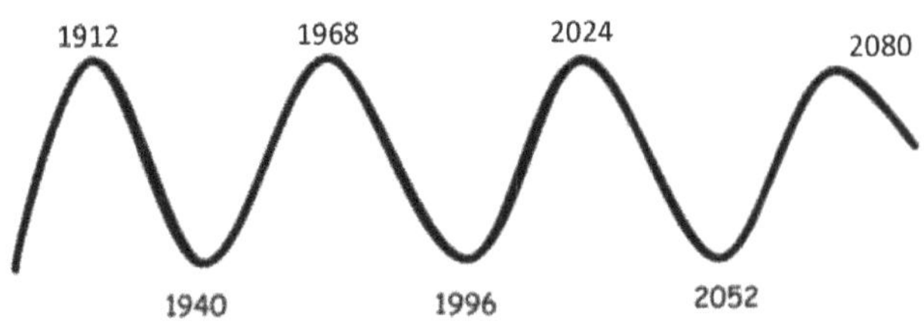

Figure 2.1. *Fifty-six-year economic cycles*

2.4.2. *The structure of economic megacycles*

Each 56-year cycle can be divided into two major phases: the first 28 years of stagnation or recession, followed by 28 years of growth. During the initial phase of stagnation, the energy consumption experiences a decreasing deviation from the logistic growth curve. This phase is typically marked by slower growth or even contractions, as the existing economic model is disrupted by new technological innovations that have yet to fully diffuse through society. These changes often result in substantial shifts in production methods, labor markets and societal structures.

The second half of the cycle is characterized by increasing deviation from the sigmoid curve, signifying robust energy consumption and economic growth. This is a result of the wide adoption and integration of the new technologies that emerged in the first phase. As these technologies spread across industries and regions, they begin to have a significant impact on productivity, ultimately sparking the growth cycle. Within each 28-year phase, the economy experiences smaller subperiods of approximately seven years, suggesting that, even within longer megacycles, shorter term fluctuations do exist (Marchetti 1986; Modis 2017).

2.4.3. *Technology as a catalyst for megacycles*

At the heart of each economic megacycle is the emergence of new key technologies. These innovations lead to the discovery of cheaper energy sources, the development of new transportation infrastructures and the introduction of novel means of production and consumption. For instance, the canal systems developed in the early 19th century gave way to railroads, which were later replaced by highways and airlines. In today's era, the rise of Maglev trains, which can reach speeds of 600 km per hour, signals the impending dawn of a new transportation infrastructure that will fuel future economic growth.

The cyclical nature of economic growth can be traced back to the introduction and diffusion of these technological advancements. It often takes several decades for a new technology to be widely adopted and to contribute meaningfully to productivity. This delay accounts for the stagnation or slower growth seen in the first half of each megacycle, whereas the rapid expansion that follows reflects the transformative power of these innovations once they have been fully integrated into the economy (Perilla Jiménez 2020).

2.4.4. *Historical patterns of energy and economic growth*

The first notable megacycle occurred between 1800 and 1856. During this period, energy production shifted from traditional sources such as wood and dried manure to water and wind power. Technological advancements, such as the use of water and wind mills, facilitated the rise of factories and new forms of transportation, such as horse-drawn carriage. As of these technologies matured and England emerged as a dominant global power, driving economic growth (Crafts et al. 1989).

The second megacycle, spanning 1856–1912, saw the widespread adoption of steam engines and coal. These technologies powered the economic expansion of the late 19th and early 20th centuries, with coal making up 50% of the energy mix by the end of this period. The United States, fueled by industrialization, became the new global economic leader (Rosenberg and Trajtenberg 2004).

From 1912 to 1968, the introduction of the internal combustion engine and the rise of oil as a major energy source drove the next economic cycle. Oil became central to the global economy, accounting for approximately 40% of the energy mix by 1968. This period also saw the rise of new powers, notably Europe and Japan, as they rebuilt their economies after World War II (Skare et al. 2021).

The recent megacycle, from 1968 to 2024, has been marked by the widespread adoption of information technology (IT) and the rise of natural gas as a significant energy source. IT revolutionized countless sectors, laying the groundwork for the digital economy that emerged in the late 20th century. The global energy mix in 2022 reflects the evolving energy landscape, with 27% of energy coming from coal, 31% from oil, 24% from natural gas and 12% from renewable sources (Modis 2017). China, fueled by rapid industrialization and technological innovation, has emerged as the dominant global economic force.

2.5. The future of economic megacycles

Since the world has approached the end of the current megacycle in 2024, new technologies and energy sources are beginning to take shape. The next megacycle may be driven by the continued rise of renewable energy, advancements in AI and the development of new transportation infrastructures such as Maglev trains. Additionally, new sectors of the economy are emerging, dominated by companies and technologies that did not exist before the 21st century, such as smartphones, social media platforms, electric vehicles and blockchain technologies (Lanteri 2021).

2.5.1. *The 2024–2080 megacycle: a new era of exponential change and growth*

The year 2024 marked the dawn of a new era that will shape the trajectory of humanity for the remainder of the century. This period, the beginning of a new 56-year megacycle, promises profound transformations across all aspects of human life, driven by exponential technological advances. Similar to previous cycles in history, 2024–2080 will witness the stagnation phase from 2024 to 2052, followed by a phase of robust economic growth from 2052 to 2080. New technologies – especially in energy, AI and biotechnology – will take center stage, just as IT and telecommunications have revolutionized the last few decades. These innovations will redefine not only economies but also geopolitics, societal structures and even the balance of global power (Ben-Ishai et al. 2024).

2.5.2. *Stagnation phase: 2024–2052*

The years following 2024 will bring about what may initially appear to be a period of economic stagnation, much like the stagnation observed in the initial phase of earlier megacycles. During this time, new technologies will begin to emerge and evolve, yet they will not immediately impact productivity on a large scale. This will be a phase of discovery and implementation, where breakthroughs in nuclear fusion, AI, quantum computing and biotechnology will begin to transform industries but will require time to fully mature and diffuse across businesses and households (Gorham 2020).

The most significant technological advancement of this period will likely be the widespread commercial use of nuclear fusion. In November 2022, the first successful test of nuclear fusion was conducted in the United States, providing a glimpse into the future of energy production. By the 2040s, nuclear fusion is expected to become a commercially viable source of cheap, clean and virtually inexhaustible energy. The global energy landscape will undergo a radical shift as fusion energy displaces fossil fuels, drastically reducing reliance on oil, coal and natural gas. This shift will lead to geopolitical instability, as many fossil-fuel-dependent countries will see their revenues and influence wane. Nevertheless, the transition to nuclear fusion will be essential for the development of economies and the survival of households and businesses in the long term (Takeda et al. 2023).

Another critical aspect of the stagnation phase will be the ongoing global debt crisis. As the world reaches the end of the current debt cycle, many currencies will depreciate, and demand for gold as a safe haven for wealth will increase. Historically, when the demand for money exceeds the actual supply in the banking system, capital flight occurs, often leading to inflation. This dynamic will play out once again, resulting in debt payments being made in devalued currencies and placing additional stress on global financial systems (Cebiroğlu and Unger 2019).

2.5.3. *Growth phase: 2052–2080*

After 2052, the new technologies that emerged during the stagnation phase will have become fully integrated into the global economy, ushering in a period of exponential economic growth. Similar to the widespread adoption of IT and telecommunications after 1996, the technologies of the future – nuclear fusion, AI, quantum computing, 3D printing and new material sciences – will be used by every business and household, driving productivity and creating new industries (Matyushok et al. 2021).

One of the most transformative aspects of this new megacycle will be the rise of AI. By the end of the 2020s, companies will have either fully integrated AI into their operations or will have fallen behind. AI will permeate every aspect of life, from personalized tutoring systems for children to professional assistants for adults. These AI-driven tools will greatly enhance human productivity, allowing individuals to achieve more than ever before in less time. Personal AI tutors, for instance, will revolutionize education by providing students with personalized learning experiences, enabling them to acquire more knowledge and skills than in any previous generation. In healthcare, AI will enable earlier diagnoses, more effective treatments and overall improved well-being (Alowais et al. 2023).

Another key driver of growth will be advancements in 3D printing and quantum computing. These technologies will redefine industries by enabling the rapid and efficient production of complex materials and solving previously unsolvable problems in science and engineering. The combination of AI, 3D printing and quantum computing will result in a new wave of innovation, fostering the creation of new economic sectors and transforming existing ones (Gyongyosi and Imre 2019; Shahrubudin et al. 2019; Abdelaal 2024).

Moreover, the development and widespread use of clean energy from nuclear fusion will provide the foundation for this growth. Cheap and stable energy will fuel industrial processes, enable the growth of new industries and reduce the environmental impact of human activity. Societies will become more energy efficient, and the cost of living will decrease as energy becomes more abundant and accessible (Windsor 2019).

2.5.4. *Geopolitical and societal implications*

While the economic megacycle evolves with a degree of predictability, the geopolitical landscape will face significant challenges. The conflict between democratic systems of governance and illiberal regimes will intensify, as countries with authoritarian governments continue to channel wealth into military build-ups rather than improving the standard of living for their citizens. These geopolitical tensions will pose risks to global stability, especially as new technologies such as AI and biotechnology can be used for both constructive and destructive purposes.

Internally, many nations will experience growing political polarization, with extreme political movements on both the left and right fighting for control of state power. These movements will often target individual liberties and democratic institutions, creating further division within societies. However, these internal conflicts are unlikely to disrupt the broader economic megacycle, which tends to unfold with regularity every 5.5 decades.

Amidst these challenges, nations that embrace technological innovation and modernization will have the opportunity to thrive. By investing in new technologies and creating internationally tradable products and services, countries can position themselves as leaders in the new global economy. Additionally, cultural diplomacy and the strategic use of cultural heritage will allow nations to enhance their influence on the international stage (Bekkers 2023; Luo and Van Assche 2023).

2.5.5. *Role of labor and automation*

A key challenge for economies in the coming decades will be the balance between labor and automation. While an influx of cheap labor may provide short-term economic benefits, it can also slow down modernization by reducing the incentive to invest in automation and technology. In the long term, economic growth will depend on increased productivity, which can be achieved only through automation and technological innovation.

As AI and automation technologies advance, they will not only increase muscle power, as previous industrial revolutions did, but also enhance mental power. Machines will be able to perform not only physical tasks but also cognitive tasks, allowing businesses to produce more with fewer workers. This shift will require significant adjustments in the labor market, as workers will need to adapt to new roles that require higher levels of education and skill (Acemoglu and Restrepo 2019).

2.6. Conclusions

The 56-year economic megacycle model offers a framework for understanding the relationship between technological revolutions, energy consumption and economic growth. By examining historical patterns, we can see how each cycle is driven by the emergence of new technologies that take time to fully integrate into the economy. As these technologies mature, they trigger periods of robust growth, which are followed by stagnation as the cycle begins again. In the future, it is clear that new technologies and energy sources will continue to drive economic cycles, transforming society and reshaping the global economic landscape.

The megacycle from 2024 to 2080 will be a period of profound transformation. The technologies that emerge in the next three decades will revolutionize economies, societies and geopolitics. As nuclear fusion becomes a viable energy source, AI permeates every industry and quantum computing unlocks new possibilities, humanity will experience unprecedented growth in productivity and well-being. However, these advances will also present new challenges, including geopolitical tensions, internal political strife and the need to adapt to a rapidly changing labor market. Ultimately, the nations and individuals who embrace innovation and modernization will be best positioned to thrive in this new era of exponential growth.

2.7. References

Abdelaal, M. (2024). AI in manufacturing: Market analysis and opportunities. *arXiv:2407.05426*. doi: 10.48550/arXiv.2407.05426.

Acemoglu, D. and Restrepo, P. (2019). Automation and new tasks: How technology displaces and reinstates labor. *Journal of Economic Perspectives*, 33(2), 3–30.

Alowais, S.A., Alghamdi, S.S., Alsuhebany, N., Alqahtani, T., Alshaya, A.I., Almohareb, S.N., Aldairem, A., Alrashed, M., Bin Saleh, K., Badreldin, H.A. et al. (2023). Revolutionizing healthcare: The role of artificial intelligence in clinical practice. *BMC Medical Education*, 23(1), 689.

Bekkers, E. (2023). The impact of geopolitical conflicts on trade, growth, and innovation. *arXiv:2203.12173v2*. doi: 10.48550/arXiv.2203.12173.

Ben-Ishai, G., Dean, J., Manyika, J., Porat, R., Varian, H., Walker, K. (2024). AI and the opportunity for shared prosperity: Lessons from the history of technology and the economy. *arXiv:2401.09718v3*. doi: 10.48550/arXiv.2401.09718.

Cebiroğlu, G. and Unger, S. (2019). On the relationship of money supply, consumer demand, demographics and debt. *International Journal of Public Policy*, 15(3–4), 187–205.

Crafts, N.F.R., Leybourne, S.J., Mills, T.C. (1989). Trends and cycles in British industrial production, 1700–1913. *Journal of the Royal Statistical Society. Series A*, 152(1), 43–60.

Dafermos, Y., Gabor, D., Michell, J. (2023). Institutional supercycles: An evolutionary macro-finance approach. *New Political Economy*, 28(5), 693–712.

Furman, J. and Seamans, R. (2019). AI and the economy. *Innovation Policy and the Economy*, 19(1), 161–191.

Gorham, C. (2020). The 4th industrial revolution effect on the enterprise cyber strategy. *arXiv:2006.07488*. doi: 10.48550/arXiv.2006.07488.

Gyongyosi, L. and Imre, S. (2019). A survey on quantum computing technology. *Computer Science Review*, 31(C), 51–71.

Henderson, R. (2021). Innovation in the 21st century: Architectural change, purpose, and the challenges of our time. *Management Science*, 67(9), 5479–5488.

Hung, H.F. (2022). The virus, the dollar, and the global order: The COVID-19 crisis in comparative perspective. *Development and Change*, 53(6), 1177–1199.

Lanteri, A. (2021). Strategic drivers for the fourth industrial revolution. *Thunderbird International Business Review*, 63(3), 273–283.

Lo, A.W. (2021). The financial system red in tooth and claw: 75 years of co-evolving markets and technology. *Financial Analysts Journal*, 77(3), 5–33.

Luo, Y. and Van Assche, A. (2023). The rise of techno-geopolitical uncertainty: Implications of the United States CHIPS and Science Act. *Journal of International Business Studies*, 54(8), 1423–1440.

Marchetti, C. (1986). Fifty-year pulsation in human affairs: Analysis of some physical indicators. *Futures*, 18(3), 376–388.

Matyushok, V., Krasavina, V., Berezin, A., García, J.S. (2021). The global economy in technological transformation conditions: A review of modern trends. *Economic Research-Ekonomska Istraživanja*, 34(1), 1471–1497.

Modis, T. (2017). A hard-science approach to Kondratieff's economic cycle. *Technological Forecasting and Social Change*, 122, 63–70.

Perilla Jiménez, J.R. (2020). Testing the impact of technology diffusion and innovation on long-run growth using cointegration techniques. *Journal of International Trade and Economic Development*, 29(6), 748–773.

Reinhart, C.M., Reinhart, V., Trebesch, C. (2016). Global cycles: Capital flows, commodities, and sovereign defaults, 1815–2015. *American Economic Review*, 106(5), 574–580.

Rosenberg, N. and Trajtenberg, M. (2004). A general-purpose technology at work: The Corliss steam engine in the late-nineteenth-century United States. *Journal of Economic History*, 64(1), 61–99.

Shahrubudin, N., Lee, T.C., Ramlan, R.J.P.M. (2019). An overview on 3D printing technology: Technological, materials, and applications. *Procedia Manufacturing*, 35, 1286–1296.

Skare, M., Porada-Rochon, M., Blazevic-Buric, S. (2021). Energy cycles: Nature, turning points and role in England economic growth from 1700 to 2018. *Acta Montanistica Slovaca*, 26(2), 281–302.

Smith Stegen, K. (2018). Redrawing the geopolitical map: International relations and renewable energies. In *The Geopolitics of Renewables*, Scholten, D. (ed.). Springer, Cham.

Takeda, S., Keeley, A.R., Managi, S. (2023). How many years away is fusion energy? A review. *Journal of Fusion Energy*, 42(1), 16.

Windsor, C. (2019). Can the development of fusion energy be accelerated? An introduction to the proceedings. *Philosophical Transactions. Series A, Mathematical, Physical, and Engineering Sciences*, 377(2141), 20170446.

3

Modeling Functioning as a Determinant of Wellbeing: A Mediation Analysis

The purpose of this chapter is to explore the relationships of functioning as a determinant of well-being to social trust, satisfaction with life and feelings of safety. Furthermore, it investigates the mediating role of feelings of safety walking alone in the local area after dark in the relationship among social trust, satisfaction with life and functioning. The analysis was based on the 2012 European Social Survey datasets for France, Poland, Spain and Sweden. The models of the separate path analyses provided acceptable model fit for France, Spain and Sweden, and adequate model fit for Poland. In all countries, functioning was positively predicted by feelings of safety and satisfaction with life, demonstrating strong direct effects with the latter. Feelings of safety were positively affected by the two items of social trust and satisfaction with life. The findings showed weak mediation effects of social trust and satisfaction with life by feelings of safety. However, a strong total effect of satisfaction with life on functioning was observed in all countries. The resulting low percentages of the total variation explained by the models with feelings of safety and functioning as the mediating and dependent variables (DVs), respectively, indicate that further research is necessary.

3.1. Introduction

The measurement of well-being provides an important indicator of the welfare of nations and opportunities for policy making. A module on personal and social wellbeing was first included in the 2006 (Round 3) questionnaire of the European Social Survey (ESS) and was repeated with certain changes in 2012 (Round 6). On the basis of theoretical models and statistical analyses, the 2012 ESS measurement of well-being (New Economics Foundation 2009; European Social Survey 2013, 2015; Jeffrey et al. 2015) comprises 35 items defined in six key dimensions: evaluative well-being (two items), emotional well-being (six items), functioning

Chapter written by Anastasia CHARALAMPI and Catherine MICHALOPOULOU.

(14 items), vitality (four items), community well-being (five items) and supportive relationships (four items). Functioning is described by "feelings of autonomy, competence, engagement, meaning and purpose, self-esteem, optimism and resilience" (Jeffrey et al. 2015, p. 4). In parallel, positive functioning is described as comprising competence, autonomy, engagement, meaning and purpose of life (Panek 2015).

In previous work (Charalampi et al. 2023), the dimension of functioning as a determinant of well-being was investigated to assess its cross-national comparability on the basis of the 2012 ESS datasets (Charalampi et al. 2021). Standardized overall measurements of a common seven-item unidimensional structure of functioning were created, and the investigation of their psychometric properties resulted in providing reliable and valid scales for 14 countries: Denmark, France, Germany, Hungary, Ireland, the Netherlands, Norway, Poland, Portugal, the Russian Federation, Slovenia, Spain, Sweden and the UK.

The OECD (2020, p. 20) measurement of current well-being comprises 11 key "dimensions", which they:

> Relate to material conditions that shape people's economic options (income and wealth, housing, work and job quality) and quality-of-life factors that encompass how well people are (and how well they feel they are), what they know and can do, and how healthy and safe their places of living are (health, knowledge and skills, environmental quality, subjective wellbeing, safety) [... and] how connected and engaged people are, and how and with whom they spend their time (work–life balance, social connections, civic engagement).

Life satisfaction is considered an indicator of subjective well-being (European Social Survey 2015; OECD 2020, p. 138) and can provide valuable insights into the meaning and validity of well-being measurement (Huppert et al. 2009). The standard National Crime survey self-perceived question for the measurement of fear of crime (Forde 1993) reporting on feelings of safety when walking alone at night comprises one of the safety indicators (OECD 2020, p. 150).

Social trust provides an important indicator of a country's political culture. According to the literature, there are linkages between interpersonal difference in subjective well-being measurement and social trust (Helliwell and Putnam 2004) and between social trust and a range of health outcomes within and among countries (Kawachi 2016). In agreement with this, studies link social trust to subjective well-being (Yip et al. 2007), showing that trust and a sense of belonging contribute to subjective well-being (Helliwell and Wang 2011).

This chapter aims to explore the relationship of functioning as a determinant of well-being to social trust, satisfaction with life and feelings of safety. Furthermore, it investigates the mediating role of feelings of safety walking alone in the local area after dark in the relationship among social trust, satisfaction with life and functioning.

3.2. Methods

3.2.1. *Procedure and participants*

The analysis was based on the 2012 (Round 6) ESS datasets (European Social Survey European Research Infrastructure (ESS ERIC) 2023) for France, Poland, Spain and Sweden. The ESS implements all of the strict methodological prerequisites for over-time and cross-national comparability (Kish 1994; Carey 2000) by applying probability sampling, minimum effective achieved sample sizes in all participating countries and a maximum target nonresponse rate of 30% (The ESS Sampling Expert Panel 2016).

The survey defines the survey population in all rounds as all persons aged 15+ residing within private households in each country, regardless of their nationality, citizenship or language. The realized samples and a summary of the participants' demographic and social characteristics are presented in Table 3.1. As shown, gender was almost equally distributed, with the exception of France, where the sample included more women than men. The mean age ranged from 46 to 52 years. More than 43.3% of the participants were married, the majority had completed secondary education or lower and at least 43.6% were in paid work.

Country	*N*	Men (%)	Women (%)	Age Mean (SD)	Married (%)	Secondary education or lower (%)	In paid Work (%)
France	1,968	44.8	55.2	51.8 (18.5)	43.3	70.9	47.0
Poland	1,898	47.9	52.1	46.1 (18.8)	57.6	75.4	48.2
Spain	1,889	48.3	51.7	47.6 (18.0)	53.6	72.8	43.6
Sweden	1,847	51.3	48.7	47.8 (19.0)	45.6	57.4	54.1

Table 3.1. *The demographic and social characteristics of participants: European Social Survey (2012). The reference period for the respondent's main activity was defined as during the last 7 days*

3.2.2. Measures and item selection

In Table 3.2, the 2012 ESS measurement considered for the analyses are presented in the order appearing in the questionnaire. There are three items measuring social trust in the core questionnaire. The first item is worded as "Using this card, generally speaking, would you say that most people can be trusted, or that you can't be too careful in dealing with people?" and is measured on a scale ranging from 0 to 10: "most people can be trusted (10)" or "you cannot be too careful (0)". The second item is worded as "Using this card, do you think that most people would try to take advantage of you if they got the chance, or would they try to be fair?" and is measured on a scale ranging from 0 to 10: "most people would try to take advantage of me (0)"/"try to be fair (10)". The third item is worded as "Would you say that most of the time, people try to be helpful or that they are mostly looking out for themselves?", which measured on a scale ranging from 0–10: "most of the time, people try to be helpful (10)" or "look out for themselves (0)". Also included in the core questionnaire, the satisfaction with life question is as follows: "All things considered, how satisfied are you with your life as a whole nowadays, on a scale 0–10 where 0 means extremely dissatisfied and 10 means extremely satisfied?". Since all of the aforementioned variables were assigned a 0–10 scale, their level of measurement was considered as interval.

In the core questionnaire, the standard National Crime survey self-perceived question measuring the fear of crime is worded as "How safe do you – or would you feel walking alone in this area after dark?". There are four possible response categories, which are defined as follows: very safe (1), safe (2), unsafe (3) and very unsafe (4). The order of the response categories was reversed before the analyses so as low and high values would indicate lower and higher feelings of safety, respectively. The level of measurement was considered ordinal.

As mentioned previously, in previous work (Charalampi et al. 2023), a seven-item unidimensional construct was created to measure functioning as a determinant of well-being via questions of the personal and social well-being module included in the 2012 ESS questionnaire. The scale comprises five positively (F1 and F3–F6) and two negatively (F7 and F8) worded items. The scoring of the positively worded items was reversed before the analysis to achieve correspondence between the ordering of the response categories. The response categories range from 1 to 5 and are defined as follows: 1 (agree strongly); 2 (agree); 3 (neither agree nor disagree); 4 (disagree); and 5 (disagree strongly). Therefore, the level of measurement was considered as pseudo-interval (Charalampi 2018; Charalampi et al. 2019, 2020).

	ESS quest.	Aligned scale	Label
Social trust			
Most people can be trusted or you can't be too careful	A3	0–10	Social trust 1
Most people would try to take advantage of me or try to be fair	A4	0–10	Social trust 2
Most of the time people try to be helpful or mostly look for themselves	A5	0–10	Social trust 3
How satisfied are you with life as a whole?	B20	0–10	Satisfaction with life
Feelings of safety walking alone in the local area after dark	C6	1–4 (R)	Feelings of safety
Functioning scale			Functioning
Free to decide how to live my life	D16	1–5 (R)	
Feel accomplishment from what I do	D18	1–5 (R)	
Feel what I do in life is valuable	D23	1–5 (R)	
Always optimistic about my future	D2	1–5 (R)	
Feel very positive about myself	D3	1–5 (R)	
At times I feel as if I am a failure	D4	1–5	
When things go wrong in my life it takes a long time for me to get back to normal	D19	1–5	
R = these items were reversed before analysis.			

Table 3.2. *The 2012 European Social Survey (ESS) measurements used in the analyses*

Considering the countries under investigation in the present work, the composite reliability of this scale was 0.704, 0.724, 0.705 and 0.761 for France, Poland, Spain and Sweden, respectively, thus providing reliable overall measurements (Charalampi et al. 2023).

Moreover, evidence of adequate convergent validity was provided (Charalampi et al. 2023). Therefore, this scale was proven to be both reliable and valid in all countries under consideration.

3.2.3. *Statistical analyses*

Initially, univariate analyses were performed. Bivariate correlation analyses were performed. Pearson and Spearman's correlation coefficients were used for interval and categorical measures, respectively.

Before performing path analysis, a number of preliminary decisions, tests and procedures were considered, referring to the adequacy of the sample size for performing these analyses and how outliers and missing values were dealt with.

Kline (1998) suggested that a sample size of 10 times the number of parameters in a model is adequate for performing path analysis and that a sample size of 20 times the number of parameters in path analysis is the best. However, path analysis is considered to be a large sample method (Tabachnick and Fidell 2007). Missing data analysis and data screening for outliers were performed for all samples and was based on the variables' boxplots. Cases were eliminated if they appeared in the boxplots as outliers (Thompson 2005; Tabachnick and Fidell 2007; Brown 2015). The size and pattern of missing values for each variable were investigated. Missing data had to be replaced because complete datasets are required for SPSS Amos.

In Figure 3.1, the theoretical structure of the path analysis model under consideration is defined as follows: the three questions on social trust and the single measurement of satisfaction with life define the independent variables (IVs), the question on feelings of safety, the mediator (intervening) variable and the overall unidimensional measurement of functioning constituted the DV. Because there was no theory to indicate which background variables may be used as controls, feelings of safety and functioning by the socioeconomic variables were tested (Table 3.A1). Given that feelings of safety and functioning by gender and employment status were significant in most countries, it was decided to use them as controls.

Univariate statistics were computed for each measure, and their distributional properties were inspected (testing for normality) to determine the appropriateness of the methods to be used. Separate path analyses were performed with maximum likelihood for each country. Standardized indirect effects were considered the "index of mediation" (Preacher and Hayes 2008, p. 38; see also Cheung 2009), and they were tested with bootstrapping methods.

To generate bootstrap confidence intervals for the standardized indirect effects, 5,000 bootstrap samples were used (Preacher and Hayes 2008; Cheung 2009). A standardized indirect effect was considered statistically significant only if its 95% bootstrap confidence interval excluded zero (Hayes 2018).

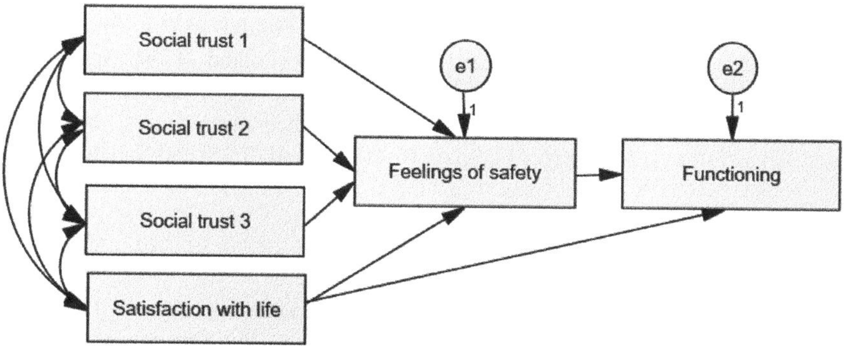

Figure 3.1. *The theoretical structure of the path analysis models tested: European Social Survey, 2012*

The evaluation of the path models was based on the goodness-of-fit indices. Model fit is to be considered as adequate if χ^2 tests are not significant. Comparative fit index (CFI) and Tucker–Lewis index (TLI) values are greater than or close to 0.95, and the root-mean-square error approximation (RMSEA) is ≤ 0.06 with a 90% confidence interval (CI) upper limit ≤ 0.06 (Bollen 1989; Hu and Bentler 1999; Schmitt 2011; Brown 2015). Model fit is considered acceptable if χ^2 tests are not significant, CFI and TLI values are > 0.90 and RMSEA < 0.08 with the 90% CI upper limit < 0.08 (Hu and Bentler 1999; Marsh et al. 2004).

Statistical analyses and path analyses were performed using IBM SPSS Statistics Version 29 and IBM SPSS Amos Version 29, respectively.

3.3. Results

3.3.1. *Univariate analysis*

In Table 3.3, the frequency distributions and univariate statistics of the 2012 ESS measurements of functioning, feelings of safety, social trust and satisfaction with life are presented for France, Poland, Spain and Sweden.

The findings showed on average relatively high levels of functioning (Table 3.3). On the basis of their mean scores on functioning, countries may be classified as follows: Spain (3.71), Poland (3.89), France (3.93) and Sweden (3.97). In all countries, the median showed that the respondents felt safe walking alone in the local area after dark. On average, the levels of social trust were moderate, with social trust 2 presenting the highest levels. On the basis of their mean scores, countries may be classified as follows: social trust 1: Poland (4.12), France (4.45), Spain (5.13) and Sweden (6.01); social trust 2: Poland (4.96), Spain (5.43), France (5.82) and Sweden (6.53); and social trust 3: Poland (3.74), Spain (4.72), France (4.73) and Sweden (5.96). In all countries, the levels of satisfaction with life were higher than those of social trust and based on their mean scores, they may be classified as follows: France (6.41), Spain (6.91), Poland (7.15) and Sweden (7.88).

3.3.2. *Bivariate analysis: correlation analysis*

In Table 3.4, bivariate correlations of functioning to social trust, satisfaction with life and feelings of safety are presented. As shown, the first social trust item (social trust 1) was significantly related to functioning in all countries, with the respective correlations ranging from 0.115 (France) to 0.161 (Sweden). The second social trust item (social trust 2) was significantly related to functioning in all countries, with the respective correlations ranging from 0.105 (Poland) to 0.174 (France). The third social trust item (social trust 3) was significantly related to functioning in all countries, with correlations ranging from 0.067 (Poland) to 0.155 (Sweden). The satisfaction with life variable was significantly related to functioning in all countries, with the respective correlations ranging from 0.318 (France) to 0.447 (Spain). The feeling of safety variable was significantly related to functioning in all countries, with the respective correlations ranging from 0.112 (France) to 0.167 (Poland). All of the correlations were positive.

3.3.3. *Multivariate analysis: mediation analysis*

The sample sizes (Table 3.1) ranged from 1,847 (Sweden) to 1,968 (France) and were considered large enough for carrying out path analyses separately in each country. The screening of samples detected a negligible number of outlying cases, ranging overall from 3 to 14 cases, and it was decided not to reject them from the analysis.

The size of missing values (Table 3.3) ranged from 0.1% (France, Spain) to 4.7% (Poland). All missing values were replaced by the mean values of each variable because complete datasets were required for SPSS Amos.

In every country, the respondents used the full range of possible responses for all of the variables (Table 3.3). Overall, non-normality was not severe (skewness > 2; kurtosis > 7) for any interval measured variable, as the skewness and kurtosis values ranged from −1.231 (Sweden) to 0.367 (Poland) and from −0.663 (Poland) to 2.412 (Sweden), respectively.

Country/variable	Mean/ Median	SD	95% CI	Frequency (%) of response categories												Skew.	Kurt.
				0	1	2	3	4	5	6	7	8	9	10	NA		
France																	
Functioning	3.93	0.908	3.89–3.97		1.8	5.3	18.0	47.1	27.0						0.8	–0.871	0.784
Feelings of safety	3				8.8	16.7	40.2	32.8							1.5		
Social trust 1	4.45	2.115	4.35–4.54	6.5	3.0	8.1	14.3	12.5	27.5	11.5	9.5	5.3	1.1	0.6	0.1	–0.219	–0.220
Social trust 2	5.82	2.074	5.73–5.91	2.7	0.9	2.8	6.3	7.2	25.3	14.3	18.2	15.3	3.9	3.0	0.1	–0.509	0.390
Social trust 3	4.73	2.134	4.64–4.83	3.9	2.7	8.6	12.9	13.6	24.9	12.9	10.0	7.3	1.6	1.6	–	–0.061	–0.183
Satisfaction with life	6.41	2.456	6.30–6.52	3.4	1.7	3.2	6.1	5.4	12.3	10.1	18.0	22.6	9.2	7.9	0.1	–0.769	0.075
Poland																	
Functioning	3.89	0.802	3.85–3.92		0.6	5.6	17.8	52.5	18.8						4.7	–0.679	0.567
Feelings of safety	3				1.8	14.5	57.6	23.7							2.4		
Social trust 1	4.12	2.420	4.00–4.23	9.9	6.6	10.2	13.1	11.2	22.6	8.2	8.7	6.4	1.7	1.1	0.3	0.016	–0.663
Social trust 2	4.96	2.366	4.84–5.07	4.7	4.2	7.1	11.1	9.2	24.7	8.6	13.4	10.8	2.7	2.3	1.2	–0.184	–0.494
Social trust 3	3.74	2.355	3.63–3.85	8.4	9.4	15.4	15.5	10.5	18.5	6.5	7.3	3.8	1.5	1.4	1.8	0.367	–0.404
Satisfaction with life	7.15	2.245	7.05–7.26	1.7	0.8	1.4	4.2	4.0	11.9	6.8	17.1	24.1	13.0	14.4	0.6	–0.953	0.729
Spain																	
Functioning	3.71	0.870	3.67–3.75		1.3	7.9	23.5	49.7	14.8						2.8	–0.639	0.359
Feelings of safety	3				4.0	18.1	51.0	25.6							1.3		
Social trust 1	5.13	2.130	5.04–5.23	4.9	2.0	4.6	9.4	10.2	24.5	16.7	16.5	7.7	1.9	1.5	0.1	–0.476	0.132
Social trust 2	5.43	2.130	5.33–5.53	3.5	2.0	4.1	8.7	8.4	24.4	14.7	18.2	11.5	2.0	2.2	0.3	–0.458	0.134
Social trust 3	4.72	2.193	4.62–4.83	4.3	3.5	7.9	13.7	12.2	23.0	13.1	11.4	7.0	2.1	1.4	0.4	–0.086	–0.320
Satisfaction with life	6.91	2.325	6.80–7.02	2.4	0.8	2.3	3.9	4.1	11.1	10.8	17.6	22.6	11.1	13.0	0.3	–0.907	0.640

Table 3.3. *The frequency distribution and univariate statistics of the 2012 European Social Survey measurements of functioning, feelings of safety, social trust and satisfaction with life for France, Poland, Spain and Sweden*

				Frequency (%) of response categories													
Country/variable	**Mean/ Median**	**SD**	**95% CI**	**0**	**1**	**2**	**3**	**4**	**5**	**6**	**7**	**8**	**9**	**10**	**NA**	**Skew.**	**Kurt.**
Sweden																	
Functioning	3.97	0.745	3.93–4.00		0.4	3.7	16.4	57.4	21.3						0.8	–0.669	0.876
Feelings of safety	3				2.6	11.2	41.9	44.1							0.2		
Social trust 1	6.01	2.097	5.92–6.11	2.3	1.1	2.8	7.1	7.5	16.6	12.9	23.6	19.4	4.4	2.1	0.2	–0.711	0.276
Social trust 2	6.53	1.859	6.44–6.61	0.9	0.6	1.5	4.1	5.1	15.6	12.9	25.2	23.8	6.9	3.1	0.3	–0.784	0.788
Social trust 3	5.96	1.954	5.87–6.05	1.2	0.6	3.5	7.4	7.9	16.8	16.2	24.3	16.2	3.9	1.8	0.2	–0.554	0.086
Satisfaction with life	7.88	1.688	7.80–7.96	0.4	0.1	0.3	1.7	1.8	5.5	5.4	17.5	29.9	21.0	16.2	0.2	–1.231	2.412

Table 3.3. *(continued)*

	Functioning			
Variable	**France**	**Poland**	**Spain**	**Sweden**
Social trust 1	0.115*	0.116*	0.126*	0.161*
Social trust 2	0.174*	0.105*	0.138*	0.157*
Social trust 3	0.132*	0.067**	0.112*	0.155*
Satisfaction with life	0.318*	0.326*	0.447*	0.423*
Feelings of safety[a]	0.112*	0.167*	0.120*	0.152*

[a]Spearman's correlation coefficients: $*p < 0.001$. $**p < 0.05$.

Table 3.4. *The relation of functioning to social trust items, satisfaction with life and feelings of safety: Pearson's correlation coefficients*

The path analyses results for France, Poland, Spain and Sweden are presented in Table 3.5. In Table 3.6, the goodness-of-fit indices for the path analyses models performed with maximum likelihood are presented for each country. As shown, the models of France, Spain and Sweden provided acceptable model fit and that of Poland adequate model fit.

			β			
Model			**France**	**Poland**	**Spain**	**Sweden**
Feelings of safety	←	Social trust 1	0.095	0.042	0.071	0.153
Feelings of safety	←	Social trust 2	0.119	0.060	0.041	0.078
Feelings of safety	←	Social trust 3	–0.024	–0.026	0.051	–0.003
Feelings of safety	←	Satisfaction with life	0.075	0.083	0.040	0.112
DV: Functioning	←	Feelings of safety	0.060	0.109	0.070	0.072
DV: Functioning	←	Satisfaction with life	0.308	0.298	0.432	0.405
		Variable	R^2			
		Feelings of safety	0.143	0.052	0.094	0.168
		Functioning	0.106	0.124	0.202	0.197

Table 3.5. *Path analyses performed with maximum likelihood: standardized coefficients and squared multiple correlations*

Country	χ^2 (*df*)	*p*	CFI	TLI	RMSEA (90% CI)
France	19.271 (3)	0.000	0.990	0.905	0.053 (0.032–0.076)
Poland	7.874 (3)	0.049	0.996	0.964	0.029 (0.002–0.055)
Spain	10.187 (3)	0.017	0.996	0.963	0.036 (0.013–0.061)
Sweden	13.625 (3)	0.003	0.995	0.955	0.044 (0.022–0.069)

Model fit is considered adequate if χ^2 is not significant, CFI and TLI values greater than or close to 0.95 and RMSEA $\leq$ 0.06 with the 90% CI upper limit $\leq$ 0.06. Model fit is considered acceptable if χ^2 is not significant, CFI > 0.90, TLI > 0.90 and RMSEA < 0.08 with the 90% CI upper limit < 0.08. *df* = degrees of freedom; CFI = comparative fit index; TLI = Tucker–Lewis index; RMSEA = root-mean-square error of approximation; CI = confidence interval.

Table 3.6. *Path analyses performed with maximum likelihood: goodness-of-fit indices*

As shown in Table 3.5, in all countries, functioning was positively predicted by feelings of safety, as well as by satisfaction with life. The standardized direct effect of satisfaction with life on functioning for France, Poland, Spain and Sweden was 0.308, 0.298, 0.432 and 0.405, respectively.

In all countries, feelings of safety were positively affected by social trust 1, social trust 2 and satisfaction with life and negatively affected by social trust 3, except for Spain, where the reverse was true.

The squared multiple correlations for functioning and feelings of safety models ranged from 0.106 (France) to 0.202 (Spain) and from 0.052 (Poland) to 0.168 (Sweden), respectively.

In Table 3.7, the mediating effects are presented for each country. As indicated, weak simple mediation effects of social trust 1 by feelings of safety were detected in the cases of France, Spain and Sweden, with significant standardized indirect effects ranging from 0.005 (Spain) to 0.011 (Sweden). Furthermore, weak simple mediation effects of social trust 2 by feelings of safety were detected in the cases of France, Poland and Sweden, with significant standardized indirect effects ranging from 0.006 (Sweden) to 0.007 (France and Poland). Moreover, weak simple mediation effects of social trust 3 by feelings of safety were detected in the case of Spain, with a significant standardized indirect effect of 0.004.

Additionally, weak simple mediation effects of satisfaction with life by feelings of safety were observed in the cases of France, Poland and Sweden, with significant standardized indirect effects ranging from 0.004 (France) to 0.009 (Poland). The standardized total effect of satisfaction with life on functioning for France, Poland, Spain and Sweden were 0.312, 0.307, 0.435 and 0.413, respectively.

There were no mediating effects for social trust 1 in the case of Poland; for social trust 2 in the case of Spain; for social trust 3 in the cases of France, Poland and Sweden; and for satisfaction with life in the case of Spain.

	France			Poland		
Variables	**SIE**	**95% CI**	***p* value**	**SIE**	**95% CI**	***p* value**
Social trust 1	0.006	0.001, 0.013	0.009	0.005	0.000, 0.011	0.069
Social trust 2	0.007	0.002, 0.015	0.011	0.007	0.001, 0.014	0.016
Social trust 3	–0.001	–0.006, 0.001	0.230	–0.003	–0.010, 0.002	0.259
Satisfaction with life	0.004	0.001, 0.011	0.009	0.009	0.004, 0.017	0.000
	Spain			**Sweden**		
Social trust 1	0.005	0.001, 0.012	0.010	0.011	0.004, 0.021	0.003
Social trust 2	0.003	–0.001, 0.010	0.105	0.006	0.001, 0.013	0.006
Social trust 3	0.004	0.000, 0.009	0.029	0.000	–0.005, 0.004	0.860
Satisfaction with life	0.003	0.000, 0.008	0.065	0.008	0.003, 0.016	0.003

Table 3.7. *Path analyses: standardized indirect effects (SIE), their 95% bootstrap confidence intervals (CI) and significance*

3.4. Conclusions

In this chapter, the relationship of functioning as a determinant of well-being to social trust, satisfaction with life and feelings of safety was investigated. Moreover, the mediating role of feelings of safety walking alone in the local area after dark in the relationship among social trust, satisfaction with life and functioning was also investigated.

The findings showed that the three social trust items, satisfaction with life and feelings of safety were significantly related to functioning in all countries. Overall, all of the correlations were positive, ranging from 0.067 (Poland) to 0.447 (Spain). In all countries, satisfaction with life was strongly correlated to functioning.

The models of the separate path analyses provided acceptable model fit for France, Spain and Sweden and adequate model fit for Poland. In all countries, functioning was positively predicted by feelings of safety and satisfaction with life.

In all countries, strong direct effects of satisfaction with life on functioning were observed. Furthermore, in all countries, feelings of safety were positively affected by social trust 1, social trust 2 and satisfaction with life and negatively affected by social trust 3, except for Spain, where the reverse was true.

The findings showed weak mediation effects of social trust 1 by feelings of safety in France, Spain and Sweden. Furthermore, weak mediation effects were detected in the case of social trust 2 through feelings of safety in France, Poland and Sweden. Moreover, weak mediation effects were detected in the case of social trust 3 through feelings of safety in Spain. Although weak mediation effects were detected in the case of satisfaction with life by feelings of safety in France, Poland and Sweden, the total effect of satisfaction with life on functioning was strong in all countries.

Certainly, the resulting low percentages of the total variation explained by the models with feelings of safety and functioning as the mediating and DVs, respectively, indicate that in future research, additional social indicators should be considered to provide a more coherent interpretation.

3.5. References

Bollen, K.A. (1989). *Structural Equations with Latent Variables*. John Wiley & Sons, New York.

Brown, T.A. (2015). *Confirmatory Factor Analysis for Applied Research*, 2nd edition. Guilford Press, New York.

Carey, S. (ed.) (2000). *Measuring Adult Literacy: The International Adult Literacy Survey (IALS) in the European Context*. Office for National Statistics, London.

Charalampi, A. (2018). The importance of items' level of measurement in investigating the structure and assessing the psychometric properties of multidimensional constructs. PhD Thesis, Panteion University of Social and Political Sciences, Athens.

Charalampi, A., Michalopoulou, C., Richardson, C. (2019). Determining the structure and assessing the psychometric properties of multidimensional scales constructed from ordinal and pseudo-interval items. *Communications in Statistics: Case Studies, Data Analysis and Applications*, 5(1), 26–38. doi: 10.1080/23737484.2019.1579683.

Charalampi, A., Michalopoulou, C., Richardson, C. (2020). Validation of the 2012 European Social Survey measurement of wellbeing in seventeen European countries. *Applied Research in Quality of Life*, 15, 73–105. doi: 10.1007/s11482-018-9666-4.

Charalampi, A., Tsiganou, J., Michalopoulou, C. (2021). Investigating the relation of functioning as a determinant of wellbeing to political and social trust in three Balkan countries. In *Yearbook of UNWE*, Nikolova, C., Todorova, E., Lambovska, M., Nedev, T. (eds). University of National and World Economy, Sofia. doi: 10.37075/YB.2021.1.12.

Charalampi, A., Michalopoulou, C., Richardson, C. (2023). Exploring cross-national comparability of unidimensional constructs. In *Quantitative Demography and Health Estimates: Healthy Life Expectancy, Templates for Direct Estimates from Life Tables and Other Applications*, Skiadas, C.H. and Skiadas, C. (eds). Springer, Cham. doi: 10.1007/978-3-031-28697-1.

Cheung, M.W.L. (2009). Comparison of methods for constructing confidence intervals of standardized indirect effects. *Behavior Research Methods*, 41, 425–438. doi: 10.3758/BRM.41.2.425.

ESS Sampling Expert Panel (2016). Sampling guidelines: Principles and implementation for the European Social Survey. ESS ERIC, London [Online]. Available at: www.europeansocialsurvey.org/ [Accessed 2 June 2016].

European Social Survey (2013). Round 6 module on personal and social wellbeing – Final module in template. Centre for Comparative Social Surveys, City University of London, London.

European Social Survey (2015). *Measuring and Reporting on Europeans' Wellbeing: Findings from the European Social Survey*. ESS ERIC, London.

European Social Survey European Research Infrastructure (ESS ERIC) (2023). ESS6 – Integrated file, edition 2.5. Document, Sikt – Norwegian Agency for Shared Services in Education and Research, Trondheim. doi: 10.18712/ess6e02_5.

Forde, D.R. (1993). Perceived crime, fear of crime, and walking alone at night. *Psychological Reports*, 73(2), 403–407. doi: 10.2466/pr0.1993.73.2.403.

Hayes, A.F. (2018). *Introduction to Mediation, Moderation, and Conditional Process Analysis: A Regression-Based Approach*, 2nd edition. Guilford Press, New York.

Helliwell, J.F. and Putnam, R.D. (2004). The social context of well-being. *Philosophical Transactions of the Royal Society of London. Series B, Biological Sciences*, 359(1449), 1435–1446. doi: 10.1098/rstb.2004.1522.

Helliwell, J.F. and Wang, S. (2011) Trust and well-being. *International Journal of Wellbeing*, 1(1), 42–78. doi: 10.5502/ijw.v1i1.3.

Hu, L. and Bentler, P.M. (1999) Cutoff criteria for fit indexes in covariance structure analysis: Conventional criteria versus new alternatives. *Structural Equation Modeling: A Multidisciplinary Journal*, 6(1), 1–55. doi: 10.1080/10705519909540118.

Huppert, F.A., Marks, N., Clark, A., Siegrist, J., Stutzer, A., Vittersø, J., Wahrendorf, M. (2009) Measuring well-being across Europe: Description of the ESS well-being module and preliminary findings. *Social Indicators Research*, 91(3), 301–315. doi: 10.1007/s11205-008-9346-0.

Jeffrey, K., Abdallah, S., Quick, A. (2015). *Europeans' Personal and Social Wellbeing: Topline Results from Round 6 of the European Social Survey*. ESS Topline Result Series, London.

Kawachi, I. (2016) Trust and public health. In *Handbook on Social and Political Trust*, Uslaner, R. (ed.). Oxford University Press, New York.

Kish, L. (1994) Multipopulation survey designs: Five types with seven shared aspects. *International Statistical Review*, 62(2), 167–186.

Kline, R.B. (1998). *Principles and Practice of Structural Equation Modeling*. Guilford Press, New York.

Marsh, H.W., Hau, K.T., Wen, Z. (2004). In search of golden rules: Comment on hypotheses-testing approaches to setting cutoff values for fit indexes and dangers in overgeneralizing Hu and Bentler's (1999) findings. *Structural Equation Modeling: A Multidisciplinary Journal*, 11(3), 320–341. doi: 10.1207/s15328007sem1103_2.

New Economics Foundation (2009). National accounts of well-being: Bringing real wealth onto the balance sheet. *NEF* [Online]. Available at: https://neweconomics.org/uploads/files/2027fb05fed1554aea_uim6vd4c5.pdf [Accessed 5 May 2015].

OECD (2020). How's life? In *2020: Measuring Well-Being*. OECD Publishing, Paris. doi: 10.1787/9870c393-en.

Panek, T. (2015) Subjective personal and social well-being in the European countries. In *Hopes and Anxieties in Europe*, Sztabiński, P.W., Domański, H., Sztabiński, F. (eds). Peter Lang Publishing, Frankfurt.

Preacher, K.J. and Hayes, A.F. (2008). Contemporary approaches to assessing mediation in communication research. In *The Sage Sourcebook of Advanced Data Analysis Methods for Communication Research*, Hayes, A.F., Slater, M.D., Snyder, L.B. (eds). Sage Publications, Thousand Oaks.

Schmitt, T.A. (2011). Current methodological considerations in exploratory and confirmatory factor analysis. *Journal of Psychoeducational Assessment*, 29(4), 304–321. doi: 10.1177/0734282911406653.

Tabachnick, B.G. and Fidell, L.S. (2007). *Using Multivariate Statistics*. Pearson Allyn & Bacon, Upper Saddle River.

Thompson, B. (2005). *Exploratory and Confirmatory Factor Analysis: Understanding Concepts and Applications*. American Psychological Association, Washington, D.C.

Yip, W., Subramanian, S.V., Mitchell, A.D., Lee, D.T.S., Wang, J., Kawachi, I. (2007). Does social capital enhance health and well-being? Evidence from rural China. *Social Science and Medicine*, 64(1), 35–49. doi: 10.1016/j.socscimed.2006.08.027.

3.6. Appendix

Country/variable	Gender	Age	Marital status	Domicile	Level of educational attainment	Employment status	Household's Income
France							
Feelings of safety	√*	√**	√*	√*	√*	√*	√*
Functioning						√*	
Poland							
Feelings of safety	√*	√**	√**	√*		√*	
Functioning	√*				√*	√*	√*
Spain							
Feelings of safety	√*	√*	√*	√*	√*	√*	√**
Functioning	√**			√**		√*	√*
Sweden							
Feelings of safety	√*	√*	√*	√*	√*	√*	√*
Functioning	√*		√*		√**	√*	√*

*$p < .001$, **$p < .05$. Gender: 1 = male, 2 = female; marital status: 1 = legally married, 2 = in a legally registered civil union, 3 = legally separated, 4 = legally divorced/civil union dissolved, 5 = widowed/civil partner died; 6 = none of these (never married or in legally registered civil union); domicile; 1 = a big city; 2 = the suburbs or outskirts of a big city, 3 = a town or a small city, 4 = a country village, 5 = a farm or home in the countryside; level of educational attainment: a detail coding frame based on the International Standard Classification of Education (ISCED) including values ranging from "not completed ISCED level 1" to "ISCED 6, doctoral degree"; employment status: 1 = in paid work (or away temporarily) (employee, self-employed, working for your family business), 2 = in education (not paid for by employer) even if no vacation, 3 = unemployed and actively looking for a job, 4 = unemployed, wanting a job but not actively looking for a job, 5 = permanently sick or disabled, 6 = retired, 7 = in community or military service, 8 = doing housework, looking after children or other persons, 9 = other; household's income: ten income range categories corresponding broadly to deciles of the actual household income range in each country (1 = J, 2 = R, 3 = C, 4 = M, 5 = F, 6 = S, 7 = K, 8 = P, 9 = D, 10 = H).

Table 3.A1. *Significance of feelings of safety and functioning according to socio-economic variables: European Social Survey (2012)*

4

Cross-Cultural Issues in Psychological Assessment: A Multistrategy Approach

The issue of culturally and ethnically unbiased psychological tests has been widely faced in the areas of abilities and attitudes, but less so in other areas, which frequently rely on self-reported symptom measures to assess and monitor symptom change. A very convenient situation consists of relying on scales for cross-cultural bias when people with different demographic characteristics and culturally divergent groups are compared (Poortinga 1989).

Various approaches to comparability in cross-cultural studies have been developed, with a privileged psychometric approach consisting of assessing factor equivalence (Asparouhov and Muthén 2014). Most often, a single strategy is adopted, satisfactorily addressing some contexts but sometimes leaving a few issues still unanswered. A multistrategy approach has been suggested, where the potential flaws of a single technique may be amended by additional methods (Hui and Triandis 1985). In our study, we explore the advantages of applying more than one method for comparing suicide risk among Italian and Indian young adults.

4.1. Introduction

Behavioral and psychological research often consists of the analysis of unobservable constructs, a compound of items whose assessment also relies on self-report measures, especially in the case of symptoms. The need for commonly shared scales in the worldwide scientific community imposes the assessment of groups in a complex comparison. Hence, the need for a well-developed measure requires the optimal properties of invariance, namely, measurement invariance (MI) (Poortinga 1989; Dong and Dumas 2020). Invariance properties ascertain that a scale returns the same pattern of responses regardless of the group of respondents.

Chapter written by Franca CRIPPA, Giulia GOTTI, Raffaella CALATI, Mariangela ZENGA, Kainaat DANYAL and Naved IQBAL.

Then, the metric remains the same, with or without a common origin and/or the need for a linear transformation. MI implies that a cultural difference in the construct is converted into a corresponding difference in the measurement.

By now, in cross-cultural equivalence, the study of factorial structure has become a scientific cornerstone (Beckstead et al. 2008; Asparouhov and Muthén 2014) since it addresses validity at its core. However, the complexity of the theme calls for a wider and polyhedric perspective. Disentangling the sociocultural context's constellational effect on psychological factors requires a strategic approach to assess construct invariance and to identify possible bias (Beckstead et al. 2008). Our analysis sketches a multimethod perspective (Hui and Triandis 1983, 1985; Triandis 1999), moving from the possible contribution of a plain but comprehensive standard direct analysis in section 4.2, to the role of differential item functioning (DIF) in section 4.3, based on current knowledge on factorial structures. Our research focuses on suicide risk among young adults, namely, university students, in India and Italy, given the substantial rates of major mood disorders among college and university students. In fact, cross-cultural research on suicide risk in different contexts can strongly contribute to preventive actions in light of both personal- and cultural-specific characteristics.

4.2. Suicide risk among university students: India and Italy in direct comparison

A common analytical strategy in cross-cultural studies consists of a straightforward juxtaposition of measures from the populations and groups involved, implying scalar equivalence. Notwithstanding its apparent simplicity, the favor encountered by this approach lies in simultaneous monitoring of the factual convergence of a wide variety of measures. From this perspective, a study on suicide risk among Italian and Indian university students was performed with young adults aged 18–35 years. Sadly, suicide represents the fourth leading cause of death in youths aged 15–29 years (World Health Organization 2024b). The age-standardized suicide rate (per 100,000 population) in India and Italy equals 12.9 [9.3–16.5] and 4.3 [4.0–6.9], respectively, with no availability of age-related rate for India (World Health Organization 2024a). Italian subjects were recruited from April 2020 to July 2021 (Magliocca et al. 2024), Indian subjects were recruited from September 2021 to September 2022, and the samples consisted of 1,665 participants and 402 students, all of whom signed an informed consent form.

The project was approved by the Research Ethics Committees of the University of Milan-Bicocca (Prot. 0025172/20 of 23/4/2020), the University of Eastern Piedmont (Prot. 803/CE, study CE 165/20, 01/07/2020) and the Jamia Millia Islamia University of New Delhi (Prot. Psy052, 28/07/2022).

STUDENTS' CITIZENSHIP	Indian n=402	Italian n=1,665	Indian vs Italian
	Socio-demographic characteristics		
Age	22.32 ±2.93	22.01 ±2.57	-1.41 ^{ns}
Women/men ratio (%)	262	434	-
Single/in relationship ratio (%)	347	94	-
Belief in God yes/no-don't know ratio (%)	458	54	-
	Clinical characteristics		
Contact with mental health professionals	72 17.9%	685 41.1%	75.29**
Presence of depression	216 53.7%	735 44.1%	11.98***
Intensity of suicidal thoughts	1.39 ±2.54	0.58 ±1.55	-6.79***
High intensity of suicidal thoughts	44 10.9%	51 3.1%	48.88***
	Perceived Social Support		
Family	19.02±7.03	20.21±7.11	-3.36**
Significant Others	18.72 ±7.94	23.41±5.97	-11.41**
Friends	19.39±7.11	21.13±6.60	-4.56**
Total	57.12±17.65	64.74±15.76	-8.13**

$^{*}p < 0.05$; $^{**}p < 0.01$; $^{***}p < 0.001$

Table 4.1. *Some participants' characteristics in a direct comparison*

The participants' sociodemographic data were collected, together with clinical information on previous and current physical and mind wellness (Table 4.1). A set of questionnaires assessing psychological/psychiatric conditions, somatic pain and social measures were then administered, representing the core of the psychological measure considered.

In line with official data on suicide mortality, Indian students displayed a worse clinical picture in almost all measurements of psychological/psychiatric measures than Italian students did: higher suicidal ideation (SI) (26.37% vs. 20.24%), higher and more frequent state (92% vs. 63.6%) and trait (95.3% vs. 75.5%) anxiety, depression (53.7% vs 4.4.1%), and current (18.7% vs. 8.2%) and habitual (18.2% vs. 9.8%) mental pain. Similarly, suicidal thoughts were also more intense and frequent in Indian students than in Italian students (10.9% vs. 3.1%). Consistently, Indian participants also reported slightly lower self-esteem and less fear of death. Quite surprisingly, however, social measures revealed greater perceived support by Indian youth, even in the presence of SI, a result that contradicts expectations.

4.3. Merging techniques: A better way in cross-cultural studies?

The concept of cross-cultural equivalence has been debated in the literature as susceptible to different declinations, for example, functional, conceptual and metric (Poortinga 1989). Hui and Triandis (1985) highlighted two specific types, both crucial to psychological testing: construct operationalization on the one hand, which mostly refers to construct validity and studies with covariance/correlation structures, and item equivalence on the other hand, which involves item characteristics curves. Suicidal risk is, even if not exclusively, related to depression symptoms and should be monitored for primary prevention. Henceforth, we focus on MI issues in the case of the depression scale, namely, the Beck Depression Inventory-II (BDI-II) (Beck et al. 1996). The scale consists of 21 items, with a total score ranging from 0 to 63 and a higher score indicating greater severity of depressive symptoms investigated in the previous 2 weeks. A score equal to or above 14 indicates the presence of depression – mild, moderate or severe – while a score below this cutoff indicates the absence of depression. Current SI was assessed on the basis of item 9 of the BDI-II, recoded as dichotomous, as the absence or presence of any suicidal options.

In the framework of the structural equation model literature, the validity of the BDI-II in terms of covariance/correlation scale structure has been extensively confirmed by means of both traditional confirmative factor analysis (CFA) and its advancement, multiple group CFA (MG-CFA) (Asparouhov and Muthén 2014; Dere et al. 2015). This is the case for university students in northern America, with quite different cultural heritage such as Western and Chinese subgroups, who showed a strong MI for BDI–II across both gender and culture (Dere et al. 2015). A bifactor model allows for the distinction between somatic and cognitive symptoms, despite some discrepancies, which, in the authors' opinion, requires enlarging the set of personal characteristics. With respect to the Indian case, depression measures have faced the factorial structure in Indian adolescents compared, once again, to Western adolescents. The psychometric properties of the BDI have hence been studied among Indian adolescents, reaching a bifactorial structure estimation, somatic symptoms and mood-negative cognitions, in line with most findings in other cultures, notwithstanding an actual factor ranging from 2 to 7 (Basker et al. 2007).

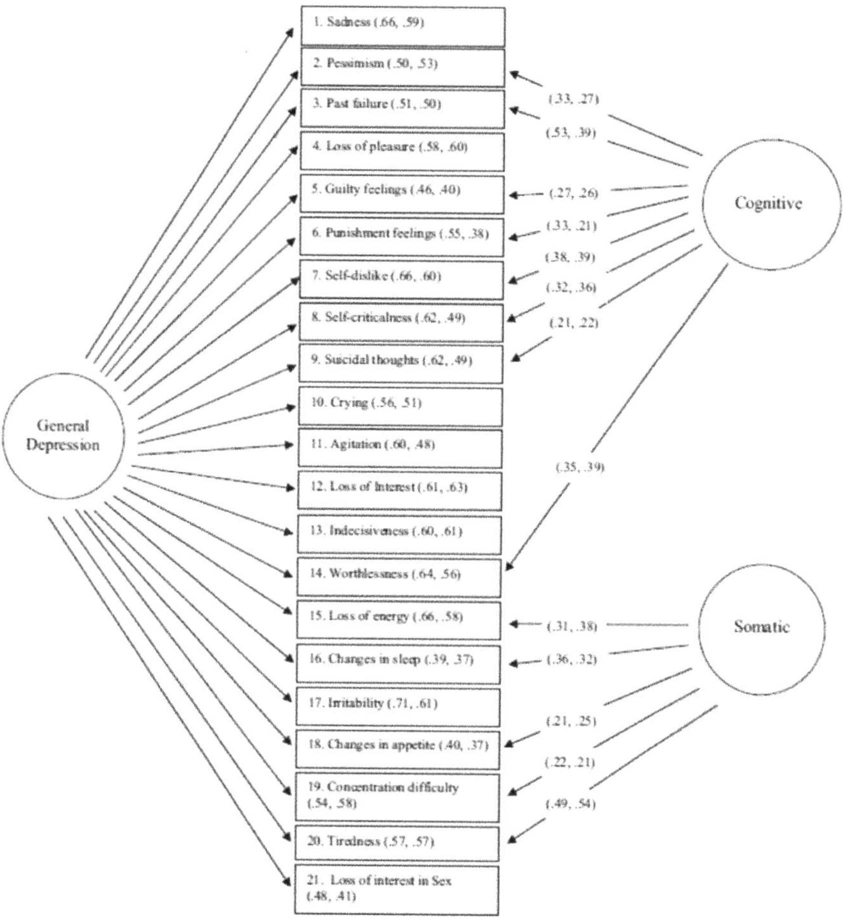

Figure 4.1. *The bifactorial structure for a cross-cultural university students application. Source: Dere et al. (2015, p. 9)*

As mentioned above, the cornerstone statistical methods for MI are factorial structure techniques, and some criticalities may still remain, namely, some instability possibly ascribable to a specific item. In this context, the psychometric analysis of MI may turn to DIF to explore if, when and where the pattern of responses changes according to respondents (Mehta 1996).

4.4. Do different people respond in the same way to common items?

As seen above, MI requires similar response patterns irrespective of whichever respondents are involved. Considering more than one group and focusing on items, the issue becomes checking group similarity in items functioning and, when disregarded, identifying possible sources of differential functioning, either homogeneous or not, to achieve comparability (Tsutsumi et al. 2009). This multigroup analysis can be carried out within the frame of item–response theory (IRT), namely, within DIF (Bock and Zimoski 1997).

For an item response, the simplest assessment format includes only a pair of exhaustive and mutually exclusive alternatives via a dichotomous approach:

$$Pr[X_{ni} = 1|\beta_n - \delta_i] = \frac{exp(\beta_n - \delta_i)}{1 + exp(\beta_n - \delta_i)} \quad [4.1]$$

Expression [4.1], the simple logistic model (SLM), gives the probability of the presence x_{ni} reported by the nth subject when replying to the ith item. Both parameters, the item difficulty δ_i and the person's characteristics β_n, are measured along a shared continuum.

In our type of measurement, however, response options are ordinal, as is often the case in psychology, especially in self-report assessment. Wright and Masters (1982) show that Rasch models can be extended to polytomous models:

$$Pr[X = x] = \frac{exp\sum_{k=0}^{x}(\beta_n - \delta_{ki})}{\sum_{j=0}^{m_i} exp\sum_{k=0}^{j}\left(\beta_n - \delta_{k_i}\right)} \quad [4.2]$$

where δ_{k_i} is the kth threshold location of item i on a latent continuum, β_n is the location of person n on the same continuum, and m_i is the maximum score for item i (Wright and Masters 1982).

Logistic regression in DIF analysis allows the investigation of both dichotomously and polytomously scored items, in the latter case with a limited number of groups, usually no more than three. Therefore, it suits our comparison, with two groups.

The DIF logistic regression takes the following form:

$$Y = \beta_0 + \beta_1 X_1 + \beta_2 X_2 + \beta_3 X_1 X_2 \qquad [4.3]$$

where Y is the response, the natural log of the odds ratio; β_s are the coefficients for the independent variables. The intercept β_0 expresses the probability of a category of response when X_1 and X_2 are constrained to zero. X_1 is the group matching variable, usually the overall total scale score. X_2 is a dummy variable for group membership, which is dichotomous in our case. The interaction between a group and the matching score is given by X_1 X_2. The two groups are identified as reference and focal. When the logistic regression curves are the same, no DIF is evident. The logistic regression shows DIF when two people of matched characteristics exhibit a different probability of assuming the same item category.

The DIF can be uniform when the sign of the difference remains the same; otherwise, the DIF is non-uniform. Chi-square difference tests compare parameters across the two groups, if not equal, showing DIF to some extent (Osterlind and Everson 2009).

We performed DIF analysis for ordinal data via Jamovi Project Software (version 2.5) (Jamovi 2024). In the case of the BDI-II scale, results were in line with an overall stability of the items behavior across the two cultures (Metha 1996). An illustrative example concerning pessimism is provided by item 2 (Figure 4.2). However, the ICC plots, cumulative and adjacent, for the reference and focal groups were reasonably close and did not overlap perfectly. In fact, the closeness between the continuous and dotted lines was nearly narrow, showing very similar behavior for each item option.

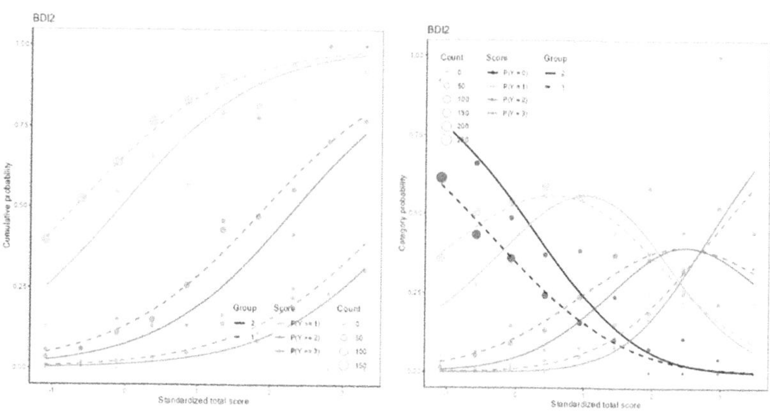

Figure 4.2. *ICC plot for the BDI-II scale, item 2, and cumulative and adjusted ICC plots. For a color version of this figure, see www.iste.co.uk/dimotikalis/data5.zip*

	Statistic	*p*	Adj.*p*
MSPSS_1	159.05	<0.001	<0.001
MSPSS_2	87.97	<0.001	<0.001
MSPSS_3	24.13	<0.001	<0.001
MSPSS_4	46.01	<0.001	<0.001
MSPSS_5	20.10	<0.001	<0.001
MSPSS_6	27.34	<0.001	<0.001
MSPSS_7	13.73	0.001	0.001
MSPSS_8	37.58	<0.001	<0.001
MSPSS_9	6.85	0.033	0.033
MSPSS_10	50.79	<0.001	<0.001
MSPSS_11	29.83	<0.001	<0.001
MSPSS_12	12.56	0.002	0.002

Table 4.2. *Likelihood ratio chi-square statistics for the MSPSS scale. *Adj.p = p value adjusted by the likelihood ratio test using multiple comparisons*

Let us recall the results of the cross-cultural direct comparison in section 4.2. One outcome, in particular, did revert to our expectation, namely, greater perceived social support by the Indian youths, who suffered more than the Italian students under several points of view.

To gain deeper insight into this apparent contradiction, we investigated the responses to the *Multidimensional Scale for Perceived Social Support* (MSPSS). The statistical fit analysis showed a difference for all items (Table 4.2).

The results of the fit measures are further highlighted by means of ICC plots that converge in the same direction as a homogeneous DIF, that is, without crossing of any sort. An illustrative case is provided by item 2, which expresses the extent to which the respondent perceives the presence in their life of a close person in which to confide happiness and sorrow. In the ICC plot, both adjacent and cumulative, focal and reference curves look quite distant, as the red double arrows illustrate (Figure 4.3), showing homogeneous DIF for several specific categories of the item.

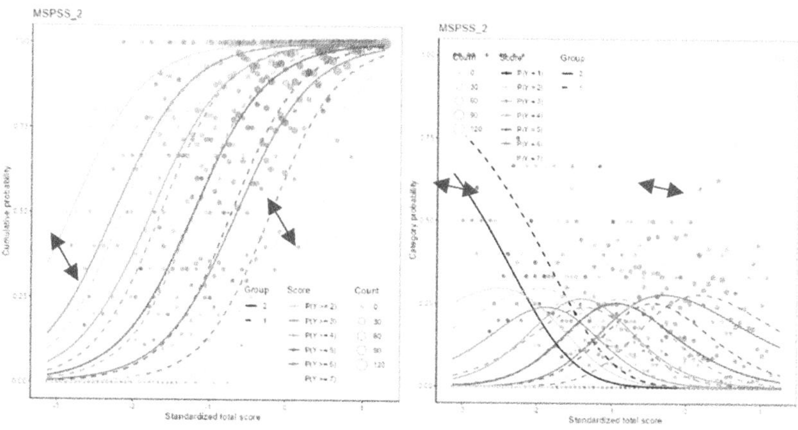

Figure 4.3. *ICC plot, cumulative and adjacent, for the MPSS scale for social support, item 2. For a color version of this figure, see www.iste.co.uk/dimotikalis/data5.zip*

4.5. Conclusions

Cross-cultural analysis poses several challenges and many interrogatives from an analytical perspective. On the one hand, the efforts and advances of some methodological strategies, such as structural equation models or IRT, have both set a cornerstone and pushed their advances to the frontier of multigroup investigation. On the other hand, the aforementioned perspectives may leave some issues unanswered to a lesser or greater extent. The two main methods may complement each other, but they may still require the contribution of additional techniques, such as direct comparisons and confounding effect analysis.

In our chapter, we have sketched a few lines of investigation on the basis of a comprehensive, direct cross-cultural study. This initial step allowed us to gain a polyhedric scenery of the phenomena involved, clarifying the following directions. In our area of research, suicide risk, the ultimate aim is to adapt prevention and intervention to culture-specific, therefore person-specific, differences.

4.6. References

Asparouhov, T. and Muthén, B. (2014). Multiple-group factor analysis alignment. *Structural Equation Modeling: A Multidisciplinary Journal*, 21, 495–508.

Basker, M., Moses, P.D., Russell, S., Russell, P.S.S. (2007). The psychometric properties of Beck Depression Inventory for adolescent depression in a primary-care paediatric setting in India. *Child and Adolescent Psychiatry and Mental Health*, 1, 1–7.

Beck, A.T., Steer, R.A., Brown, G.K. (1996). *Manual for Beck Depression Inventory-II*. Psychological Corporation, San Antonio, TX.

Beckstead, J.W., Yang, C.Y., Lengacher, C.A. (2008). Assessing cross-cultural validity of scales: A methodological review and illustrative example. *International Journal of Nursing Studies*, 145(1), 110–119.

Bock, R.D. and Zimowski, M.F. (1997). Multiple group IRT. In *Handbook of Modern Item Response Theory*, van der Linden, W.J. and Hambleton, R.K. (eds). Springer, New York.

Dere, J., Watters, C.A., Yu, S.C.M., Bagby, R.M., Ryder, A.G., Harkness, K.L. (2015). Cross-cultural examination of measurement invariance of the Beck Depression Inventory–II. *Psychological Assessment*, 27(1), 68–81.

Dong, Y. and Dumas, D. (2020). Are personality measures valid for different populations? A systematic review of measurement invariance across cultures, gender, and age. *Personality and Individual Differences*, 160, 109956.

Hui, C.H. and Triandis, H.C. (1983). Multistrategy approach to cross-cultural research: The case of locus of control. *Journal of Cross-Cultural Psychology*, 14(1), 65–83.

Hui, C.H. and Triandis, H.C. (1985). Measurement in cross-cultural psychology: A review and comparison of strategies. *Journal of Cross-Cultural Psychology*, 16(2), 131–152.

Jamovi (2024). The Jamovi Project [Online]. Available at https://www.jamovi.org.

Magliocca, S., Romano, D., Joiner, T.E., Madeddu, F., Calati, R., Zeppegno, P., Gramaglia, C. (2024). The interpersonal psychological theory of suicide in Italian university students: Validation of the INQ-15 and the AcSS-FAD. *Assessment*, 31, 1070–1088.

Mehta, P.D. (1996). An item response investigation of the Beck Depression Inventory. PhD Thesis, University of Houston, TX.

Osterlind, S.J. and Everson, H.T. (2009). *Differential Item Functioning*. Sage Publications, New York.

Poortinga, Y.H. (1989). Equivalence of cross-cultural data: An overview of basic issues. *International Journal of Psychology*, 24(6), 737–756.

Triandis, H.C. (1999). Cross-cultural psychology. *Asian Journal of Social Psychology*, 2(1), 127–143.

Tsutsumi, A., Iwata, N., Watanabe, N., De Jonge, J., Pikhart, H., Fernández-López, J.A., Xu, L., Peter, R., Knutsson, A., Niedhammer, I. et al. (2009). Application of item response theory to achieve cross-cultural comparability of occupational stress measurement. *International Journal of Methods in Psychiatric Research*, 18(1), 58–67.

World Health Organization (2024a). Suicide rates, age-standardized [Online]. Available at: https://www.who.int/data/gho/data/themes/mental-health/suicide-rates [Accessed 20 July 2024].

World Health Organization (2024b). Suicide mortality rate (per 100 000 population) [Online]. Available at: https://data.who.int/indicators/i/F08B4FD/16BBF41 [Accessed 2 July 2024].

Wright, B.D. and Masters, G.N. (1982). *Rating Scale Analysis*. MESA Press, Chicago, IL.

5

A Control Chart for Zero-Inflated Semi-Continuous Data

Data sets that contain an excessive number of zeros appear in several fields of applications. In the literature, we find several approaches to modeling zero-inflated count data, but modeling and monitoring semi-continuous data with many zeros remains an open challenge. The traditional control charts used to monitor processes over time, that is, to detect deviations from the expected behavior, are not suitable for dealing with data sets with an excessive number of zeros. In this chapter, we consider a zero-inflated Lomax distribution as a possible model for these types of data, and then, we implement and analyze the performance of a Shewhart control chart for process monitoring.

5.1. Introduction

In many real applications, we are faced with data sets with an excessive number of zeros that can occur for different reasons. We can have in the data set structural zeros, when the zero observations correspond effectively to a measurement equal to zero and/or zeros due to measurement noise or other factors, such as missing data, lack of precision of the measurement equipment that has certain limits of detection, or individuals of the sample non-exposed to the event. Some examples of this type of data sets are found, for instance, in health service visits data made by patients in a year; in insurance claims data, where many claims are zero (no claims) and the positive claims follow a skewed distribution; in medical studies, where data often exhibit a combination of zero values (no disease occurrence) and positive measurements; in chromatography applications when evaluating compound concentrations, for example, pesticide residues in food or water samples.

Chapter written by Fernanda Otília FIGUEIREDO, Adelaide FIGUEIREDO and M. Ivette GOMES.

For a color version of all figures in this chapter, see www.iste.co.uk/dimotikalis/data5.zip

And how can we model this type of data set? In the literature, we find several approaches that allow for frequent zero observations, and among them, the most common are zero-inflated models and hurdle models in case of count data, and the use of zero-inflated distributions to model semi-continuous data, that is, data from a continuous distribution with one or more than one point of mass.

5.1.1. *Zero-inflated and hurdle models for count data*

Zero-inflated models for count data assume that there are two different processes that can produce a zero, that is, we can have structural zeros when the measure is effectively zero, and a subpopulation of zeros within the data due to other factors. To account for both types of zeros, these models assume a mixture of two components: the zero and the non-zero component. The model estimates the probability of one observation belonging to each component, and the distribution of the non-zero values. This type of model has been used, for instance, in health care to model the number of days of hospitalization of patients, in sports to model the number of times in the last month that one has participated in sports activities, and so on.

The hurdle models assume that there is only one process by which a zero can be produced, that is, they assume that the zero observations correspond effectively to a measurement equal to zero. In these models, we have a Bernoulli variable that predicts whether the value of the measurement variable is zero or greater than zero, and then, the conditional distribution of the positive values is governed by a truncated-at-zero distribution. These models have been used in health services to model the number of emergency room visits made by patients in a year, and in a context of school attendance to model the number of days absent, among other applications. Although these two models for count data differ in their assumptions and the way they model the data, several studies point out that the differences between them are not very significant, and they essentially differ in the way the zero observations are interpreted. For more details see, for instance, Feng (2021).

5.1.2. *Inflated distributions for semi-continuous data*

To model semi-continuous data, we find in the literature the use of some inflated distributions in different applications. For instance, the zero-inflated beta distribution to model proportions in $[0,1[$ that arise in a health-related framework (see Maravelakis et al. (2022)); the inflated-beta distribution with two points of mass, at zero and one, to model a data set of indicators of qualified persons in priority services in some municipal districts (see Ospina and Ferrari (2010)); the inflated-Pareto distribution with a point of mass at 0.5, the limit of detection of a chromatograph, to model measurements obtained by chromatography, and afterwards implement variables and attributes acceptance-sampling plans for reducing the risk associated with chemical compounds (see Figueiredo et al. (2018a, b)). Other approaches for dealing with zero-inflated semi-continuous data and different applications of these models can be found in Liu (2019).

The remainder of the chapter is organized as follows. In section 5.2, we present some motivation for the use of the zero-inflated Lomax distribution together with some properties of this distribution. In section 5.3, a Shewhart-type control chart is proposed for monitoring zero-inflated Lomax data, and its performance under some scenarios is analyzed in section 5.4. Finally, some conclusions are drawn in section 5.5.

5.2. Zero-inflated Lomax distribution

Data sets with non-negative values from a skewed and/or heavy-tailed continuous distribution and with a large percentage of zeros are frequent in various fields. Among other possible examples, we refer to some applications in the following fields: in ecology when analyzing the abundance of species in a certain area; in hydrology when we register the daily precipitation levels; in actuarial sciences when we deal with insurance claims data; in health care when we have a data set of monthly medical costs for heart failure patients in a hospital; in chromatography when estimating concentrations of harmful chemical compounds.

As noted in Min and Agresti (2002), most of the methods in the literature for semi-continuous data analysis do not assume a highly skewed and heavy-tailed data distribution, and therefore this framework remains an open area for future research, important, for example, for modeling health expenditure and compliance data. In this work, we focus on the Lomax and zero-inflated Lomax distributions to model semi-continuous data. The Lomax distribution, also called a Pareto type-II distribution, is a special case of the generalized Pareto distribution that has been shifted so that its support begins at zero. This distribution has been used with success in business, economics, actuarial sciences, internet traffic and in other areas for modeling positive continuous data from a heavy-tailed distribution. Therefore, modeling positive continuous data from a heavy-tailed distribution with a point of mass at zero, using a zero-inflated Lomax (ZILomax) distribution, can be a good option in several contexts. To monitor such data, we implement a Shewhart chart to detect deviations from the expected process behavior and we analyze its performance. We note that several control charts based on zero-inflated count data have already been studied in the literature (for a detailed review, see, for instance, Mahmood and Xie (2019)), but very few are for monitoring semi-continuous data.

5.2.1. *The Lomax and the zero-inflated Lomax distributions*

A random variable X has a Lomax distribution with shape parameter $\xi > 0$ and scale parameter $\lambda > 0$, here denoted $X \sim \text{Lomax}(\xi, \lambda)$, if its probability density function (p.d.f.) and cumulative distribution function (c.d.f.) are, respectively, given by:

$$f_{Lomax}(x;\xi,\lambda) = \frac{1}{\xi}\lambda^{1/\xi}(x+\lambda)^{-1/\xi-1},\ x \geq 0,$$

and

$$F_{Lomax}(x;\xi,\lambda) = 1 - \lambda^{1/\xi}(x+\lambda)^{-1/\xi},\ x \geq 0.$$

A random variable X with a zero-inflated Lomax distribution has an extra parameter $\phi \in]0,1[$, the inflation parameter, here denoted $X \sim \text{ZILomax}(\phi,\xi,\lambda)$, and has a mixed probability distribution given by:

$$f_{ZILomax}(x;\phi,\xi,\lambda) = \begin{cases} \phi, & x = 0, \\ (1-\phi) f_{Lomax}(x;\xi,\lambda), & x > 0, \end{cases} \qquad [5.1]$$

and the associated c.d.f. is given by:

$$F_{ZILomax}(x;\phi,\xi,\lambda) = \phi + (1-\phi)F_{Lomax}(x;\xi,\lambda),\ x \geq 0. \qquad [5.2]$$

5.2.2. *Maximum likelihood estimates*

The parameters ϕ, ξ and λ of the ZILomax(ϕ,ξ,λ) distribution can be estimated by maximum likelihood (ML). To obtain a simple closed-form for the ML estimates (MLE), in the following we are going to consider, without loss of generality, a ZILomax distribution with scale parameter $\lambda = 1$, in [5.1] and [5.2], that is a two-parameter ZILomax(ϕ,ξ) distribution, that corresponds to a shifted Pareto standard distribution. Thus, for a random variable $X \sim \text{ZILomax}(\phi,\xi)$ we have:

$$f_{ZILomax}(x;\phi,\xi) = \begin{cases} \phi, & x = 0, \\ (1-\phi)\frac{1}{\xi}(x+1)^{-1/\xi-1}, & x > 0, \end{cases} \qquad [5.3]$$

and

$$F_{ZILomax}(x;\phi,\xi) = \phi + (1-\phi)\left(1-(x+1)^{-1/\xi}\right),\ x \geq 0. \qquad [5.4]$$

In this case, the mean value and the variance are, respectively, given by:

$$E(X) = (1-\phi)\frac{\xi}{1-\xi},\ \xi < 1, \qquad [5.5]$$

and

$$V(X) = (1-\phi)\left(\frac{\xi}{1-\xi}\right)^2\left(\frac{1}{1-2\xi}+\phi\right), \xi < 1/2. \quad [5.6]$$

Given an observed sample of size n from a ZILomax(ϕ, ξ) distribution, say $(x_1, x_2, \cdots, x_n)$, the likelihood function is given by:

$$L(\phi, \xi) = \prod_{i=1}^{n_1} \phi \prod_{i=1}^{n-n_1} (1-\phi)\frac{1}{\xi}(x_i+1)^{-1/\xi-1},$$

where n_1 are the number of observations equal to 0 in the sample of size n, and consequently, $n_2 = n - n_1$ are the number of positive observations. From the system of likelihood equations:

$$\begin{cases} \frac{\mathrm{d}}{\mathrm{d}\phi} \ln L(\phi, \xi) = 0 \\ \frac{\mathrm{d}}{\mathrm{d}\xi} \ln L(\phi, \xi) = 0 \end{cases} \Longleftrightarrow \begin{cases} n_1/\phi - n_2/(1-\phi) = 0, \\ n_2/\xi + \sum_{i=1}^{n_2} \ln(x_i+1)/\xi^2 = 0, \end{cases}$$

we obtain the ML estimates of ϕ and ξ,

$$\hat{\phi} = n_1/n \text{ and } \hat{\xi} = \sum_{i=1}^{n_2} \ln(x_i+1)/n_2, \quad [5.7]$$

that are, respectively, the proportion of zero observations in the sample, and the average of the logarithm of the observations $x_i + 1$ with $x_i > 0$.

5.3. Shewhart control chart for monitoring zero-inflated Lomax data

We are going to assume, without loss of generality, the data process comes from a ZILomax(ϕ, ξ) distribution, defined by equations [5.3] and [5.4].

For the development of any control chart, the process parameters must be known, in our case the parameters ϕ and ξ. In practice, these parameters are rarely known, and will be accurately estimated by ML from a large in-control historical data set, called a phase-I reference sample, and using the estimates given by the expressions in [5.7]. During what is known as Phase-I analysis, the (estimated) control limits of the chart are determined, and the corresponding control chart is applied retrospectively to confirm the process was in-control when the reference sample was collected. Otherwise, if the chart triggers a signal, the observations outside the control limits are discarded, new estimates of the parameters are obtained, and the process is repeated.

In Phase-II, the value of the parameters ϕ and ξ will be assumed known, equal to the previous estimates, and its value will be denoted by ϕ_0 and ξ_0. Then, a (Phase-II) control chart is implemented for real-time monitoring. In our case, we will implement a control chart for individual observations, obtained by plotting the values of the recorded observations:

$$X_i \sim \text{ZILomax}(\phi = \tau\phi_0, \xi = \delta\xi_0), \;\; i = 1, 2, ...$$

where ϕ_0 and ξ_0 are the in-control parameter values, and τ and δ are the magnitude of possible shifts in these parameters, respectively. If $\delta = 1$ and $\tau = 1$, the process is in-control (IC); otherwise, the process is out-of-control (OOC) due to a shift in ϕ and/or ξ, and consequently, we have a shift in the assumed process mean value, $\mu = \mu_0 = (1 - \phi_0)\xi_0/(1 - \xi_0)$, given by [5.5].

When the parameters are estimated, it is important to note that the performance of the control chart differs from the performance of the corresponding chart with known parameters due to the variability of the estimates. In the case of estimated parameters, the control limits of the chart must be considered random variables. However, the analysis of the effect of the parameters' estimation is out of the scope of this work.

In many practical situations, the main aim is to detect changes in the process mean level μ_0, occurred by changes in ϕ and/or ξ. In particular, the detection of increases is of greater interest when an increase is associated with the presence of an assignable cause leading to process deterioration. Thus, we will focus on an upper-sided Shewhart control chart. A two-sided control chart would be similarly implemented. The upper control limit (UCL) of the upper-sided Shewhart control chart with known parameters, ϕ_0 and ξ_0, is usually determined in order to obtain a chart with a desired performance, say, with a given false alarm rate (FAR), usually 0.27%.

The probability that an observation X_i, $i = 1, 2, 3, ...$ exceeds the upper-control limit, that is, the chart triggers an OOC signal, is given by:

$$\beta = \beta(\phi, \xi) = P(X_i > \text{UCL}) = (1 - \phi)(\text{UCL} + 1)^{-1/\xi},$$

and the FAR of the chart is given by $\alpha = \beta(\phi_0, \xi_0)$. Thus, for a given FAR α, the upper-control limit is obtained by:

$$\text{UCL} = ((1 - \phi_0)/\alpha)^{\xi_0} - 1.$$

5.4. Performance of the proposed control chart

The run length (RL) of a control chart is the number of points plotted on the chart until it triggers an OOC signal for the first time, and the performance of a control chart is usually evaluated by the properties of its RL distribution, in particular, by some of its parameters. The RL of the upper-sided ZILomax Shewhart control chart with known parameters has a geometric distribution with parameter β, the probability defined before. The average run length (ARL) and the standard deviation run length (SDRL) of the chart with known parameters are two commonly used measures of performance, and are given by ARL=$1/\beta$ and SDRL=$\sqrt{1-\beta}/\beta$. When the process is in-control, the ARL (ARL_0) must be large, and when the process is OOC, the ARL must be as small as possible. The in-control ARL of our chart is directly related with the FAR, that is, ARL_0=1/FAR.

Although the ARL jointly with the SDRL are the most common metrics of performance, due to the high asymmetry of the RL distribution in most of the cases, the percentiles of the RL distribution are also considered in the evaluation of the properties of the chart, and in particular, the median RL (MRL). The MRL of the upper-sided ZILomax Shewhart-type control chart is given by:

$$MRL = \left\lceil -\ln 2/\ln\left(1-(1-\phi)(\text{UCL}+1)^{-1/\xi}\right)\right\rceil,$$

where $\lceil x \rceil$ denotes the rounded-up integer of x.

To illustrate the performance of the previous control chart, we determined the control limit of the chart that corresponds to an ARL_0=370.4 (FAR=0.27%) and we considered four scenarios for the in-control parameters:

- Scenario #1: $\phi_0 = 0.75$ and $\xi_0 = 0.25 \implies$ UCL=2.10202;
- Scenario #2: $\phi_0 = 0.6$ and $\xi_0 = 0.25 \implies$ UCL=2.48878;
- Scenario #3: $\phi_0 = 0.5$ and $\xi_0 = 0.25 \implies$ UCL=2.68894;
- Scenario #4: $\phi_0 = 0.4$ and $\xi_0 = 0.25 \implies$ UCL=2.86097.

To describe the OOC situation, we considered different magnitudes of shifts in the inflation and shape parameters: $\phi = \tau\phi_0$ and $\xi = \delta\xi_0$ for some values of $\tau < 1$ and/or $\delta > 1$. Note that we are interested in detecting increases in the mean value $\mu_0 = (1-\phi_0)\xi_0/(1-\xi_0)$ of the process. If $\delta \geq 1$ and/or $\tau \leq 1$ (not both equal to 1), we surely have an increase in the mean of the process. For these scenarios, we will present the ARL and the MRL profiles of the chart in Figures 5.1–5.4, for $1 \leq \delta \leq 2$ and $\tau = 1, 0.9, 0.8, 0.75, 0.5$. When the process is in-control ($\delta = \tau = 1$), ARL $=$ 370.4 and MRL $=$ 257.

From Figure 5.1, corresponding to scenario 1, with fixed in-control parameters $\xi_0 = 0.25$ and $\phi_0 = 0.75$ (a very large percentage of zeros in the distribution), we observe the following behavior in the performance of the chart:

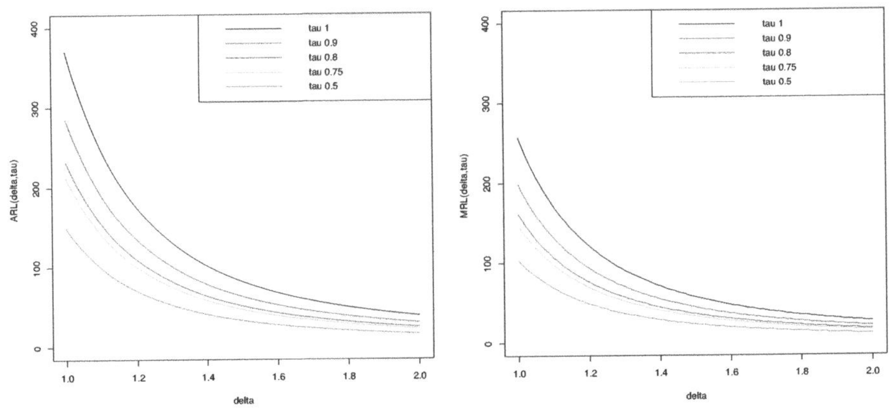

Figure 5.1. *ARL (left) and MRL (right) profiles. Data: $X \sim$ZILomax($\phi = \tau\phi_0, \xi = \delta\xi_0$), with in-control parameters $\phi_0 = 0.75$, $\xi_0 = 0.25$*

– If only ξ increases (that is if $\delta > 1$ and $\tau = 1$), the ARL (and the MRL) decreases quickly with δ. As the larger is δ, on average (in median terms) fewer observations are necessary to be collected to detect the change.

– If only ϕ decreases (that is if $\delta = 1$ and $\tau < 1$), the ARL and the MRL also decreases with τ. For instance, if $\tau = 0.9$ (it corresponds to a decrease of 10% in ϕ_0), the ARL and the MRL values are larger than the ones we obtain if $\tau = 0.5$ (since it corresponds to a larger decrease, 50%, in ϕ_0).

– If ξ increases and ϕ decreases (that is if $\delta > 1$ and $\tau < 1$), the ARL as well as the MRL decreases more quickly as it would be expected since it corresponds to a larger increase in the mean value μ_0.

When we compare the results obtained for the different scenarios, shown in Figures 5.1–5.4, where the parameter ϕ_0 associated with the percentage of zeros in the sample varies from 0.75 to 0.4, we can draw the following conclusions:

– The ARL and the MRL behavior is similar for all the scenarios, that is, if ξ increases and/or ϕ decreases (that is if $\delta > 1$ and/or $\tau < 1$), the ARL as well as the MRL has a decreasing behavior.

– The smaller the value of ϕ_0, the closer the ARL (and MRL) curves are for the different values of τ, that is, reductions of different magnitudes in the parameter ϕ lead to similar changes in the process mean value, and hence to similar ARL (MRL) values.

– If $\delta > 1$ and $\tau = 1$, the lower the in-control value ϕ_0, the smaller the number of samples needed to detect the change, and as expected, these values decrease with δ for fixed ϕ_0, as we can see from the values presented in Table 5.1.

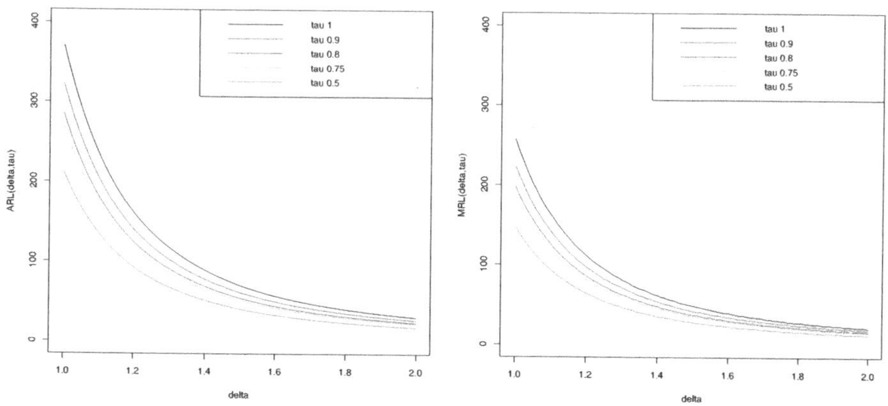

Figure 5.2. *ARL (left) and MRL (right) profiles. Data:* X *∼ZILomax*($\phi = \tau\phi_0, \xi = \delta\xi_0$), *with in-control parameters* $\phi_0 = 0.6$, $\xi_0 = 0.25$

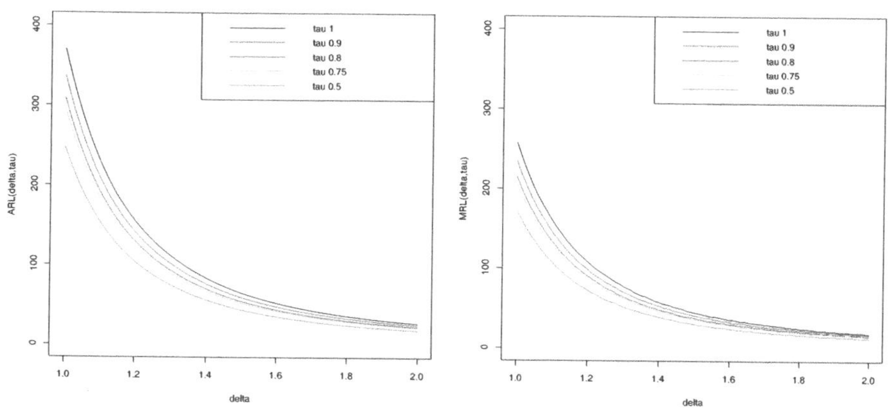

Figure 5.3. *ARL (left) and MRL (right) profiles. Data:* X *∼ZILomax*($\phi = \tau\phi_0, \xi = \delta\xi_0$), *with in-control parameters* $\phi_0 = 0.5$, $\xi_0 = 0.25$

– If $\delta = 1$ and $\tau < 1$, the lower the in-control value ϕ_0, the greater the number of samples needed to detect the change, but as expected, these values decrease with τ, but slowly as ϕ_0 increases, as we can see from the values presented in Table 5.2.

– Tables 5.3–5.6 show some ARL and MRL values obtained for the different scenarios and for changes in both parameters ($\delta > 1$ and $\tau < 1$).

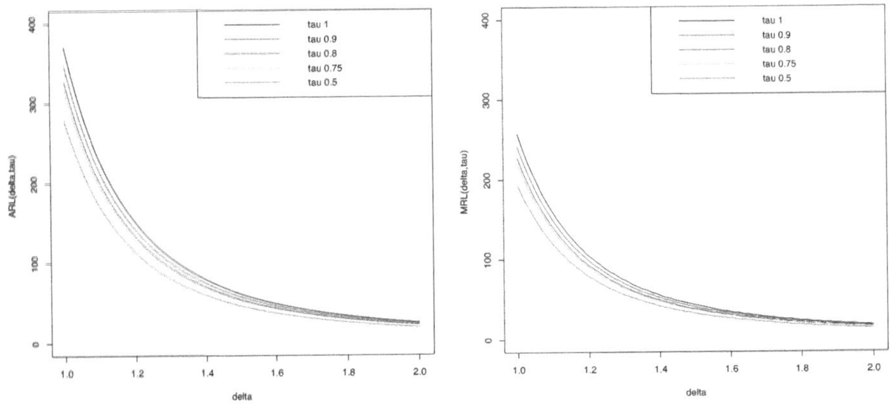

Figure 5.4. *ARL (left) and MRL (right) profiles. Data: X ~ZILomax($\phi = \tau\phi_0, \xi = \delta\xi_0$), with in-control parameters $\phi_0 = 0.4$, $\xi_0 = 0.25$*

	ARL values				MRL values			
δ	$\phi_0 = 0.75$	$\phi_0 = 0.6$	$\phi_0 = 0.5$	$\phi_0 = 0.4$	$\phi_0 = 0.75$	$\phi_0 = 0.6$	$\phi_0 = 0.5$	$\phi_0 = 0.4$
1.1	245	235	230	227	170	163	160	157
1.2	174	161	155	150	121	112	108	104
1.3	130	117	111	106	90	81	77	74
1.4	102	89	83	79	71	62	58	55
1.5	82	70	65	61	57	49	45	43
1.6	68	57	52	49	47	40	36	34
1.7	57	47	43	40	40	33	30	28
1.8	49	40	36	34	34	28	25	23
1.9	43	35	31	29	30	24	22	20
2.0	38	30	27	25	27	21	19	17

Table 5.1. *ARL and MRL in case of $\delta > 1$ and $\tau = 1$ (i.e., if only ξ increases)*

5.5. Conclusions

In this work, we studied the performance of an upper-sided Shewhart-type control chart for individual observations to monitor zero-inflated Lomax processes. The use of the zero-inflated Lomax distribution was motivated by the need for having a distribution that accounts for highly skewed and heavy-tailed data, a framework that arises in many areas of application, and due to the fact that the Pareto-type distributions have an important role in the statistics of extremes. The performance of the implemented control chart was studied under several scenarios, and in all of them we observed an interesting performance to detect increases in the process mean value. The development of control charts for non-individual observations and the analysis of the effect of parameter estimation on the performance of the chart will be considered in a future research.

	ARL values				MRL values			
τ	$\phi_0 = 0.75$	$\phi_0 = 0.6$	$\phi_0 = 0.5$	$\phi_0 = 0.4$	$\phi_0 = 0.75$	$\phi_0 = 0.6$	$\phi_0 = 0.5$	$\phi_0 = 0.4$
0.9	285	322	337	347	198	223	234	241
0.8	231	285	308	327	161	198	214	227
0.75	212	269	296	317	147	187	206	220
0.5	148	212	246	275	103	147	171	193

Table 5.2. *ARL and MRL in case of $\delta = 1$ and $\tau < 1$ (i.e., if only ϕ decreases)*

	ARL values				MRL values			
δ	$\tau = 0.9$	$\tau = 0.8$	$\tau = 0.75$	$\tau = 0.5$	$\tau = 0.9$	$\tau = 0.8$	$\tau = 0.75$	$\tau = 0.5$
1.1	189	153	140	98	131	106	97	68
1.2	134	109	100	70	93	76	69	48
1.3	100	81	74	52	70	57	52	36
1.4	78	63	58	41	54	44	40	28
1.5	63	51	47	33	44	36	33	23
1.6	52	42	39	27	36	30	27	19
1.7	44	36	33	23	31	25	23	16
1.8	38	31	28	20	27	22	20	14
1.9	33	27	25	17	23	19	17	12
2.0	30	24	22	15	21	17	15	11

Table 5.3. *ARL and MRL for scenario 1 ($\xi_0 = 0.25, \phi_0 = 0.75$) and some values of $\delta > 1$ and $\tau < 1$*

	ARL values				MRL values			
δ	$\tau = 0.9$	$\tau = 0.8$	$\tau = 0.75$	$\tau = 0.5$	$\tau = 0.9$	$\tau = 0.8$	$\tau = 0.75$	$\tau = 0.5$
1.1	204	181	171	134	142	126	119	93
1.2	140	124	117	92	97	86	81	64
1.3	102	90	85	67	71	62	59	46
1.4	77	68	65	51	54	48	45	35
1.5	61	54	51	40	42	37	35	28
1.6	49	44	41	32	34	30	29	23
1.7	41	36	34	27	29	25	24	19
1.8	35	31	29	23	24	22	20	16
1.9	30	27	25	20	21	19	18	14
2.0	26	23	22	17	18	16	15	12

Table 5.4. *ARL and MRL for scenario 2 ($\xi_0 = 0.25, \phi_0 = 0.6$) and some values of $\delta > 1$ and $\tau < 1$*

	ARL values				MRL values			
δ	$\tau = 0.9$	$\tau = 0.8$	$\tau = 0.75$	$\tau = 0.5$	$\tau = 0.9$	$\tau = 0.8$	$\tau = 0.75$	$\tau = 0.5$
1.1	209	192	184	154	145	133	128	107
1.2	141	129	124	103	98	90	86	72
1.3	101	93	89	74	70	64	62	51
1.4	76	69	67	56	53	48	46	39
1.5	59	54	52	43	41	38	36	30
1.6	48	44	42	35	33	30	29	24
1.7	39	36	35	29	27	25	24	20
1.8	33	30	29	24	23	21	20	17
1.9	28	26	25	21	20	18	17	15
2.0	25	23	22	18	17	16	15	13

Table 5.5. *ARL and MRL for scenario 3 ($\xi_0 = 0.25, \phi_0 = 0.5$) and some values of $\delta > 1$ and $\tau < 1$*

	ARL values				MRL values			
δ	$\tau = 0.9$	$\tau = 0.8$	$\tau = 0.75$	$\tau = 0.5$	$\tau = 0.9$	$\tau = 0.8$	$\tau = 0.75$	$\tau = 0.5$
1.1	212	200	194	170	147	139	135	118
1.2	141	133	129	113	98	92	90	78
1.3	100	94	91	80	69	65	63	55
1.4	74	70	68	59	52	49	47	41
1.5	57	54	52	46	40	38	36	32
1.6	46	43	42	37	32	30	29	26
1.7	38	35	34	30	26	25	24	21
1.8	31	30	29	25	22	21	20	18
1.9	27	25	25	21	19	18	17	15
2.0	23	22	21	19	16	15	15	13

Table 5.6. *ARL and MRL for scenario 4 ($\xi_0 = 0.25, \phi_0 = 0.4$) and some values of $\delta > 1$ and $\tau < 1$*

5.6. Acknowledgments

This work is partially financed by national funds through FCT - Fundação para a Ciência e a Tecnologia, under the scope of the projects UID/00006/2025, UIDB/00006/2020 (https://doi.org/10.54499/UIDB/00006/2020) (CEAUL) and LA/P/0063/2020 (https://doi.org/ 10.54499/LA/P/0063/2020).

5.7. References

Feng, C.X. (2021). A comparison of zero-inflated and hurdle models for modeling zero-inflated count data. *Journal of Statistical Distributions and Applications*, 8(8), 1–19.

Figueiredo, F., Figueiredo, A., Gomes, M.I. (2018a). Acceptance-sampling plans for reducing the risk associated with chemical compounds. In *Recent Studies on Risk Analysis and Statistical Modeling*, Oliveira, T.A., Kitsos, C.P., Oliveira, A., Grilo, L.M. (eds). Springer, Cham.

Figueiredo, F., Figueiredo, A., Gomes, M.I. (2018b). Design of sampling plans for sensory evaluation. *AIP Conf. Proc.*, 2040–110006.

Liu, L., Shih, Y-C.T., Strawderman, R.L., Zhang, D., Johnson, B.A. Chai, H. (2019). Statistical analysis of zero-inflated nonnegative continuous data: A review. *Statistical Science*, 34(2), 253–279.

Mahmood, T. and Xie, M. (2019). Models and monitoring of zero-inflated processes: The past and current trends. *Quality and Reliability Engineering International*, 35, 2540–2557.

Maravelakis, P.E., Rakitzis, A.C., Castagliola, P. (2022). Exponentially weighed moving average charts for monitoring zero-inflated proportions with applications in health care. *Statistical Methods in Medical Research*, 31(5), 959–977.

Min, Y. and Agresti, A. (2002). Modeling nonnegative data with clumping at zero: A survey. *Journal of the Iranian Statistical Society*, 1, 7–33.

Ospina, R. and Ferrari, S.L.P. (2010). Inflated beta distributions. *Statistical Papers*, 51, 111–126.

6

Further Results on Location Invariant Estimation of the Weibull Tail Coefficient

Among the large variety of parameters of extreme events, we shall here emphasize the *Weibull tail-coefficient* (WTC), which can be defined as the index of regular variation of a regularly varying hazard function, $H(x) := -\ln(1 - F(x))$. The WTC is thus deeply linked to a positive *extreme value index* (EVI), the index of regular variation of $\overline{F}(x) := 1 - F(x)$ and several estimators of a positive EVI, based on *generalized means*, which are generalizations of the classical Hill EVI-estimators that have recently been used for the WTC-estimation. Contrarily to the EVI and the WTC, most of the aforementioned estimators are not location invariant. In this chapter, location-invariant WTC-estimators are considered and studied for finite samples, through Monte Carlo simulations. Those estimators are dependent on an extra tuning parameter and are highly flexible. Adequate choices of the tuning parameters under play are here put forward. Some concluding remarks are further provided.

6.1. Introduction

Let us assume that we have access to a sample $\underline{\mathbf{X}}_n = (X_1, \ldots, X_n)$ of n *independent, identically distributed* (IID) or even stationary weakly dependent *random variables* (RVs) from a *cumulative distribution function* (CDF) F. As usual, let us denote by $X_{1:n} \leq \cdots \leq X_{n:n}$ the associated ascending *order statistics* (OSs), and further assume to be under the framework of the *extremal types theorem* (ETT), that is, assume that there exist sequences of real constants $\{a_n > 0\}$ and $\{b_n \in \mathbb{R}\}$ such that $(X_{n:n} - b_n)/a_n$, the maximum, linearly normalized, converges in distribution to a non-degenerate RV. Then (Fisher and Tippett (1928); Gnedenko

Chapter written by M. Ivette GOMES, Frederico CAEIRO and Lígia HENRIQUES-RODRIGUES.
For a color version of all figures in this chapter, see www.iste.co.uk/dimotikalis/data5.zip

(1943)), the limit CDF is necessarily of the type of the *general extreme value* (GEV), given by:

$$G_\xi(x) \equiv \mathrm{GEV}_\xi(x) = \begin{cases} \mathrm{e}^{-(1+\xi x)^{-1/\xi}}, \ 1+\xi x > 0, & \text{if } \xi \neq 0, \\ \mathrm{e}^{-\mathrm{e}^{-x}}, \ x \in \mathbb{R}, & \text{if } \xi = 0. \end{cases} \qquad [6.1]$$

It is then said that the CDF F belongs to the *max-domain of attraction* of G_ξ, and the notation $F \in \mathcal{D}_\mathcal{M}(\mathrm{GEV}_\xi)$ is used, where ξ, in [6.1], is the EVI, the primary parameter of extreme and large events. The EVI measures the heaviness of the *right-tail function* (RTF):

$$\overline{F}(x) := 1 - F(x), \qquad [6.2]$$

and the heavier the right-tail, the larger ξ is.

Under a semi-parametric framework and for heavy tails ($\xi > 0$), the approach considered in this chapter, we work in the whole:

$$\mathcal{D}_\mathcal{M}{}^+ := \mathcal{D}_\mathcal{M}(\mathrm{GEV}_{\xi>0}), \qquad [6.3]$$

and, with $\overline{F}(\cdot)$ defined in [6.2] and $\mathcal{D}_\mathcal{M}{}^+$ defined in [6.3]:

$$F \in \mathcal{D}_\mathcal{M}{}^+ \iff \overline{F} \in \mathcal{R}_{-1/\xi}, \qquad [6.4]$$

where $\mathcal{R}_\alpha$ denotes the set of regularly varying functions with index α, that is, positive measurable functions $g(\cdot)$ such that $g(tx)/g(t) \to x^\alpha$, as $t \to \infty$ and for all $x > 0$ (see Bingham et al. (1987), for further details on the notion of regular variation).

The estimation of any parameter of extreme and large events is then based on the k upper observations above the random threshold $X_{n-k:n}$ (see the books by Beirlant et al. (2004), de Haan and Ferreira (2006) and Gomes et al. (2013b)), being the estimation based on an intermediate number of OSs, that is, a value of $k \in [1, n)$, such that:

$$k = k_n \to \infty, \qquad k/n \to 0 \quad (k = o(n)), \qquad \text{as } n \to \infty.$$

Among the large variety of parameters of extreme events, we shall here emphasize the WTC, θ, which can be defined as the reciprocal of the index of regular variation of a regularly varying hazard function:

$$H(x) := -\log(1 - F(x)) \in \mathcal{R}_{1/\theta},\ \theta \in \mathbb{R}^+,$$

just as $-1/\xi > 0$ is the index of regular variation of $\overline{F}$, as can be seen in [6.4]. The WTC is thus deeply linked to a positive EVI, and several estimators of a positive EVI, based on *generalized means* (GMs), which are generalizations of the classical Hill EVI-estimators (Hill (1975)), have recently been used for the WTC-estimation (Caeiro et al. (2022a, b); Henriques-Rodrigues et al. (2024)).

Contrarily to the EVI and the WTC, most of the aforementioned estimators are scale invariant but not location invariant. In this chapter, after some details on GMs EVI and WTC-estimation, in section 6.2, and along the lines of Gomes et al. (2025), specific GMs location-invariant WTC-estimators are put forward in section 6.3 and a large-scale simulation is developed in section 6.4. Those estimators are dependent on an extra tuning parameter and are highly flexible. Adequate choices of the tuning parameters under play are put forward here. Section 6.5 concludes with some comments and mentions several open research topics.

6.2. Hill and GMs EVI and WTC-estimators

For heavy-tailed models, the classical EVI-estimators are the Hill (H) estimators (Hill (1975)), with the functional form:

$$\mathrm{H}(k) \equiv \mathrm{H}(k; \underline{\mathbf{X}}_n) \equiv \mathrm{H}_{k,n} := \frac{1}{k}\sum_{i=1}^{k} V_{ik}, \qquad 1 \le k < n, \qquad [6.5]$$

where

$$V_{ik} := \ln X_{n-i+1:n} - \ln X_{n-k:n},\ 1 \le i \le k < n. \qquad [6.6]$$

Hill EVI-estimators, the averages of the log-excesses, in [6.6], are highly efficient at the optimal k, in the sense of minimal *mean squared error* (MSE), but depend strongly on the choice of k, being thus very diverse in the number of alternative estimators (see Gomes and Guillou (2015) and Fedotenkov (2020), one of the most recent overview articles on the topic).

6.2.1. *Power-mean-of-exponent-p (PM$_p$) and Holder's mean-of-order-p (MO$_p \equiv \mathrm{H}_p$) EVI estimation*

Beyond the average, in [6.5], the p-moments of log-excesses, that is,

$$M_{k,n}^{(p)} := \frac{1}{k}\sum_{i=1}^{k} \left\{ \ln X_{n-i+1:n} - \ln X_{n-k:n} \right\}^p,\ p \ge 1,\ \left[M_{k,n}^{(1)} \equiv \mathrm{H}_{k,n}\right]$$

introduced in Dekkers et al. (1989), have also played a relevant role in the EVI-estimation and can more generally be parameterized in any $p \in \mathbb{R} \setminus \{0\}$. And, as far as we know, one of the first GMs to be considered was the *power mean of exponent* p (PM_p) *of the log-excesses*, introduced in Gomes and Martins (1999), also considered in Segers (2001), and further studied in Gomes and Martins (2001). This class of EVI-estimators has the functional form:

$$\mathrm{PM}_p(k) \equiv \mathrm{PM}_p(k; \underline{\mathbf{X}}_n) \equiv \mathrm{PM}_{k,n,p} := \left(\frac{M_{k,n}^{(p)}}{\Gamma(p+1)}\right)^{1/p}, \quad \text{for } p > 0, \qquad [6.7]$$

with $\mathrm{PM}_1(k) \equiv \mathrm{H}(k)$, $\Gamma(\cdot)$ denoting the complete Gamma function and can be considered for any $p > -1$. Details on the asymptotic behavior and finite sample properties of the PM_p EVI-estimators can be found in Gomes and Martins (2001).

Further note that we can write:

$$\mathrm{H}(k) = \sum_{i=1}^{k} \ln\left(\frac{X_{n-i+1:n}}{X_{n-k:n}}\right)^{1/k} = \ln\left(\prod_{i=1}^{k} \frac{X_{n-i+1:n}}{X_{n-k:n}}\right)^{1/k}.$$

The H EVI-estimator at level k is thus the logarithm of the *geometric mean* (or *mean-of-order-*0) of:

$$U_{ik} := \frac{X_{n-i+1:n}}{X_{n-k:n}}, \quad 1 \le i \le k < n. \qquad [6.8]$$

Brilhante et al. (2013, 2014), and almost simultaneously Paulauskas and Vaičiulis (2013) and Beran et al. (2014), considered as basic statistics, the *mean-of-order-p* (MO_p) of U_{ik}, $1 \le i \le k$, in [6.8], for $p \ge 0$. And more generally, Gomes and Caeiro (2014), and also Caeiro et al. (2016), considered those same statistics for any $p \in \mathbb{R}$, that is:

$$\mathrm{M}_p(k) = \begin{cases} \left(\frac{1}{k}\sum_{i=1}^{k} U_{ik}^p\right)^{1/p}, & \text{if } p \neq 0, \\ \left(\prod_{i=1}^{k} U_{ik}\right)^{1/k}, & \text{if } p = 0, \end{cases}$$

and the associated class of MO_p EVI-estimators:

$$\text{H}_p(k) \equiv \text{H}_p(k; \underline{\mathbf{X}}_n) \equiv \text{H}_{k,n,p} := \begin{cases} \left(1 - \text{M}_p^{-p}(k)\right)/p, & \text{if } p < 1/\xi, \\ & p \neq 0, \\ \ln \text{M}_0(k) = \text{H}(k), & \text{if } p = 0. \end{cases} \qquad [6.9]$$

6.2.2. *WTC estimation*

The simplest WTC-estimators were introduced in Gardes and Girard (2006) (GGH), with H standing for Hill, and are given by:

$$\widehat{\theta}_{\text{H}}^{\text{GG}}(k) \equiv \widehat{\theta}_{\text{H}}^{\text{GG}}(k; \underline{\mathbf{X}}_n) := \frac{\ln(n/k)}{k} \sum_{i=1}^{k} V_{i,k} = \ln(n/k)\text{H}_{k,n}, \qquad [6.10]$$

with $\text{H}_{k,n}$ the already defined H EVI estimators in [6.5]. Further notice that we can also replace $1/\ln(n/k)$, in [6.10], by an asymptotically equivalent function, like:

$$T_n = \frac{1}{k} \sum_{i=1}^{k} \ln \ln \left(\tfrac{n+1}{i}\right) - \ln \ln \left(\tfrac{n+1}{k+1}\right) \sim \frac{1}{\ln(n/k)},$$

as proposed in Beirlant et al. (1996), and further studied in Girard (2004). We then come to the WTC-estimators (GH):

$$\widehat{\theta}_{\text{H}}^{\text{G}}(k) \equiv \widehat{\theta}_{\text{H}}^{\text{G}}(k; \underline{\mathbf{X}}_n) := \frac{\text{H}_{k,n}}{T_n} = \frac{\text{H}_{k,n}}{\frac{1}{k}\sum_{i=1}^{k} \ln \ln \left(\frac{n+1}{i}\right) - \ln \ln \left(\frac{n+1}{k+1}\right)}. \qquad [6.11]$$

A first approach to the use of GMs in the WTC-estimation was recently performed in Caeiro et al. (2022a, b), where, with $\text{H}_p(k)$ and $\widehat{\theta}_{\text{H}}^{\text{GG}}(k)$, respectively, given in [6.9] and [6.10]:

$$\widehat{\theta}_{\text{H}_p}^{\text{GG}}(k) \equiv \widehat{\theta}_{\text{H}_p}^{\text{GG}}(k; \underline{\mathbf{X}}_n), \qquad [6.12]$$

also called GGH_p WTC-estimators, were considered.

More generally, Henriques-Rodrigues et al. (2024) extended the above-mentioned results, studying the asymptotic and finite sample behavior of three additional GMs WTC-estimators, involving not only, $\text{H}_p(k)$, in [6.9] but also $\text{PM}_p(k)$, in [6.7], and both GG and G functionals, respectively, given in [6.10] and [6.11], as a function of the H EVI estimators, in [6.5].

For an adequate choice of p, the new GMs WTC-estimators:

$$\widehat{\theta}^{\mathrm{G}}_{\mathrm{PM}_p}(k) \equiv \widehat{\theta}^{\mathrm{G}}_{\mathrm{PM}_p}(k; \underline{\mathbf{X}}_n) := \frac{\mathrm{PM}_{k,n,p}}{T_n}, \qquad [6.13]$$

now also called GPM_p WTC-estimators, outperformed all other estimators in terms of bias and MSE for almost all models considered in Henriques-Rodrigues et al. (2024), and are the ones used here in the simulations performed in section 6.4.

6.3. Classes of PORT-GMs (PGMs) WTC-estimators

The aforementioned classes of GMs EVI and WTC-estimators depend not only on k but also on the *tuning* parameter $p \in \mathbb{R}$, are highly flexible, but, as often desired, they are not location-invariant, depending strongly on possible shifts in the model underlying the data, contrarily to what happens to the EVI and to the WTC, which are independent of shifts in the data (see Gomes et al. (2025) for a proof).

Just as done in Gomes et al. (2025), it is thus sensible to suggest the use of the classes of PORT-GMs WTC-estimators, where PORT stands for *peaks over a random threshold*. They are similar in spirit to the PORT-H EVI-estimators, studied in Araújo Santos et al. (2006), and further considered in Gomes et al. (2008), among other more recent articles, like Gomes et al. (2013c, 2016b).

All classes of PORT estimators are based on a *sample of excesses* over a random threshold $X_{n_s:n}$, $n_s := \lfloor ns \rfloor + 1, 0 \le s < 1$:

$$\underline{\mathbf{X}}_n^{(s)} := \left(X_{n-j+1:n} - X_{n_s:n}, \quad 1 \le j \le n - n_s\right) \qquad [6.14]$$

rather than on the available sample $\underline{\mathbf{X}}_n$, where $\lfloor x \rfloor$ denotes the integer part of x. And the PORT $\mathrm{H}_p \equiv \mathrm{MO}_p$ EVI estimators, introduced and studied both theoretically and for finite samples in Gomes et al. (2016b), may even compare favorably, both asymptotically and for finite samples, with the PORT versions of the second-order *minimum-variance reduced-bias* (MVRB) EVI-estimators in Caeiro et al. (2005), provided that we adequately choose the vector, (p, s), of tuning parameters. We can have $s = 0$, if the underlying CDF has a finite left endpoint, $x_{_F} := \inf\{x : F(x) > 0\}$ (the random threshold can then be the minimum) and $0 < s < 1$, for CDFs with finite or infinite left endpoint $x_{_F}$ (the random threshold is an empirical quantile).

For $0 \leq s < 1$ and $k < n - n_s$, the PORT-GMs classes of WTC-estimators have the same functional form of the GMs classes of WTC-estimators, but with $\underline{\mathbf{X}}_n = (X_1, \ldots, X_n)$ replaced by the sample of excesses $\underline{\mathbf{X}}_n^{(s)}$, in [6.14]. With $\bullet$ standing for both PM_p and H_p, respectively, given in [6.7] and [6.9], and with $*$ standing for both the GG and the G functionals, respectively, given in [6.10] and [6.11], they are thus given by:

$$\widehat{\theta}_{\bullet}^{*}(k) \equiv \widehat{\theta}_{\bullet}^{*}(k; \underline{\mathbf{X}}_n^{(s)}). \qquad [6.15]$$

For $(\bullet, *) = (\mathrm{H}_p, \mathrm{GG})$, in [6.15], one gets the GGH_p WTC-estimator, already defined in [6.12], and a similar comment applies to the choice $(\bullet, *) = (\mathrm{PM}_p, \mathrm{G})$, in [6.15], which leads to the GPM_p WTC-estimator, in [6.13]. These estimators are now invariant for both changes of scale and location in the data, and depend on the extra *tuning parameter* s, which provides even more flexible classes of WTC-estimators, as will be seen in section 6.4, where Monte Carlo studies are developed for different models.

6.4. Monte Carlo simulation of the PORT-GPM$_p$ (PGPM$_p$) WTC-estimators

Just as an illustration of several Monte Carlo simulation studies based on $r = 1,000$ replicates of samples of size $n = 1,000$, we first present, in Figures 6.1 to 6.4, the patterns of simulated *expected values* (E) and MSE of the GH, GGH and the PGH, PGGH and PGPM_p WTC-estimators, for a shift $s = 0.1$, and, respectively, for a Gamma(0.5) $(\theta = 1)$, $p = 2.75, 3, 3.25$, a Gamma(0.75) $(\theta = 1)$, $p = 1.5, 1.75, 2$, a half–normal $(\theta = 0.5)$, $p = 3, 3.5, 4$, and a two parameter (or shifted) exponential (Johnson et al. (1994)) $(\theta = 1)$, $p = 0.75, 0.9, 1.1$ models.

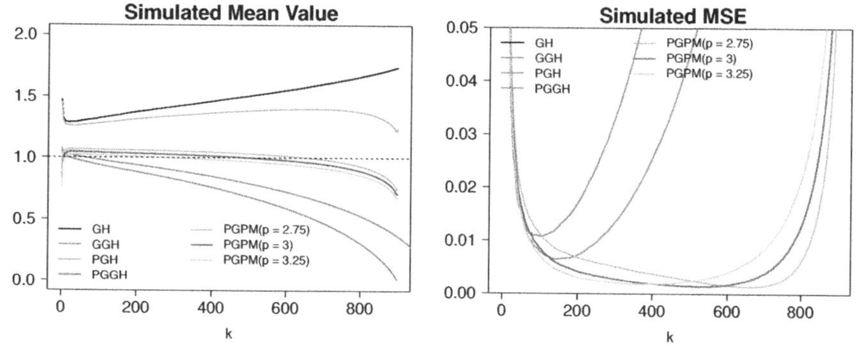

Figure 6.1. *Simulated mean values (left) and MSEs (right) of the PORT GPM$_p$ WTC-estimators from samples of size $n = 1{,}000$ from a Gamma(0.5) parent ($\theta = 1$) and $s = 0.1$*

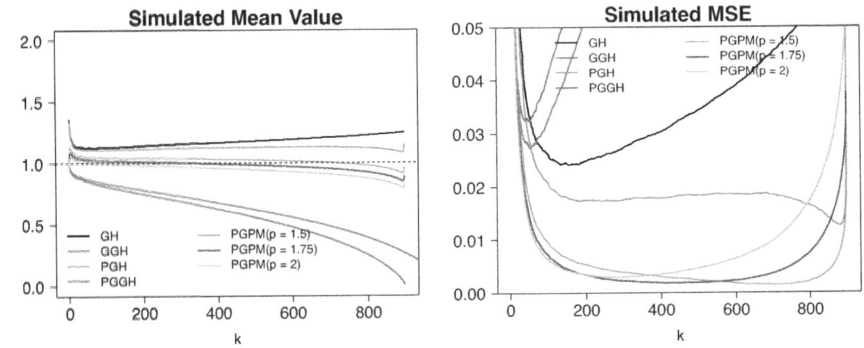

Figure 6.2. *Simulated mean values (left) and MSEs (right) of the PORT GPM$_p$ WTC-estimators from samples of size $n = 1{,}000$ from a Gamma(0.75) parent ($\theta = 1$) and $s = 0.1$*

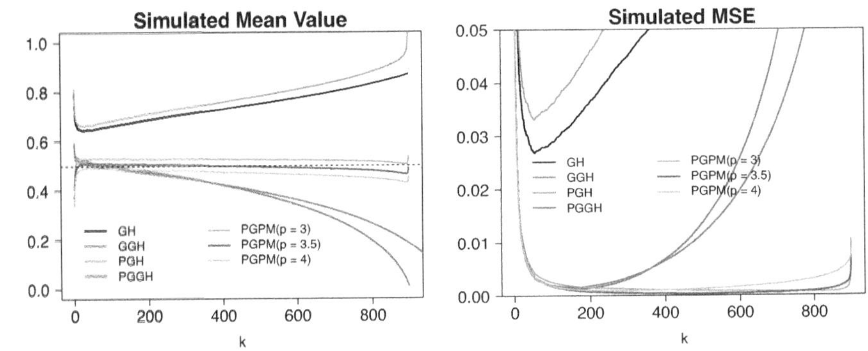

Figure 6.3. *Simulated mean values (left) and MSEs (right) of the PORT GPM$_p$ WTC-estimators from samples of size $n = 1{,}000$ from a half-normal parent ($\theta = 0.5$) and $s = 0.1$*

The choice of excesses over a low quantile, like the one associated with $s = 0.1$, are usually the ones providing smaller bias and MSE, in general. But indeed, for the aforementioned models, with a finite left endpoint, it would be even possible to choose $s = 0$ and to have a slightly larger sample size for the sample of excesses, in [6.14], and more reliable results as can be seen in Figure 6.5, for a Gamma(0.5) model, Figure 6.6, for a Gamma(0.75) model, and in Figure 6.7 for a half-normal model.

As noted by Caeiro et al. (2022b), the GH estimator evidences no bias for samples drawn from the one-parameter exponential model (the two-parameter model with location parameter equal to 0). Thus, to achieve the smallest MSE, we need to select a threshold close to the minimum of the sample. Due to the memoryless property, for this model, there is no advantage in basing the inference on the sample $\underline{\mathbf{X}}_n^{(s)}$, in [6.14], of excesses over a random threshold. Conversely, for the two-parameter exponential distribution, the situation is different, as the GH estimator is biased (Figure 6.4). Inference should be based on the excesses over a random threshold, which follows a one-parameter exponential distribution.

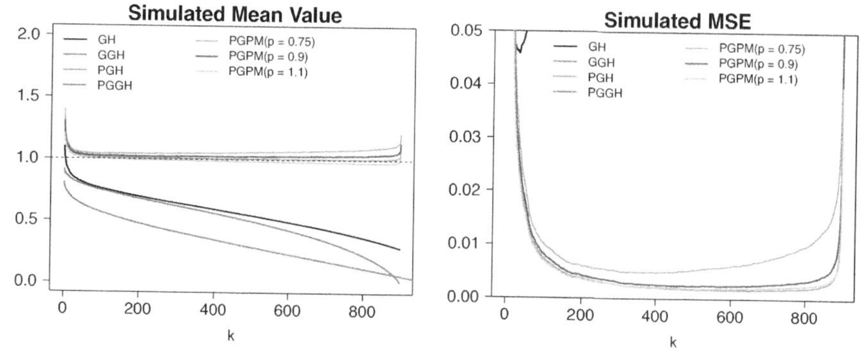

Figure 6.4. *Simulated mean values (left) and MSEs (right) of the PORT GPM$_p$ WTC-estimators from samples of size $n = 1000$ from a Exp(1,1) parent ($\theta = 1$) and $s = 0.1$*

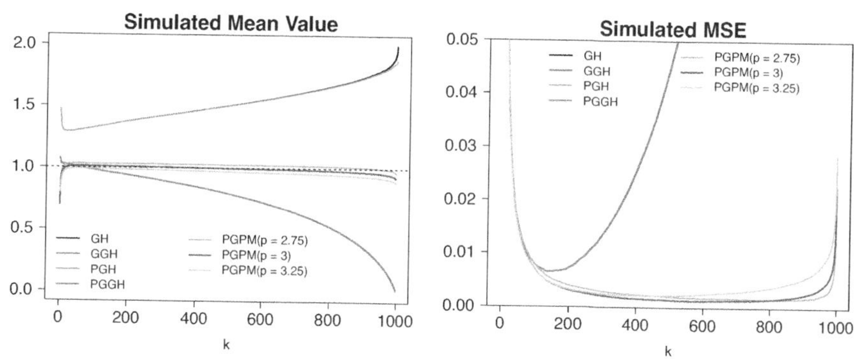

Figure 6.5. *Simulated mean values (left) and MSEs (right) of the PORT GPM$_p$ WTC-estimators from samples of size $n = 1000$ from a Gamma(0.5) parent ($\theta = 1$) and $s = 0$*

Regarding bias and MSE patterns, as a function of k, similar results were obtained for other simulated models and are available from the authors.

The information of the simulated mean values of the PORT WTC-estimators, at optimal levels, in the sense of minimal MSE, for the models under study with $s = 0.1$, is summarized in Table 6.1 and the corresponding simulated root MSE (RMSE) also computed at optimal levels is presented in Table 6.2. The values providing the smallest absolute bias and RMSE are highlighted in bold.

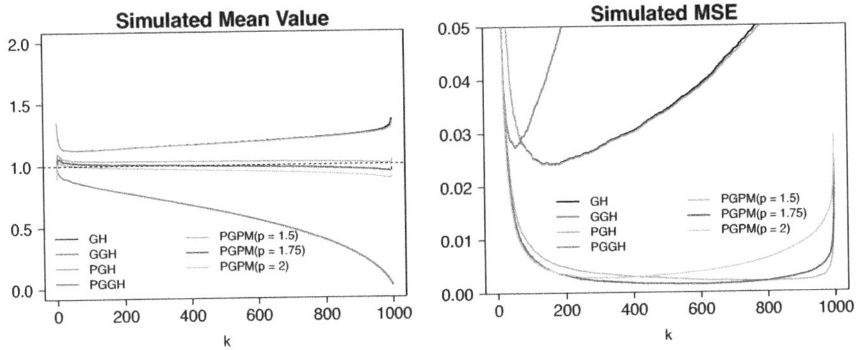

Figure 6.6. *Simulated mean values (left) and MSEs (right) of the PORT GPM_p WTC-estimators from samples of size $n = 1{,}000$ from a Gamma(0.75) parent ($\theta = 1$) and $s = 0$*

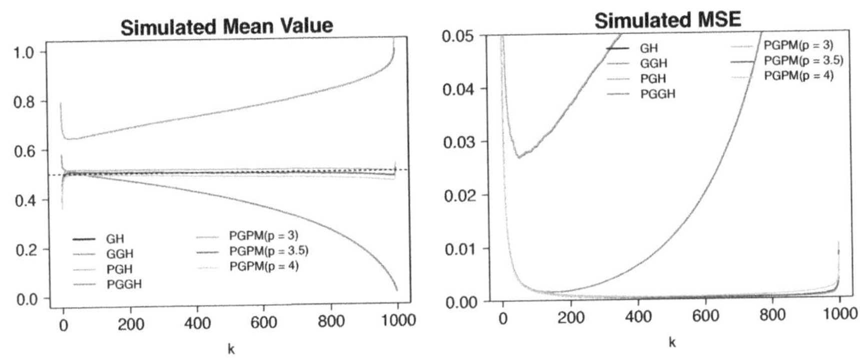

Figure 6.7. *Simulated mean values (left) and MSEs (right) of the PORT GPM_p WTC-estimators from samples of size $n = 1{,}000$ from a half-normal parent ($\theta = 0.5$) and $s = 0$*

A few general comments: For all k, and now with a location-invariant behavior, the PORT-methodology enables a clear reduction in MSE, as well as in bias, for an adequate choice of the tuning parameter s, with the obtention of estimates closer to the target. Indeed, the PORT-GPM_p, considered as a function of (k, p, s), could beat most of the other WTC-estimators. The choice of the tuning parameters can be done through heuristic sample-path stability algorithms, like the ones in Gomes et al. (2013c) and Neves et al. (2015). Alternatively, it is also sensible to use a bootstrap algorithm of the type of the ones in Gomes et al. (2011) and Gomes et al. (2012, 2013a), among others. See also Caeiro and Gomes (2016) and Gomes et al. (2016a), where R-scripts are provided.

n	100	200	500	1000	2000	5000
Gamma(0.5) parent, $\theta = 1$						
PGH	1.3322	1.3095	1.2576	1.2199	1.1969	1.1661
PPGH	0.8685	0.8910	0.9291	0.9344	0.9488	0.9623
PGPM(p=2.75)	**0.9926**	**0.9993**	**0.9987**	**0.9996**	**1.0001**	**0.9980**
PGPM(p=3)	0.9659	0.9834	0.9866	0.9939	0.9965	0.9971
PGPM(p=3.25)	0.9599	0.9703	0.9817	0.9859	0.9911	0.9963
Gamma(0.75) parent, $\theta = 1$						
PGH	1.1352	1.126	1.1029	1.0846	1.082	1.0641
PPGH	0.8032	0.8273	0.8475	0.8591	0.8684	0.8882
PGPM(p=1.5)	**1.0002**	**1.0044**	**0.9979**	**0.9986**	**0.9963**	**1.0022**
PGPM(p=1.75)	0.9805	0.9741	0.9837	0.9886	0.9930	0.9929
PGPM(p=2)	0.9520	0.9576	0.9696	0.9666	0.9756	0.9810
Half-normal parent, $\theta = 0.5$						
PGH	0.7362	0.6888	0.6913	0.6697	0.6584	0.6439
PPGH	0.4643	0.4697	0.4813	0.4856	0.4894	0.493
PGPM(p=3)	0.5639	0.5602	0.5585	0.5553	0.5522	0.5471
PGPM(p=3.5)	0.5248	0.5227	0.5175	0.5119	0.5079	0.5054
PGPM(p=4)	**0.4962**	**0.4926**	**0.4962**	**0.4958**	**0.4975**	**0.4969**
Exponential(1,1) parent, $\theta = 1$						
PGH	**1.019**	**1.0059**	**0.9988**	**0.9991**	**1.0012**	**0.9997**
PPGH	0.7555	0.7875	0.7865	0.8146	0.8256	0.8411
PGPM(p=0.75)	1.0711	1.0617	1.0547	1.0469	1.0404	1.0374
PGPM(p=0.9)	1.0364	1.0259	1.0226	1.0236	1.0222	1.0186
PGPM(p=1.1)	0.9975	0.9841	0.9763	0.9818	0.9805	0.9821

Table 6.1. *Simulated mean values of the PORT WTC-estimators under study computed at the simulated optimal level* ($s = 0.1$)

6.5. Overall comments and open research topics

– It is clear that GMs, often dependent on an extra parameter $p \in \mathbb{R}$, can be used, surely with success, in the estimation of any parameter of extreme events, like the WTC. And alternative reliable WTC-estimators based on the GM EVI-estimators in Paulauskas and Vaičiulis (2017) can in the future also play a relevant role in the estimation of those parameters.

– Moreover, the lack of efficiency of the H_p EVI-estimators for $p < 0$ together with the results obtained by Stehlík (2010), related to the robustness of the MO_{-1} EVI-estimators, deserves a further discussion of the topic *robustness vs. efficiency*.

– There is nowadays no doubt that risk analyses related to extreme events are challenging and require the combined expertise of statisticians and domain experts in climatology, dynamical systems, hydrology, finance, insurance, medicine, sports and many other fields. In our opinion, even *statistics of univariate extremes* and the WTC-estimation is still a quite lively topic of research of high relevance in risk modeling.

n	100	200	500	1000	2000	5000
Gamma(0.5) parent, $\theta = 1$						
PGH	0.4027	0.3499	0.2875	0.2433	0.2157	0.1826
PPGH	0.2081	0.1625	0.1253	0.1039	0.0795	0.0592
PGPM(p=2.75)	**0.1137**	**0.0774**	**0.0496**	**0.0354**	**0.0243**	**0.0157**
PGPM(p=3)	0.1157	0.0793	0.0513	0.0361	0.0258	0.0160
PGPM(p=3.25)	0.1219	0.0844	0.057	0.0424	0.0305	0.0202
Gamma(0.75) parent, $\theta = 1$						
PGH	0.1990	0.1602	0.1326	0.1099	0.0973	0.0764
PPGH	0.2770	0.2318	0.1989	0.1811	0.1566	0.1361
PGPM(p=1.5)	0.1215	**0.0816**	**0.0535**	**0.0375**	**0.0269**	**0.0169**
PGPM(p=1.75)	**0.1192**	0.0820	0.0565	0.0393	0.0310	0.0205
PGPM(p=2)	0.1247	0.0938	0.0685	0.0548	0.0428	0.0328
Half-normal parent, $\theta = 0.5$						
PGH	0.2717	0.2318	0.2067	0.1861	0.1725	0.1536
PPGH	0.0841	0.0691	0.0469	0.0354	0.027	0.0181
PGPM(p=3)	0.0929	0.0767	0.0655	0.0607	0.0568	0.0517
PGPM(p=3.5)	0.0663	0.0479	0.0335	0.0247	0.0191	0.0133
PGPM(p=4)	**0.0563**	**0.0400**	**0.0252**	**0.0186**	**0.0138**	**0.0090**
Exponential(1,1) parent, $\theta = 1$						
PGH	0.1368	0.0863	**0.0547**	**0.0388**	**0.0284**	**0.0171**
PPGH	0.3107	0.2788	0.2523	0.2254	0.2098	0.1859
PGPM(p=0.75)	0.1674	0.1146	0.0845	0.0679	0.0568	0.0471
PGPM(p=0.9)	0.147	0.0942	0.0612	0.0468	0.0378	0.0269
PGPM(p=1.1)	**0.1306**	**0.0844**	0.0578	0.0443	0.0342	0.0251

Table 6.2. *Simulated RMSE of the PORT WTC-estimators under study computed at the simulated optimal level* ($s = 0.1$)

– Resampling methodologies, like the jackknife, the generalized jackknife and the bootstrap, have been fruitfully used in the estimation of the EVI, the extremal index and the value at risk, but can also be used in the reliable estimation of many other parameters of extreme events, either in an univariate or multivariate framework, a topic still under development in what regards the estimation of the WTC.

– Topics like threshold selection and the PORT methodology under a semi-parametric framework are still quite challenging.

– For some of the GMs estimators, non-regular frameworks, where a non-degenerate non-normal asymptotic behavior can appear, still deserve further attention (see Gomes et al. (2022), among others). The challenge is not to go beyond the value of p that leads to consistency. Several algorithms have already been conceived and are able to partially perform such a goal, but this is a topic that is still under investigation, being part of an interesting "tale of the tails".

6.6. Acknowledgments

This work is funded by national funds through the FCT Ð Fundação para a Ciência e a Tecnologia, I.P., under the scope of the projects UID/00006/2025 and UIDB/00006/2020 (https://doi.org/10.54499/UIDB/00006/2020) (CEAUL), projects UID/00297/2025, UIDB/00297/2020 (https://doi.org/10.54499/UIDB/00297/2020) and UIDP/00297/2020 (https://doi.org/ 10.54499/UIDP/00297/2020) (Center for Mathematics and Applications) and projects UID/MAT/04674/2025 and UIDB/MAT/04674/2020 (https://doi.org/10.54499/UIDB/04674/2020) (CIMA). The first and third authors are also financed, respectively, by HiTEc Cost Action CA21163 and by project 10.54499/CEECINST/00054/2018/CP1522/CT0003 (https://doi.org/10.54499/CEECINST/00054/2018/CP1522/CT0003).

6.7. References

Araújo Santos, P., Fraga Alves, M.I., Gomes, M.I. (2006). Peaks over random threshold methodology for tail index and quantile estimation. *Revstat – Statistical Journal*, 4(3), 227–247.

Beirlant, J., Teugels, J.L., Vynckier, P. (1996). *Practical Analysis of Extreme Values*. Leuven University Press, Leuven.

Beirlant, J., Goegebeur, Y., Segers, J., Teugels, J.L. (2004). *Statistics of Extremes: Theory and Applications*. Wiley, Chichester.

Beran, J., Schell, D., Stehlík, M. (2014). The harmonic moment tail index estimator: Asymptotic distribution and robustness. *Annals of the Institute of Statistical Mathematics*, 66(1), 193–220.

Bingham, N., Goldie, C.M., Teugels, J.L. (1987). *Regular Variation*. Cambridge University Press, Cambridge.

Brilhante, M.F., Gomes, M.I., Pestana, D. (2013). A simple generalization of the Hill estimator. *Computational Statistics and Data Analysis*, 57(1), 518–535.

Brilhante, M.F., Gomes, M.I., Pestana, D. (2014). The mean-of-order p extreme value index estimator revisited. In *New Advances in Statistical Modeling and Applications*, Pacheco, A., Santos, R., Oliveira, M.R., Paulino, C.D. (eds). Springer-Verlag, Berlin and Heidelberg.

Caeiro, F. and Gomes, M.I. (2015). Threshold selection in extreme value analysis. In *Extreme Value Modeling and Risk Analysis: Methods and Applications*, Dey, D. and Yan, J. (eds). Chapman-Hall/CRC, Boca Raton.

Caeiro, F., Gomes, M.I., Pestana, D. (2005). Direct reduction of bias of the classical Hill estimator. *Revstat – Statistical Journal*, 3(2), 113–136.

Caeiro, F., Gomes, M.I., Beirlant, J., de Wet, T. (2016). Mean-of-order-p reduced-bias extreme value index estimation under a third-order framework. *Extremes*, 19(4), 561–589.

Caeiro, F., Gomes, M.I., Henriques-Rodrigues, L. (2022a). Estimation of the Weibull Tail Coefficient through the power mean-of-order-p. In *Recent Developments in Statistics and Data Science*, Bispo, R., Henriques-Rodrigues, L., Alpizar-Jara, R., De Carvalho, M. (eds). Springer, Cham.

Caeiro, F., Henriques-Rodrigues, L., Gomes, M.I. (2022b). The use of generalized means in the estimation of the Weibull tail coefficient. *Computational and Mathematical Methods*, 7290822. doi:10.1155/2022/7290822.

Dekkers, A.L.M., Einmahl, J.H.J., de Haan, L. (1989). A moment estimator for the index of an extreme-value distribution. *The Annals of Statistics*, 17, 1833–1855.

Fedotenkov, I. (2020). A review of more than one hundred Pareto-tail index estimators. *Statistica*, 80(3), 245–299.

Fisher, R.A. and Tippett, L.H.C. (1928). Limiting forms of the frequency distributions of the largest or smallest member of a sample. *Proceedings of the Cambridge Philosophical Society*, 24, 180–190.

Gardes, L. and Girard, S. (2006). Comparison of Weibull tail-coefficient estimators. *Revstat – Statistical Journal*, 4(2), 163–188.

Girard, S. (2004). A Hill type estimator of the Weibull tail-coefficient. *Communications in Statistics – Theory and Methods*, 33(2), 205–234.

Gnedenko, B.V. (1943). Sur la distribution limite du terme maximum d'une série aléatoire. *Annals of Mathematics*, 44, 423–453.

Gomes, M.I. and Caeiro, F. (2014). Efficiency of partially reduced-bias mean-of-order-p versus minimum-variance reduced-bias extreme value index estimation. In *Proceedings of COMPSTAT 2014*, Gilli, M., Gonzalez-Rodriguez, G., Nieto-Reyes, A. (eds). The International Statistical Institute/International Association for Statistical Computing, The Hague.

Gomes, M.I. and Guillou, A. (2015). Extreme value theory and statistics of univariate extremes: A review. *International Statistical Review*, 83(2), 263–292.

Gomes, M.I. and Martins, M.J. (1999). Efficient alternatives to the Hill estimator. In *Extreme Values and Additive Laws*, Gomes, M.I., Pestana, D., Canto e Castro, L., Fraga Alves, M.I., Martins, M.J. (eds). CEAUL Editions, Lisbon.

Gomes, M.I. and Martins, M.J. (2001). Generalizations of the Hill estimator – asymptotic versus finite sample behaviour. *Journal of Statistical Planning and Inference*, 93, 161–180.

Gomes, M.I., Fraga Alves, M.I., Araújo Santos, P. (2008). PORT Hill and moment estimators for heavy-tailed models. *Communications in Statistics – Simulation & Computation*, 37, 1281–1306.

Gomes, M.I., Mendonça, S., Pestana, D. (2011). Adaptive reduced-bias tail index and VaR estimation via the bootstrap methodology. *Communications in Statistics – Theory and Methods*, 40(16), 2946–2968.

Gomes, M.I., Figueiredo, F., Neves, M.M. (2012). Adaptive estimation of heavy right tails: The bootstrap methodology in action. *Extremes*, 15, 463–489.

Gomes, M.I., Figueiredo, F., Neves, M.M. (2013a). Adaptive choice of thresholds and the bootstrap methodology: An empirical study. In *Advances in Regression, Survival Analysis, Extreme Values, Markov Processes and Other Statistical Applications*, Lita da Silva, J., Caeiro, F., Natário, I., Braumann, C.A. (eds). Springer-Verlag, Berlin and Heidelberg.

Gomes, M.I., Fraga Alves, M.I., Neves, C. (2013b). *Análise de Valores Extremos: Uma Introdução*. Edições SPE and INE, Lisbon.

Gomes, M.I., Henriques-Rodrigues, L., Fraga Alves, M.I., Manjunath, B.G. (2013c). Adaptive PORT-MVRB estimation: An empirical comparison of two heuristic algorithms. *Journal of Statistical Computation and Simulation*, 83(6), 1129–1144.

Gomes, M.I., Caeiro, F., Henriques-Rodrigues, L., Manjunath, B.G. (2016a). Bootstrap methods in statistics of extremes. In *Extreme Events in Finance: A Handbook of Extreme Value Theory and its Applications*, Longin, F. (ed.). John Wiley & Sons, Hoboken, NJ.

Gomes, M.I., Henriques-Rodrigues, L., Manjunath, B.G. (2016b). Mean-of-order-p location-invariant extreme value index estimation. *Revstat – Statistical Journal*, 14(3), 273–296.

Gomes, M.I., Henriques-Rodrigues, L., Pestana, D. (2022). Non-regular frameworks and the mean-of-order-p extreme value index estimation. *Journal of Statistical Theory and Practice*, 16(3).

Gomes, M.I., Caeiro, F., Henriques-Rodrigues, L. (2025). Peaks Over Random Thresholds (PORT) estimation of the Weibull tail coefficient. In *New Frontiers in Statistics and Data Science. SPE 2023*, Henriques-Rodrigues, L., Menezes, R., Meira-Machado, L., Faria, S. and De Carvalho, M. (eds). Springer, Cham.

de Haan, L. and Ferreira, A. (2006). *Extreme Value Theory: An Introduction*. Springer Science + Business Media, New York.

Henriques-Rodrigues, L., Caeiro, F., Gomes, M.I. (2024). Improvements in the estimation of the Weibull tail coefficient – A comparative study. *Mathematical Methods in the Applied Sciences*, 47(11), 8255–8274. doi: 10.1002/mma.10013.

Hill, B.M. (1975). A simple general approach to inference about the tail of a distribution. *The Annals of Statistics*, 3, 1163–1174.

Johnson, N.L., Kotz, S., Balakrishnan, N. (1994). *Continuous Univariate Distributions*, Volume 1. John Wiley & Sons, New York.

Neves, M.M., Gomes, M.I., Figueiredo, F., Prata-Gomes, D. (2015). Modeling extreme events: Sample fraction adaptive choice in parameter estimation. *Journal of Statistical Theory and Practice*, 9(1), 184–199.

Paulauskas, V. and Vaičiulis, M. (2013). On an improvement of Hill and some other estimators. *Lithuanian Mathematical Journal*, 53(3), 336–355.

Paulauskas, V. and Vaičiulis, M. (2017). A class of new tail index estimators. *Annals Institute of Statistical Mathematics*, 69(2), 461–487.

Segers, J. (2001). Residual estimators. *Journal of Statistical Planning and Inference*, 98(1–2), 15–27.

Stehlík, M., Potocky, R., Waldl, H., Fabián, Z. (2010). On the favourable estimation of fitting heavy tailed data. *Computational Statistics*, 25, 485–503.

7

What Can we Learn from Malta? An Exploration of Gender Disparities in Education, Work and Money in Europe

This chapter examines the evolution of gender inequality in the domains of education, work and income across European Union (EU) Member States from 2010 to 2021, employing temporal trajectory analysis to identify trends and shifts over time. The study uses comprehensive datasets covering key indicators such as labor force and education participation and poverty rate. By constructing temporal trajectories for these indicators, the research delineates patterns of progress and regression in gender equality across different countries and sectors. The analysis reveals significant variations in the pace and direction of change, highlighting both areas of substantial improvement and persistent gender disparities. The findings suggest that while some EU countries have made notable strides toward gender equality, that is, Malta, others continue to experience considerable challenges. The results underscore the importance of sustained and targeted interventions to address specific barriers to gender equality, ensuring comprehensive and inclusive progress in all Member States.

7.1. Introduction

Equality between women and men is vital to economic and social growth and is a fundamental value of the EU. To reach the objectives set by the EU in the Europe 2020–2025 growth strategy, address current economic and social challenges, secure social justice and achieve smart and sustainable development, gender equality has to play a pivotal role in the political debate in Europe (EIGE 2023). The European Institute for Gender Equality created the Gender Equality Index, the only index that provides a comprehensive map of differences in outcomes between women and men at the individual level in the EU and across Member States. The index supports

Chapter written by Erika GRAMMATICA, Francesca GRESELIN and Mariangela ZENGA.

evidence-based policy making and indicates where political priorities should be shifted to accelerate the process of achieving a gender-equal Europe. As a result of the index, scores for each Member State and an EU average are presented to enable a detailed assessment of how close the EU and Member States have come toward achieving gender equality in each of the critical domains and within the EU policy agenda. In 2021, with an average score of 70.2 (where 1 stands for no gender equality and 100 for full gender equality), the EU is on track toward a society based on gender equality. Despite 50 years of policies and actions at the European level, the Member States have still not managed to fully overcome gender gaps (EIGE 2023). The definition of gender equality adopted by the index is a pragmatic one that can encompass several different perspectives: "equal share of assets and equal dignity and integrity between women and men" (EIGE 2013). Given these premises, the present study explores and analyzes the evolution of gender inequality in the three main contexts of education, work and money for the 27 EU member countries in the last decade. This study aims to assess whether there is a dynamic toward gender equality in the considered countries by looking for similarities and differences between them through a graphical approach using temporal trajectories. A reduction of the problem dimension was performed through a principal component analysis (PCA), prior to the dynamic trajectory analysis. This technique allows the extraction of several latent components lower than the original variables, choosing the first two components in a bi-dimensional plot on a Cartesian plane. Thus, the trajectory for each country is subsumed and represented by joining the points in the new coordinates, over the years. By plotting trajectories for more than one country on the same figure, we obtain very informative graphs both on the evolution of the countries over time and in a comparative manner. In a more quantitative approach, we further calculated the center of gravity of each trajectory. It serves as a representative point for each country, and summarizes all the measurements in the three considered dimensions, over the entire period. In this scenario, the center of gravity may function as a concise measurement, indicating the central point of the trajectory, with its coordinates averaged for each unit.

The remainder of this chapter is organized as follows. Section 7.2 introduces and discusses the gender gap in education, work and financial resources. Section 7.3 describes the Gender Equality Index and the variables we adopted for our assessment. Section 7.4 presents the methodology used for dynamic analysis of trajectories. Section 7.5 shows the results of the PCA, while the trajectory analysis containing the main evidence is illustrated in section 7.6. Finally, a brief discussion and some concluding remarks are presented in section 7.7.

7.2. Gender gap: education, work and money

Access to and participation in education and training is crucial for everyone's social mobility and changes in the labor market. Despite progress in participation, gender inequalities and segregation persist in the field of education, limiting women's and men's access to certain sectors of the labor market (EIGE 2023).

The labor market reflects gender disparities, including differences in employment opportunities, remuneration and career progression between men and women. Despite societal advances, gender-based distinctions persist in various aspects. Men and women often occupy different industries, with women disproportionately in lower paying sectors such as healthcare, education and administration, while men dominate higher paying fields such as technology and finance (Wharton 2012).

The gender pay gap is well-documented, illustrating income differences between men and women. Women, on average, earn less than men for comparable work or roles. This wage differential can be attributed to various factors, including occupational segregation, discriminatory practices and the influence of motherhood on the career trajectories of women (Correll et al. 2007).

The concept of the glass ceiling symbolizes unseen barriers impeding women's professional advancement, leading to under-representation in executive roles despite improvements.

Work–life balance poses challenges for women with caregiving responsibilities due to societal expectations, affecting their professional progression.

Gender-based discrimination and bias persist in recruitment, hiring and promotions, influenced by stereotypes. Women often engage in informal or part-time employment, lacking job security and progression opportunities.

Gender inequality in financial resources and the at-risk-of-poverty rate are complex and multidimensional issues that reflect the gender disparities in many societies. These phenomena can be influenced by a number of factors, including wage differences, access to education and employment opportunities, as well as traditionally assigned gender roles in society.

Women, consistently earning less than men for equivalent work, face a significant financial resource gap, which puts them at an elevated risk of poverty (Boll and Lagemann 2019).

Education remains a key determinant of economic success, and barriers to quality education for girls persist in many parts of the world. This lack of educational opportunities directly contributes to income inequality, as women may find themselves in lower paid positions or face discrimination in the labor market (Unesco 2022).

Addressing gender inequality requires a multi-pronged effort, including changes in government policies, business practices and social mindsets. Measures such as promoting equal pay, access to education, promoting inclusive company policies and sharing caregiving responsibilities can help reduce these inequalities. Furthermore, raising awareness and promoting a culture that values gender equality is the key to addressing the deep roots of these problems.

7.3. Gender Equality Index

The structure of the conceptual framework of the Gender Equality Index consists of eight domains (Figure 7.1), the first six (work, money, knowledge, time, power, health) being combined into a core index and an additional two satellite domains (intersecting inequalities and violence). The satellite domains are conceptually related to gender equality, but cannot be included in the core index because they measure an illustrative phenomenon – that is, a phenomenon that only applies to a selected group of the population. Each domain includes different indicators, which were detected on women and men.

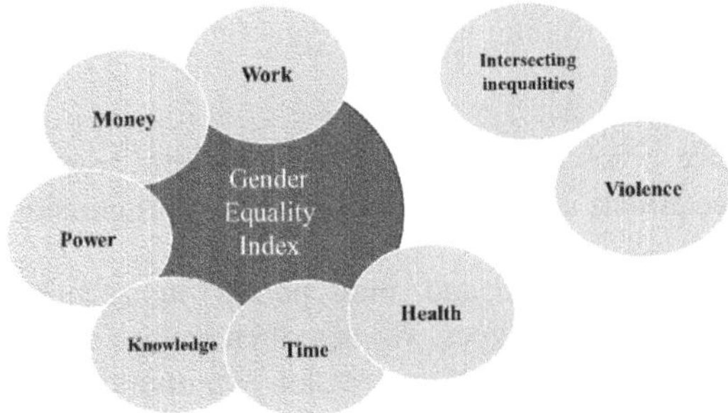

Figure 7.1. *Domains of the Gender Equality Index. Source: European Institute for Gender Equality*

In this study, the Gender Equality Index was taken into consideration to analyze the dynamics of gender equality in different countries and over time. Attention was focused on the domains of work, money and knowledge.

The domain of work measures the extent to which women and men can benefit from equal access to employment and good working conditions. This domain, in line with the central political aspects, analyzes not only the models relating to the methods of access of women and men to the labor market but also the conditions of permanence, identifying some gender models existing within the market of work: participation, segregation and quality of work.

The domain of money measures gender inequalities in access to financial resources and in the economic situation of women and men.

The knowledge domain measures gender inequalities in educational outcomes, participation in education and training throughout life.

Domain measured	Concept measured	Indicator	Source
Work	FTE employment	Full-time equivalent employment rate (%, 15+ population)	Eurostat, EU labour force survey
	Duration of working life	Duration of working life (years, 15+ population)	Eurostat, EU labour force survey
Money	Income	Mean equivalised net income (PPS, 16+ population)	Eurostat, EU statistics on income and living conditions
	Not at risk of poverty	At-risk-of-poverty rate (%, 16+ population)	Eurostat, EU statistics on income and living conditions
Knowledge	Tertiary education	Graduates of tertiary education (%, 15+ population)	Eurostat, EU labour force survey
	Lifelong learning	People participating in formal or non-formal education and training (%, 15+ population)	Eurostat, EU labour force survey

Table 7.1. *Concepts measured and indicators used in the respective domains*

The FTE employment rate takes into account the higher incidence of part-time employment among women and is obtained by comparing each worker's average number of hours with the average of a full-time worker.

The duration of working life indicator (DWL) measures the number of years a person aged 15 is expected to be active in the labor market throughout his/her life.

Equivalized disposable income in PPS (purchasing power standard) is the total income of a household, after tax and other deductions, that is available for spending or saving, divided by the number of household members converted into equalized adults; household members are equalized or made equivalent by weighting each according to their age using the so-called modified OECD equivalence scale.

The at-risk-of-poverty rate is the share of people with an equivalized disposable income (after social transfers) below the at-risk-of-poverty threshold, which is set at 60% of the national median equivalized disposable income after social transfers.

Educational attainment measures the share of high-educated people among men and women; people with tertiary education as their highest level successfully completed (levels 5–8), percentage from total +15 population.

The last variable, referred as Lifelong learning, reports the percentage of people participating in formal or non-formal education and training, in the last 4 weeks.

7.4. Three-way data approach based on principal component analysis

Starting from the EIGE variables, indicator ratios were constructed to distinguish whether gender inequality favors women or men. For each variable in the domains, the variable for women was compared to that for men minus one:

$$\frac{Variable\ women}{Variable\ men} - 1 \qquad [7.1]$$

When the result is equal to 0 we are in a situation of gender equality, when the result is greater than 0, there is gender inequality in favor of women and when the result is less than 0, there is gender inequality in favor of men.

In this study, a set of variables for countries belonging to the EU is observed for 8 years (2010, 2012, 2015, 2017, 2018, 2019, 2020, 2021). These data form a multivariate time array X (D'Urso 2000; Kiers 2000; Rizzi and Vichi 1995), the structure of which is:

$$X \equiv \{x_{ijt} : i = 1, \ldots, I; j = 1, \ldots, J; t = 1, \ldots, T\}$$

where i is a statistical unit (i.e. a state), j is one of the indices that relate women to men and t is an occasion (i.e. a year within the 2010–2021 period), X_{ijt} represents the jth variable observed in the ith unit at time t. In a time array, we have the same units in which we observe the same variables at different times (D'Urso 2000).

The entities along the horizontal axis are indicated by the first index (i), those along the vertical axis by the second index (j) and those along the depth axis by the third index (t) (Kiers 2000).

Such three-way data can be rearranged to obtain time trajectories (Coppi and Zanella 1978; Coppi 1986; D'Urso 2000), thereby displaying the paths of the countries over time on a J-dimensional space. The three sets of entities define the three "ways" or three "dimensions" of the three-way array.

The time array X can be represented by a bi-dimensional matrix (stacked matrix) by combining two of the three indices i, j, t in the rows and assigning the other index to the columns. The various types of stacked matrices are: $X_i \equiv \{x_{ijt} : j = 1, \ldots, J; t = 1, \ldots, T\}$, with dimension TxJ, $X_j \equiv \{x_{ijt} : i = 1, \ldots, I; t = 1, \ldots, T\}$, with dimension TxI and $X_t \equiv \{x_{ijt} : i = 1, \ldots, I; j = 1, \ldots, J\}$, with dimension IxJ. The X can be seen as a set of bi-dimensional matrices that represent the slices of the "parallelepiped of data". In particular, we have I matrices X_i, J matrices X_j and T matrices X_t (D'Urso 2000). Rizzi and Vichi (1995) highlight the value of reorganizing dataset X into a consolidated two-way format for effective data analysis. They explore alternative strategies to represent X as a comprehensive two-way matrix, with the selection of a specific approach hinging on the analysis' objectives. The strategy we use to re-arrange X comprises two steps. In the first step, the observed values of the J variables on all I units in t are selected from the multivariate time array X, thus obtaining an $I \times J$ matrix which is called "frontal slice" (Rizzi and Vichi 1995; D'Urso 2000):

$$X_{..t} \equiv \{x_{ijt} : i = 1, \ldots, I; j = 1, \ldots, J; t = 1, \ldots, T\}$$
$$(t = 1, \ldots, T)$$

Frontal slice $X_{..t}$ is an $I \times J$ matrix including J variables observed on I units in t, with $t = 1, \ldots T$. Consequently, the multivariate time array X can be seen as a set of T slices. In the second step, slices are stacked on top of each other to obtain the $\tilde{X}$ matrix with $I \cdot T$ rows and J columns, as shown in Figure 7.2.

The generic row of $\tilde{X}$, denoted by x_{it}, contains the observed values for unit i in t:

$$x_{it} \equiv x_{i1t}, \ldots x_{iJt}$$

Considering that countries are the I units in this study, the matrix displaying the time trajectory of country i is obtained by selecting the J-dimensional vectors x_{it}, with $t = 1 \ldots, T$, from $\tilde{X}$ (D'Urso 2000):

$$\tilde{X}_i \equiv \{x_{it} : t = 1, \ldots, T\}$$

A time trajectory $\tilde{X}_i$ can be achieved for each country i, with $i = 1, \ldots, I$, and then such trajectories can be compared to detect the dissimilarities among countries. D'Urso (2000) compares the time trajectories of different statistical units by using a geometric setting in which each unit i is located on T parallel J-dimensional spaces. However, a comparison between time trajectories is easier when the synthesis of the $\tilde{X}$ is carried out via PCA (Jolliffe 2002) to reduce the number of variables J.

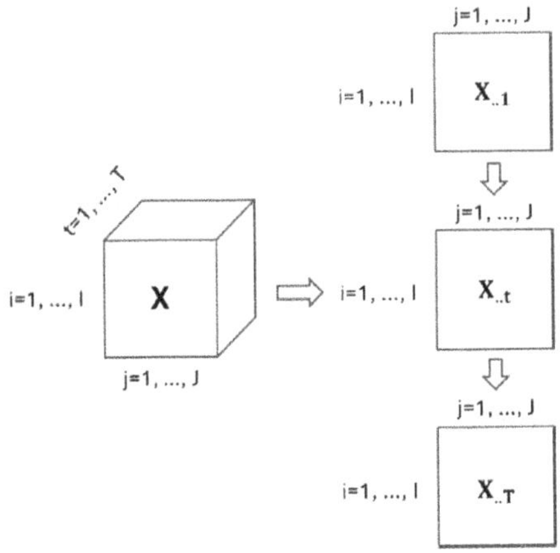

Figure 7.2. *Representation of X as a matrix consisting of slices stacked on top of each other*

7.5. Evidence from principal component analysis

The aim of applying PCA to a data set with J variables is to reduce its dimensions by transforming the original J variables into new Q variables, with Q less than J. Such new variables are obtained in a way that ensures the loss in statistical information is minimized for each Q (with $Q = 1, \ldots, J-1$) as measured by the proportion of total variance that is not explained by the new Q variables.

These new Q variables, referred to as PCs, are uncorrelated with each other by construction. A PC, indicated by y, is given by the linear combination $y = \sum_{j=1}^{J} a_j x_j = \tilde{X}_a$, where x_j is the jth column of $\tilde{X}$ and $a = a_1, \ldots, a_J$ is a vector of coefficients (Jolliffe and Cadima 2016).

The application of the PCA allows us to achieve four possible pieces of evidence:

1) similarity between Member States of the EU;

2) individuation of groups of domain indicators;

3) association of EU Member States with some specific indicators;

4) evolution of gender inequalities in the domains of education, work and money in the period considered using the time trajectory.

The analysis was carried out on the ratios (see equation [7.1]) of women to men calculated from the six variables of the domains of education, work and money for each year and for the Member States of the EU to identify the latent components that group these ratios. Two principal components with eigenvalues greater than 1, together explaining 69% of the variance, have been identified. The first component, explaining 45%, was labeled "participation in work and education", while the second component, explaining 24%, was labeled "financial resources".

Indicators	PC1 (45%)	PC2 (24%)	
FTE employment	0.992		**Participation in work and education**
Duration of working life	0.847		
Graduates of tertiary education	0.756		
Lifelong learning	0.634		
Income		0.883	**Financial resources**
Risk-of-poverty rate		-0.869	

Table 7.2. *Results of PCA*

7.6. Results of trajectory analysis

In the same two-dimensional plan, it is possible to visualize a couple of coordinates for each year of each country representing the two components obtained by the PCA. The union of these coordinates draws a single trajectory for each country defining the route over the time between participation in work/education and financial resources.

However, when all countries are represented in the same Cartesian plane, each quarter of the plot displays a group of countries in common situations. In the first quarter, countries with high values of participation in work/education and financial resources are shown; the second quarter is for countries with high values of economic resources but low values of participation in work/education. In the third quarter, countries with difficult situations are plotted. They have low values for both participation in work/education and financial resources, and finally, in the fourth quarter, it is possible to find countries with an intermediate position given by low values of economic resources and high values for participation in work/education.

Figure 7.3 plots all the countries in the same graph using a bubble chart that represents the barycenter. Through the bubble graph, it is possible to get a static representation based on the barycenter of the Member States of the EU; the larger the bubble, the bigger the variability in the path that the country takes over the years. The first component is represented on the abscissa axis, while the second component is on the ordinate axis. The participation of women in the labor market and education compared to that of men increases moving toward the right; on the other hand, financial resources for women compared to men increase the higher you move.

Malta is the country that shows the greatest variability in its temporal trajectory.

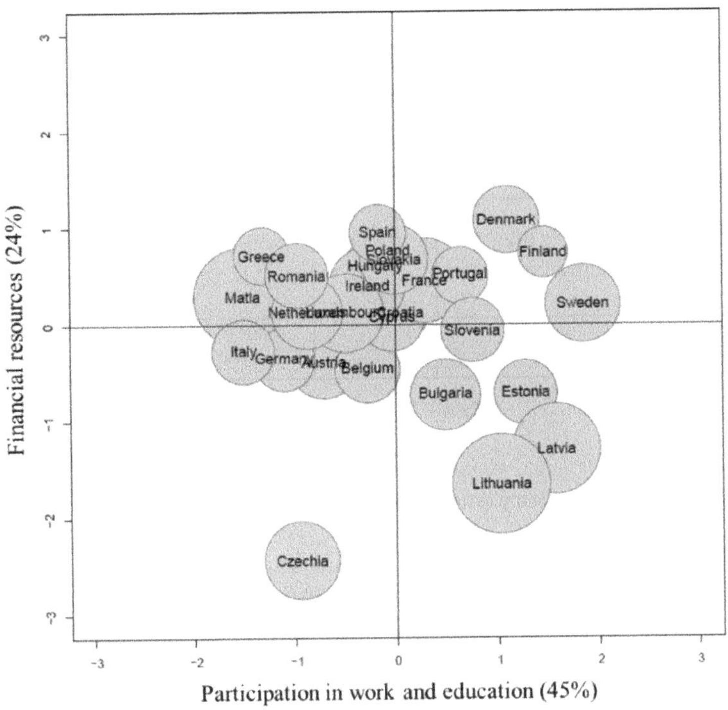

Figure 7.3. *Bubble chart for all countries (2010–2021)*

Malta is located in the third quadrant, where the situation of women's financial resources compared to men is favorable. Considering the entire temporal trajectory, from 2010 to 2021, Malta has recorded significant improvements in women's participation in the labor market and education, as shown in Figure 7.4.

In recent decades, Malta has implemented several internal policies to improve gender equality. Key initiatives include introducing gender mainstreaming into all government policies and measures to promote work–life balance, such as improving parental leave, paternity leave and care services to children through the implementation, in 2021, of the "Regulation on Work–Life Balance". The government has also focused on increasing women's participation in the labor market through various employment programs and incentives. Additionally, Malta has actively worked to reduce the gender pay gap and improve gender representation in decision-making roles (Human Rights Malta).

In the realm of education, Malta has launched initiatives to inspire more girls to engage in studies and careers in science, technology, engineering and mathematics

(STEM). This also involves training teachers to recognize and combat gender bias in the classroom. It has also provided scholarships and grants specifically for women to pursue higher education, particularly in fields in which they are underrepresented (EIGE 2024).

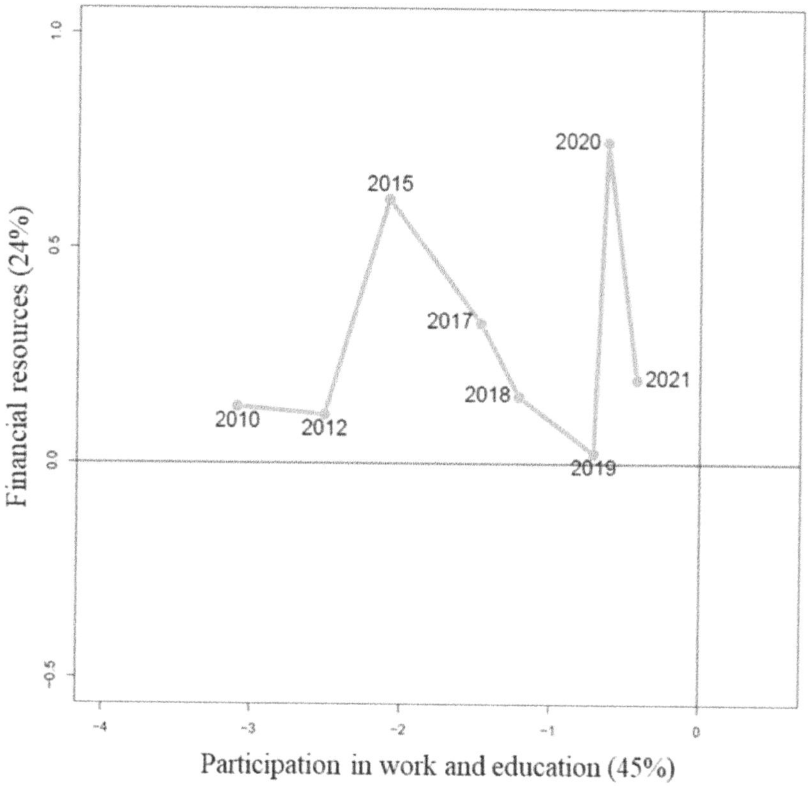

Figure 7.4. *Malta's trajectory from 2010 to 2021*

To mitigate gender disparities in financial resources, Malta has implemented programs designed to enhance financial literacy among women, equipping them with the knowledge and skills necessary for effective financial management. It has also provided grants, loans and business support services aimed at female entrepreneurs. These initiatives support women in launching and expanding their enterprises, thus enhancing their economic self-sufficiency. Furthermore, Malta has worked on reforms of the welfare and pension system to ensure that women, who often have interrupted career paths due to caring responsibilities, receive fair and adequate benefits (EIGE 2024).

7.7. Conclusions

This study has examined the multifaceted dimensions of gender inequality in education, employment and financial resources in countries of the EU using statistical techniques to analyze temporal trajectories. The findings underscore a persistent and complex landscape in which gender disparities persist despite advances in policy and awareness.

PCA was used to uncover the relationship between gender inequality indicators in the three reference areas. However, trajectory analysis was used as an exploratory method to examine the evolution over time of these indicators in each Member State of the EU, thus identifying similarities among the states.

Malta is a country from which others can learn, as it has evolved and improved significantly. Over the period from 2010 to 2021, the country has made notable advancements in women's participation in the labor force and education. These improvements stem from comprehensive national policies promoting gender equality, such as gender mainstreaming across government strategies and initiatives to support work–life balance through enhanced parental leave and childcare services. Malta has also focused on increasing the participation of the female labor force through employment programs and addressing the gender pay gap. In education, efforts include initiatives to encourage girls in STEM fields, teacher training to combat gender bias and scholarships to support women in underrepresented academic disciplines.

Looking ahead, addressing gender inequality requires comprehensive approaches that integrate policy coherence across the education, employment and financial sectors. This includes fostering inclusive educational environments, promoting equitable career opportunities and enhancing financial literacy and access to capital for women. In addition, fostering a culture of gender equality through awareness campaigns and social advocacy can contribute to changing social norms and attitudes toward greater inclusivity and fairness.

In conclusion, while progress has been made, the journey toward gender equality in the EU remains ongoing and necessitates continued commitment across all levels of society and governance to achieve substantive and lasting change.

7.8. Acknowledgments

Research carried out within the MUSA – Multilayered Urban Sustainability Action – project, funded by the European Union – NextGenerationEU, under the National Recovery and Resilience Plan (NRRP) Mission 4 Component 2 Investment Line 1.5: Strengthening of research structures and creation of R&D "innovation ecosystems", set up of "territorial leaders in R&D".

7.9. References

Boll, C. and Lagemann, A. (2019). The gender pay gap in EU countries: New evidence based on EU-SES 2014 data. *Intereconomics*, 54, 101–105.

Coppi, R. (1986). Analysis of three-way data matrices based on pairwise relation measures. In *Procedings in Computational Statistics*, De Antoni, F., Lauro, N., Rizzi, A. (eds). Physica-Verlag, 129–139. doi: 10.1007/978-3-642-46890-2_20.

Coppi, R. and Zannella, F. (1978). L'analisi fattoriale di una serie temporale multipla relativa allo stesso insieme di unita statistiche. *Atti della XXIX Riunione Scientifica della SIS*, Bologna.

Correll, S.J., Benard, S., Paik, I. (2007). Getting a job: Is there a motherhood penalty? *American Journal of Sociology*, 112(5), 1297–1338.

D'Urso, P. (2000). Dissimilarity measures for time trajectories. *Journal of the Italian Statistical Society*, 9(1), 54–65.

EIGE (2013). Gender Equality Index: Main findings. EIGE [Online]. Available at: https://eige.europa.eu/sites/default/files/documents/mh-02-13-275-en-c.pdf.

EIGE (2023). Gender Equality Index 2023: Towards a green transition in transport and energy. EIGE [Online]. Available at: https://eige.europa.eu/publications-resources/publications/gender-equality-index-2023-towards-green-transition-transport-and-energy?language content entity=en.

EIGE (2024). Gender equality in academia and research – GEAR tool. EIGE [Online]. Available at: https://eige.europa.eu/gender-mainstreaming/toolkits/gear/step-step-guide?language content entity=en.

Human Rights Directorate (n.d.). [Online]. Available at: https://humanrights.gov.mt/en/Pages/Gender%20Equality/European%20Affairs/Gender-Equality-Index-2020-Malta.aspx.

Jolliffe, I.T. (2002). *Principal Component Analysis*. Springer, New York.

Jolliffe, I.T. and Cadima, J. (2016). Principal component analysis: A review and recent developments. *Philosophical Transactions of the Royal Society A*, 374(2065), 20150202. doi: 10.1098/rsta.2015.0202.

Kiers, H.A.L. (2000). Towards a standardized notation and terminology in multiway analysis. *Journal of Chemometrics*, 14(3), 105–122.

Rizzi, A. and Vichi, M. (1995). Representation, synthesis, variability and data preprocessing of a three-way data set. *Computational Statistics & Data Analysis*, 19(2), 203–222.

Unesco (2022). Deepening the debate on those still left behind. Gender Report [Online]. Available at: https://www.unesco.org/gem-report/en/2022-gender-report.

Wharton, A.S. (2012). Work and family in the 21st century: Four research domains. *Sociology Compass*, 6(3), 219–235.

8

Financial Analysis of a Public Hospital: The Case of the Corfu General Hospital

This chapter conducts a 10-year financial analysis of the Corfu General Hospital in Greece to provide information for making appropriate administrative decisions. The financial analysis was conducted using the ratios method, with data sourced from the hospital's published financial statements. The Corfu General Hospital has demonstrated improvement in all categories of ratios during the review period, despite fluctuations. It has satisfactory liquidity, and as a public organization, it relies on equity, demonstrating increased efficiency. However, it is experiencing significant delays in repaying its creditors and collecting its receivables. The financial analysis of the hospital's financial position reveals a profitable dynamic in terms of its sustainability for the future.

8.1. Introduction

The health sector is of the utmost importance to both society and the state. In Greece, the Ministry of Health oversees the 13 health regions and is responsible for providing public health services. The Greek National Health System (NHS), established under Law 1397/83, ensures that all citizens receive primary, secondary and tertiary healthcare. It is the state's duty to provide health services to all citizens equally, regardless of their economic, social or professional status. Public hospitals belong to the NHS and are non-profit organizations that operate as legal entities under public law, supervised by the relevant Health District of Health Services (FEK 143/A/07.10.1983 n.d.). Hospitals' income comes mainly from the state budget, public and private insurance agencies, direct patient payments, European Union programs, real estate utilization and donations (Dikaios and Chletsos 1999). However, the efficient use of resources involved in healthcare systems to ensure

---

Chapter written by Margarita IOANNIDOU and George MATALLIOTAKIS.

their sustainable operation is a relevant topic for both managers and policymakers of the healthcare industry (Lee 2016). Furthermore, financially stable hospitals are better able to maintain reliable systems and provide resources for quality improvement (Akinleye et al. 2019). Hospital profitability refers to the successful business performance achieved by treating patients and carrying out other business activities during a fiscal year (Cho and Chu 2016).

Healthcare systems worldwide face ongoing pressure to control costs and enhance care quality (Stadhouders et al. 2019). In Greece, particularly over the past decade, the NHS has faced significant challenges due to the global economic recession and the COVID-19 pandemic. From 2009 to September 2019, Greece experienced a deep financial crisis, resulting in the implementation of reforms aimed at addressing long-standing issues in the health system. Furthermore, the emergence of the COVID-19 pandemic in 2020 posed a new challenge to the already strained health system. Despite the economic crisis that preceded it, measures were put in place to safeguard public health, including a full vaccination program, implementation of measures to reduce virus transmission, reorganization of hospital operations, expansion of hospital capacity and provision of financial support to avoid the collapse of health facilities.

8.2. Materials and methods

This chapter conducts a longitudinal financial analysis of the Corfu General Hospital over a decade, from 2012 to 2021. The hospital serves the health needs of a densely populated and highly visited island. The analysis is based on its published financial statements. Financial ratios are used to examine the hospital's liquidity, capital structure and sustainability, activity and efficiency (Vasiliou and Iriotis 2015).

8.3. Results

8.3.1. *Liquidity ratios*

After reviewing the data, it appears that there is not a significant difference between the general and specific liquidity indicators, as the value of stocks represents only a small percentage of the hospital's current assets.

However, the liquidity ratio stands out as significantly different from the other indicators. This disparity occurs because the hospital's needs exceed its available assets by a large margin. Consequently, when this is not considered in the assessment of its liquidity, the ability to repay its short-term obligations appears significantly diminished.

During the review period, the hospital's cash liquidity ratio started quite low, indicating that there was not enough cash to pay overdue debts. However, in 2015, the ratio improved significantly and continued to increase, reaching its peak in 2020. Notably, in 2016, reserves grew substantially, whereas short-term liabilities decreased. Generally, short-term liabilities showed a downward trend from 2012 to 2021. From 2015 onward, the hospital did not face any liquidity issues, as it had enough funds to meet its obligations to creditors. However, in 2020 and 2021, there was a decline in the hospital's funds and the ratio.

	Current Ratio	**Quick Ratio**	**Absolute Liquid Ratio**
2012	1.49	1.45	0.14
2013	1.98	1.93	0.39
2014	4.49	4.43	0.22
2015	4.35	4.30	0.56
2016	4.61	4.56	1.85
2017	8.62	8.51	2.77
2018	7.56	7.45	2.67
2019	5.67	5.46	2.51
2020	10.20	9.92	2.83
2021	11.07	10.82	1.86
Average	**6.004**	**5.883**	**1.58**

Table 8.1. *Liquidity ratios*

8.3.2. *Financial structure and viability ratios*

On the basis of the analysis of the hospital's capital structure indicators, it is evident that since 2012, the hospital has been reducing its reliance on foreign capital and predominantly using its own resources to finance its assets. This trend provides security to the hospital's creditors. Furthermore, the ratio of the owner's equity to fixed assets has been showing a moderate increase over time, indicating that the hospital has been financing its fixed assets through its equity. This upward trend reflects the hospital's consistent policy regarding its assets financing.

Additionally, the analysis of the ratio of the owner's equity to total assets indicates that the hospital relies primarily on its own resources, with only a small portion of its assets being financed by short-term creditors. This demonstrates the security of the hospital's creditors and the stable equity management policy maintained by management, even during the period of the financial crisis in the country and the COVID-19 pandemic.

The ratio of owner's equity to total liabilities fluctuated significantly during the review period, reaching its lowest point in 2012 and its peak in 2021, with a 416.44% increase by the end of the period. This was driven by the rising trend in equity capital prices and a decrease in foreign capital prices, impacting the ratio's price formation. The debt-to-assets ratio consistently remained at low levels, with a downward trend in the later years. The ratio's price remained stable at its minimum value in 2020–2021 due to the gradual decrease in foreign capital, which was influenced by consistent administrative policy.

	Ratio of owner's equity to fixed assets	**Ratio of owner's equity to total assets**	**Ratio of owner's equity to total liabilities**	**Debt-to-assets assets ratio**
2012	1.07	0.86	5.90	0.14
2013	1.05	0.89	8.46	0.10
2014	1.24	0.92	12.23	0.07
2015	1.38	0.90	8.64	0.09
2016	1.25	0.91	10.71	0.08
2017	1.42	0.95	17.56	0.05
2018	1.44	0.94	15.26	0.05
2019	1.26	0.93	13.96	0.06
2020	1.44	0.96	23.50	0.04
2021	1.58	0.96	24.57	0.04
Average	**1.313**	**0.922**	**14.079**	**0.071**

Table 8.2. *Financial structure and viability ratios*

8.3.3. *Activity ratios*

The inventory turnover ratio increased slightly in the first 2 years, remained stable for the following 3 years, and then significantly decreased over the next 5 years. From 2017 onward, there was a trend of increased stockpiling, requiring additional investment, but it did not affect the hospital's liquidity. Overall, stock management improved during the economic crisis, declined gradually and tended to increase stockpiling during the pandemic.

The accounts receivables turnover ratio fluctuated significantly during the review period. In 2013, sales revenue steeply declined, leading to a significant decrease in the ratio's price from the previous year. A higher 2020 value indicates improved claim management, leading to reduced risk. The payables turnover ratio fluctuated at low levels over time, with the time to cover the hospital's obligations increasing. From 2017 onward, there was a slight increase. Comparing the payables turnover ratio with the accounts receivables turnover ratio, the hospital pays its liabilities much faster than it collects its claims, negatively affecting its liquidity and financial position.

	Inventory turnover ratio	**Accounts receivables turnover ratio**	**Payables turnover ratio**
2012	14.07	0.46	0.66
2013	14.75	0.07	0.60
2014	14.74	0.26	0.78
2015	12.45	0.20	0.63
2016	14.80	0.25	0.71
2017	12.16	0.36	0.94
2018	10.45	0.30	1.20
2019	7.08	0.49	1.16
2020	5.99	0.55	1.45
2021	6.66	0.46	1.78
Average	**11.31**	**0.34**	**0.991**

Table 8.3. *Activity ratios*

8.3.4. *Profitability ratios*

The gross profit margin of hospitals has consistently improved over the past decade, demonstrating resilience despite fluctuations. While the margin was negative from 2012 to 2014 due to higher costs of goods sold than sales revenue, it has since remained consistently positive, reaching its peak in 2021. Fluctuations in the ratio seem to be more influenced by changes in sales revenue than by the cost of sales, which have remained relatively stable over the decade. Furthermore, the hospital has navigated significant fluctuations in the net profit margin, with the lowest value recorded in 2013. Despite this, the hospital has maintained satisfactory values at high levels over the years. In addition, the return on assets ratio fluctuated before stabilizing, with a steady increase in the average amount of the hospital's assets during the first 5 years followed by successive ups and downs. Overall, the profitability of the hospital's assets seems to have stabilized at satisfactory levels. Finally, the hospital's return-to-equity ratio has maintained a positive trend, reflecting its capacity for profitable performance and long-term success.

	Gross Profit Margin	Net Profit Margin	Return on Assets	Return on Equity
2012	-22.18%	51.45%	4.09%	5.09%
2013	-516.66%	-133.86%	-1.55%	-1.87%
2014	-10.16%	216.96%	12.94%	15.25%
2015	19.02%	121.77%	7.88%	9.49%
2016	14.34%	191.69%	13.63%	16.79%
2017	33.30%	97.60%	8.37%	10.16%
2018	22.72%	47.96%	3.83%	4.57%
2019	38.80%	70.23%	7.61%	9.10%
2020	43.25%	47.52%	5.79%	6.81%
2021	52.09%	53.79%	7.25%	8.17%
Average	**-32.55%**	**76.51%**	**6.98%**	**8.36%**

Table 8.4. *Profitability ratios*

8.4. Discussion

The examination of liquidity ratios revealed that the hospital's liquidity was satisfactory during the first few years of the decade but lower than that in subsequent years. There was a general upward trend in liquidity levels over the years. The hospital's total assets showed an overall upward trend, with a 9.3% increase at the end of the period. Compared with those in 2012, hospitals also experienced significant increases in their assets and stock value, with increases of 292.7% and 95.5%, respectively. Receivables increased by 136.1% at the end of the period, whereas total liabilities decreased by 65.85%. The hospital's net profit fluctuated before a 142.2% increase was recorded. The examination of the hospital's financial structure and viability ratios reveals positive progress and gradual improvement over time. Throughout the decade, the hospital relied on gradually increasing equity capital, whereas liabilities declined and were minimized by the end of the decade, leading to an overall improvement in the hospital's financial position.

Examining the hospital's activity ratios, it is observed that over the past decade, the administration has been implementing a stockpiling policy, leading to a steady increase in funds immobilization for longer periods of time.

The analysis of the accounts receivable turnover ratio has shown an increasing trend in the accounts receivable collection period. This should ideally be minimized to reduce vulnerability and enhance the utilization of funds. The accounts receivable collection period reached an unfavorable level in 2013 because of a significant decrease in sales that year. Furthermore, the payables turnover ratio was found to be lower than the accounts receivables turnover ratio, indicating that the hospital makes its payments more quickly than it collects its claims. However, despite some improvements, there are still significant delays in both collecting receivables from customers and paying suppliers, which require attention and resolution.

The overall efficiency of the hospital, despite fluctuations in the first 5 years of the review period and a notably negative value in 2013, seems to be consistently positive. Both gross and net profit margins during the pandemic are particularly satisfactory. As a result, the return on assets ratio and the return on equity ratio suggest that Corfu Hospital has a profitable outlook, which does not raise concerns about its sustainability in the future.

8.5. References

Akinleye, D.D., McNutt, L.A., Lazariu, V., McLaughlin, C.C. (2019). Correlation between hospital finances and quality and safety of patient care. *PLOS One*, 14, e0219124. doi: 10.1371/journal.pone.0219124.

Cho, H.W. and Chu, C. (2016). What would be a better strategy for National University Hospital management? *Osong Public Health and Research Perspectives*, 7(3), 139–140. doi: 10.1016/j.phrp.2016.05.003.

Dikaios, K. and Chletsos, M. (1999). *Healthcare Services – Hospital, Peculiarities and Challenges, Vol. B.* Greek Open University, Patra.

Hellenic Republic. (1983). Law 1397/1983 – National Healthcare System (FEK A 143/07.10. 1983). *Official Journal of the Hellenic Republic.*

Lee, D.H. (2016). Comparison of efficiency of healthcare systems of countries with global competitiveness using data envelopment analysis. *Global Business Finance Review*, 21, 46–55. doi: 10.17549/gbfr.2016.21.1.46.

Stadhouders, N., Kruse, F., Tanke, M., Koolman, X., Jeurissen, P. (2019). Effective healthcare cost-containment policies: A systematic review. *Health Policy*, 123, 71–79. doi: 10.1016/j.healthpol.2018.10.015.

Vasiliou, D. and Iriotis, N. (2015). *Financial Management Theory and Practice*. Rosili, Athens.

9

EWMA Control Charts for Skewed Distributions

In this chapter, the skewness correction (SC) method is applied to the exponentially weighted moving average (EWMA) control chart, which is called the skewness correction EWMA (SC_{EWMA}) control chart, to monitor the non-normal process. The performance of the newly proposed SC_{EWMA} chart is compared and contrasted with those of weighted variance EWMA (WV_{EWMA}), weighted standard deviation EWMA (WSD_{EWMA}) and the classic EWMA control limits based on the degree of skewness and varying smoothing parameters. The comparison is made with respect to their *Type-I* errors by using the Monte Carlo simulation technique with data generated from the lognormal, gamma and Weibull distributions. The newly proposed SC_{EWMA} chart is expected to produce strong results and hence can be used as an alternative to the most commonly used WV_{EWMA} chart.

9.1. Introduction

A control chart is a statistical device that is used basically for studying and controlling repetitive processes. This concept was proposed by Walter A. Shewhart of the Bell Telephone Laboratories in the 1920s. Shewhart shows that control charts may serve first to define the goal or standard for a process that the management would like to attain; second, they may be used as an instrument for attaining that goal; and third, they may serve as a means of judging whether the goal set by the management has been attained or not by Duncan (1986). Therefore, we can say that control charts are instruments used for specification, production and inspection in an industrial setting.

Chapter written by Derya KARAGÖZ and Moustapha Aminou TUKUR.

The classic Shewhart control charts are generally used for monitoring the process mean and variability in the characteristics of a random quality variable of interest and are based on the normality assumptions. However, real-life problems in most cases are not normally distributed. Using the $\bar{X}$ and R charts in such cases produce misleading results because the increase in the skewness of the distributions will obviously lead to a relative increase in the *Type-I* error produced due to the changes within the population (Karagoz and Hamurkaroglu 2012). For skewed distributions, to demonstrate the changes in the population, non-symmetric control limits need to be used (Bai and Choi 1995). Methods such as the weighted variance (WV) proposed by Chang and Bai (2001), weighted standard deviation (WSD) proposed by Chang and Bai (2001) and SC proposed by Chan and Cui (2003) can be used. Using these methods help the experimenter to avoid misinterpretation of results and hence produce a better output.

The classic and R control charts and all of their derivatives are generally used to detect large shifts in the process mean. Hence, they are not too reliable in situations where small shifts are of interest. To solve such problems, the EWMA control chart, which was proposed by Roberts (2000), can be used. The EWMA is a statistical method employed in process monitoring. It involves the averaging of data, with the weight assigned to each data point decreasing as it becomes more distant in time from the current measurement. In contrast, other control charts treat each data point individually.

Koyuncu and Karagoz (2018) and Karagoz and Koyuncu (2019) constructed mean and range control chart limits based on Shewhart, WV and SC methods by using simple random sampling, ranked set sampling, median ranked set sampling and neoteric ranked set sampling designs. The performance of the proposed control charts based on neoteric ranked set sampling designs was compared to those of their counterparts in ranked set sampling, median ranked set sampling and simple random sampling using the Monte Carlo simulation.

Researchers have developed an interest in the EWMA control chart after its discovery, and much work has been done in this area. Robinson and Ho (1978), Crowder (1989), and Lucas and Saccucci (1990) numerically studied the properties of EWMA control charts and proposed vital relationships between the parameters of the EWMA control charts, which are discussed in greater detail in the subsequent sections. Recently, in the case of non-normal process, the WV_{EWMA} and WSD_{EWMA} charts were proposed instead of the classic EWMA Chart by Khoo and Atta (2008). The peculiarity of this work lies in the proposition of a new method called SC_{EWMA} for skewed distributions whose behaviors are keenly studied, compared and contrasted with the existing methods and inferences made in that regard. The lognormal, gamma and Weibull distributions are considered skewed processes and are given as follows:

– The probability density function of a random variable X, which is log normally distributed, is given as follows:

$$f(x|\sigma,\mu) = \frac{1}{x\sigma\sqrt{2\pi}}\exp(-\frac{(ln(x)-\mu)^2}{2\sigma^2})$$

Here, $x > 0$, σ is the scale parameter, and μ is the location parameter.

– The probability density function of a random variable X that is gamma distributed with shape parameter α and scale parameter β is given as follows:

$$f(x|\alpha,\beta) = \frac{1}{\Gamma(\alpha)\beta\alpha}x^{\alpha-1}\, exp(-\frac{x}{\beta})$$

– The probability density function of a random variable X, which is Weibull distributed, is given as follows:

$$f(x|\beta,\lambda) = \beta\lambda^{\beta}\, x^{\beta-1}exp(-x\lambda)^{\beta}$$

Here, β is the shape parameter, and λ is the scale parameter.

The subsequent sections of this chapter comprise mainly EWMA control charts (section 9.2), EWMA control charts for skewed distributions (section 9.3), real data application of the newly proposed method (section 9.4), the simulation study (section 9.5), the results and discussions for the EWMA control charts (section 9.7), and finally, the conclusion of this study (section 9.8).

9.2. Exponentially weighted moving average control charts

The EWMA is a statistical technique for monitoring the process of averaging data in a way that assigns decreasing weights to data as they are further removed in time. The EWMA is based on the principle of EWMA.

In the absence of knowledge regarding the initial parameters, a time-based EWMA statistic is defined as follows (Mitra 2016):

$$G_t = \lambda\bar{X}_t + (1-\lambda)G_{(t-1)}. \quad [9.1]$$

Here, λ is a weighting or smoothing constant and lies in the interval $0 < \lambda < 1$. The starting value, which is also the process target, is given such that $G_o = \bar{\bar{X}}$.

In the absence of known parameters, the limits of the EWMA control chart are defined as follows:

$$UCL_{EWMA_t} = \bar{\bar{X}} + K\frac{\hat{\sigma}}{\sqrt{n}}\sqrt{\frac{\lambda}{(2-\lambda)}[1-(1-\lambda)^{2t}]}$$

$$CL_{EWMA_t} = \bar{\bar{X}},$$

$$LCL_{EWMA_t} = \bar{\bar{X}} - K\frac{\hat{\sigma}}{\sqrt{n}}\sqrt{\frac{\lambda}{(2-\lambda)}[1-(1-\lambda)^{2t}]} \qquad [9.2]$$

For sufficiently large values of the time variable t, the standard deviation of the random variable G_t is given by an asymptotic expression as follows:

$$\frac{\hat{\sigma}}{\sqrt{n}}\sqrt{\frac{\lambda}{(2-\lambda)}[1-(1-\lambda)^{2t}]} = \sqrt{\frac{\sigma^2}{n}\frac{\lambda}{2-\lambda}}. \qquad [9.3]$$

Consequently, the limits of the EWMA control chart in the absence of known parameters are provided in the following (Mitra 2016):

$$UCL_{EWMA} = \bar{\bar{X}} + K\frac{\hat{\sigma}}{\sqrt{n}}\sqrt{\frac{\lambda}{(2-\lambda)}}$$

$$CL_{EWMA} = \bar{\bar{X}},$$

$$LCL_{EWMA} = \bar{\bar{X}} - K\frac{\hat{\sigma}}{\sqrt{n}}\sqrt{\frac{\lambda}{(2-\lambda)}}. \qquad [9.4]$$

Here, K is a number chosen by the experimenter that is directly related to the smoothing constant. Generally, in a wide range of applications where individual measurements are involved, a well-designed EWMA as a control chart is highly recommended, particularly during the process monitoring phase (Montgomery 1997).

9.3. EMMA control charts for the non-normal process

As previously stated, the conventional EWMA control chart, which is employed to identify minor fluctuations in the process mean, assumes that the distribution of the process is symmetrical. In the event that the distribution of the process is skewed, the use of the classic EWMA control chart may not yield the desired and reliable results. This paper presents an overview of the use of EWMA control charts for the analysis of non-normal processes. Therefore, methods such as WV, WSD, and SC are preferable to EWMA control charts for achieving optimal results when analyzing non-normal processes. The following section will provide a detailed explanation of these methods.

9.3.1. *The WV_{EWMA} control chart*

The WV_{EWMA} method was developed by Khoo and Atta (2008). The limits of the WV_{EWMA} control chart in the absence of known parameters are provided in the following:

$$UCL_{WV_{EWMA}} = \bar{\bar{X}} + K\frac{\bar{R}}{d_2^*\sqrt{n}}\sqrt{2\hat{P}_x}\sqrt{\frac{\lambda}{(2-\lambda)}}$$

$$CL_{WV_{EWMA}} = \bar{\bar{X}}$$

$$LCL_{WV_{EWMA}} = \bar{\bar{X}} - K\frac{\bar{R}}{d_2^*\sqrt{n}}\sqrt{2(1-\hat{P}_x)}\sqrt{\frac{\lambda}{(2-\lambda)}}. \quad [9.5]$$

The values of the constants K and λ are obtained depending on the desired conditions of the average run length, as described in the previous sections. Here, d_2^* is the control chart constant for the chart based on *WV* and $P_x = P(X \leq \bar{X})$ is the probability that the quality variable *X* will be less than or equal to its mean. The constant d_2^*, which is defined as the mean of the relative range, is obtained under the non-normality assumption. This value can be computed via numerical integration once the distribution is specified by Bai and Choi (1995).

9.3.2. *The WSD_{EWMA} control chart*

This method was proposed by Atta and Ramli (2011). In the absence of known parameters, the limits of the WSD_{EWMA} control chart are computed using the following formulations (Atta and Ramli 2011).

$$UCL_{WSD_{EWMA}} = \bar{\bar{X}} + K\frac{\bar{R}}{d_2^*\sqrt{n}}2\hat{P}_x\sqrt{\frac{\lambda}{(2-\lambda)}}$$

$$CL_{WSD_{EWMA}} = \bar{\bar{X}}$$

$$LCL_{WSD_{EWMA}} = \bar{\bar{X}} - K\frac{\bar{R}}{d_2^*\sqrt{n}}2(1-\hat{P}_x)\sqrt{\frac{\lambda}{(2-\lambda)}} \quad [9.6]$$

Here, the constant $d_2^* = P_x d_2\big(2n(1-P_x)\big) + (1-P_x)d_2(2P_x)$, where $d_2(n)$ is d_2 for the normal distribution when the sample size is equal to n (Khoo et al. 2009). The value of this constant is computed by Chang and Bai (2001).

9.3.3. *Newly proposed SCEWMA control chart*

Given the EWMA defined above, the limits of the SC_{EWMA} control chart in the absence of known parameters are proposed as follows:

$$UCL_{SC_{EWMA}} = \bar{\bar{X}} + (K + c_4^*)\frac{\bar{R}}{d_2^*\sqrt{n}}\sqrt{\frac{\lambda}{(2-\lambda)}}$$

$$CL_{SC_{EWMA}} = \bar{\bar{X}}$$

$$LCL_{SC_{EWMA}} = \bar{\bar{X}} + (-K + c_4^*)\frac{\bar{R}}{d_2^*\sqrt{n}}\sqrt{\frac{\lambda}{(2-\lambda)}} \quad [9.7]$$

where c_4^* and d_2^* are the control chart constants for the SC method. The constant c_4^* is obtained as follows:

$$c_4^* = \frac{\frac{4}{3}k_3(\bar{X})}{1+0.2k_3^2(\bar{X})} \quad [9.8]$$

where $k_3(\bar{X})$ is the skewness of the subgroup mean $\bar{X}$.

9.4. Real data

The real data used in this section were taken from the quality control department of a company engaged in the production of veterinary drugs (Prabawani et al. 2020). The number of bacterial colonies in the product (which is a quality characteristic of aquaculture medicine) was considered as the quality variable used to construct the control charts. Eight samples were taken from each test, and the residual values of the sampled data were calculated. The residual values for these samples are given in Table 9.1.

The EWMA control limits for the residuals of the dataset are obtained via both the aforementioned and the proposed methods and are given in Table 9.2. The results show that the control limit value becomes narrower when the values of the parameters L and λ are small. As a result, the number of out-of-control points (T) also increases with narrowing control limits. The EWMA control chart of each method without control points is shown in Figure 9.1. The figures show that the EWMA control limits are not affected by the presence of outliers. In Figure 9.1(a), the process is controlled with WSD_{EWMA} and SC_{EWMA} charts, whereas the other charts are not controlled for the smaller values of the parameters L and λ. The control chart becomes more sensitive with smaller values of the parameters L and λ. In Figure 9.1(b), the process is in control with the SC_{EWMA} chart, whereas the other charts are not.

Subgroup	Residuals							
1	–0.3000	–0.4000	0.2000	–0.9100	0.2000	0.2000	0.7000	–0.2000
2	–1.7800	0.3000	1.2000	–1.9300	0.3000	0.9000	–0.4000	–1.2000
3	–0.2900	0.8000	1.1000	0.0000	0.0000	12.900	13.900	0.0000
4	0.4000	0.3000	–1.1700	–0.5000	0.1000	–0.5000	–0.5000	0.1000
5	–0.7600	0.6000	1.8000	–0.5300	0.0000	–0.5200	0.5000	1.0000
6	–0.7400	0.6000	1.8000	–0.3700	0.0000	–0.3000	0.5000	1.0000
7	–0.3000	0.3000	0.2000	0.2000	–0.3000	–0.5000	0.5000	–0.1000
8	–0.3000	1.1000	–0.2000	–0.1000	0.6000	–0.3000	0.5000	1.4000
9	–0.5000	0.7000	–0.8000	0.3000	1.5000	–0.7400	–0.1000	1.3000
10	–0.6000	0.2000	–0.6000	–0.1000	0.1000	–0.4000	0.6000	0.1000
11	–0.8000	0.1000	–0.3000	–1.0000	0.3000	–0.4000	7.8000	0.0000
12	–1.1000	–0.2000	0.3000	–1.1000	–0.4000	0.2000	0.1000	0.2000
13	–0.6000	0.2000	0.4000	–0.4000	–0.3000	–0.1000	0.3000	0.4000
14	–0.5000	0.8000	1.1000	–0.6000	0.8000	1.2000	–0.6000	–0.2000
15	–0.3000	0.2000	0.1000	–1.0000	–0.1000	0.1000	0.3000	–0.7000
16	0.8000	1.0000	–0.1000	0.3000	–0.1000	–0.7000	0.5000	–0.2000
17	1.2000	0.2000	–0.4000	–0.4000	–0.7400	0.5000	0.4000	–0.6000
18	0.2000	–0.3000	0.3000	–0.2000	–0.5000	0.6000	0.3000	–0.2000
19	–0.3000	0.1000	–0.4000	0.1000	0.4000	–0.2000	0.1000	–0.5000
20	0.1000	0.1000	–0.5000	–0.1000	–0.5000	0.3000	0.2000	–0.3000

Table 9.1. *Residuals in the number of bacterial colonies*

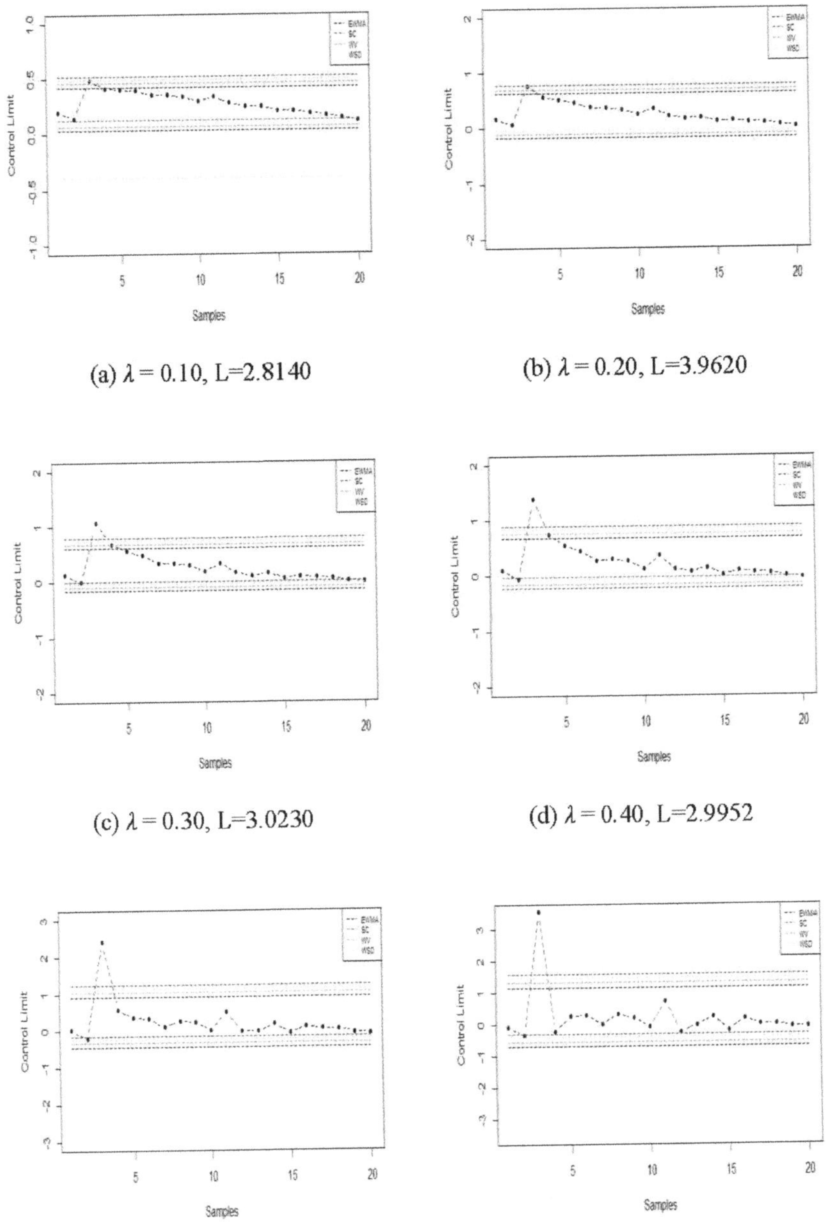

(a) $\lambda = 0.10$, L=2.8140

(b) $\lambda = 0.20$, L=3.9620

(c) $\lambda = 0.30$, L=3.0230

(d) $\lambda = 0.40$, L=2.9952

(e) $\lambda = 0.70$, L=3.0870

(f) $\lambda = 1.00$, L=3.0900

Figure 9.1. *EWMA control charts for residuals. For a color version of this figure, see www.iste.co.uk/dimotikalis/data5.zip*

		EWMA			WV_{EWMA}			WSD_{EWMA}			SC_{EWMA}		
λ	L	*UCL*	*LCL*	T	*UCL*	*LCL*	T	*UCL*	*LCL*	T	*UCL*	*LCL*	T
1.00	3.090	1.1600	–0.7048	1	1.3317	–0.5495	1	1.4809	–0.3931	1	1.5959	–0.3135	2
0.70	3.087	0.9112	–0.4559	1	1.0370	–0.3420	1	1.1464	–0.2274	1	1.2310	–0.1688	2
0.40	2.995	0.6795	–0.2243	2	0.7627	–0.1490	1	0.8350	–0.0732	1	0.8971	–0.0283	3
0.30	3.023	0.6108	–0.1556	2	0.6814	–0.0917	1	0.7427	–0.0275	1	0.7937	0.0090	3
0.20	3.962	0.6261	–0.1709	1	0.6995	–0.1045	1	0.7633	–0.0377	1	0.7735	–0.0426	0
0.10	2.814	0.4224	0.0328	1	0.4583	0.0653	1	0.4895	0.0979	0	0.5220	0.1230	1

Table 9.2. *Control limits for residuals in the number of bacterial colonies*

9.5. Simulation study

Here, the newly developed SC_{EWMA} control chart is compared with existing heuristic WV_{EWMA}, WSD_{EWMA} and classic EWMA control charts using a Monte Carlo simulation under lognormal, gamma and Weibull distributions. The comparison of these charts performances is made based on their *Type-I* errors, which is the probability of detecting an out-of-control situation even though the process is in control. The *type-I* error is also called the false alarm detection rate. The Monte Carlo simulation program is written in MATLAB 2016b 64-bit version 9.1.0. The experimental design, the simulation study and the results obtained from the simulation studies are subsequently discussed.

Throughout the scope of this work, the quality variable under investigation is assumed to either be gamma distributed with a shape parameter (α) and scale parameter (β), Weibull distributed with a scale parameter (λ) and shape parameter (β) or lognormal distributed with a location parameter (μ) and scale parameter (σ). For the gamma distribution, the skewness is affected only by the shape parameter (α); hence, throughout this work, the scale parameter (β) is given a constant value of 1. For the Weibull distribution, the skewness is affected only by the shape parameter (β); hence, the scale parameter (λ) is given a constant value of 1. Finally, for the lognormal distribution, the skewness is affected only by the scale parameter (σ); hence, the location parameter (μ) is given a constant value of 0. The skewness values, the varying parameters and their corresponding probabilities are given in Table 9.3. The probabilities are taken to two decimal places and are also obtained from the Monte Carlo simulation. The EWMA statistic is set up following the steps provided in section 9.3. The in-control ARL used for this study is 370, which is equivalent to a *Type-I* error (α) of 0.0027 for the classic Shewhart method when the process is in control. In the coding, however, an α *Type-1* error is used instead of an ARL because the relationship $ARL = 1/\alpha$ exists between them.

The optimal ordered pairs of (λ,K) used for this study are given in Table 9.4. Some of these optimal pairs are in the interval $0.05 < \lambda < 0.25$, which was studied by Borror et al. (1999) and found to be the best smoothing parameter interval corresponding to the in-control *Type-I* error of 0.0027 or ARL of 370 for the classic Shewhart charts.

	Lognormal		**Weibull**		**Gamma**	
k_3	σ	*PX*	β	*PX*	α	*PX*
0.50	0.16	0.53	2.15	0.54	16.00	0.53
1.00	0.32	0.56	1.57	0.57	4.00	0.57
1.50	0.44	0.59	1.20	0.61	1.80	0.60
2.00	0.54	0.61	1.00	0.63	1.00	0.63
2.50	0.66	0.63	0.86	0.66	0.64	0.66
3.00	0.72	0.64	0.77	0.68	0.44	0.69

Table 9.3. *Varying parameters and their probabilities for lognormal, Weibull and gamma distributions*

λ	0.10	0.20	0.30	0.40	0.70
K	2.6952	2.8537	2.9286	2.9614	3.0000

Table 9.4. *Values of the smoothing and control chart constants*

The subgroup sizes used for this work are $n = 3, 5, 7$ and 10, which are chosen to represent small, medium and large subgroup sizes, respectively. The WV constant (d_2^{WV}) and WSD constant (d_2^{WSD}) were computed and given by Chang and Bai (2001). The d_2 and C_4^* constants used for the various subgroup sizes when the distribution is normal were calculated and given by Karagoz (2018). Note that the $\widehat{P_x}$ used for the WV and WSD methods are computed simultaneously within the simulation program.

9.6. Simulation algorithm

As previously mentioned, the Monte Carlo simulation technique is used throughout the scope of this work. The algorithmic steps used for the simulation are as follows:

– N independent identically distributed (*i.i.d.*) pseudorandom numbers are generated from gamma ($gamma(\alpha,1)$), Weibull ($weibull(1,\lambda)$) and lognormal ($lognormal(0,\sigma)$) distributions for each of the subgroup sample sizes $n = 3, 5, 7, 10$.

– The above process is repeated 100 times, and its mean, grand mean, range and mean of the range are computed.

– The $\widehat{P}_X$ value is then obtained from the randomly generated data in the previous step.

– The lower and upper control limits for the classic EWMA, SC_{EWMA}, WV_{EWMA} and WSD_{EWMA} are computed.

– The EWMA test statistics G_t is computed for all 100 subgroups of size n generated above.

– The EWMA test statistics G_t are checked to either be within the control limits computed above or not for each of the methods, and their *type-I* errors are obtained and recorded.

– The above steps are repeated 10,000 times, which is the simulation size, and the mean of the 10,000 *type-I* errors for each method is computed and recorded.

Importantly, small changes are made to the program to suit the various smoothing parameters.

9.7. Results and discussion

After successfully executing the programs, the results obtained are tabulated as follows in hierarchical order of the subgroup sizes n.

For $n = 3$, when the smoothing parameter was in the interval $0.10 \le \lambda \le 0.20$, the Weibull distribution produced the smallest results, which were very close to the expected control value of 0.0027. The WV_{EWMA} emerged as the most suitable method to be used. As an alternative, the WSD_{EWMA} could also be used if the experimenter feels like doing so because it also produced good readings. As the smoothing parameter is increased to the interval $0.30 \le \lambda \le 0.40$, the Weibull distribution produced the smallest results for the *Type-I* error. Compared with WV_{EWMA}, WSD_{EWMA} yielded better readings in most cases, especially when the skewness was extremely small. These two methods could be used as alternatives to each other depending on the obligations put in place by the management of the place where the experiment is being carried out. As the smoothing parameter was further increased to a higher value of $\lambda = 0.70$, the Weibull distribution produced the smallest readings when the skewness was less than or equal to 1.50. As the skewness is increased beyond 1.50, the gamma distribution overtook the former and produced the smallest results. WSD_{EWMA} produced the smallest readings when the skewness was less than or equal to 1.50. SC_{EWMA}, which was the proposed method, emerged as the one with the smallest *Type-I* errors for all the distributions when the skewness was greater than 1.50. These two methods could be used as alternatives to each other under this circumstance.

		Gamma				**Weibull**				**Lognormal**			
λ	k_3	*EWMA*	SC_{EWMA}	WV_{EWMA}	WSD_{EWMA}	*EWMA*	SC_{EWMA}	WV_{EWMA}	WSD_{EWMA}	*EWMA*	SC_{EWMA}	WV_{EWMA}	WSD_{EWMA}
	0.50	0.0030	0.0043	0.0030	0.0032	0.0031	0.0045	0.0029	0.0029	0.0031	0.0042	0.0029	0.0030
	1.00	0.0040	0.0089	0.0029	0.0037	0.0041	0.0090	0.0031	0.0037	0.0042	0.0090	0.0031	0.0040
	1.50	0.0060	0.0173	0.0033	0.0057	0.0065	0.0177	0.0031	0.0056	0.0058	0.0158	0.0029	0.0049
0.1	2.00	0.0090	0.0273	0.0034	0.0089	0.0093	0.0273	0.0035	0.0090	0.0083	0.0236	0.0031	0.0065
	2.50	0.0140	0.0379	0.0039	0.0147	0.0137	0.0378	0.0036	0.0129	0.0117	0.0332	0.0033	0.0095
	3.00	0.2080	0.0472	0.0044	0.0240	0.0176	0.0448	0.0032	0.0172	0.0142	0.0378	0.0036	0.0096
	0.50	0.0030	0.0038	0.0030	0.0030	0.0032	0.0040	0.0029	0.0027	0.0034	0.0038	0.0031	0.0030
	1.00	0.0050	0.0065	0.0029	0.0032	0.0045	0.0067	0.0029	0.0032	0.0050	0.0069	0.0034	0.0036
	1.50	0.0070	0.0113	0.0029	0.0040	0.0071	0.0117	0.0027	0.0039	0.0070	0.0110	0.0032	0.0041
0.2	2.00	0.011	0.0172	0.0033	0.0061	0.0109	0.018	0.0032	0.0063	0.0099	0.0156	0.0035	0.0051
	2.50	0.0160	0.0228	0.0034	0.0096	0.0154	0.0236	0.0033	0.0084	0.0142	0.0215	0.0040	0.0073
	3.00	0.0230	0.0272	0.0038	0.0160	0.0204	0.0264	0.0034	0.0111	0.0164	0.0232	0.0043	0.0066
	0.50	0.0030	0.0035	0.0030	0.0029	0.0030	0.0031	0.0025	0.0022	0.0034	0.0034	0.0030	0.0029
	1.00	0.0050	0.0051	0.0028	0.0027	0.0047	0.0050	0.0028	0.0026	0.0054	0.0055	0.0034	0.0034
	1.50	0.0080	0.0080	0.0031	0.0031	0.0079	0.0080	0.0028	0.0030	0.0076	0.0085	0.0034	0.0036
0.3	2.00	0.0120	0.0118	0.0036	0.0045	0.0121	0.0116	0.0035	0.0043	0.0105	0.0111	0.0038	0.0043
	2.50	0.0180	0.0139	0.0040	0.0061	0.017	0.0141	0.0038	0.0052	0.0154	0.0142	0.0048	0.0059
	3.00	0.0250	0.0149	0.0044	0.0094	0.0220	0.0153	0.0041	0.0068	0.018	0.0151	0.0051	0.0052
	0.50	0.0030	0.0032	0.0030	0.0027	0.0029	0.0029	0.0025	0.0021	0.0034	0.0032	0.0029	0.0028
	1.00	0.005	0.0043	0.0030	0.0026	0.0050	0.0040	0.0029	0.0023	0.0056	0.0045	0.0034	0.0030
	1.50	0.0090	0.0060	0.0035	0.0028	0.0087	0.0060	0.0032	0.0025	0.0085	0.0065	0.0038	0.0034
0.4	2.00	0.0130	0.0077	0.0041	0.0034	0.0134	0.0078	0.0042	0.0035	0.0121	0.0086	0.0046	0.0041
	2.50	0.0200	0.0086	0.0048	0.0044	0.019	0.0091	0.0048	0.0040	0.0167	0.0105	0.0055	0.0053
	3.00	0.0270	0.0075	0.0054	0.0055	0.0239	0.0087	0.0052	0.0046	0.0194	0.0107	0.0061	0.0048
	0.50	0.0040	0.0028	0.0031	0.0026	0.0033	0.0022	0.0025	0.0019	0.0039	0.003	0.0032	0.0028
	1.00	0.0060	0.0030	0.0036	0.0025	0.0060	0.0022	0.0033	0.0021	0.0069	0.0035	0.0042	0.0033
	1.50	0.0110	0.0030	0.0048	0.0029	0.0112	0.0025	0.0045	0.0025	0.0107	0.0044	0.0053	0.0038
0.7	2.00	0.0170	0.0026	0.0059	0.0034	0.0166	0.0027	0.006	0.0034	0.0144	0.0048	0.0061	0.0045
	2.50	0.0230	0.0025	0.0069	0.0039	0.0228	0.0029	0.0068	0.0041	0.0198	0.005	0.0076	0.0058
	3.00	0.0310	0.0029	0.0080	0.0044	0.0278	0.0031	0.0074	0.0047	0.0225	0.0049	0.0084	0.0057

Table 9.5. *The results of p for the EWMA charts under skewed distributions for n = 3*

The results obtained are tabulated in Table 9.5 for all of the distributions and illustrated graphically for some cases below.

For $n = 5$ and $n = 7$, when the smoothing parameter was $\lambda = 0.10$, the lognormal distribution produced the smallest results. When the smoothing parameter was increased to $\lambda = 0.20$, the Weibull distribution produced the smallest results. The WV_{EWMA} emerged as the most suitable method to be used. As an alternative, the classic EWMA could also be used if the experimenter feels like doing so because it also produced strong readings when the skewness was smaller than or equal to 1.50. As the smoothing parameter had been increased to the interval $0.30 \leq \lambda \leq 0.40$, the Weibull distribution produced the smallest results for the *Type-1* error. The WV_{EWMA} gave the best results for *Type-1* error. WSD_{EWMA} produced good readings when the skewness was less than or equal to 1.50 for the first situation, whereas SC_{EWMA} produced better results for the latter. This method could be used as an alternative to the former when the skewness is less than or equal to 1.50. As the smoothing parameter is increased to $\lambda = 0.70$, the gamma distribution produced the smallest results for the *Type-1* error. The SC_{EWMA}, which was the proposed method, gave the smallest readings for the *Type-1* error. It was closely followed by WSD_{EWMA}, which could be used as an alternative to SC_{EWMA}.

The results obtained are tabulated in Tables 9.6 and 9.7 for all of the distributions and are illustrated graphically for some cases below.

For $n = 10$, when the smoothing parameter was in the interval $0.10 \leq \lambda \leq 0.20$, the lognormal distribution produced the smallest overall results for the *Type-1* error. The WV_{EWMA} also produced the best readings for the *Type-1* error. This method was followed by the classic EWMA method when the skewness was less than or equal to 1.50. Under this skewness, the latter could be used as an alternative to the former. When the smoothing parameter was in the interval $0.30 \leq \lambda \leq 0.40$, the Weibull distribution produced the overall smallest readings for the *Type-1* error. The WV_{EWMA} also produced the best results for *Type-1* error. It was closely followed by the SC_{EWMA} method, which produced good results when the skewness was less than or equal to 1.50. The latter can therefore be used as an alternative to the former under such skewness. When the smoothing parameter was further increased to $\lambda = 0.70$, the gamma distribution produced the overall smallest readings for the *Type-1* error. SC_{EWMA}, which was the proposed method, performed best and produced the best results for *Type-1* error. It was followed by WV_{EWMA}, which produced considerably good results. Under these experimental conditions, WV_{EWMA} could be used as an alternative to SC_{EWMA}.

		Gamma				Weibull				Lognormal			
λ	k_3	*EWMA*	SC_{EWMA}	WV_{EWMA}	WSD_{EWMA}	*EWMA*	SC_{EWMA}	WV_{EWMA}	WSD_{EWMA}	*EWMA*	SC_{EWMA}	WV_{EWMA}	WSD_{EWMA}
0.1	0.50	0.0029	0.0035	0.0028	0.0031	0.0031	0.0038	0.0028	0.0032	0.0032	0.0036	0.0029	0.0032
	1.00	0.0041	0.0065	0.0031	0.0047	0.0037	0.0062	0.0029	0.0047	0.0039	0.0062	0.003	0.0044
	1.50	0.0056	0.0108	0.0033	0.0074	0.0057	0.0113	0.0031	0.0079	0.0052	0.0105	0.0030	0.0063
	2.00	0.0083	0.0180	0.0039	0.0129	0.0079	0.0179	0.0038	0.0126	0.0068	0.0151	0.0031	0.0085
	2.50	0.0118	0.0258	0.0042	0.0205	0.0117	0.0261	0.0038	0.0184	0.0099	0.0238	0.0034	0.0126
	3.00	0.0171	0.0351	0.0048	0.0332	0.0149	0.0332	0.0037	0.0243	0.0119	0.0286	0.0036	0.0157
0.2	0.50	0.0032	0.0034	0.0029	0.0032	0.0032	0.0034	0.0028	0.0031	0.0032	0.0033	0.0029	0.0031
	1.00	0.0042	0.0050	0.0028	0.0040	0.0041	0.0047	0.0028	0.0040	0.0043	0.0050	0.0031	0.0041
	1.50	0.0059	0.0076	0.0029	0.0060	0.0063	0.0082	0.0028	0.0066	0.0058	0.0075	0.0030	0.0053
	2.00	0.0089	0.0116	0.0032	0.0097	0.0090	0.0117	0.0032	0.0098	0.0079	0.0106	0.0030	0.0068
	2.50	0.0129	0.0167	0.0033	0.0163	0.0129	0.0166	0.0031	0.0138	0.0114	0.0158	0.0035	0.0101
	3.00	0.0187	0.0217	0.0037	0.0266	0.0166	0.0206	0.0030	0.0185	0.0139	0.0187	0.0038	0.0124
0.3	0.50	0.0030	0.0030	0.0027	0.0029	0.0030	0.0030	0.0026	0.0028	0.0031	0.0030	0.0027	0.0029
	1.00	0.0041	0.0039	0.0026	0.0034	0.0041	0.0038	0.0026	0.0035	0.0044	0.0042	0.0029	0.0036
	1.50	0.0065	0.0057	0.0028	0.0049	0.0064	0.0057	0.0024	0.0048	0.0063	0.0059	0.003	0.0047
	2.00	0.0096	0.0079	0.003	0.0074	0.0096	0.0081	0.003	0.0075	0.0086	0.0077	0.0032	0.0056
	2.50	0.0144	0.0111	0.0032	0.0124	0.0137	0.0108	0.003	0.0103	0.0121	0.0111	0.0037	0.0078
	3.00	0.0203	0.0130	0.0035	0.0198	0.0181	0.0132	0.0033	0.0137	0.0147	0.0128	0.0042	0.0096
0.4	0.50	0.0030	0.0028	0.0026	0.0027	0.0030	0.0027	0.0024	0.0025	0.0031	0.0029	0.0027	0.0028
	1.00	0.0044	0.0035	0.0027	0.0032	0.0043	0.0034	0.0026	0.0032	0.0048	0.0037	0.0030	0.0034
	1.50	0.0068	0.0046	0.0028	0.0043	0.007	0.0044	0.0026	0.0041	0.0070	0.0050	0.0032	0.0043
	2.00	0.0107	0.0059	0.0032	0.0060	0.0106	0.0059	0.0032	0.0059	0.0095	0.0066	0.0036	0.0052
	2.50	0.0154	0.0070	0.0035	0.0089	0.015	0.0076	0.0034	0.0079	0.0136	0.0085	0.0044	0.0069
	3.00	0.0218	0.0080	0.0038	0.0145	0.0192	0.0089	0.0038	0.0103	0.0159	0.0095	0.0048	0.0081
0.7	0.50	0.0033	0.0027	0.0028	0.0027	0.0029	0.0022	0.0023	0.0021	0.0034	0.0028	0.0029	0.0029
	1.00	0.0054	0.0027	0.0030	0.0028	0.0051	0.0024	0.0027	0.0025	0.0056	0.0031	0.0035	0.0033
	1.50	0.0084	0.0028	0.0035	0.0032	0.0089	0.0025	0.0033	0.0029	0.0084	0.0035	0.0039	0.0038
	2.00	0.0132	0.0027	0.0044	0.0038	0.0133	0.0028	0.0044	0.0038	0.0117	0.0042	0.0048	0.0046
	2.50	0.0188	0.0024	0.0051	0.0043	0.0183	0.0029	0.005	0.0043	0.0162	0.0048	0.0059	0.0057
	3.00	0.0258	0.0024	0.0058	0.0053	0.0232	0.0031	0.0056	0.0050	0.0189	0.0050	0.0066	0.0064

Table 9.6. *The results of p for the EWMA charts under skewed distributions for n = 5*

λ	k_3	Gamma				Weibull				Lognormal			
		$EWMA$	SC_{EWMA}	WV_{EWMA}	WSD_{EWMA}	$EWMA$	SC_{EWMA}	WV_{EWMA}	WSD_{EWMA}	$EWMA$	SC_{EWMA}	WV_{EWMA}	WSD_{EWMA}
0.1	0.50	0.0030	0.0033	0.0029	0.0033	0.0031	0.0034	0.0028	0.0034	0.0031	0.0034	0.0029	0.0033
	1.00	0.0038	0.0051	0.0029	0.0046	0.0041	0.0051	0.0031	0.0052	0.0034	0.0051	0.0029	0.0044
	1.50	0.0049	0.0081	0.0032	0.0075	0.0054	0.0088	0.0032	0.0085	0.0045	0.0080	0.0029	0.0062
	2.00	0.0071	0.0131	0.0038	0.0132	0.007	0.013	0.0037	0.0133	0.0059	0.0120	0.0031	0.0086
	2.50	0.0096	0.0189	0.0043	0.0220	0.0100	0.0196	0.004	0.0195	0.0082	0.0187	0.0036	0.013
	3.00	0.0138	0.0264	0.0052	0.0346	0.0123	0.0253	0.0041	0.0257	0.0098	0.0220	0.0036	0.0155
0.2	0.50	0.0031	0.0032	0.0029	0.0031	0.0031	0.0030	0.0027	0.0032	0.0029	0.0031	0.0028	0.0030
	1.00	0.0041	0.0043	0.0029	0.0043	0.0041	0.0042	0.0029	0.0047	0.0038	0.0043	0.0029	0.0041
	1.50	0.0054	0.0062	0.0030	0.0066	0.0059	0.0063	0.0030	0.0071	0.0052	0.0063	0.0030	0.0055
	2.00	0.0079	0.0092	0.0032	0.011	0.0077	0.009	0.0032	0.0111	0.0068	0.0088	0.0031	0.0073
	2.50	0.0111	0.0125	0.0035	0.0183	0.0106	0.0129	0.0032	0.0158	0.0095	0.0127	0.0034	0.0107
	3.00	0.0154	0.0169	0.0039	0.0296	0.0137	0.0164	0.0033	0.0210	0.0115	0.0151	0.0038	0.0130
0.3	0.50	0.0030	0.0029	0.0027	0.0030	0.0029	0.0027	0.0024	0.0028	0.0028	0.0027	0.0026	0.0028
	1.00	0.0040	0.0036	0.0027	0.0037	0.0041	0.0034	0.0027	0.0039	0.0040	0.0037	0.0028	0.0037
	1.50	0.0054	0.0047	0.0026	0.0053	0.0062	0.0049	0.0027	0.0059	0.0055	0.0048	0.0029	0.0046
	2.00	0.0082	0.0064	0.0028	0.0087	0.0084	0.0067	0.0031	0.0091	0.0073	0.0064	0.0030	0.0061
	2.50	0.0118	0.0087	0.003	0.0147	0.0114	0.0089	0.0028	0.0125	0.0104	0.0091	0.0035	0.0086
	3.00	0.0162	0.0111	0.0032	0.0240	0.0148	0.0110	0.0030	0.0167	0.0122	0.0108	0.0037	0.0105
0.4	0.50	0.0029	0.0027	0.0026	0.0027	0.0027	0.0026	0.0023	0.0024	0.0032	0.0030	0.0028	0.0029
	1.00	0.0041	0.0032	0.0026	0.0034	0.0044	0.0033	0.0026	0.0031	0.0046	0.0037	0.0029	0.0033
	1.50	0.0059	0.0039	0.0025	0.0046	0.0071	0.0045	0.0026	0.0041	0.0069	0.0050	0.0032	0.0043
	2.00	0.0090	0.0050	0.0029	0.0073	0.0107	0.0059	0.0032	0.0059	0.0093	0.0064	0.0035	0.0052
	2.50	0.0127	0.0061	0.0031	0.0119	0.0151	0.0076	0.0034	0.0079	0.0136	0.0087	0.0044	0.0070
	3.00	0.0176	0.0075	0.0034	0.0193	0.0198	0.0087	0.0039	0.0103	0.0158	0.0095	0.0047	0.0081
0.7	0.50	0.0033	0.0027	0.0028	0.0027	0.0031	0.0023	0.0024	0.0025	0.0033	0.0028	0.0028	0.0028
	1.00	0.0052	0.0027	0.0029	0.0028	0.0046	0.0024	0.0026	0.0029	0.0054	0.0030	0.0033	0.0031
	1.50	0.0087	0.0029	0.0036	0.0033	0.0077	0.0026	0.0029	0.0036	0.0084	0.0035	0.0038	0.0037
	2.00	0.0132	0.0027	0.0043	0.0036	0.0110	0.0026	0.0034	0.0044	0.0118	0.0042	0.0049	0.0047
	2.50	0.0191	0.0026	0.0052	0.0044	0.0154	0.003	0.0041	0.0055	0.0164	0.005	0.0061	0.0059
	3.00	0.0259	0.0025	0.0060	0.0053	0.0194	0.0032	0.0046	0.0066	0.0190	0.0051	0.0068	0.0066

Table 9.7. *The results of p for the EWMA charts under the skewed distributions for n = 7*

9.8. Conclusion

This work focused mainly on proposing a new method of control charts for skewed distribution which was called the SC_{EWMA}. The performance of this newly proposed method was compared with that of existing control chart methods for skewed distributions using specifically known skewed distributions and precise sampling conditions. In a nutshell, it can be deducted from above that the EWMA methods for skewed distributions are highly affected by the values of the smoothing parameter λ and the sample size n used for the subgroups. It can also be confirmed in Choobineh and Ballard (1987) and Chang and Bai (2001) that if extremely small or medium shifts in the process mean are of interest, then WV_{EWMA} should be preferred to the others. If larger shifts are of interest, then our proposed method of SC_{EWMA} should be preferred for obtaining optimal solutions from the production process.

		Gamma				**Weibull**				**Lognormal**			
λ	k_3	*EWMA*	SC_{EWMA}	WV_{EWMA}	WSD_{EWMA}	*EWMA*	SC_{EWMA}	WV_{EWMA}	WSD_{EWMA}	*EWMA*	SC_{EWMA}	WV_{EWMA}	WSD_{EWMA}
0.1	0.50	0.0028	0.0030	0.0027	0.0031	0.0033	0.0031	0.0027	0.0036	0.0028	0.003	0.0027	0.0031
	1.00	0.0034	0.0042	0.0028	0.0046	0.0041	0.0046	0.0033	0.0058	0.0034	0.0044	0.0030	0.0043
	1.50	0.0045	0.0065	0.0033	0.0080	0.0048	0.0066	0.0034	0.0088	0.0042	0.0063	0.0031	0.0061
	2.00	0.0063	0.0099	0.0041	0.0138	0.0063	0.0097	0.004	0.0135	0.0051	0.0092	0.0034	0.0081
	2.50	0.0084	0.0142	0.0049	0.0222	0.0078	0.0144	0.0043	0.0196	0.0066	0.0141	0.0036	0.0113
	3.00	0.0106	0.019	0.0057	0.0334	0.0098	0.0186	0.0045	0.0251	0.0077	0.0175	0.0040	0.0140
0.2	0.50	0.0031	0.0031	0.0029	0.0033	0.0031	0.0029	0.0025	0.0034	0.0030	0.0030	0.0028	0.0031
	1.00	0.0037	0.0038	0.0028	0.0044	0.0040	0.0036	0.0028	0.0048	0.0036	0.0038	0.0029	0.0041
	1.50	0.0049	0.0050	0.0030	0.0069	0.0054	0.0053	0.0031	0.0078	0.0045	0.0050	0.0030	0.0053
	2.00	0.0067	0.0069	0.0033	0.0115	0.0066	0.0069	0.0033	0.0116	0.0055	0.0069	0.0030	0.0067
	2.50	0.0092	0.0100	0.0041	0.0195	0.0086	0.0099	0.0034	0.0166	0.0075	0.0099	0.0034	0.0093
	3.00	0.0123	0.0129	0.0046	0.0298	0.0111	0.0127	0.0037	0.0216	0.0092	0.0118	0.0036	0.0114
0.3	0.50	0.0028	0.0026	0.0026	0.0028	0.0031	0.0027	0.0025	0.0032	0.0029	0.0028	0.0027	0.0029
	1.00	0.0037	0.0032	0.0026	0.0039	0.0039	0.0031	0.0026	0.0043	0.0039	0.0034	0.0029	0.0037
	1.50	0.0050	0.0041	0.0027	0.0059	0.0053	0.0041	0.0026	0.0066	0.0046	0.0041	0.0027	0.0046
	2.00	0.0070	0.0051	0.0029	0.0096	0.007	0.0052	0.0029	0.0097	0.0061	0.0053	0.0029	0.0057
	2.50	0.0097	0.0069	0.0033	0.0159	0.0092	0.0069	0.0029	0.0132	0.0087	0.0075	0.0035	0.0077
	3.00	0.0127	0.0086	0.0035	0.0249	0.0118	0.0087	0.0031	0.0176	0.0102	0.0088	0.0037	0.0092
0.4	0.50	0.0028	0.0026	0.0025	0.0027	0.0031	0.0026	0.0024	0.0030	0.0027	0.0025	0.0025	0.0026
	1.00	0.0037	0.0028	0.0024	0.0034	0.0040	0.0028	0.0025	0.0040	0.0036	0.0030	0.0027	0.0033
	1.50	0.0053	0.0034	0.0026	0.0051	0.0058	0.0034	0.0025	0.0056	0.0050	0.0038	0.0028	0.0043
	2.00	0.0074	0.0042	0.0027	0.0081	0.0077	0.0044	0.0029	0.0085	0.0064	0.0045	0.0029	0.0050
	2.50	0.0102	0.0053	0.0030	0.0135	0.0101	0.0054	0.0028	0.0112	0.0091	0.0061	0.0035	0.0067
	3.00	0.0137	0.0062	0.0031	0.0213	0.0124	0.0066	0.0030	0.0147	0.0106	0.0070	0.0038	0.0079
0.7	0.50	0.0028	0.0025	0.0025	0.0026	0.0032	0.0024	0.0024	0.0029	0.0029	0.0026	0.0026	0.0027
	1.00	0.0041	0.0026	0.0026	0.0031	0.0044	0.0024	0.0025	0.0033	0.0041	0.0028	0.0029	0.0031
	1.50	0.0062	0.0027	0.0028	0.004	0.0065	0.0026	0.0025	0.0041	0.0059	0.0031	0.0031	0.0036
	2.00	0.0091	0.0027	0.0029	0.0056	0.0090	0.0027	0.0030	0.0056	0.0078	0.0036	0.0035	0.0041
	2.50	0.0126	0.0028	0.0033	0.0081	0.0121	0.0029	0.0033	0.0068	0.0111	0.0042	0.0043	0.0050
	3.00	0.0166	0.0027	0.0037	0.0121	0.0154	0.0032	0.0037	0.0084	0.0129	0.0047	0.0048	0.0058

Table 9.8. *The results of p for the EWMA charts under the skewed distributions for n = 10*

9.9. References

Atta, A.M.A. and Ramli, R. (2011). A comparison study on the performances of $\bar{X}$, EWMA and CUSUM control charts for skewed distributions using weighted standard deviations methods. *Journal of Science and Technology*, 3(2), 77–88.

Bai, D.S. and Choi, I.S. (1995). $\bar{X}$ and R control charts for skewed populations. *Journal of Quality Technology*, 27(2), 120–131.

Borror, C.M., Montgomery, D.C., Runger, G.C. (1999). Robustness of the EWMA control chart to non-normality. *Journal of Quality Technology*, 31(3), 309–316.

Chan, L.K. and Cui, H.J. (2003). Skewness correction $\bar{X}$ and R charts for skewed distributions. *Naval Research Logistics*, 50(6), 555–573.

Chang, Y.S. and Bai, D.S. (2001). Control charts for positively-skewed populations with weighted standard deviations. *Quality and Reliability Engineering International*, 17(5), 397–406.

Choobineh, F. and Ballard, J.L. (1987). Control-limits of QC charts for skewed distributions using weighted variance. *IEEE Transactions on Reliability*, 36(4), 473–477.

Crowder, S.V. (1989). Design of exponentially weighted moving average schemes. *Journal of Quality Technology*, 21(3), 155–162.

Duncan, A.J. (1986). *Quality Control and Industrial Statistics*, 5th edition. Richard D. Irwin, Inc., Homewood.

Karagöz, D. (2018). Robust $\bar{X}$ control chart for monitoring the skewed and contaminated process. *Hacettepe Journal of Mathematics and Statistics*, 47(1), 223–242.

Karagöz, D. and Hamurkaroglu, C. (2012). Control charts for skewed distributions: Weibull, gamma, and lognormal. *Metodološki zvezki – Advances in Methodology and Statistics*, 9(2), 95–106.

Karagöz, D. and Koyuncu, N. (2019). New ranked set sampling schemes for range charts limits under bivariate skewed distributions. *Soft Computing*, 23(5), 1573–1587.

Khoo, M.B.C. and Atta, A.M.A. (2008). An EWMA control chart for monitoring the mean of skewed populations using weighted variance. In *Proceedings of the IEEE International Conference on Industrial Engineering and Engineering Management*, Singapore.

Khoo, M.B.C., Atta, A.M.A., Chen, C.H. (2009). Proposed X and S control charts for skewed distributions. In *Proceedings of the IEEE International Conference on Industrial Engineering and Engineering Management*, Hong Kong.

Koyuncu, N. and Karagöz, D. (2018). New mean charts for bivariate asymmetric distributions using different ranked set sampling designs. *Quality Technology and Quantitative Management*, 15(5), 602–621.

Lucas, J.M. and Saccucci, M.S. (1990). Exponentially weighted moving average control schemes: Properties and enhancements. *Technometrics*, 32(1), 1–12.

Mitra, A. (2016). *Fundamentals of Quality Control and Improvement*, 4th edition. John Wiley & Sons, Hoboken.

Montgomery, D.C. (1997). *Introduction to Statistical Quality Control*, 4th edition. John Wiley & Sons, New York.

Prabawani, N.A., Mashuri, M., Irhamah. (2020). Performance of robust EWMA control chart for variability process using non-normal data. *Journal of Physics: Conference Series*, 1511(1), 012007. doi: 10.1088/1742-6596/1511/1/012054.

Roberts, S.W. (2000). Control chart tests based on geometric moving averages. *Technometrics*, 42(1), 97–101.

Robinson, P.B. and Ho, T.Y. (1978). Average run lengths of geometric moving average charts by numerical methods. *Technometrics*, 20(1), 85–93.

10

Assessing the Impact of Renewable Energy Sources on Energy Economics: A Non-Linear Regression Analysis of Hellenic Energy Exchange Market Clearing Prices

The impact of renewable energy sources (RESs) on energy economics, specifically within the Hellenic Energy Exchange (HEnEx), is a crucial metric for evaluating the overall assimilation of RES into society's energy landscape. This chapter strives to capture the correlation between the market clearing price (MCP) of the day-ahead market (DAM) and RES production originating from the island of Crete through the application of nonlinear regression techniques. The objective was accomplished with the use of data provided publicly by HEnEx and the application of advanced algorithms. More specifically, this chapter evaluates the performance of sparse autoencoders and compares their efficiency with that of Spearman's rank. The obtained results show the effectiveness of the adopted methodologies, offering insights that are invaluable for policymakers, energy market participants and stakeholders alike.

10.1. Introduction

HEnEx serves as the Nominated Electricity Market Operator (Hellenic Energy Exchange S.A. 2023), overseeing the monitoring and scheduling of all electrical energy trades within Greece and the interconnected markets. Since its inception,

---

Chapter written by Emmanuel KARAPIDAKIS, Yiannis KATSIGIANNIS, Konstantinos BLAZAKIS, Marios NIKOLOGIANNIS, George MATALLIOTAKIS, Georgios STAVRAKAKIS, Nikos VENIANAKIS and Paolo BONFINI.

For a color version of all figures in this chapter, see www.iste.co.uk/dimotikalis/data5.zip.

there has been a noticeable increase in the traded volumes of RES, both in terms of the amount of energy traded and its proportion within the energy mix. The implications of this trend can be analyzed using data from the Energy Trading Spot System (ETSS), a platform developed and maintained by HEnEx. ETSS provides comprehensive data for all types of energy markets, including the DAM and the intraday market, along with its subcategories.

In the DAM, participants include various suppliers (low-, medium-, and high-voltage distributors); consumers from the island of Crete; hydro stations; and exporters to Albania, Turkey, Italy, North Macedonia and Bulgaria. Sellers encompass all producers, RES stations, lignite and natural gas power plants; imported energy from the aforementioned countries; and energy production from Crete, whether renewable or conventional (diesel or mazut power plants). The participation share of each participant fluctuates over time, significantly influencing the market dynamics and the determination of the MCP.

Various methods have been employed to determine the correlation between the market price and its components, encompassing both linear (Falkoni and Krajacic 2016; Busu et al., 2019; Massa and Rosellón 2020) and nonlinear approaches (Bahadur and Paffenroth 2020; Niu 2021; Xiu et al. 2022; Savargaonkar et al. 2024). These methods recognize that each participant's impact varies and depends on multiple factors.

Neural networks have also been utilized for similar purposes, aiming to uncover hidden patterns and correlations. Among these, sparse autoencoders, a type of artificial neural network designed to learn efficient representations of input data, have been employed in various applications. These include forecasting (Gugulothu and Subramanian 2019; Chen et al. 2019), estimating the long-term state of charge for energy storage (Savargaonkar et al. 2021) and electricity consumption pattern analysis (Li et al. 2022).

Sparse autoencoders are a type of autoencoder that imposes a sparsity constraint on the hidden units, meaning that only a small number of neurons are activated at any given time. This results in a more efficient and often more interpretable latent representation. The sparsity constraint helps capture essential patterns and structures in the data, making sparse autoencoders particularly useful for nonlinear regression tasks.

Sparse autoencoders use encoders to map input data to a latent-space representation and decoders to reconstruct the input data from this representation. By reducing the dimensionality of the data while preserving essential nonlinear relationships, sparse autoencoders aid in identifying significant correlation patterns. This dimensionality reduction is a key feature, enabling the model to capture the most important features of the input data while discarding noise and redundant information. Consequently, the model requires fewer parameters and performs faster computations, enhancing efficiency during both training and inference.

Moreover, the sparsity constraint helps avoid overfitting by forcing the model to learn robust and generalizable features. The latent representations produced are often more interpretable and meaningful, capturing the underlying structures in the data. The encoder learns a compact representation of the data, often revealing patterns and structures not immediately apparent in the original high-dimensional space.

Sparse autoencoders were deployed to assess the correlation between the participants situated in the island of Crete and the HEnEx market results. The transactional data from the DAM trades were used as input for this survey (EnExGroup 2024), with Crete's participation being exclusive to the specific market.

10.2. Methodology

For both methods (Spearman's rank, sparse autoencoder), normalization of the data was executed to maintain uniform weight updates, preventing skewed weight distributions. Equation [10.1] was used as a scaler:

$$\bar{y} = \frac{y_i - \bar{y}}{\sigma f_y} \qquad [10.1]$$

In equation [10.1], y_i represents the original data, $\bar{y}$ denotes the normalized data, $\bar{y}$ represents the sample mean and σf_y represents the sample's standard deviation.

10.2.1. *Spearman's rank*

As part of the time series analysis of the available data, a classical additive decomposition was performed. This method models the time series as the sum of three components: the trend series, the seasonal series and the residuals. These components are represented by equation [10.2]:

$$x_i = Tr_i + Sl_i + Rd_i \qquad [10.2]$$

This decomposition is useful for identifying trends, seasonality and irregularities in the data, aiding in forecasting and analysis tasks. The trend component captures the long-term progression or directionality of the time series, representing the underlying pattern in the data, abstracted from short-term fluctuations and noise. The seasonal component represents periodic fluctuations that occur at regular intervals within the time series data. The residual component contains the remaining variation in the data that cannot be explained by the trend or seasonality, representing the random noise or irregularities present in the time series after removing the trend and seasonal effects. An expected outcome of the decomposition is the formation of this component as white noise or randomness.

A stationary time series is a series of data points collected sequentially over time where statistical properties such as the mean, variance, and covariance remain constant. In a stationary time series, the mean of the series remains constant over time, showing no upward or downward trend. The variance (or standard deviation) of the series remains constant over time, meaning that the spread of data points around the mean does not change.

Additionally, the autocovariance between observations at different time lags remains constant, indicating that the relationship between past and future values does not change over time.

Stationary time series tend to exhibit more predictable patterns, allowing models built on stationary data to often provide more accurate forecasts, as they assume that the underlying patterns will continue into the future.

The methodology employs classical decomposition for all the time series being analyzed and computes their correlation with the MCP using the three coefficients, aiming to capture both short-term and long-term dependencies.

Spearman's rank correlation coefficient is a non-parametric measure that evaluates the strength and direction of the association between two ranked variables. It measures how well the relationship between the two variables can be described using a monotonic function, with values ranging from -1 to 1. Spearman's coefficient is computed using equation [10.3]:

$$r = 1 - \frac{6 * \Sigma l_i^2}{m * (m^2 - 1)} \qquad [10.3]$$

where m represents the number of elements and l_i represents the difference between the ranks of the corresponding variables. The associated assumptions for Spearman's rank correlation coefficient are that the data can be ordinal, interval or ratio, but they are converted to ranks.

Additionally, the relationship between variables must be monotonic, meaning it consistently increases or decreases. Scaling ensures that the gradients are neither too large nor too small, promoting faster and more stable convergence during training. Additionally, when input features have different scales, they can lead to disproportionately large or small weights during training.

10.2.2. *Sparse autoencoder*

For the training of the model, the time series used includes the hourly electricity demand of the island, the conventional and renewable hourly production, and the subtraction of imported and exported hourly power between the island and the mainland's grid.

The encoder part of an autoencoder is responsible for compressing the input data into a lower dimensional representation. This compressed representation is often referred to as the "latent space". The encoder essentially learns to extract the most important features from the input data.

Then, applying a sparsity constraint to the hidden layers can be achieved through regularization techniques such as L1 regularization or KL divergence. The L1 regularization technique was applied in this survey, and afterwards, the model was trained using a reconstruction loss (e.g. the mean squared error between the input and the reconstructed output).

The model was regularized to enforce sparsity, ensuring that only a small fraction of the neurons is active for any given input.

Once trained, the encoder part of the autoencoder was used to map new data points to their latent representations. This latent space effectively captures the nonlinear relationships within the data.

The regression model input characteristics were derived from the latent representations. This could be a neural network or another nonlinear model, such as a basic linear regression model.

Utilizing these features, a regression model was trained to predict the dependent variable. Table 10.1 shows the hyperparameters used for the autoencoder model used in this survey.

Parameters	**Values**
Encoding dimension	3
Epochs	50
Batch size	512
Optimizer	adam
Activation function (encoder)	relu
Activation function (decoder)	sigmoid

Table 10.1. *Sparse autoencoder hyperparameters*

10.3. Results

Using equation [10.3] on the decomposed data, Spearman's coefficients were calculated and are presented in Figures 10.1–10.3.

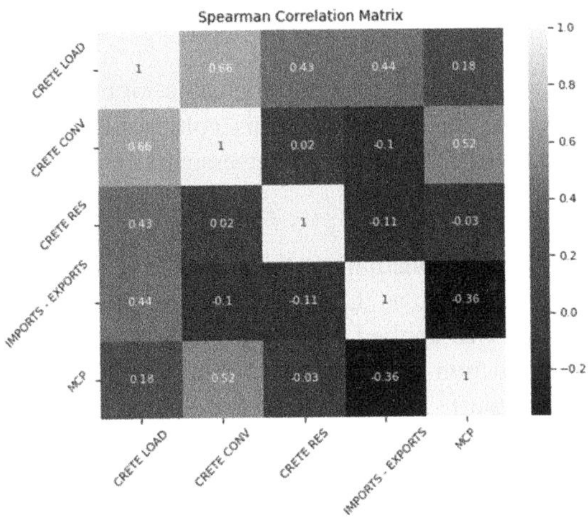

Figure 10.1. *Spearman's correlation matrix for the original data*

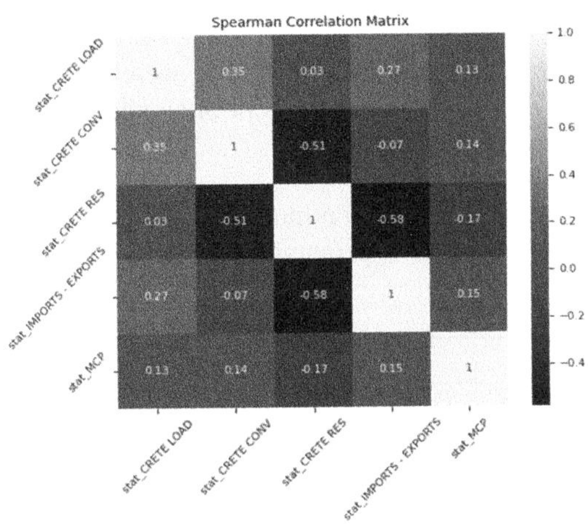

Figure 10.2. *Spearman's correlation matrix for the stationary data*

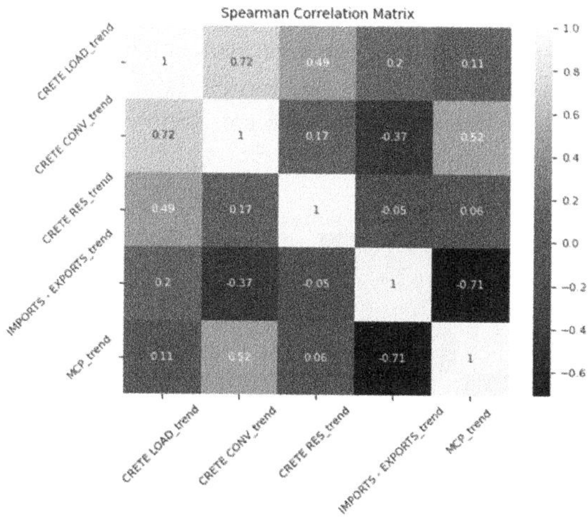

Figure 10.3. *Spearman's correlation matrix for the trend data*

The positive correlation of 0.52 between CRETE_CONV and MCP signifies a notable and consistent association between conventional energy production and increasing market clearing prices. The Spearman's correlation matrix for trend components reveals that the Crete load has a low positive correlation of 0.11 with the trend component of MCP, suggesting that increases in the energy load trend may have a slight, but not particularly strong, association with increases in the MCP trend. Conversely, the Crete Conventional trend exhibits a moderate positive correlation of 0.52 with the MCP trend series, indicating a stronger, more reliable relationship between the trend in conventional energy production and the MCP, which is consistent with the findings of the other two coefficients. The Crete RES trend series presents a very low positive correlation of 0.06 with the MCP trend series, implying a negligible monotonic relationship between the trend components of renewable energy production and market clearing prices. Finally, the strong negative correlation of −0.71 between the trend of imports and exports net position and the MCP trend suggests a robust inverse relationship, where an increase in the trend of imports and exports corresponds to a decrease in the MCP trend, or vice versa.

The stationary Crete load exhibits a low positive correlation of 0.13, reflecting a weak but positive short-term association with market clearing prices. Similarly, stat_CRETE_CONV displays a low positive correlation of 0.14 with stationary MCP, indicating a similarly weak association between short-term variations in conventional energy production and market clearing prices. In contrast, stationary Crete_RES shows a low negative correlation of −0.17 with stationary MCP, suggesting a slight inverse short-term relationship with market clearing prices.

Additionally, stationary import–export has a low positive correlation of 0.15 with stationary MCP, signifying a weak positive association in the short term. These correlations highlight the non-trending and more erratic fluctuations that can occur in the energy market. Figure 10.4 shows the correlation between the MCP and the features created by the autoencoder.

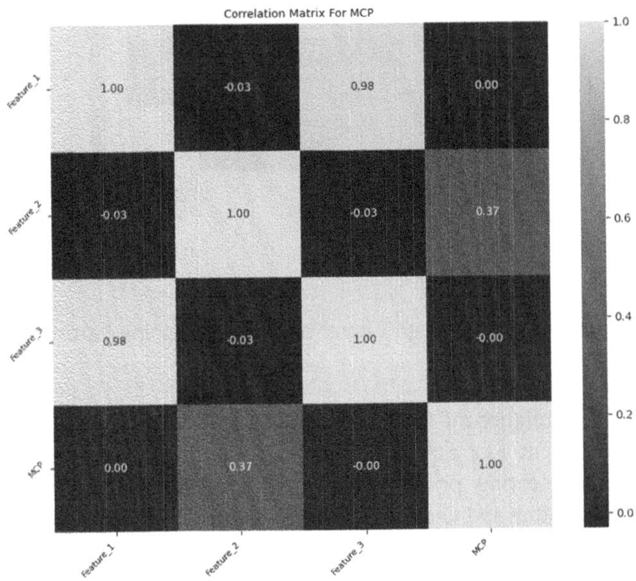

Figure 10.4. *Correlation matrix with a sparse autoencoder*

Remarkably, the sole non-negative absolute value observed is a modest 0.37 between MCP and feature 2, which is relatively negligible and virtually insignificant. This finding underscores the autoencoder's general inability to identify correlation, in stark contrast to Spearman's rank method, which proved more adept at discerning relationships within the components of the decomposed time series. The constrained data range further hinders overall effectiveness, since the specific participants' market shares could influence the outcomes. Furthermore, the features generated by the autoencoder remain abstract, lacking any clear interpretative value.

10.4. Discussion

Spearman's rank successfully identified strong long-term correlations, as evidenced by the moderate positive correlation of 0.52 between the Cretan conventional production trend series and the MCP trend data, suggesting a robust, reliable relationship between the trends in conventional energy production and market clearing prices. Similarly, the strong negative correlation of −0.71 between the trend part of the import–export difference and the MCP trend data indicates a significant inverse relationship, suggesting that as the trend of imports and exports increases, the trend of the MCP decreases, or vice versa. Additionally, it captured weak short-term correlations between Cretan participants and the MCP, offering insightful results that could inform market policy adjustments and enhance social welfare. Across all three decomposed components, Crete RES presented very weak correlation levels, indicating minimal market impact. This is attributed to the low absolute number of scheduled trades and the relatively small scale compared with the national renewable energy production, including large-scale hydropower plants. Conversely, the sparse autoencoder failed to detect underlying patterns in the data or interpret them meaningfully. This suggests that either a larger dataset, both in scale and time period, should be employed or the method should be reconsidered entirely.

10.5. Conclusions

In this chapter, the correlation between a subset of market participants on the Greek energy exchange, specifically producers and suppliers located on the island of Crete, was examined. The correlation between their traded volumes and the MCP was calculated using two methods: Spearman's rank and the sparse autoencoder. The contrast in the effectiveness of these methods is evident, as only Spearman's rank succeeded in capturing and identifying significant results.

The notable conclusions pertain to the substantial long-term correlations between conventional production and the MCP, as well as between the net position of imports and exports and the MCP. In all the cases, the electricity load and local renewable energy production showed no significant impact on the MCP. The sparse autoencoder failed to provide a complementary perspective or even validate the findings obtained via Spearman's coefficient, suggesting that larger data volumes and alternative training methods might be necessary.

10.6. Acknowledgments

This work received financial support from the project "Enhancing resilience of Cretan power system using distributed energy resources (CResDER)" (Proposal ID: 03698) financed by the Hellenic Foundation for Research and Innovation (H.F.R.I.) under the action "2nd Call for H.F.R.I. Research Projects to support Faculty Members and Researchers".

10.7. References

Bahadur, N. and Paffenroth, R. (2020). Dimension estimation using autoencoders with applications to financial market analysis. In *19th IEEE International Conference on Machine Learning and Applications (ICMLA)*, Miami, FL. doi: 10.1109/ICMLA51294.2020.00088.

Busu, M., ClodniȚchi, R., MureȘan, M.L. (2019). A correlation analysis of the spot market prices of the Romanian electricity sector. *Management & Marketing. Challenges for the Knowledge Society*, 14(1), 150–162. doi: 10.2478/mmcks-2019-0010.

Chen, H., Wang, S., Wang, S., Li, Y. (2019). Day-ahead aggregated load forecasting based on two-terminal sparse coding and deep neural network fusion. *Electric Power Systems Research*, 177, 105987. doi: 10.1016/j.epsr.2019.105987.

EnExGroup. (2024). Day-ahead market [Online]. Available at: https://www.enexgroup.gr/web/guest/markets-publications-el-day-ahead-market. [Accessed 24 April 2024].

Falkoni, A. and Krajacic, G. (2016). Linear correlation and regression between the meteorological data and the electricity demand of the Dubrovnik region in a short-term scale. *Thermal Science*, 20(4), 1073–1889. doi: 10.2298/TSCI151209157F.

Gugulothu, N. and Subramanian, E. (2019). Load forecasting in energy markets: An approach using sparse neural networks. In *Proceedings of the Tenth ACM International Conference on Future Energy Systems, e-Energy '19*. Association for Computing Machinery, New York. doi: 10.1145/3307772.3330167.

Hellenic Energy Exchange S.A. (2023). *HEnEx Spot Trading Rulebook: Day-Ahead & Intra-Day Markets Trading Rulebook v. 1.8*. Hellenic Energy Exchange S.A., Athens.

Li, T., Wang, Z., Zhao, W. (2022). Comparison and application potential analysis of autoencoder-based electricity pattern mining algorithms for large-scale demand response. *Technological Forecasting and Social Change*, 177, 121523. doi: 10.1016/j.techfore.2022.121523.

Massa, R. and Rosellón, J. (2020). Linear and nonlinear Granger causality between electricity production and economic performance in Mexico. *Energy Policy*, 142, 111476. doi: 10.1016/j.enpol.2020.111476.

Niu, H. (2021). Correlations between crude oil and stocks prices of renewable energy and technology companies: A multiscale time-dependent analysis. *Energy*, 221, 119800. doi: 10.1016/j.energy.2021.119800.

Savargaonkar, M., Oyewole, I., Chehade, A. (2021). Sparse autoencoded long short-term memory network for state-of-charge estimations. In *IEEE Transportation Electrification Conference & Expo (ITEC)*, Chicago, IL. doi: 10.1109/ITEC51675.2021.9490070.

Savargaonkar, M., Oyewole, I., Chehade, A., Hussein, A.A. (2024). Uncorrelated sparse autoencoder with long short-term memory for state-of-charge estimations in lithium-ion battery cells. *IEEE Transactions on Automation Science and Engineering*, 21(1), 15–26. doi: 10.1109/TASE.2022.3222759.

Xiu, X., Miao, Z., Yang, Y., Liu, W. (2022) Deep canonical correlation analysis using sparsity-constrained optimization for nonlinear process monitoring. *IEEE Transactions on Industrial Informatics*, 18(10), 6690–6699. doi: 10.1109/TII.2021.3121770.

11

Enhancing Energy Market Stability: Comparative Analysis of Forecasting Techniques for Market Clearing Prices in the Day-Ahead Market

Forecasting the energy market's clearing price (MCP) contributes to price stabilization, crisis mitigation and facilitating the smooth and reliable operation of the system. In this context, this survey endeavors to develop a robust forecasting technique tailored for the day-ahead market (DAM), utilizing a publicly accessible data subset. The subset concerns the trades originating or delivered to the island of Crete, evaluating the forecast methods under limited data availability. This study examines and compares the performance of sophisticated algorithms such as the LightGBM, multihead CNN and LSTM. The results prove the suitability of the advanced methods for day-ahead MCP forecasting, especially the multihead CNN, which has the highest performance, paving the way for more effective and efficient market operations, thereby fostering greater resilience and stability in the energy sector.

11.1. Introduction

Forecasting the MCP holds significant value for governmental agencies by mitigating price fluctuations, enhancing responsiveness to rapid market shifts and ensuring safe and efficient system operations. Similarly, businesses derive benefits from forecasting techniques, leveraging them to refine bidding strategies, anticipate

---

Chapter written by Emmanuel KARAPIDAKIS, Yiannis KATSIGIANNIS, Konstantinos BLAZAKIS, Marios NIKOLOGIANNIS, George MATALLIOTAKIS, Georgios STAVRAKAKIS, Nikos VENIANAKIS and Nikolaos SCHETAKIS.

For a color version of all figures in this chapter, see www.iste.co.uk/dimotikalis/data5.zip.

financial outcomes and strengthen the viability of their operational plans. Moreover, precise forecasting methods validate the influence of energy producers and suppliers, providing a clear understanding of how factors such as renewable energy sources (RESs), fuel costs and daily demand from both short-term and long-term market behaviors.

Machine learning methods have gained popularity, particularly in the economics and finance sectors, owing to their ability to manage large data volumes and their extensive capabilities. In energy economics, they are primarily used for forecasting purposes, such as forecasting electricity load profiles (Behm et al. 2020), consumption and production of market participants (Mhlanga 2023), bidding strategies (Santos et al. 2023) and closing prices. In this study, the performance of sophisticated algorithms such as the LightGBM, multihead CNN and LSTM were examined.

The LightGBM is a tree-based gradient-boosting algorithm widely used for machine learning tasks in the energy market (Park and Hwang 2021; Park et al. 2021; Wang et al. 2021; Yao et al. 2022). The LightGBM is designed to handle large datasets efficiently, offering excellent performance in both speed and accuracy. It uses histogram-based learning, which groups data into bins or histograms during training, reducing memory usage and computational requirements. This optimization makes LightGBM ideal for large-scale, real-time or distributed machine-learning tasks.

Moreover, LightGMB employs gradient-based one-side sampling (GOSS) to focus on instances with larger gradients during training, speeding up the process while maintaining model performance. The LightGBM can bundle exclusive features together, reducing the number of unique values in a dataset, which saves memory and enhances efficiency, particularly for categorical features. The number of tree estimators, the maximum number of leaves on a tree and the learning rate were determined for the purpose of tuning hyperparameters.

Convolutional neural networks (CNNs) are commonly used for tasks such as natural language processing, image and video recognition, recommender systems, text and image classification, and handling financial time series data. In the energy sector, they have been frequently deployed for forecasting energy loads and market prices (Shao et al. 2020; Guo et al. 2020; Aslam et al. 2021; Rick and Berton 2022; Wang et al. 2023).

The fundamental layers of a standard CNN include convolutional layers, pooling layers, dropout layers, flattening layers and fully connected layers. The convolutional layer convolves the input data to create feature maps by sliding small filters (kernels) over the data, where each kernel has learnable weights. Elementwise multiplication is performed at each position, producing a new layer for each kernel.

The depth of the convolutional layer, which is determined by the number of kernels, is a crucial hyperparameter that is chosen on the basis of the available data.

After the convolutional layer, pooling layers perform downsampling operations on the feature maps, integrating sets of elements into a single value (e.g. maximum or average value). This pooling operation helps eliminate noise and improves performance. CNNs excel at successively extracting higher level features by applying different kernels of various sizes and depths, repeating these layers multiple times.

Dropout layers can be added after convolutional and pooling layers to prevent overfitting by randomly omitting certain components during training. The final pooled layer is flattened into a single vector, which is then connected to a fully connected layer and subsequently to the output layer. The output layer aggregates the probabilities for each class, providing a classification estimate for the given input.

An extension of the CNN model involves creating distinct sub-CNN models, or individual heads, for each input variable, known as a multihead CNN (MHCNN) model. This variant requires adjustments in model preparation and dataset training and testing. Each input is processed by an independent CNN, enhancing feature extraction by focusing on one input at a time. Each convolutional head can be tailored to the specific properties of its corresponding input. The model's configuration, including the number of layers and associated hyperparameters, is modified to align with this methodology.

Long short-term memory networks (LSTMs) incorporate feedback connections, significantly enhancing memory retention capabilities. LSTMs are flexible, handling both individual data points, such as images, and entire data sequences. Applications of LSTMs include speech recognition, handwriting recognition, anomaly detection in network traffic and intrusion detection systems (IDSs). In the energy landscape, LSTMs are used for forecasting electricity load, energy consumption and energy-related commodity prices (Gundu and Simon 2021; Memarzadeh and Keynia 2021; Manowska and Bluszcz 2022; Meng et al. 2022; Jailani et al. 2023; Brik and Ouakdi 2024).

A typical LSTM unit consists of a cell, an output gate, a forget gate (which determines which information to discard) and an input gate (which analyzes pertinent data for memory updates). These gates control the flow of information into and out of the cell, allowing the cell to maintain values for arbitrarily long periods.

LSTM networks are well suited for tasks involving forecasting, classification and processing on the basis of time series data, especially when dealing with problems where unknown duration lags exist between crucial events. They address the vanishing gradient issue that can occur during the training of traditional recurrent neural networks (RNNs). Their ability to manage long-term dependencies gives them an advantage over RNNs, hidden Markov models and other sequence-learning techniques.

11.2. Methodology

Before running the proposed algorithms, data preprocessing is needed. Scaling data are essential for enhancing the efficiency of applied methods. This ensures that the gradients are neither too large nor too small, promoting faster and more stable convergence during training.

Additionally, when input features have different scales, it can lead to disproportionately large or small weights during training. Normalization helps maintain uniform weight updates, preventing skewed weight distributions. Equation [11.1] was used as a scaler:

$$x' = \frac{x-\mu_x}{\sigma_x} \qquad [11.1]$$

In equation [11.1], x represents the original data, x' represents the normalized data, μ_x signifies the sample mean and σ_x denotes the sample's standard deviation.

To forecast MCP future values, a Cretan time series dataset with various features from November 2021 until December 2023 was used.

The input data include the consumption and production of electrical energy on the island of Crete, which is categorized separately from other participants in the energy exchange. Local production types encompass conventional methods, such as fuel-based generation and RES. Previous day, MCP values in the same hour, time and data on the net position of imports and exports to and from the island of Crete were also considered. All of the data were recorded at hourly intervals.

In Figure 11.1, the whole MCP time series and a zoom version of the whole time series are depicted.

Compared with those in 2023, the last two months of 2021 and the whole of 2022 were noted with increased prices and high fluctuations, whereas seasonality on a weekly basis can be identified by zooming in on the data.

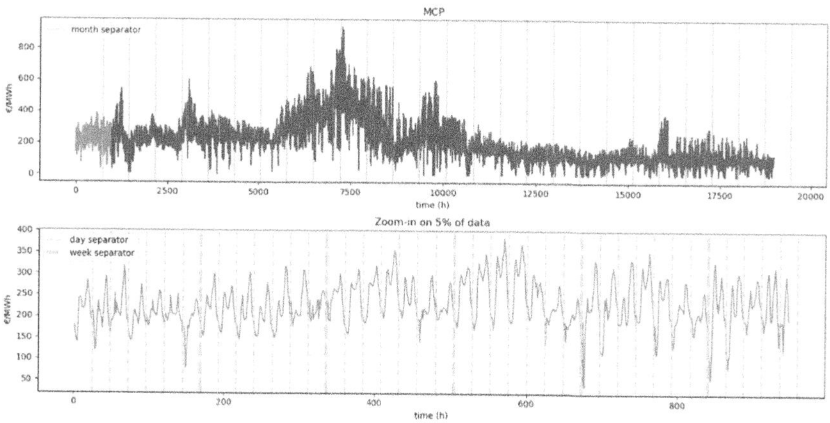

Figure 11.1. *MCP time series*

In this study, a conservative protocol called rolling origin cross-validation (ROCV) was employed. In this approach, a 5-ROCV was applied, and for each fold, a contiguous portion of the entire dataset was used, while the remaining portion was disregarded. The method is named because the origin of each subdataset shifts to later timesteps with each fold. Within each fold, the subdataset is split into training, validation and test sets.

In Figure 11.2, the blue, orange and red segments represent the training, validation and test set, respectively, for the second fold of the 5-ROCV applied in this work. The gray segment indicates the portion of data disregarded for that fold. The illustrated data pertain to the whole MCP series.

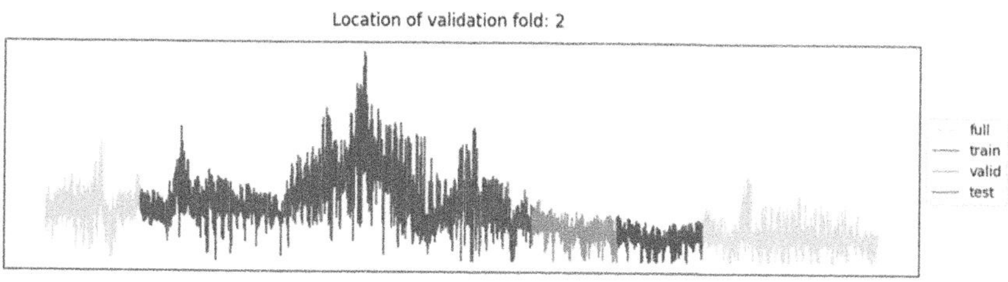

Figure 11.2. *MCP sets for the second fold of 5-ROCV*

The forecasted values are the MCPs for the next 24 hours (i.e. one day ahead).

Windowing the dataset resulted, for each folding, in the data shape summarized in Table 11.1.

Set	x shape	y shape
Train	(8,922, 24, 6)	(8,922, 24)
Validation	(1,874, 24, 6)	(1,874, 24)
Test	(1,876, 24, 6)	(1,876, 24)

Table 11.1. *Windowed dataset shapes*

At this stage, the proposed algorithms are deployed. The forecasts from separate windows are combined into one series to provide a thorough overview of all of the predictions made for the entire dataset. To accomplish this combination, the mean value of the forecasts, standard deviations, min/max predictions and accounting for overlapping prediction windows are recorded at each timestep.

11.3. Results

Figure 11.3 shows the forecast of the LightGBM. The solid green curve shows the mean value of the prediction at each timestep. The dark-shaded area indicates the standard deviation (1-σ), whereas the light-shaded area represents the range of minimum to maximum predictions (min/max). Generally, the prediction window closest to a given target timestep t provides the most accurate prediction, with minimal deviation from the true value within the shaded area. Conversely, the window furthest in time exhibits the greatest deviation from the true value.

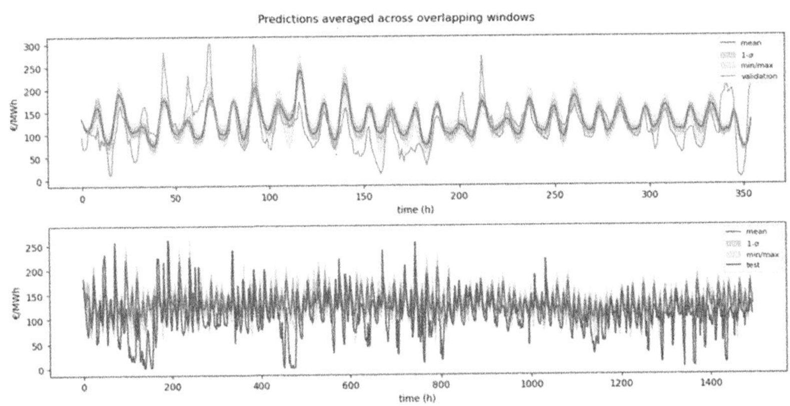

Figure 11.3. *Averaged predictions for LightGBM*

The model's mean predictions align closely with the validation series, indicating that the model effectively captures the underlying patterns in the validation data. The minimal deviations between the predicted mean and the validation series suggest a good fit. However, there are instances, particularly at the peaks, where the predictions do not perfectly match the actual data.

In contrast, the mean predicted values and the actual test series diverge from the validation image. The increased width of the dark-shaded area signifies high uncertainty in the model's predictions. Additionally, the broader range of the light-shaded area, representing the min/max predictions, indicates greater variability in the model's output.

The wider dark-shaded area in the test series predictions further indicates the model's reduced certainty about its predictions during this period.

Similarly, Figure 11.4 illustrates the results of the MHCNN forecast.

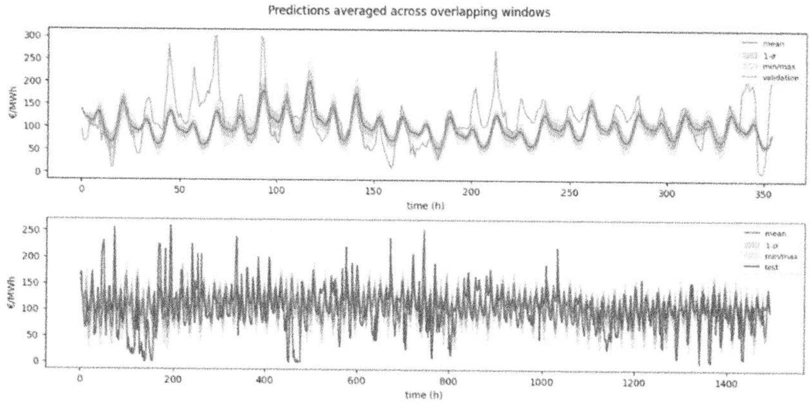

Figure 11.4. *Averaged predictions for the MHCNN*

For the validation series, the mean prediction closely follows the actual data, although it does not perfectly match the peak values. The standard deviation is relatively small, as indicated by the narrower dark green shaded areas, reflecting confidence in the model's predictions during the validation phase.

In contrast, for the test series, the mean prediction struggles to consistently capture the actual pattern, as evidenced by more frequent deviations. Additionally, the increased width of both the standard deviation and min/max prediction bands indicates relatively high uncertainty and variability in the model's forecasts on the test data.

Figure 11.5 presents the LSTM results against the validation and test data.

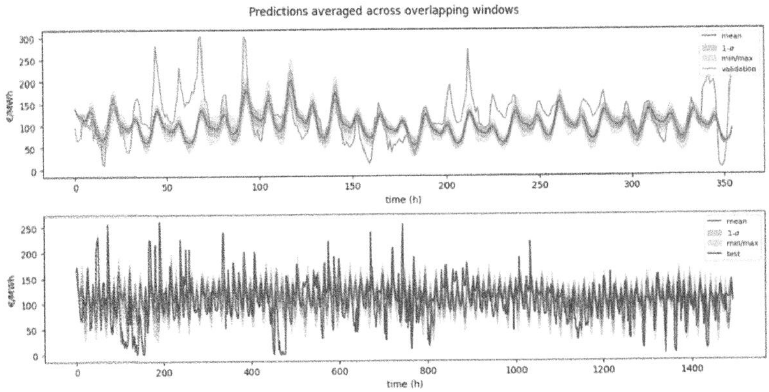

Figure 11.5. *Averaged predictions for LSTM*

Like the MHCNN, the mean forecast in the validation series graph closely follows the actual data, with the standard deviation indicating a reasonable level of confidence in the predictions. However, deviations occur, especially at the peaks, where the forecast does not capture the exact magnitude of the actual data.

In the test series graph, the model's predictions exhibit high variability and less accuracy, a common trait among all forecast models. The wider standard deviation and min/max prediction regions reflect greater uncertainty in the model's ability to accurately forecast the test data.

Table 11.2 summarizes all of the forecasting methods' mean absolute error (MAE) and root mean square error (RMSE) values.

	MAE	RMSE
LightGBM	33.63	43.77
MHCNN	30.50	39.90
LSTM	31.37	40.81

Table 11.2. *Forecasting performance*

Notably, almost every model shows comparable forecasting performance for the energy MCP with the MHCNN accomplishing the best forecasting performance.

More analytically, the MHCNN has an MAE improvement of 2.77% and 9.30% compared with the LSTM and LightGBM, respectively, whereas it has an RMSE improvement of 2.22% and 8.84% compared with the LSTM and LightGBM, respectively.

11.4. Discussion

All three models exhibit comparable forecasting results, with the MHCNN prevailing as the best forecasting performance.

The increase in the standard deviation and the range of the min/max predictions in the test series for all of the models indicates relatively high uncertainty and variability, suggesting that more investigation is needed to improve the models' generalization capabilities.

The MHCNN achieved the lowest MAE (30.50) and RMSE (39.90). This suggests that the MHCNN has the best forecasting capability and is likely the most reliable model for future forecasts among the three models evaluated. The model's effectiveness was satisfactory given the limited scale of data and could be applied to similar cases of incomplete knowledge. Increased data availability could significantly enhance the accuracy of the results.

11.5. Conclusions

In this study, EnEx data from Crete were used to forecast the MCP for the next day. The dataset includes the hourly electrical energy inputs required and produced by various sources from November 2021 until December 2023. The forecasting models employed were the LightGBM, MHCNN and LSTM, and the models' performance was evaluated using the MAE and RMSE metrics. Overall, the MHCNN outperformed the other models, achieving the lowest MAE and RMSE values. Developments in the medium-term energy MCP will be crucial to the price stabilization, crisis mitigation and facilitating the smooth and reliable operation of the system.

11.6. Acknowledgments

This work received financial support from the project "Enhancing resilience of Cretan power system using distributed energy resources (CResDER)" (Proposal ID: 03698), financed by the Hellenic Foundation for Research and Innovation (H.F.R.I.) under the action "2nd Call for H.F.R.I. Research Projects to support Faculty Members and Researchers".

11.7. References

Aslam, S., Ayub, N., Farooq, U., Alvi, M.J., Albogamy, F.R., Rukh, G., Haider, S.I., Azar, A.T., Bukhsh, R. (2021) Towards electric price and load forecasting using CNN-based ensembler in smart grid. *Sustainability*, 13(22), 12653. doi: 10.3390/su132212653.

Behm, C., Nolting, L., Praktiknjo, A. (2020). How to model European electricity load profiles using artificial neural networks. *Applied Energy*, 277, 115564. doi: 10.1016/j.apenergy.2020.115564.

Brik, H. and Ouakdi, J.E. (2024) Interplay of volatility and geopolitical tensions in clean energy markets: A comprehensive GARCH-LSTM forecasting approach. *International Journal of Energy Economics and Policy*, 14(4), 92–107. doi: 10.32479/ijeep.16075.

EnExGroup (2024). Day-ahead market [Online]. Available at: https://www.enexgroup.gr/web/guest/markets-publications-el-day-ahead-market.

Gundu, V. and Simon, S.P. (2021). PSO–LSTM for short term forecast of heterogeneous time series electricity price signals. *Journal of Ambient Intelligence and Humanized Computing*, 12(2), 2375–2385. doi: 10.1007/s12652-020-02353-9.

Guo, X., Zhao, Q., Zheng, D., Ning, Y., Gao, Y. (2020). A short-term load forecasting model of multi-scale CNN-LSTM hybrid neural network considering the real-time electricity price. *Energy Reports*, 6(9), 1046–1053. doi: 10.1016/j.egyr.2020.11.078.

Jailani, N.L.M., Dhanasegaran, J.K., Alkawsi, G., Alkahtani, A.A., Phing, C.C., Baashar, Y., Capretz, L.F., Al-Shetwi, A.Q., Tiong, S.K. (2023). Investigating the power of LSTM-based models in solar energy forecasting. *Processes*, 11(5), 1382. doi: 10.3390/pr11051382.

Manowska, A. and Bluszcz, A. (2022). Forecasting crude oil consumption in Poland based on LSTM recurrent neural network. *Energies*, 15(13), 4885. doi: 10.3390/en15134885.

Memarzadeh, G. and Keynia, F. (2021). Short-term electricity load and price forecasting by a new optimal LSTM-NN based prediction algorithm. *Electric Power Systems Research*, 192, 106995. doi: 10.1016/j.epsr.2020.106995.

Meng, A., Wang, P., Zhai, G., Zeng, C., Chen, S., Yang, X., Yin, H. (2022). Electricity price forecasting with high penetration of renewable energy using attention-based LSTM network trained by crisscross optimization. *Energy*, 254(Part A), 124212. doi: 10.1016/j.energy.2022.124212.

Mhlanga, D. (2023). Artificial intelligence and machine learning for energy consumption and production in emerging markets: A review. *Energies*, 16(2), 745. doi: 10.3390/en16020745.

Park, J. and Hwang, E. (2021). A two-step multistep-ahead electricity load forecasting scheme based on LightGBM and attention-BiLSTM. *Sensors*, 21(22), 7697. doi: 10.3390/s21227697.

Park, S., Jung, S., Jung, S., Rho, S., Hwang, E. (2021). Sliding window-based LightGBM model for electric load forecasting using anomaly repair. *Journal of Supercomputing*, 77(11), 12857–12878. doi: 10.1007/s11227-021-03787-4.

Rick, R. and Berton, L. (2022). Energy forecasting model based on CNN-LSTM-AE for many time series with unequal lengths. *Engineering Applications of Artificial Intelligence*, 113(C), 104998. doi: 10.1016/j.engappai.2022.104998.

Santos, P., Rezende, I., Soares, T., Miranda, V. (2023). Evaluation of different bidding strategies for a battery energy storage system performing energy arbitrage – A neural network approach. In *19th International Conference on the European Energy Market (EEM)*, Lappeenranta. doi: 10.1109/EEM58374.2023.10161915.

Shao, X., Kim, C.S., Sontakke, P. (2020). Accurate deep model for electricity consumption forecasting using multi-channel and multi-scale feature fusion CNN–LSTM. *Energies*, 13(8), 1881. doi: 10.3390/en13081881.

Wang, Y., Chen, J., Chen, X., Zeng, X., Kong, Y., Sun, S., Guo, Y., Liu, Y. (2021). Short-term load forecasting for industrial customers based on TCN-LightGBM. *IEEE Transactions on Power Systems*, 36(3), 1984–1997. doi: 10.1109/TPWRS.2020.3028133.

Wang, D., Gan, J., Mao, J., Chen, F., Yu, L. (2023). Forecasting power demand in China with a CNN-LSTM model including multimodal information. *Energy*, 263(Part E), 126012. doi: 10.1016/j.energy.2022.126012.

Yao, X., Fu, X., Zong, C. (2022). Short-term load forecasting method based on feature preference strategy and LightGBM-XGboost. *IEEE Access*, 10, 75257–75268. doi: 10.1109/ACCESS.2022.3192011.

12

Using the Coxian Continuous-Time Hidden Markov Model to Analyze Lombardy Region Wards for Older Individuals

Healthcare managers are under increased pressure to maintain high-quality care within already strained healthcare systems across Europe. This adversity has arisen from increasing aging populations, where the care of older people is of vital concern. This research investigates the healthcare system for older people in Italy's Lombardy region to model, understand the flow of patients through the system and uncover any potential issues about their care. The Coxian phase-type distribution and Coxian continuous-time hidden Markov model will be applied to uncover different patient pathways through Lombardy region hospitals.

The findings show that the Coxian continuous-time hidden Markov model uncovers more information when it is applied to Lombardy region data. The model highlights different patient pathways or management systems across hospitals.

The Coxian phase-type distribution is able to uncover patient pathways through the healthcare system, providing healthcare providers with insight into the flow of patients through the hospital system. However, patients may flow through hospital systems via different pathways; some may be in the hospital for a short period of time and leave the hospital after a day or two, whereas others may stay in the hospital much longer. The Coxian continuous-time hidden Markov model can uncover these different pathways. This provides a greater understanding of the system, enabling more efficient resource allocation and highlighting potential areas of further investigation, such as patients having to wait over four weeks before they are discharged or have ward/hospital transfers. The longer lengths of stay could be due to the complex nature of patient care, or it may lead to poor use of resources and inefficiency within the healthcare system and harm to the patient.

Chapter written by Hannah MITCHELL, Adele H. MARSHALL and Mariangela ZENGA.

The analysis has value as a management tool to highlight potential issues that require further investigation to run a more efficient healthcare system. It also has value in decision-making and resource allocation.

12.1. Introduction

Healthcare systems across Europe have come under increased pressure and scrutiny in recent years, with governments requesting that hospitals deliver the highest standard of care to their citizens while managing and achieving tight performance measures and budgets. The mantra of the national healthcare system across Europe is that it is available to everyone as a right regardless of whom the individual is (Active Citizenship Network 2002). Such systems are under pressure, as, across the globe, healthcare providers are experiencing an increasing older population, with life expectancy increasing consistently since the 1950s by approximately 2.5 years per decade and is expected to continue to do so (Siddall and Kjaeserud 2007).

Within Europe, the fastest growing age group of residents is 80 years old and older. It is predicted that by 2030, almost 12% of all Europeans will be over 75 years old, with 7% over 80 years old (in 2019, the proportion of 80-year-olds was 5.8% (Eurostat 2019)). It is also predicted that one-third of Europe's population will be over 60 years of age, whereas 13% will be under 16 years of age. This will be particularly evident within Italy, which has the third largest proportion of elderly people in the world, behind Japan and Monaco (Statista Research Department 2021). This leads to several questions that need to be considered, for example, how do hospitals cope with a growing number of older patients? Most healthcare systems across Europe are funded through tax revenue and insurance premiums, both of which are received from the workforce. With the population getting older, the workforce will continue to diminish. Therefore, the tax revenue and insurance premiums decline at a time when the budgets required by the healthcare system need to increase to provide high-quality care. The care of older people is therefore a major concern that needs to be addressed.

The Italian healthcare system "Sevizio Sanitario Nazionale" was established in 1978, providing universal healthcare coverage throughout the Italian state to all citizens regardless of the individual's social status (France et al. 2005). In the early 1990s, major reforms took place that transferred power from the central state government to each of the regions within Italy. Each region was given a certain amount of control over how the health services in their region run in terms of administration and organizational responsibilities. Healthcare systems are financed by national and regional taxes where the state has the overall power to set what it deems an essential level of care. This transfer of power was performed to ensure that the regions have more sensitivity in controlling expenditures and promoting efficiency, quality and patient satisfaction. This has led to each region's healthcare differing in terms of infrastructure and expenditure.

Modeling patient flow in a healthcare system has been seen as an important aspect in understanding the system, with the length of stay of patients used to help measure the usage of hospital resources and help managers run a more efficient and effective hospital. The Coxian phase-type distribution (Neuts 1981) and the Coxian continuous-time hidden Markov model will be applied to data from Lombardy wards for older people. This will provide a more detailed understanding of the healthcare system for older people and enable healthcare providers to identify any potential issues with respect to the running of the system.

This research will investigate the healthcare system for older people in Italy's Lombardy region to model, understand the flow of patients through the system and uncover potential issues related to care.

This paper is organized as follows: first, the Coxian phase-type distribution, the continuous-time hidden Markov models and the Coxian continuous-time hidden Markov models are introduced; then, the data and results are presented. Finally, conclusions and practical implications conclude this chapter.

12.2. Methodology

The model presented in this chapter aims to capture more information about the flow of subjects through a system by incorporating a dynamic latent factor within it. The models utilized to achieve this are the Coxian phase-type distribution (CPT) and continuous-time hidden Markov (CTHMM) models.

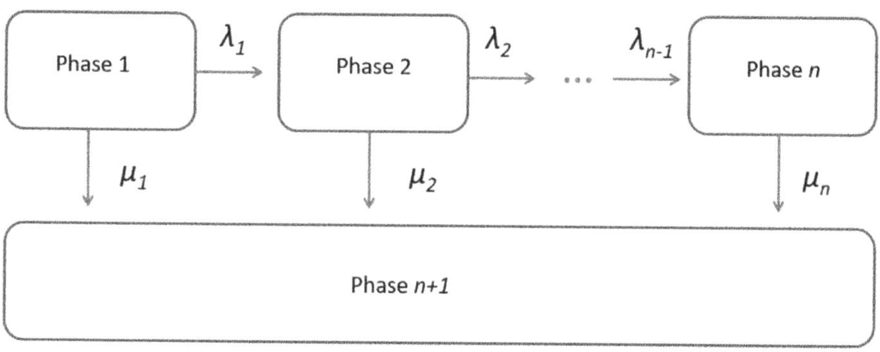

Figure 12.1. *Coxian phase-type distribution*

CPT is a popular modeling technique for representing survival distributions and, as such, is used regularly in the field of healthcare modeling but is not limited to this area (Faddy 1994; Faddy and McClean 1999; McClean et al. 2008; Shaw and Marshall 2007; Marshall et al. 2002). Figure 12.1 provides an illustration of an n-phase Coxian phase-type distribution.

Let $(X(T); t > 0)$ be a latent Markov chain in continuous time T with states $1, 2, \dots, n, n+1$ and $X(0) = 1$ for $i = 1, 2, \dots, n-1$.

$$\text{prob}\{X(t + \delta t) = i + 1|X(t) = i\} = \lambda_i \delta t + o(\delta t)$$

and for $i = 1,2, \dots,n$

$$\text{prob}\{X(t + \delta t) = n + 1|X(t) = i\} = \mu_i \delta t + o(\delta t)b$$

where states $1, 2, \dots, n$ are latent (transient) states of the process, state $n + 1$ is the absorbing state, λ_i represents the transition from state i to state $(i + 1)$ and μ_i represents the transition from state i to the absorbing state $(n + 1)$. The probability density function of T can be written as follows:

$f(t) = \mathbf{p}\exp\{\mathbf{Q}t\}\mathbf{q}$ where $\mathbf{Q}$ is the matrix of transition rates between states:

$$\mathbf{Q} = \begin{pmatrix} -(\lambda_1 + \mu_1) & \lambda_1 & 0 & \dots & 0 & 0 \\ 0 & -(\lambda_2 + \mu_2) & \lambda_2 & \dots & 0 & 0 \\ . & . & . & & . & . \\ . & . & . & & . & . \\ . & . & . & & . & . \\ 0 & 0 & 0 & \dots & -(\lambda_{n-1} + \mu_{n-1}) & \lambda_{n-1} \\ 0 & 0 & 0 & \dots & 0 & -\mu_n \end{pmatrix},$$

and $q = -Qe = (\mu_1, \mu_2, \dots, \mu_n)^T$ and $\mathbf{p} = (1, 0, \dots, 0)$.

The CTHMM is a probabilistic model consisting of a hidden process and an observed stochastic process. This model can be used to infer the hidden state from what is observed. It was initially developed for use in speech recognition (Rabiner 1989), but its applications have spread to a range of different fields (Bureau et al. 2003; Cooper and Lipsitch 2004; Hassan and Nath 2005; Bhar and Hamori 2006; Beyreuther et al. 2008; Wall and Li 2009; Gupta and Dhingra 2012). These applications use the hidden Markov model to infer a component of a system that has an effect but cannot be measured. Formally, the CTHMM is defined by three parameters, $\lambda = (\boldsymbol{P},\boldsymbol{B},\boldsymbol{\pi})$, where $\boldsymbol{P}$ is the probability matrix (size $k \times k$, where k is the number of hidden states), which stores the probability of transitioning to state s_j following hidden state s_i (Rabiner 1989). This probability matrix is defined by a transition rate matrix $\boldsymbol{A}$ and the time difference t between observations as $\mathrm{P(t)} = \exp(\mathrm{A}t)$. $\mathrm{P}(t)$ is a matrix representing the probabilities of movement between each of the states. The initial distribution is given by $\pi = \{\pi_i\}$, where $\pi_i = P(q_1 = s_i)$ for $1 \le i \le k$. This is the probability that the first hidden state q_1 is hidden state s_i. The observation matrix, $\boldsymbol{B}$, stores the probability of the $\widehat{\mathrm{R}}$th observation being produced from the hidden state s_i, independent of point t, given by $\mathrm{B} = \{\mathrm{b_i}(\widehat{\mathrm{R}})\}$, where $\mathrm{b_i}(\widehat{\mathrm{R}}) = P(x_t = v_{\widehat{R}} | q_t = s_i)$ is the probability of the observation x_t at time t being equal to $v_{\widehat{R}}$ given the hidden state $q_t = s_i$, where $v_{\widehat{R}}$ is the $\widehat{\mathrm{R}}$th observation that is produced. Figure 12.2 illustrates the CTHMM, where the hidden states are represented by s and the observations by O. At each instantaneous time an observation occurs, the hidden state may change, governed by the transition matrix $\boldsymbol{P}$. The observation at time t is generated by some process whose state s_t is hidden from the observer.

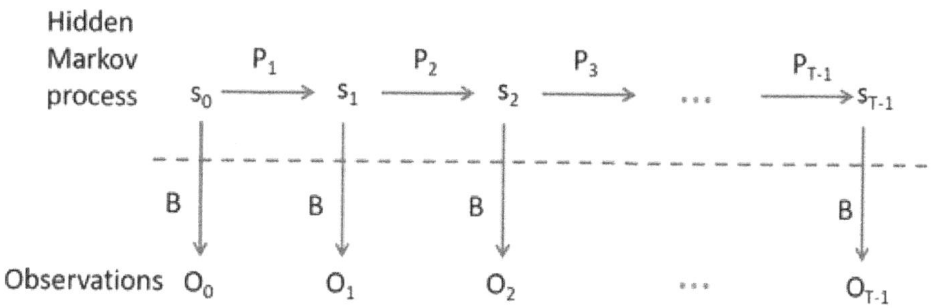

Figure 12.2. *The hidden Markov model*

Combining the Coxian phase-type distribution with the CTHMM to incorporate the dynamic nature of the underlying latent factor of the system highlights the hidden factors that affect the system (Mitchell et al. 2021). Such effects and their influence on flow cannot be measured directly. This will increase the accuracy of modeling the system and provide healthcare providers with more knowledge and understanding of how the system is running. Let $\mathbf{O} = (o_1, \ldots, o_T)$ and $\mathbf{q} = (q_1, \ldots, q_T)$ be the observed data and the hidden underlying state sequence, respectively, for each of the different time points up to time T. The likelihood function for the incomplete data is defined by $P(\boldsymbol{O}|\lambda)$, while the likelihood function for the complete data is given by $P(\boldsymbol{O},\boldsymbol{q}|\lambda)$. The incomplete data are seen as the hidden aspect. The expected log-likelihood $Q(\lambda,\lambda')$ is therefore defined as:

$$Q(\lambda, \lambda') = \sum_{q \in Q} \log \pi_{q_0} P(\boldsymbol{O}, \boldsymbol{q}|\lambda') + \sum_{q \in Q} \left(\sum_{t=2}^{T} \log \mathbf{P}_{q_{t-1}, q_t} \right) P(\boldsymbol{O}, \boldsymbol{q}|\lambda') + \sum_{q \in Q} \left(\sum_{t=1}^{T} \log \mathrm{b}_{q_t}(o_t) \right) P(\boldsymbol{O}, \boldsymbol{q}|\lambda')$$

where λ' are the previous estimates of the parameters, π_{q_0} is the probability of being in the initial state, P_{q_{t-1}, q_t} is the hidden probability matrix, which contains the probability of moving between each of the hidden states, and b_{q_t} is the probability of the observations belonging to each of the hidden states as given by the probability density function used to model the observations. The parameters within the expected log-likelihood are in three independent parts and can thus be optimized individually. Finally, the Coxian hidden Markov model is optimized via the Baum–Welch algorithm and the expectation–maximization (EM) algorithm (Baum and Petrie 1966; Baum et al. 1970; Dempster et al. 1977).

Coxian-CTHMM is illustrated in Figure 12.3, where each of the hidden states is linked to a Coxian phase-type distribution. This example shows two hidden states with n_1 and n_2 phase Coxian phase-type distributions. The model is however generalizable. Combining the CTHMM with the Coxian phase-type distribution allows the two models to interact with each other and will allow for a more in-depth analysis of the flow of subjects through a system, as it will show how latent variables that cannot be observed can affect the system.

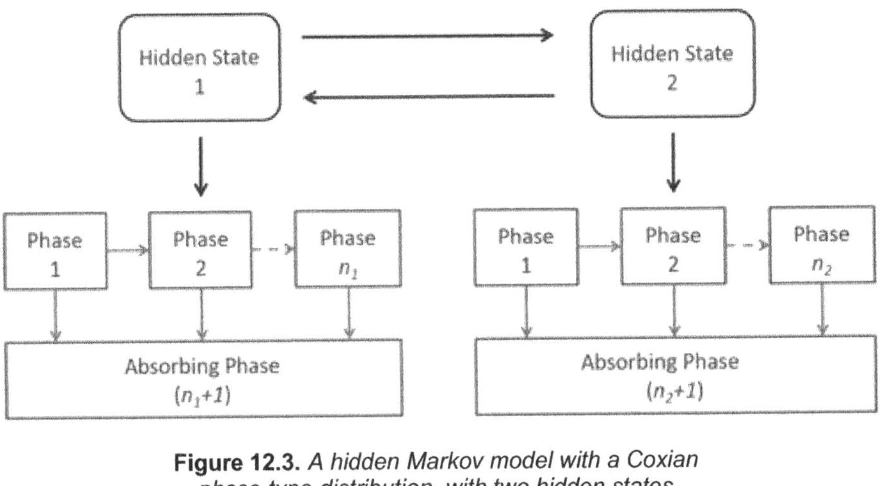

Figure 12.3. *A hidden Markov model with a Coxian phase-type distribution, with two hidden states*

12.3. Data and results

12.3.1. *Data*

With the reforms of the Italian healthcare system in the 1990s, the Lombardy regional government used this power to set up a quasimarket within its healthcare sector. The aim is to improve the quality of services and control healthcare expenditures. This allowed the introduction of competition within the healthcare system, as individuals can request which hospital they wish to receive treatment from rather than receiving treatment from certain hospitals due to catchment areas (Nuti et al. 2012). The healthcare system in the Lombardy region comprises approximately 17% of all Italian hospitals, 12 of which have specialist wards for older people. These wards are analyzed in this chapter.

The data used in this investigation consisted of length of stay information for 8,769 patients aged 65 years or older who received treatment in a Lombardy ward for older people in 2015. There were no day-of-hospital cases, with all patients classified as having ordinary admissions and slightly more female patients (58%), with an overall average age of 83.9 years. The patients were found to have a mean and median length of stay of 11.2 days and 9 days, respectively, with 96.1% of patients discharged within 30 days. The Coxian phase-type distribution and Coxian-continuous-time hidden Markov model (Coxian-CTHMM) will be applied to these data to uncover more information about the healthcare system for older patients in Lombardy, Italy. The Coxian-CTHMM model presented in this chapter aims to capture more information about the flow of patients through Lombardy hospital wards for older people by incorporating a dynamic latent factor within it. Incorporating a dynamic latent factor into the model will enable non-directly observable variables that affect patient flow, such as quality of care, to be considered. The Viterbi algorithm (Baum et al. 1966, 1970) can then be used to separate the data into two groups according to the hidden states, from which the characteristics within each of the hidden states can be seen and analyzed.

12.3.2. *Results*

To obtain the optimal fit of the Coxian phase-type distribution to each of the 12 hospital wards, the Akaike information criterion (AIC) (Schwarz 1978) was used. The distribution was initially fitted using the one-phase Coxian phase-type distribution and built by sequentially adding additional phases (one at a time) to the distribution until the AIC indicated that an optimum had been reached (Mitchell et al. 2021). For example, the five-phase Coxian phase-type distribution was deemed optimal for hospital 2, whereas the four-phase Coxian phase-type distribution was considered optimal for hospital 9[1].

For hospital 2, it is possible that the first phase could represent admission followed by diagnosis in the second phase. Some patients leave the hospital ward at this phase (phase 2) at a rate of $\hat{\mu}_2 = 0.0594$, with the majority of patients transitioning straight through the third and fourth phases, as the rates of leaving the system are $\hat{\mu}_3 = 0.000$ and $\hat{\mu}_4 = 0.000$, respectively, into the fifth phase. Given that these parameter values are approximately 0, suggesting that patients spend no time at all in them, the two phases could be collapsed down into one phase, representing treatment, as no patients leave the hospital from either of these phases but instead move into phase 5. The patients then all transition through to the fifth phase at a rate of 0.290. This final phase could represent rehabilitation. Hospital 9, however, shows that patients leave the system from the first and last phases. This potentially shows that patients who leave at the same phase as hospital 2 except hospital 9 have admissions and diagnoses at the first phase.

The Coxian phase-type distribution is able to provide an overview of the flow through the hospital ward, but there are different ways in which patients can flow through the hospital system, for example, some patients may only stay in the hospital a day or two leaving from the first phase of the Coxian phase-type distribution, whereas other patients will leave from the final phase. To uncover if there are different pathways within the healthcare system, the Coxian-CTHMM with two hidden states is applied to each of the hospital wards. The hidden states in this model represent an unobservable variable that influences patient flow, which could include, for example, quality of care. This will provide healthcare providers with a better understanding of the healthcare system for older patients. Similar to fitting the Coxian phase-type distribution, the fitting of the Coxian-CTHMM is conducted in a sequential manner. Each Coxian phase-type distribution within the hidden states was independently sequentially built, that is, a two-phase Coxian phase-type distribution in one hidden state and a three-phase Coxian phase-type distribution in the other hidden state (Mitchell et al. 2021). This sequential building of the model continues until the AIC shows that the optimal model has been obtained. The AIC results for hospitals 2 and 9 and the parameter estimates for the optimal models are provided in Table 12.1. According to the AIC, the optimal model for hospital 2 is the model that has a hidden state with a one-phase Coxian phase-type distribution and a second hidden state with a three-phase Coxian phase distribution. Hospital 9 has an optimal model with two hidden states consisting of two and eight phases. Table 12.1 outlines the Coxian phase-type distribution parameters obtained from each of the hidden states. This suggests that the incorporation of the Coxian-CTHMM captures the

1 In this chapter, the focus will be on the hospital 2 and hospital 9, the results for the 12 hospital wards can be given on request.

presence of different patient pathways. Hidden state 1 represents patients who generally tend to have longer lengths of stay. It could be assumed that longer lengths of stay may represent a poorer quality of care, particularly if the patients are having to wait because their place of discharge is not ready (Bottle et al. 2013). However, the patient's condition or diagnosis is an important contributing factor to their length of stay, as some patients may have complex treatment needs that require them to stay in the hospital longer, which should be considered, particularly when considering older patients.

Hidden state 1 phases	Hidden state 2 phases	-log-likelihood		AIC	
		Hospital 2	Hospital 9	Hospital 2	Hospital 9
1	1	−1,810.7	−4,386.9	3,631.4	8,723.8
1	2	−1,740.6	−4,081.2	3,495.2	8,176.4
2	2	−1,740.5	−4,080.8	3,499.2	8,179.6
1	3	−1,733.3	−4,013.0	**3,484.6**	8,044
2	3	−1,733.2	−4,011.8	3,488.4	8,045.6
1	4	−1,731.8	−3,995.8	3,485.6	8,013.6
2	4	−1,729.3	−3,993.1	3,484.6	8,012.2
1	5	–	−3,986.9	–	7,999.8
2	5	–	−3,982.7	–	7,995.4
1	6	–	−3,980.2	–	7,990.4
2	6	–	−3,975.6	–	7,985.2
1	7	–	−3,975.3	–	7,984.6
2	7	–	−3,971.8	–	7,981.6
1	8	–	−3,972.1	–	7,982.2
2	8	–	−3,969.6	–	**7,981.2**
1	9	–	−3,970.7	–	7,983.4
2	9	–	−3,968.3	–	7,982.6
3	7	–	−3,969.7	–	7,981.4
3	8	–	−3,967.9	–	7,981.8
3	9	–	−3,966.8	–	7,983.6

Table 12.1. *Log-likelihood, AIC (values in bold represent the AIC for the best model) of the Coxian-CTHMM for hospitals 2 and 9*

The distribution and results obtained for hospitals 2 and 9 are reported in Tables 12.2 and 12.3 and Figure 12.4. In particular, for hospital 2, the estimation for the first hidden state shows that individuals enter the hospital and then leave at rates of $\hat{\mu}_1 = 0.2477$ and $\hat{\mu}_2 = 0.1138$, respectively. In contrast to the first hidden state, the second hidden state shows that individuals transition through the healthcare system at a much faster rate, suggesting that fewer resources are used within this group of patients. In hospital 2, a very small number of patients leave the second phase before transitioning through to the final phase.

In Table 12.3, for hospital 9, within the second hidden state, patients transition directly through to the second phase, where some patients leave the hospital system, with the remainder of patients transitioning to the eighth phase before they leave hospital 9.

	Parameter estimates
Hidden state 1	$\hat{\mu}_1 = 0.2477$
Hidden state 2	$\hat{\mu}_1 = 2.1830e^{-6}, \hat{\mu}_2 = 7.086e^{-4}, \hat{\mu}_3 = 0.1786$ $\hat{\lambda}_1 = 0.1586, \hat{\lambda}_2 = 0.1580$

Table 12.2. *Parameter estimates of the Coxian-CTHMM for hospital 2*

	Parameter estimates
Hidden state 1	$\hat{\mu}_1 = 6.2164e^{-161}, \hat{\mu}_2 = 0.1138$ $\hat{\lambda}_1 = 0.1138$
Hidden state 1	$\hat{\mu}_1 = 2.0000e^{-323}, \hat{\mu}_2 = 0.0280, \hat{\mu}_3 = 3.7653e^{-76}$, $\hat{\mu}_4 = 5.0696e^{-68}$, $\hat{\mu}_5 = 3.7969e^{-40}, \hat{\mu}_6 = 2.4939e^{-17}$, $\hat{\mu}_7 = 2.5453e^{-04}, \hat{\mu}_8 = 1.0054, \hat{\lambda}_1 = 0.8360, \hat{\lambda}_2 = 0.8080, \hat{\lambda}_3 =$ $0.2072, \hat{\lambda}_4 = 1.0029, \hat{\lambda}_5 = 1.0029, \hat{\lambda}_6 = 1.0029, \hat{\lambda}_7 = 1.0027$

Table 12.3. *Parameter estimates of the Coxian-CTHMM for hospital 9*

After the Coxian-CTHMM is fitted to each of the different wards within the Lombardy region, some of the hospitals have similar patterns of flow through the hospital system. In particular, hospitals can be grouped according to two main patterns observed in patient flows, which we refer to as two different systems. Hospital wards 1, 8, 9 and 11 have similar patterns and are thus referred to as the first system; hospital wards 2, 10, 4, 7 and 12 are in the second system; and hospital ward 3 has a different system behavior (hospital wards 5 and 6 had very few inpatients) than all of the other wards. Coxian-CTHMM was applied to each of these grouped systems to uncover the differences in patient flow pathways and to discover the effect that grouping hospitals into the two systems may have on understanding the healthcare system in Lombardy. For System I, the two- and six-phase Coxians within the two hidden states were considered optimal, whereas for System II, the five- and six-phase Coxians within the two hidden states were deemed as most optimal. The result for System I is similar to the individual Coxian-CTHMM results for each of the individual hospitals within this system. For System II, the result obtained was different from the individual hospital's Coxian-CTHMM results. This is due to the effect of combining hospital patients' arrivals. These hospitals have similar underlying pathways as those of the Coxian-CTHMM applied to them individually, but the characteristics within the hospitals are different, which affects the results given when the hospitals are combined, for example, the median length of stays for the hospitals within this system ranges from 5–21 days. The majority of these hospitals are public, ranging from hospital company to an institute of scientific hospital care, one of which is a private institution with some public beds. This is potentially the cause of the difference in results.

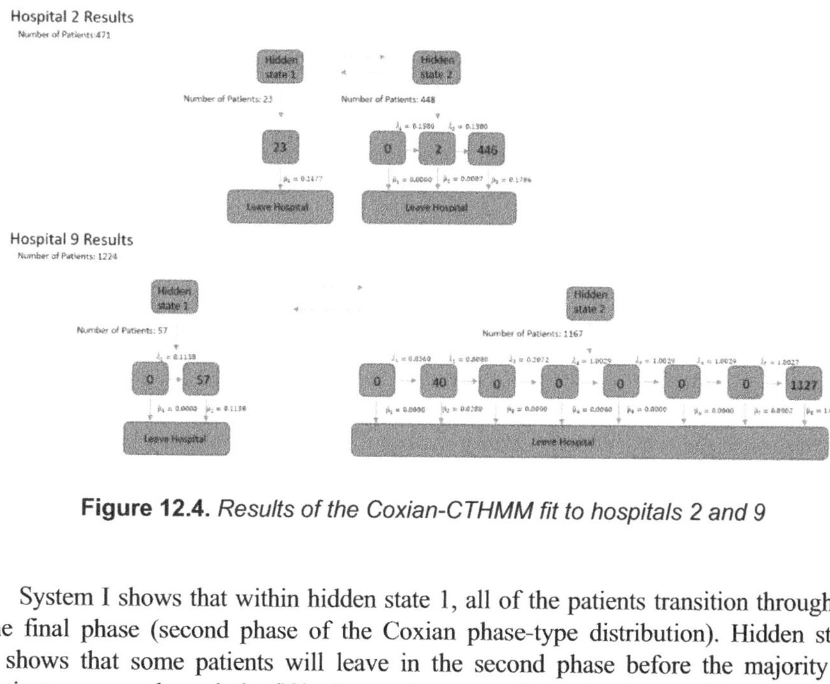

Figure 12.4. *Results of the Coxian-CTHMM fit to hospitals 2 and 9*

System I shows that within hidden state 1, all of the patients transition through to the final phase (second phase of the Coxian phase-type distribution). Hidden state 2 shows that some patients will leave in the second phase before the majority of patients process through the fifth phase, where a small number leave, with the majority leaving through the final phase. This could highlight that after admission and diagnosis, some patients will leave at this stage, whereas the majority will be admitted, receive treatment and require some form of long-term care. Hidden state 2 accounts for the majority of patients within these wards, and they tend to spend less time within the hospital than patients who are in hidden state 1. The diagnoses of the patients within hidden state 1 show that all of those with infectious diseases in System 1 are in this hidden state. There are also slightly higher proportions of those with neoplasms and ill-defined conditions within this hidden state than within hidden state 2. Among those in hidden state 1, 96% had secondary conditions, with 98% requiring some form of surgery, whereas in hidden state 2, 89% had secondary conditions and 87% required surgery. For healthcare managers, patients who will be using more resources should be taken into account in terms of budgeting and bed numbers. An investigation into the treatment needs of patients should be undertaken, as this may flag the need to investigate social care resources within the area. The other main system, System II (which accounts for five hospital wards), shows that the two hidden states observed are very similar. They are represented by a five- and six-phase Coxian phase-type distribution. Within hidden state 1 some patients will leave at the third phase, but the majority will leave at the final fifth phase. Within hidden state 2, some patients leave the second phase, with the majority continuing to the final sixth phase. Healthcare managers in charge of these hospitals should note that there is still the potential to spend longer in hospitals than they need because patients wait for transfers within these systems but that these hospitals are able to transfer and move some of these patients quite quickly, as they are able to leave from the second or third phase within the hidden states. Patients in both of these hidden states have similar main diagnoses, secondary needs and surgical requirements. However, some patients who have respiratory or circulatory issues spend more than 30 days within the hospital and are then transferred to another ward, are transferred to rehabilitation or are voluntarily left with home hospitalization care.

Table 12.4 shows the breakdown by destination of each of the hidden states within the two systems as partitioned by the Viterbi algorithm. This breakdown can provide important information to healthcare providers by flagging potential inefficiencies within the healthcare system that need to be investigated, for example, if large proportions of patients are waiting to be discharged to a nursing home. The proportion of patients who die within each of the hidden states should also be assessed, as this variable has been seen as a proxy for quality of care (Goodacre et al. 2015). Therefore, if one of the hidden states has a large proportion who is dying, then this could serve as an indicator of poor quality of care. However, the treatment plan of the patient should be checked, and risk adjustments should be made.

System 1 shows that of those patients who are transferred to rehabilitation, a nursing home, hospital transfer or voluntary home care, more than 7% are in hidden state 1. The conditions within these system destination groups show that most patients who are transferred to rehabilitation, a nursing home, hospital transfer or voluntary home care are being treated for circulatory or respiratory conditions or infectious diseases. Although it accounts for only 7% of patients, the length of stay in some cases is over four weeks. This could be due to complex needs and comorbidities. However, it is a potential area of concern if it is due to their destination not being ready, as these patients will therefore be at an increased risk of iatrogenic injury (Cornwell et al. 2012). System II, however, shows a slightly more even split for patients within each of the hidden states, with the median length of stays for each of these hidden states being more similar than what is seen within System I.

Table 12.4 shows that of those within hidden state 1, 17.36% and 10.73% of patients in Systems I and II, respectively, died, accounting for 4.90% and 49.34% of the overall patient group. Previous research has shown that death is more common at the start of an individual's hospital stay, as highlighted by the results of this model (median lengths of stay are 32 and four days for Systems I and II, respectively). This finding was also reported by McClean and Millard (1993), who reported that the peak number of deaths occurred in the first week and steadily declined over time. However, within System I, hidden state 1, the median length of stay for those who died is 32 days, whereas for hidden state 2, the median length of stay is six days.

Hidden state	Destination	Patients within destination group (%)		Patients within hidden state (%)		Average median LOS (days)	
		System 1	System 2	System 1	System 2	System 1	System 2
1	Home	2.16	59.64	42.15	74.95	32	5
	Voluntary	4.6	51	0.83	0.95	35	23
	Dead	4.90	49.34	17.36	10.73	32	4
	Nursing home	7.34	27.18	13.22	3.59	17.5	5
	Ward transfer	4.3	36	7.44	5.61	32	6
	Hospital transfer	8.88	27.87	12.40	0.70	32	5
	Hospitalization (home)	–	6	–	0.04	–	8
	Rehabilitation transfer	12.28	43	5.79	3.05	36	5.5
	Voluntary hospital home care	12.5	12	0.83	0.37	13	9
2	Home	97.84	40.36	68.93	55.59	9	13
	Voluntary	95.40	48	0.63	1	4	11
	Dead	95.10	50.66	12.18	12.08	6	14
	Nursing home	92.66	72.8	6.03	10.54	10	16
	Ward transfer	95.67	63	5.94	10.76	11	16
	Hospital transfer	91.1	72.13	4.60	1.99	12	18
	Hospitalization (home)	–	93	–	0.63	–	16
	Rehabilitation transfer	87.72	56.98	1.50	4.4	12	20.5
	Voluntary hospital home care	87.50	88	0.21	2.99	9	20

Table 12.4. *Destinations of the patients separated by the Viterbi algorithm for the two main systems*

12.4. Conclusions

The Coxian phase-type distribution and Coxian-CTHMM were each applied to the 12 wards for older people within the Lombardy region. The results highlight that Coxian-CTHMM is able to provide information regarding patient flow pathways through wards, with the results implying that some hospitals within the region run in a similar fashion. Coxian-CTHMM highlighted that there are two main systems within the region, accounting for nine hospital wards. Within System I, the two-phase Coxian phase-type distribution best represented patients who had longer lengths of stay, whereas the six-phase Coxian phase-type distribution best represented patients with shorter lengths of stay. The five- and six-phase Coxian phase-type distributions were deemed optimal for System II, with very little difference in patient demographics between the two hidden states in this system. Hospital 3 appears to have different systems in place, whereas hospitals 5 and 6 appear to admit very few patients to the ward in 2015. The two main systems identified have the potential to represent different management strategies that may be in place within the two groups of hospitals and whether such strategies are best to cope with an aging population.

This chapter applies the two-hidden-state version of the model to the data, but it is generalizable to any number of hidden states, taking into account computational ability and time. It also has the potential to be used in many different applications where the length of time in a process needs to be considered along with a dynamic latent factor affecting the system.

12.5. Practice implications

The formation of the Coxian-CTHMM and its application to Lombardy wards for older people highlights healthcare providers' different patient flow pathways that older patients take when moving through the hospital system. This has the ability to enable healthcare providers to obtain a better understanding of the healthcare system they are running as well as effectively helping the managers to make comparisons and benchmarks between similarly managed wards in neighboring hospitals with the aim of improving patient quality of care.

The model was able to flag potential issues within the healthcare system that healthcare managers need to investigate further and address. Patients staying in the hospital for more than four weeks could be due to their complex treatment needs. However, the data do not allow for this to be investigated.

Within the Lombardy region's healthcare system for older people, the model, when applied to each ward individually, showed that similar systems exist across different hospitals. Two main systems appear to be in operation, with two hospitals appearing to operate separate hospital systems. The regional government and healthcare providers for each of the hospitals should discuss these findings and investigate whether similar operations are being carried out across these hospitals and if different operation systems are in action in the two hospitals that do not conform to these identified systems.

The Viterbi algorithm, which has been applied to each of the hospitals, flags that certain issues may exist with patients being transferred home, a ward transfer, rehabilitation and transfer to a nursing home. These factors should be investigated further to ascertain whether the long length of time spent in hospitals is due to the complex needs of patients or if it is due to a delay in their destinations not being ready. If these delays are due to their destinations not being ready, healthcare providers should investigate these further, as patients will be using valuable hospital resources when they should be elsewhere. When allocating budgets and bed numbers, hospital managers should consider that some patients use more resources. They should also investigate social care resources within the area so that patients' flow through the system is not delayed by a lack of care packages available to them upon departure from the hospital.

12.6. Conflict of interest

The authors declare that they have no conflict of interest.

12.7. References

Active Citizenship Network (2002). European charter of patients' rights. Document, Active Citizenship Network, Rome [Online]. Available at: https://www.activecitizenship.net/multimedia/import/images/patientsrights/fr_english.pdf [Accessed 2 June 2025].

Baum, L.E. and Petrie, T. (1966). Statistical inference for probabilistic functions of finite state Markov chains. *The Annals of Mathematical Statistics*, 37(6), 1554–1563.

Baum, L.E., Petrie, T., Soules, G., Weiss, N. (1970). A maximization technique occurring in the statistical analysis of probabilistic functions of Markov chains. *The Annals of Mathematical Statistics*, 41(1), 164–171.

Beyreuther, M. and Wassermann, J. (2008). Continuous earthquake detection and classification using discrete hidden Markov models. *Geophysical Journal International*, 175(3), 1055–1066.

Bhar, R. and Hamori, S. (2006). *Hidden Markov models: Applications to Financial Economics*. Springer, New York.

Bottle, A., Middleton, S., Kalkman, C.J., Livingston, E.H., Aylin, P. (2013). Global Comparators project: International comparison of hospital outcomes using administrative data. *Health Services Research*, 48(6), 2081–2100.

Bureau, A., Shiboski S., Hughes J.P. (2003) Applications of continuous time hidden Markov models to the study of misclassified disease outcomes. *Statistics in Medicine*, 22(3), 441–462.

Cooper, B. and Lipsitch, M. (2004). The analysis of hospital infection data using hidden Markov models. *Biostatistics (Oxford, England)*, 5(2), 223–237.

Cornwell, J., Levenson, R., Sonola, L., Poteliakhoff, E. (2012). *Continuity of Care for Older Hospital Patients: A Call for Action*. England King's Fund, London.

Dempster, A.P., Laird, N.M., Rubin, D.B. (1977). Maximum likelihood from incomplete data via the EM algorithm. *Journal of the Royal Statistical Society: Series B (Methodological)*, 39(1), 1–38.

Eurostat (2019). *Over 27 Million People Aged 80 and over in the EU*. Document, European Commission, Brussels [Online]. Available at: https://ec.europa.eu/eurostat/web/products-eurostat-news/-/edn-20170930-1 [Accessed 2 June 2025].

Faddy, M.J. (1994). Examples of fitting structured phase-type distributions. *Applied Stochastic Models and Data Analysis*, 10(4), 247–255.

Faddy, M.J. and McClean, S.I. (1999). Analysing data on lengths of stay of hospital patients using phase-type distributions. *Applied Stochastic Models in Business and Industry*, 15(4), 311–317.

Faddy, M.J. and McClean, S.I. (2005). Markov chain modelling for geriatric patient care. *Methods of Information in Medicine*, 44(3), 369–373.

Faddy, M.J., Graves, N., Pettitt, A. (2009). Modeling length of stay in hospital and other right skewed data: Comparison of phase-type, gamma and log-normal distributions. *Value in Health*, 12(2), 309–314.

France, G., Taroni, F., Donatini, A. (2005). The Italian health-care system. *Health Economics*, 14(Supplement 1), S187–S202.

Goodacre, S., Campbell, M., Carter, A. (2015). What do hospital mortality rates tell us about quality of care? *Emergency Medicine Journal*, 32(3), 244–247.

Gupta, A. and Dhingra, B. (2012). Stock market prediction using hidden Markov models. In *2012 Students Conference on Engineering and Systems (SCES)*, Allahabad.

Hassan, M.R. and Nath, B. (2005). Stock market forecasting using hidden Markov model: A new approach. In *5th International Conference on Intelligent Systems Design and Applications (ISDA'05)*, Warsaw.

Hoogerduijn, J.G., Schuurmans, M.J., Duijnstee, M.S.H., De Rooij, S.E., Grypdonck, M.F.H. (2007). A systematic review of predictors and screening instruments to identify older hospitalized patients at risk for functional decline. *Journal of Clinical Nursing*, 16(1), 46–57.

Kinsella, K. and Wan, H. (2009). U.S. census bureau. International population reports: An aging world: 2008. Technical Report, US Government Printing Office, Washington, D.C.

Lafont, C., Gérard, S., Voisin, T., Pahor, M., Vellas, B. (2011). Reducing 'iatrogenic disability' in the hospitalized frail elderly. *Journal of Nutrition, Health and Aging*, 5(8), 645–660.

Latouche, G. and Ramaswami, V. (1999). Introduction to matrix analytic methods in stochastic modeling. *Journal of Applied Mathematics and Stochastic Analysis*, 12(4), 435–436.

Macchi, L. (2021). Aging population of Italy – Statistics & facts. Statista [Online]. Available at: https://www.statista.com/topics/8379/aging-population-of-italy/#topicHeader__wrapper.

Marshall, A.H. and Zenga, M. (2009). Simulating Coxian phase-type distributions for patient survival. *International Transactions in Operational Research*, 16(2), 213–226.

Marshall, A.H., McClean, S.I., Shapcott, C.M., Millard, P.H. (2002). Modelling patient duration of stay to facilitate resource management of geriatric hospitals. *Health Care Management Science*, 5(4), 313–319.

Marshall, A.H., Zenga, M., Giordano, S. (2013). Modelling students' length of stay at university using Coxian phase-type distributions. *International Journal of Statistics and Probability*, 2(1), 73–89.

McClean, S.I. and Millard, P.H. (1993). Patterns of length of stay after admission in geriatric medicine: An event history approach. *Statistician*, 42(3), 263–274.

McClean, S.I., Young, T., Bustard, D., Millard, P.H., Barton, M. (2008). Discovery of value streams for lean healthcare, intelligent systems. In *4th International IEEE Conference Intelligent Systems*, Varna.

Mitchell, H.J., Marshall, A.H., Zenga, M. (2021). A joint likelihood approach to the analysis of length of stay data utilising the continuous-time hidden Markov model and Coxian phase-type distribution. *Journal of the Operational Research Society*, 72(11), 2529–2541.

Neuts, M.F. (1981). *Matrix-Geometric Solutions in Stochastic Models: An Algorithmic Approach*. Johns Hopkins University Press, London.

Nuti, S., Seghieri, C., Vainieri, M., Zett, S. (2012). Assessment and improvement of the Italian healthcare system: First evidence from a pilot national performance evaluation system. *Journal of Healthcare Management*, 57(3), 182–98.

Rabiner, L.R. (1989). A tutorial on hidden Markov models and selected applications in speech recognition. *Proceedings of the IEEE*, 77(2), 257–286.

Schwarz, G. (1978). Estimating the dimension of a model. *Annals of Statistics*, 6(2), 461–464.

Shaw, B. and Marshall, A.H. (2007). Modelling the flow of congestive heart failure patients through a hospital system. *Journal of the Operational Research Society*, 58(2), 212–218.

Siddall, C. and Kjaeserud, G. (2007). Healthy ageing: keystone for a sustainable European health policy in the context of demographic change. Discussion Paper, Directorate-General for Economic and Financial Affairs and DG Empl-European Commission, Brussels.

Wall, M.M. and Li, R. (2009). Multiple indicator hidden Markov model with an application to medical utilization data. *Statistics in Medicine*, 28(2), 293–310.

13

Estimators for Extreme Value Index: Advancements in Tail Inference

In statistics of extremes, the estimation of the extreme value index (EVI) is an essential requirement for further tail inference. In this chapter, we deal with the estimation of a strictly positive EVI from a Pareto-type model. Under this framework, we study a class of estimators based on the probability weighted moments. These estimators offer a robust method for estimating the EVI, providing valuable insights into the tail behavior, and allow the estimation of other tail parameters such as an extreme quantile or the probability of exceedance of a high level. Return periods serve as a crucial metric in understanding the frequency and severity of rare events, aiding in risk assessment, infrastructure planning and disaster preparation. Understanding return periods enables decision-makers to mitigate the impacts of extreme events and enhance resilience against both natural and non-natural hazards. This research contributes to advancing our understanding of extreme value estimation and its applications.

13.1. Introduction

Extreme value theory (EVT) plays a critical role in understanding, modeling and predicting extreme and rare events that have significant impacts across various domains. These events, though rare, can have significant impact in various fields such as finance, environmental science, engineering and risk management, among others. Unlike classical statistics, which typically deals with central tendencies and overall data distribution, EVT is concerned with making inference about extreme values of the variable of interest. Having a focus on the tail of the distribution, EVT provides valuable tools for risk assessment, infrastructure design and decision making. Let $X_1, X_2, \ldots, X_n$ be a sample of n independent observations from a common

Chapter written by Ayana MATEUS and Frederico CAEIRO.

For a color version of all figures in this chapter, see www.iste.co.uk/ dimotikalis/data5.zip unknown distribution function (d.f.) F. The most commonly used approaches in EVT are as follows: the block maxima, the peaks-over-threshold and the largest observations semi-parametric method. The first method arises from the Fisher–Tippett–Gnedenko theorem (Fisher and Tippett (1928)), which provides the limiting distributions of the normalized maxima from a sequence of independent and identically distributed random variables. According to this theorem, if the sample maximum, $\max(X_1, X_2, \ldots, X_n)$, after adequate linear normalization, converges in law to a non-degenerate limit d.f. G, then G is necessarily given by:

$$G_\xi(x) = \begin{cases} \exp\left(-(1+\xi x)^{-1/\xi}\right),\ 1+\xi x > 0 & \text{if } \xi \neq 0 \\ \exp(-\exp(-x)),\ x \in \mathbb{R} & \text{if } \xi = 0. \end{cases} \qquad [13.1]$$

Whenever such a limit d.f. G_ξ exists, we say that F belongs to the max-domain of attraction of G_ξ and write $F \in D_M(G_\xi)$. The shape parameter ξ in the extreme value distribution in [13.1], known as the EVI, quantifies the heaviness of the right tail of the d.f. F. The EVI is a crucial parameter in EVT as it determines the tail behavior, which is essential for modeling and predicting extreme events. The peaks-over-threshold method is associated with another important result, the Pickands–Balkema–de Haan theorem (Balkemaand de Haan (1974); Pickands III (1975)). It states that the limiting distribution of the scaled excesses over a high threshold is the generalized Pareto (GP) distribution, which is closely associated with the extreme value distribution in [13.1]. Indeed:

$$GP(x) = 1 + \ln G_\xi(x) \quad \text{if} \quad \ln G_\xi(x) > -1.$$

The last method uses the largest observations to make an inference about the right tail, assuming only that F belongs to the max-domain of attraction of $G_\xi(x)$ (see Gomes and Guillou (2015)).

The main objective of this work is to make an inference about the right tail, $\overline{F}(x) = 1 - F(x)$, using the largest observations method. We restrict our study to models $F \in D_M(G_\xi)$, with $\xi > 0$. These models are called Pareto-type or heavy tailed models. It is well-established, as stated in the literature (Beirlant et al. (2004); Embrechts et al. (1997)) that Pareto-type models possess a regularly varying tail with a negative index of regular variation equal to $-1/\xi$, that is:

$$\lim_{t\to\infty} \frac{\overline{F}(tx)}{\overline{F}(t)} = x^{-1/\xi}, \quad \forall x > 0 \qquad [13.2]$$

Consequently, we can write:

$$\overline{F}(x) = x^{-1/\xi} l(x), \qquad x \to \infty, \qquad [13.3]$$

with $l(x)$ a slowly varying function at infinity that measures the departure of $F(x)$ to the Pareto Type I distribution.

When applying Pareto-type models, one of the most popular estimators for the EVI is the one introduced by Hill (1975) and is defined as the average of the log-excesses over the threshold $t = X_{n-k:n} > 0$:

$$\hat{\xi}^H(k) := \frac{1}{k}\sum_{i=1}^{k} \ln X_{n-i+1:n} - \ln X_{n-k:n}, \qquad k = 1, 2, \ldots, n-1, \quad [13.4]$$

where $X_{i:n}$, $i = 1, \ldots, n$, denotes the ith ascending order statistics based on the sample of size n. This estimator is known to be biased, particularly when dealing with small sample sizes. The semi-parametric estimation of the EVI is challenging since it requires careful consideration of the level k. Specifically, classic estimators exhibit high variance for high thresholds $X_{n-k:n}$, that is, for small values of k and high bias for low thresholds, that is, for large values of k. Strategies such as heuristic methods, sample path stability analysis, or minimization of the mean squared error can aid in selecting an appropriate k.

The purpose of this work is to study alternative estimators of the EVI. The remainder of this chapter is summarized as follows. In the next section, we introduce a class of estimators for the EVI derived from the probability-weighted moment method and establish their asymptotic properties. Section 13.3 focuses on a Monte Carlo simulation study to evaluate the finite-sample performance of the EVI estimators discussed in the preceding section. Finally, section 13.4 presents concluding remarks.

13.2. Estimators for the tail parameters

13.2.1. *The new class of estimators for the EVI*

Our approach to estimate the EVI involves analyzing the sample of conditional relative excesses:

$$X/t|X > t, \quad \text{with} \quad t = X_{n-k:n}.$$

These excesses asymptotically follow a Pareto distribution with shape parameter $\xi > 0$. To estimate the EVI, we employ the Probability Weighted Moment (PWM) method. This method was introduced by Greenwood et al. (1979) as a useful tool to estimate distribution parameters from models that have a well-defined quantile function. The PWMs of a continuous random variable X with d.f. F are defined as:

$$M_{k,r,s} = E(X^k(F(X))^r(1 - F(X))^s) \qquad [13.5]$$

where k, r and s are real numbers. The PWM estimators are derived by equating $M_{k,r,s}$ with their respective sample moments and then solving those equations to the unknown parameters of the distribution.

Although the constants k, r and s in [13.5] can assume any real values, for convenience many authors chose $k = 1$ and the first non-negative integer values for r and s (Hosking (1986)). Additionally, when r and s are non-negative integers, it is more practical to work with one of the following PWMs:

$$c_r = M_{1,0,r} = E(X(1 - F(X))^r), \quad r = 0, 1, \cdots, \qquad [13.6]$$

or

$$d_r = M_{1,r,0} = E(X(F(X))^r), \quad r = 0, 1, \cdots. \qquad [13.7]$$

As noted in Rasmussen (2001), estimation can be more accurate if we work with PWMs c_r or d_r, with r real, not necessarily small. The estimators of the PWMs c_r and d_r, with r real, are, respectively:

$$\tilde{c}_r = \frac{1}{n}\sum_{i=1}^{n}(1 - p_{i:n})^r X_{i:n} \quad \text{and} \quad \tilde{d}_r = \frac{1}{n}\sum_{i=1}^{n} p_{i:n}^r X_{i:n}, \qquad [13.8]$$

where $p_{i:n}$ are the so-called plotting positions, that is, empirical estimates of $F(X_{i:n})$.

Recently, Chen et al. (2017) proposed the generalized probability weighted moment (GPWM), defined by:

$$M_{g,r,s} = E(g(X)(F(X))^r(1 - F(X))^s), \qquad [13.9]$$

with $g(x)$ a suitable continuous function and r and s real numbers.

The empirical version of the GPWM in [13.9] is given by:

$$m_{g,r,s} = \frac{1}{n}\sum_{i=1}^{n} g(X_{i:n})(p_{i,n})^r(1 - p_{i,n})^s. \qquad [13.10]$$

Next, for $g(x) = \ln(x)$, $r = 0$ and a real value s, we have the GPWM for the Pareto distribution:

$$M_{\ln(x),0,s} = E(\ln(X)(1 - F(X))^s) = \frac{\xi}{(1+s)^2}, s \geq -1 \qquad [13.11]$$

The corresponding estimator of the theoretical moment in [13.11] is given as:

$$\hat{M}_{\ln(x),0,s} = \frac{1}{k}\sum_{i=1}^{k}\left(\frac{i}{k}\right)^{s} \ln\frac{X_{n-i+1:n}}{X_{n-k:n}}, \qquad s > -1, \qquad [13.12]$$

By solving the equation $M_{\ln(x),0,s} = \hat{M}_{\ln(x),0,s}$ in order to the parameter ξ, we obtain the class of generalized probability weighted moment estimator for the EVI, given by:

$$\hat{\xi}^{GPWM(s)}(k) = (1+s)^2\frac{1}{k}\sum_{i=1}^{k}\left(\frac{i}{k}\right)^{s} \ln\frac{X_{n-i+1:n}}{X_{n-k:n}}, \quad s > -1 \quad k = 1, 2, \ldots, n-1.$$

[13.13]

Note that the class of estimators in [13.13] was first studied in Gomes et al. (2005) and Caeiro et al. (2025) for $s \geq 0$. The GPWM estimators generalize the Hill estimator when $s = 0$, that is, $\hat{\xi}^{H}(k) \equiv \hat{\xi}^{GPWM(0)}(k)$.

13.2.2. *Asymptotic properties of the GPWM estimators*

To derive the asymptotic results, for the class of estimators considered in [13.13], we need to assume some conditions. First, for theoretical reasons, the threshold k is often assumed to be intermediate, that is, $k = k_n \in [1, n-1]$ is assumed to be a sequence of positive integers satisfying:

$$k \to \infty \quad \text{and} \quad k/n \to 0, \quad \text{as} \quad n \to \infty. \qquad [13.14]$$

In the case of Pareto-type models, condition [13.2] is equivalent to the following first-order regular variation representation:

$$\lim_{t\to\infty}\frac{U(tx)}{U(t)} = x^{\xi}, \qquad [13.15]$$

for every $x > 0$, with

$$U(t) = F^{\leftarrow}(1 - 1/t), \quad t \geq 1, \qquad [13.16]$$

the tail quantile function and

$$F^{\leftarrow}(t) = \inf\{x : F(x) \geq t\}, \quad 0 < t < 1, \qquad [13.17]$$

the left-continuous generalized inverse function of the d.f. F. To obtain the asymptotic bias of the EVI-estimators under consideration, we need to assume a second-order condition of regular variation. We thus assume the existence of an ultimately positive regular varying function A with index $\rho \leq 0$ (de Haan and Ferreira (2006)) such that:

$$\lim_{t \to \infty} \frac{\ln U(tx) - \ln U(t) - \xi \ln x}{A(t)} = \begin{cases} \frac{x^\rho - 1}{\rho}, & \text{if } \rho < 0, \\ \ln x, & \text{if } \rho = 0, \end{cases} \quad [13.18]$$

for every $x > 0$.

THEOREM 13.1.– *Under the second-order condition and for intermediate k such that $\sqrt{k}A(n/k) \to \lambda$, finite, it holds that:*

$$\sqrt{k}\left(\hat{\xi}^{GPWM(s)}(k) - \xi\right) \xrightarrow{d} N\left(\frac{(1+s)\lambda}{1+s-\rho}, \frac{\xi^2(1+s)^2}{1+2s}\right), \quad [13.19]$$

with $s > -0.5$ and $N(\mu, \sigma^2)$ a normal random variable with mean value μ and variance σ^2.

13.2.3. *Estimating an extreme quantile*

The parameter ξ is fundamental in characterizing the tail behavior of distributions and directly influences the estimation of extreme quantiles and tail probabilities. The classical estimator of extreme quantiles is the Weissman (1978) estimator:

$$\hat{q} = X_{n-k:n} \left(\frac{k}{np}\right)^{\hat{\xi}^{GPWM(s)}(k)}. \quad [13.20]$$

13.3. Monte Carlo simulation study of the GPWM estimators

The Monte Carlo simulation study aims to provide a comprehensive evaluation of the GPWM estimators' performance across different values of the parameter s and comparing them with the Hill estimator (a particular case of the GPWM estimators with $s = 0$). This comparison seeks to identify the most effective estimator for each distribution and all computations were done using R software (R Core Team (2020)). We also present simulation results for the estimator of high quantiles in equation [13.20], for samples of the Fréchet model.

13.3.1. *Methodology*

The simulation process involves generating 5,000 samples, each consisting of $n = 500$ observations from two different distributions:

– the Fréchet(ξ) model with d.f. $F(x) = \exp(-x^{-1/\xi})$, $x > 0$, $\xi > 0$ with $\xi = 0.5$;

– the Burr(ξ,ρ) model with d.f. $F(x) = 1 - (1 + x^{-\rho/\xi})^{1/\rho}$, $x > 0$, $\xi > 0$, $\rho < 0$ with $\xi = 0.5$ and $\rho = -0.75$.

For each sample, the GPWM estimator, $\hat{\xi}^{GPWM(s)}(k)$, is calculated for different values of k ($k = 1, ..., n - 1$) and evaluated for the parameters $s = -0.1, -0.2, -0.3, -0.4$. The performance of each estimator is assessed using the simulated values of:

– the mean $(\mathrm{E}(\hat{\xi}^{GPWM(s)}(k)), k = 1, 2, \ldots, n - 1)$;

– the root mean squared error $(\mathrm{RMSE}(\hat{\xi}^{GPWM(s)}(k)), k = 1, 2, \ldots, n - 1)$.

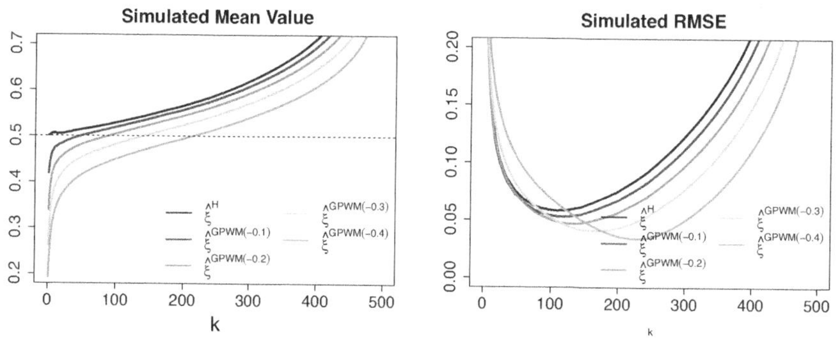

Figure 13.1. *Sample path of the simulated mean value and RMSE of the estimators ($\hat{\xi}$) for samples of size 500 from the Fréchet model*

13.3.2. *Results*

In Figures 13.1 and 13.2, we present the simulated mean value (left figure) and root mean squared error (right figure), as a function of k, for the Fréchet and Burr distributions, respectively. By using the Weissman estimator with $p = 0.002$, we present in Figure 13.3 the simulated mean and root mean square error for the Fréchet model ($q = 22$) as a function of k. Based on the results obtained from the Monte Carlo simulations, we reached the following conclusions:

– All EVI-estimators exhibit increasing bias and a peaked RMSE as a function of k. The Hill estimator also exhibits a non-negative bias.

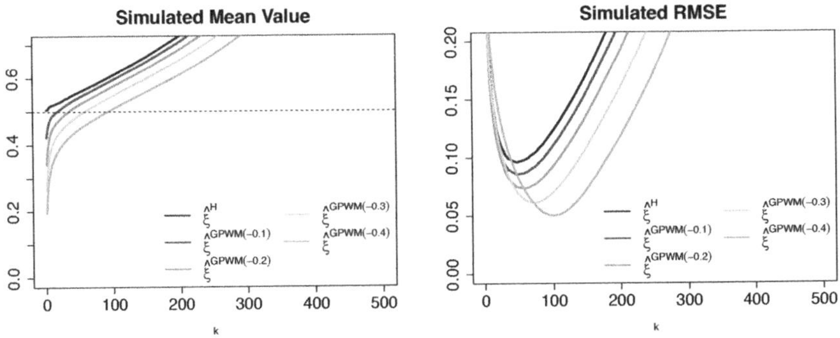

Figure 13.2. *Sample path of the simulated mean value and RMSE of the estimators ($\hat{\xi}$) for samples of size 1,000 from the Burr model*

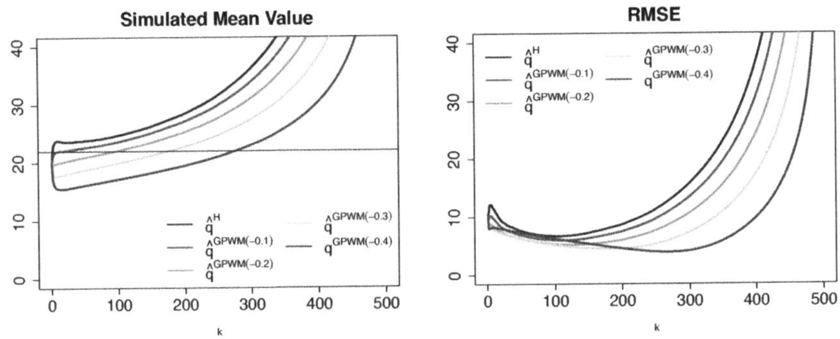

Figure 13.3. *Sample path of the simulated mean value and RMSE of a high quantile for samples of size 500 from the Fréchet model ($p = 0.002$, $q = 22$)*

– For the Fréchet and Burr models, the GPWM estimators used in this study exhibit smaller bias and a lower RMSE compared to the Hill estimator for values of k greater than 50.

– Regarding the estimation of high quantiles, the GPWM estimator with $s = -0.4$ demonstrates good performance in terms of bias and RMSE for values of k larger than 200 and smaller than 350. The estimates obtained for the RMSE are stable for values of k around 300 and are lower than those of the Hill estimator.

– These results suggest that the GPWM estimators, with an adequate value for the parameter s, are competitive against the Hill estimator.

13.4. Conclusion

In this work, we studied a class of estimators for the EVI based on the GPWM method. We examined the asymptotic distribution of the GPWM estimators within a second-order framework and validated their performance through a Monte Carlo simulation study. The results indicate that, with an adequate choice of the parameter s, these estimators can outperform the classic Hill estimator. In future research work, we intend to compare the GPWM estimators with other established estimators of the EVI, from the literature, reduce the bias of these estimators and apply them to real-world datasets.

13.5. Acknowledgments

This work is funded by national funds through the FCT – Fundação para a Ciência e a Tecnologia, I.P., under the scope of the projects UIDB/00297/2020 (https://doi.org/10.54499/UIDB/00297/2020) and UIDP/00297/2020 (https://doi.org/10.54499/UIDP/00297/2020) (Center for Mathematics and Applications).

13.6. References

Balkema, A.A. and de Haan, L. (1974). Residual life time at great age. *Annals of Probability,* 2, 792–804.

Beirlant, J., Goegebeur, Y., Segers, J., Teugels, J.F. (2004). *Statistics of Extremes: Theory and Applications*. John Wiley & Sons, Chichester.

Caeiro, F., Mateus, A., Prata Gomes, D. (2025). Tail inference with probability weighted moments. *Mathematical Methods in the Applied Sciences*. doi: 10.1002/mma.10922.

Chen, H., Cheng, W., Zhao, J., Zhao, X. (2017). Parameter estimation for generalized Pareto distribution by generalized probability weighted moment-equations. *Communications in Statistics – Simulation and Computation*, 46(10), 7761–7776.

Embrechts, P., Klüppelberg, C., Mikosch, T. (1997). *Modelling Extremal Events: For Insurance and Finance*. Springer, Berlin, Heidelberg.

Fisher, R.A. and Tippett, L.H.C. (1928). Limiting forms of the frequency distributions of the largest or smallest member of a sample. *Proceedings of the Cambridge Philosophical Society*, 24, 180–190.

Gomes, M.I. and Guillou, A. (2015). Extreme value theory and statistics of univariate extremes: A review. *International Statistical Review* 83(2), 263–292.

Gomes, M.I., Pereira, H., Miranda, M.C. (2005). Revisiting the role of the jackknife methodology in the estimation of a positive tail index. *Communications in Statistics – Theory and Methods*, 34(2), 319–335.

Greenwood, J.A., Maciunas Landwehr, J.M., Matalas, N.C., Wallis, J.R. (1979). Probability weighted moments: Definition and relation to parameters of several distributions expressable in inverse form. *Water Resources Research*, 15(5), 1049–1054.

de Haan, L. and Ferreira, A. (2006). *Extreme Value Theory*. Springer, New York.

Hill, B.M. (1975). A simple general approach to inference about the tail of a distribution. *The Annals of Statistics*, 3, 1163–1174.

Hosking, J.R.M. (1986). *The Theory of Probability Weighted Moments*. IBM, Thomas J. Watson Research Center, New York.

Pickands III, J. (1975). Statistical inference using extreme order statistics. *Ann. Statist.*, 3, 119–131.

R Core Team (2020). *R: A Language and Environment for Statistical Computing*. R Foundation for Statistical Computing, Vienna.

Rasmussen, P.F. (2001). Generalized probability weighted moments: Application to the generalized pareto distribution. *Water Resources Research*, 37(6), 1745–1751.

Weissman, I. (1978). Estimation of parameters of large quantiles based on the k largest observations. *J. Am. Stat. Assoc.*, 73, 812–815.

14

Determinants of Students' Attitude Toward History: An Empirical Approach

In the context of a multicultural and globalized world, developing a positive attitude toward history among students by investigating the factors that influence it is considered crucial. This study employs data from the EDIS scale (comprising 11 statements and four components) to investigate the influence of educational and socioeconomic factors on the attitude of 247 Greek secondary school students toward history. The econometric approach of seemingly unrelated regression was employed to derive the effects on each component, considering the correlations between them. The four components of the EDIS scale, namely, information and communication technologies (ICTs), history study strategies, broad attitude toward history and map utilization, are found to be positively and negatively influenced by various socioeconomic and educational variables, providing important evidence for the redefinition of the history curriculum in the contemporary context of constant change and population restructuring.

Highlights of this chapter:

– We model students' attitude toward history in Greek secondary schools.

– Educational and socioeconomic factors affecting the components of the EDIS scale, which evaluates students' attitude toward history, are investigated.

– Computer literacy positively affects the use of ICT on the attitude toward history and historical maps.

– Females seem more flexible in using various study strategies throughout their history.

Chapter written by Aristea MAVROGIANNI, Eleni VASILAKI and Maria GRYDAKI.

– The father's educational level positively affects almost all EDIS subscales.

– The mother's educational level negatively affects the student's broad attitude toward history.

14.1. Introduction

It is a well-documented phenomenon that students frequently exhibit a negative attitude toward history, often perceiving it as a less valuable academic discipline than others. This is partly due to the belief that history does not directly contribute to vocational rehabilitation (Dwarko 2007; Cobbold and Oppong 2010). However, contemporary attitudes are influenced by multiple factors, particularly extracurricular learning, the utilization of various sources and ICTs. It has been demonstrated that personal interest plays a pivotal role in determining students' attitudes, effort, and, ultimately, achievement in history (Bulgren et al. 2007; Snow et al. 2007; Lee and Spratley 2010). Nevertheless, further investigation is warranted to ascertain the extent to which interest influences attitude (Levstik 2011; Dan and Todd 2014). Research evidence indicates that attitude is significantly shaped by teaching techniques (Nyamwembe et al. 2013; Boadu 2015).

In recent years, interest in understanding students' attitude toward history has increased, with the intention to use this understanding to inform teaching practices. Various scholars have explored this approach, including Barton and Levstick (2004) and Cercadillo (2001). In addition, the following sources are particularly relevant when considering the impact of educational and socioeconomic factors on historical understanding (Lee and Ashby, 2000; Lee et al. 2001; Wineburg 2001; Lee and Shemilt 2004; VanSledright 2004).

The disposition toward an activity or subject is related to forming a positive or negative attitude toward it. Attitude is a concept closely related to personal interest, along with intrinsic motivation, value, perceptions and other interrelated concepts. It develops gradually and has a long-term effect on the learner's cognitive processing (Hidi and Renninger 2006). Furthermore, the latter has a positive effect on the student's motivation to learn in a subject area (Ainley et al. 2002; Osman and Hamzah 2020). The development of personal interest (Dan and Todd 2014; Zusho et al. 2005), which is derived from situational interest (Schiefele 2009) or the learner's prior experiences or knowledge in a particular domain (Hidi and Renninger 2006), is contingent upon the student's interaction with an object, event or activity (Krapp et al. 1992; Renninger et al. 1998; Schraw and Lehman 2001). When the student's experience is perceived as enjoyable and desirable, personal interest is a driving force of the bidirectional relationship between interest and knowledge. As knowledge increases, greater interest in it is generated and vice versa. Interest fuels the search for more relevant knowledge (Ainley et al. 2002; Dan and Todd 2014).

For the assessment of students' attitudes toward the teaching subject, self-assessment scales are considered more objective, as they are valid and reliable as psychometric tools. Typically, psychometric tools are in the form of a set of structured statements (Cronbach 1990; Stalikas et al. 2012), and their development, which is based on specific principles, is the subject of the applied science of psychometrics (Stalikas et al. 2012). In the present study, the self-report scale EDIS (Mavrogianni et al. 2021) was used as a psychometric tool. The term "psychometric tools" refers to instruments resulting from systematic, objective procedures based on measurable data and used for research or educational purposes.

The general methodology for transitioning from the initial stage, comprising a set of structured questions, to creating the final psychometric tool follows a series of defined steps, which involve the progressive development of the psychometrically tested valid and reliable tool. In particular, to develop the EDIS scale as a psychometric tool for educational research, the methodology of Artino et al. (2014) was employed. Following the seminal work of Mavrogianni et al. (2021), a corpus of statements on students' attitude toward history was assembled, drawing upon a preliminary literature review, classroom discussions with students, synthesis and critical evaluation of the information. The statements were subjected to a rigorous assessment of clarity, redundancy and readability process involving teams of experts and students. Finally, the students were invited to complete the statements in hard copy to ensure the formulation was accurate. After the final questionnaire was piloted on a sufficient sample of participants and appropriate statistical procedures (exploratory and confirmatory factor analyses were then evaluated for reliability, validity, and psychometric properties), the resulting instrument, the EDIS scale, comprising 11 statements, was accepted as the final psychometric instrument (Mavrogianni et al. 2021).

The subject of history is a focus of this study because, despite its contribution to students' critical thinking, it tends to be characterized by students' negative attitude. This study investigates the influence of educational and socioeconomic factors on Greek students' attitude toward history, utilizing the recently validated and reliable EDIS scale (Mavrogianni et al. 2021). In particular, this study examines the impact of educational orientation, the subject of history as a factor of orientation, foreign language proficiency, computer literacy, last grade classification, class repetition, school type and class of attendance (educational factors). With respect to socioeconomic factors, we investigate the impacts of gender, parents' educational level, parents' work conditions, the number of siblings and the mother tongue. These factors are regarded as key determinants of attitude toward history, given the profound impact of computerization on modern society and education. Furthermore, the role of the family in a multicultural society has undergone a significant transformation, with the traditional relationship between parents undergoing a process of reform.

Section 14.2 presents the related literature on the factors that affect the attitude toward history. Section 14.3 presents the research design, that is, the data and empirical strategy. Section 14.4 reports the results. Section 14.5 concludes with a summary and reflections on future developments.

14.2. Previous research

14.2.1. *Attitude toward history*

The term "attitude" is defined as the beliefs that individuals hold toward objects and people. In their 2007 study, Amengor and Fredrick proposed that an attitude is an evaluation of objects of thought, comprising three components: cognitive, affective and behavioral. The cognitive component comprises beliefs that individuals hold for the object of attitude. The affective component refers to the emotions generated by the object of thought, whereas the behavioral component consists of an individual's predispositions to act in a particular way toward the object of attitude. The attitude of teachers and learners toward the subject of history affects the teaching and learning process. In numerous instances, the educational institution's quality and the teaching staff's effectiveness are paramount in influencing students' academic attitude and interest (Hattie 2008). Therefore, attitude is central to the educational process, as it can enhance or inhibit students' behavior toward history and related activities. Despite the subject providing opportunities to develop analytical skills, critical thinking and the expression of creativity, it is often considered dull, monotonous and burdensome to students. The manner in which history is taught, with an emphasis on textbooks and a strict methodological approach, is a contributing factor to students' negative attitudes toward the subject. This is because the content tends to be presented in a static, unchanging format, consisting of an array of irrelevant dates and events that are perceived by students as being monotonous (Issar 2021).

In the research conducted by Amengor and Fredrick (2007), high school students expressed negative attitude and perceptions about history. They viewed history as a dead subject, devoid of practical application, owing to the emphasis on memorization. Furthermore, Obeidat et al. (2011) found that students perceived history as a subject with no real connection to their lives. In a study conducted by Ahmed and Maryam (2016) to examine students' attitude toward social science, the results indicated that students were more interested in studying natural science subjects because they believed it would lead to higher paying jobs. They did not perceive any meaningful connection between history and their future careers. The focus is on sciences and technology. Another study on the subject of history by Boadu (2016) recorded teachers' and students' perceptions of an overloaded syllabus.

14.2.2. *Educational factors*

Mustafina (2016) demonstrated that although teachers have incorporated ICT within classrooms, they have provided limited access to technology for students. As Izadpanah and Alavi (2016) have observed, computer technology has been integrated into the learning process in schools, is employed in a variety of school subjects, and has been found to enhance students' motivation and facilitate differentiated instruction, which in turn has been shown to further enhance motivation (Levin and Wadmany 2006). Students are utilizing technology to access information, navigate their learning and connect with a multitude of individuals and resources, both locally and globally. Students can access information in real time from experts around the globe. Teachers can guide how students can differentiate between real and fake information and can provide formative assessments (Hoffmann and Ramirez 2018). Teacher education can adapt to meet the needs of 21st-century students and teachers (Mulholland 2006; Janssen and Lozaonder 2015). In general, the integration of ICT with constructivist learning techniques has been demonstrated to enhance students' attitude toward history, particularly when it is taught in a non-traditional student-centered manner (Yilmaz 2008; Lo et al. 2009).

Private tutoring (PT) is an informal teaching activity that occurs outside of the formal school curriculum and encompasses a range of instructional approaches, including those that exceed or advance the scope of typical school learning. The relationship between PT and teachers in mainstream education is complex, which presents a challenge for more personalized learning approaches. PT assists students in comprehending challenging material, introduces them to learning opportunities outside of the school environment (Baker et al. 2001; Park et al. 2016; Addi-Raccah 2019), and alleviates parental anxiety and disillusionment with the educational system (Dawson 2010).

14.2.3. *Socioeconomic factors*

The literature review demonstrates that parental involvement in students' education is associated with improved performance. Hill and Tyson (2009) identified three categories of parental involvement: home-based involvement (e.g. assisting with homework, communicating with children about school, creating a conducive learning environment at home), school-based involvement (e.g. visiting and volunteering at school, communicating with teachers) and academic socialization (including communicating parental expectations for education and its value or utility and making preparations and plans for the future). Academic socialization refers to parents discussing the importance of academic achievement with their children, intending to foster a positive attitude toward education. This form of parental involvement is considered more important for achievement than the other two types, as it reinforces adolescents' autonomy and the internalized valuation of education. Nevertheless, assistance with homework is negatively correlated with academic outcomes (Hill and Tyson 2009). This is partly because such involvement may be a response to students not performing well, but excessive help with homework may also be understood as interfering with the child's autonomy.

The educational expectations of parents for their children (Bourdieu and Passeron 1977; Breen and Goldthorpe 1997; Tong et al. 2021) and their involvement in their children's education (Reay et al. 2005; Seginer 2006; Lareau and Weininger 2008; Hill and Tyson 2009) have been identified as playing important roles in students' development. Middle-class parents are more involved than working-class parents (Lee and Bowen 2006; Lareau 2011), whereas lower income parents are less involved in the schools of their children (La Placa and Corlyon 2016). On the one hand, parents with a higher educational level are more involved in their children's education, engage in more discussions with their children about education, and have higher educational expectations than other parents (Wang et al. 2020). On the other hand, the less direct influence of more educated mothers on their child's attitude toward history can be attributed to a combination of fostering independent thinking, reliance on diverse educational resources, time constraints and a broader social and educational environment that collectively shapes the child's perspective. According to Li and Guo (2023), the mother's educational role does not seem as important as the father's educational role, although parental accompaniment is an important determinant of children's well-being. In the same vein, a parent's educational ambitions influence children's educational attainment and attitude (Henz and Maas 1995; Paulus and Blossfeld 2007). However, research evidence shows that children do not follow parental risk attitudes and deviate from the parental norm (Wölfel and Heineck 2012).

The demographic characteristics of the home, such as family income, occupation, residence, type of school, neighborhood opportunities and learning opportunities, are affected by the father's occupation and educational level, which in turn influences the child's motivation toward education. Parents with higher levels of education ensure that their children have many educational opportunities in their communities. Highly educated parents provide more support and encouragement to their children, which enhances adolescents' academic motivation (Acharya and Joshi 2009).

Furthermore, social class and differences in the cultural and economic status of the family also have a significant impact. In more specific terms, parents with greater cultural resources are more engaged in their children's future educational expectations, whereas parents with greater economic resources are more involved in their children's current educational attainment. Social class has been found to be correlated with educational performance and level of education (Hansen and

Strømme 2021). Parents from working-class backgrounds tend to perceive education as the school's responsibility, whereas those from middle-class backgrounds tend to view it as their duty to foster the growth of their children's potential abilities. Middle-class parents are more likely to monitor their children's education and to engage with school matters, with teachers being approached when necessary to discuss any concerns.

It can be reasonably deduced from the research findings that parental education constitutes an important and significant unique predictor of a child's achievements. A meta-analysis of the literature reveals that, over an individual's lifespan, the level of parental education is a superior predictor of adult educational and occupational attainment than other demographic factors. A review of the literature reveals a paucity of studies that focus on the predictive role of the parents' educational level during middle childhood. The Columbia County Longitudinal Study, which began in 1960, provides valuable insight into this area. The study found that the parents' educational level when the child reached 8 years of age significantly predicted the educational and occupational success of the child 40 years later. These findings highlight the long-term impact of the parents' educational background on their child's future prospects. These findings lend substantial support to the assertion that parental education plays a distinctive role in predicting adult outcomes 40 years later (Dearing et al. 2004; Davis-Kean 2005; Dubow et al. 2009).

Furthermore, parental education and family interaction patterns in childhood may be directly associated with a child's subsequent academic success and achievement-oriented attitude. In the general social learning and social-cognitive framework proposed by Bandura (1986), behavioral development occurs as a consequence of observational and direct learning experiences. Such experiences give rise to the internalization of cognitive scripts, values and beliefs, which serve to guide and sustain behavioral responses over time (Anderson and Huesmann 2007). As posited by Eccles and associates (Eccles et al. 2004), this cognitive process is responsible for the emergence and persistence of achievement-related behaviors, which ultimately contribute to successful achievement. Eccles's framework places a significant emphasis on the role of children's expectations for success.

A review of the literature shows that there is a positive correlation between maternal education and children's academic achievement (Magnuson 2007; Augustine et al. 2009; Faize and Dahar 2011; Carneiro et al. 2013). The phenomenon whereby a more educated mother may exert less influence on her child's general attitude toward history can be elucidated through the application of several sociological, psychological and educational lenses.

A fathers' educational level has a significant effect on the achievement motivation of adolescents in academic areas. Achievement motivation in academic areas was greater among adolescents who were the children of postgraduate or graduate fathers than among those who were the children of intermediate or high school-educated fathers. Parents' education is one of the most important factors influencing a child's achievement motivation. Highly educated parents have greater success in providing their children with the cognitive and language skills that contribute to early success in school (Acharya and Joshi 2009; Islam and Chakrabarty 2020).

Parents with higher levels of education are frequently engaged in demanding careers that may restrict the time they are able to dedicate directly to their children on specific subjects, such as history. This is due to the inherent demands of such careers, which often require significant time and attention. Consequently, other influences, such as those exerted by peers and the media, may assume a more significant role (Milkie et al. 2004). Children of educated parents typically interact with a broader social network, which includes peers and adults with diverse perspectives. These interactions have the potential to influence their attitude toward subjects such as history to a greater extent than parental input does alone (Carbonaro 2005).

14.3. Data and methods

14.3.1. *Data*

14.3.1.1. *Questionnaire and subscales of the EDIS*

To investigate students' attitude toward history, data were collected using the 23-statement EDIS inventory in the form of a 5-point Likert-type scale (see Appendix A, section 14.6.1).[1] This inventory was then subjected to a successful reliability, validity and psychometric evaluation test with exploratory and confirmatory factor analysis (Mavrogianni et al. 2021). In the final version of the scale, 11 statements were retained, and four subscales emerged concerning the "effect of the use of ICTs on attitude toward history" (factor 1, three items), the "study strategies" of the history course (factor 2, three items), the "broad attitude" toward the subject of history (factor 3, three items) and the "effect of the use of a historical map" (factor 4, two items) (see Appendix B, section 14.6.2). Scores on the scale and its subscales were extracted in two different ways, either by considering the average values of the statements that contribute to each factor or by using the weighted averages of the items that contribute to each factor according to the specific factor loading. Table C.1 provides the descriptive statistics (number of observations, mean, standard deviation, minimum, maximum values) of the factors

1 An ethical clearance checklist was approved by the University of Crete Research Ethics Committee (decision number: 2/2018/13-03-2018) and the Greek Ministry of Education (decision number: 89964/D2/01-06-2018).

calculated in two ways, as already mentioned, along with the educational and socioeconomic variables considered in the empirical analysis.

Variable	Observation	Mean	Std. Dev.	Min	Max
F1AVER	247	3.592	1.037	1	5
F2AVER	247	3.869	1.051	1	5
F3AVER	247	3.462	1.067	1	5
F4AVER	247	2.036	0.992	1	5
F1WAVER	247	8.169	2.343	2.266	11.33
F2WAVER	247	8.432	2.287	2.175	10.875
F3WAVER	247	7.444	2.321	2.154	10.77
F4WAVER	247	3.105	1.519	1.534	7.67
School type	247	2.526	0.731	1	3
Class of attendance	247	6.385	2.264	1	9
Last grade classification	246	3.057	0.855	1	4
Educational orientation	385	0.353	0.813	0	3
History orientation	247	1.632	0.81	1	3
Class repetition	247	0.049	0.215	0	1
PC usage level	247	2.421	0.693	1	3
Language skills level	247	2.571	0.67	1	3
Gender	247	1.498	0.501	1	2
Mother tongue (Greek)	247	0.951	0.215	0	1
Number of siblings	247	2.251	0.792	1	4
Father's education level	248	4.702	1.647	1	7
Mother's education level	248	5.097	1.408	1	7
Father's work conditions	247	4.717	0.781	1	5
Mother's work conditions	247	4.267	1.234	1	5

Table 14.1. *Descriptive statistics. Authors' calculations based on EDIS database (Mavrogianni et al. 2021). F1AVER,...F4AVER reflect the averages of the components of factors 1,...4. F1WAVER,...,F4WAVER correspond to weighted averages of the components of factors 1,...4 considering the specific loading factors for each component*

14.3.1.2. *Participants*

The survey was conducted with the participation of students enrolled in secondary education, representing a diverse range of educational institutions, including secondary schools (*gymnasiums*), general high schools and vocational high schools, situated in urban, semiurban and rural areas of the prefecture of Heraklion, Crete. The participants were randomly selected from among the educational institutions that had consented to participate in the survey.[2] A total of 247 students participated, approximately equal in terms of gender (50.2% boys and 49.8% girls). Most of them (95.1%) were native speakers of Greek, whereas only a few had Greek as a second language. They were mainly attending urban schools (79.4%), as there was no willingness to participate from schools in the province. Their average age was 15.6 years, with a standard deviation of 1.3 years (age range: 12–18 years). Among the attendance variables, "level of education" was recorded because it is related both to the age maturity that adolescent students gradually attain, mainly in the older grades of high school, and to the learning differentiation between general and vocational high schools, whose direction is not directly related to the study of theoretical subjects such as history. Most students (66.8%) attended a general high school, 14.2% attended a secondary school and 19% attended a vocational high school. The variable "orientation of studies" concerned only 72 students in the second and third stages of general high school, 31.9% of whom were in the orientation of humanities studies. History is taught as a nationally examined subject with a weighting factor for admission to higher education only in the humanities orientation in the third grade of the general high school. Other attendance variables were "receiving educational assistance outside of school" (66.8% of the sample), "students' grade level based on previous grade" (different per grade level), "diagnosed learning difficulties" (9.3%) and "repeating a class" (4.9%). With respect to the students' skills, "computer use" and "language proficiency level" were recorded. The variable "computer use" was chosen to be further exploited to investigate its correlation with students' familiarity with the use of ICT throughout history. A percentage of 88.3% of the students stated that they knew how to use the computer well, very well and excellently, which is extremely high. A similar situation was observed for the variable "level of language proficiency", as only 10.1% stated that they did not know any foreign languages or knew a little, whereas approximately 90% of the student sample stated that they knew foreign languages well, very well and excellently.

---

2 Since permission was given by the principals for their school to participate in the survey, the teachers' consent was obtained to coordinate the completion of the questionnaire by students in their school's computer labs and parents consented to their children's participation.

14.3.2. *Empirical methodology*

A seemingly unrelated regression (SUR) model, proposed by Zellner (1962), is estimated. This consists of several regression equations, each having its own dependent variable and potentially different sets of exogenous explanatory variables. While each equation is a valid linear regression on its own and can be estimated separately using standard ordinary least squares (OLS) to obtain consistent estimates, it is necessary to estimate the system of linear equations simultaneously because of the assumed correlation of the error terms across the equations. The SUR method provides efficient estimates via feasible generalized least squares (FGLS) with a specific form of the variance–covariance matrix.[3] The model consists of m linear regression equations for N individuals. The jth equation for individual i is given as:

$$y_{ij} = x_{ij}^{'}\beta_j + u_{ij} \qquad [14.1]$$

With all observations stacked, the model can be rewritten as:

$$y_j = X_j\beta_j + u_j, j = 1, \ldots, m \qquad [14.2]$$

where y_j and u_j are $N{\times}1$ vectors, X_j is an $N{\times}k$ matrix and β_j is a $k{\times}1$ vector. If we stack the m equations on top of each other, the system takes the following form:

$$\begin{pmatrix} y_1 \\ y_2 \\ \vdots \\ y_m \end{pmatrix} = \begin{pmatrix} X_1 & 0 & \ldots 0 \\ 0 & X_2 & \ldots 0 \\ \vdots & \vdots & \ddots \vdots \\ 0 & 0 & \ldots X_m \end{pmatrix} \begin{pmatrix} \beta_1 \\ \beta_2 \\ \vdots \\ \beta_m \end{pmatrix} + \begin{pmatrix} u_1 \\ u_2 \\ \vdots \\ u_m \end{pmatrix} \qquad [14.3]$$

and the compact representation is as follows:

$$\boldsymbol{y} = \boldsymbol{X\beta} + \boldsymbol{u} \qquad [14.4]$$

The model assumes that the error terms u_{ij} have zero mean and are independent across observations and homoscedastic but may have cross-equation correlations within observations. Therefore, we assume that $E(u_{ij}u_{ij'}|\boldsymbol{X}) = 0$ when $j \neq j'$, whereas $E(u_{ij}u_{ij'}|\boldsymbol{X}) = \sigma_{jj'}$.

3 Two important cases in which SUR is in fact equivalent to OLS are when the error terms are in fact uncorrelated between the equations (so that they are truly unrelated) and when each equation contains exactly the same set of regressors on the right-hand side.

We estimate equation [14.2] for 247 individuals, where y_j refers to the four subscales of the EDIS, namely, (i) the use of ICT on attitude toward history (F1AVER), (ii) the study strategies of the history course (F2AVER), (iii) the broad attitude toward the subject of history (F3AVER) and (iv) the use of a historical map (F4AVER). X_j refers to the educational and socioeconomic factors that affect each of the aforementioned subscales. Notably, we drop the factors that do not significantly affect each subscale individually, reaching an SUR model where each equation does not contain exactly the same regressors.

14.4. Results

Table C.2 reports the effects of educational and socioeconomic variables on each factor of the EDIS scale.[4]

The findings reveal that the F1 factor reflecting ICT is positively affected by the usage of computers and the last grade characterization following the classification of the Ministry of Education. This set of results ties with the related literature (Levin and Wadmany 2006; Izadpanah and Alavi 2016) and common sense because the usage of technological advances (namely, ICT in our case) requires the ability to use computers (named PC usage). In addition, whether a student graduated with a high grade in the previous class was linked to the student's ability to use computers. These findings imply that students' achievements are positively associated with access to computers (Anil and Ozer 2012). On the other hand, some factors affect ICT negatively. We find evidence of an adverse relationship between the school classification and the number of students' siblings, as well as the required class repetition with ICT as a component of the EDIS scale. The school classification (secondary, general and vocational high school) seems to negatively affect the ICT factor, probably because (i) the maturity of students differs between secondary and high schools and (ii) school students with low grades in the first class of general high school tend to continue their education in vocational high school. Specifically, according to the Annual Report of Students' Assessment in Primary and Secondary Education (Matsaggouras 2019) for the 2017–2018 academic year, 61.8% of the students who left the first class of general high school moved to the second class of the vocational high school according to the figures for the subject of Modern Greek. The negative effect of the number of siblings on the ICT factor can be explained by the fact that the more children there are in the family, the less time is available for each child when parental help is needed (Li and Guo 2023). Moreover, students who have to repeat a class due to poor academic performance appear to have a less positive relationship with ICT (Hu et al. 2018).

4 The findings are qualitatively the same when the weighted averages of the items that contribute to each factor of the EDIS scale are used. The results are reported in Table C.3 in Appendix C, section 14.6.3.

	(1)	(2)	(3)	(4)
Variables	F1AVER	F2AVER	F3AVER	F4AVER
School type	–0.162**			
	(0.0718)			
Class of attendance			0.127***	
			(0.0272)	
Last grade classification	0.201**	0.317***	0.393***	0.132**
	(0.0831)	(0.0834)	(0.0766)	(0.0670)
Educational orientation		0.171***		–0.0976**
		(0.0548)		(0.0478)
History orientation			0.240***	
			(0.0678)	
Class repetition	–0.581**	–0.416*		–0.944***
	(0.275)	(0.243)		(0.245)
PC usage level	0.219**	–0.130*		0.166**
	(0.0956)	(0.0757)		(0.0804)
Language skills level		0.267**		
		(0.109)		
Gender		0.449***		
		(0.107)		
Mother tongue (Greek)				–0.819**
				(0.337)
Number of siblings	-0.152*		0.124*	
	(0.0859)		(0.0665)	
Father's educational level		0.0905**	0.127***	0.111***
		(0.0372)	(0.0391)	(0.0405)
Mother's educational level			–0.121***	
			(0.0440)	
Father's work conditions			–0.275***	
			(0.0765)	
Mother's work conditions			0.105**	
			(0.0429)	
Constant	3.223***	1.353***	1.643***	1.571***
	(0.512)	(0.350)	(0.465)	(0.428)
Observations	246	246	246	246
R-squared	0.095	0.351	0.280	0.131
Breusch–Pagan test of independence	chi-square-stat = 79.861		*p* value = 0.0000	

Table 14.2. *Effects on EDIS factors – averages. F1AVER,...F4AVER reflect the averages of the components of factors 1,...4 (Mavrogianni et al. 2021). The Breusch–Pagan test of independence shows that the four equations (columns (1)-(4)) are correlated with each other (high values of the chi-square statistic and small p values), implying that the equations should be estimated as a system and not individually. Robust standard errors in parentheses: ***p < 0.01, **p < 0.05, *p < 0.1*

With respect to the F2 factor, which refers to studying strategies of history, the findings reveal that the educational orientation that students have already chosen (regarding the second and third general high school classes), the foreign language level, the last grade characterization, the father's educational level and the gender have a positive and statistically significant effect on the way that students study history. However, PC usage and the required class repetition seem to have a negative and statistically significant effect.

The effective use of history studying strategies is linked with the personal interest that students might have because of the educational orientation they have already chosen. Additionally, history, specifically law and humanities studies (educational orientation), is one of the main subjects for students looking to enter university. Moreover, the level of language skills (foreign language level) and performance in the previous class (last grade characterization) are indicators of a student's ability to study in general and efficiently use studying strategies. In addition, the father's level of education contributes positively to the student's learning strategies, as he may share his way of studying with them. It seems, in fact, that girls more often than boys, following the example of the father, apply study strategies.[5] The findings show that the more students use electronic devices (PC usage), the less they prefer to study using traditional strategies, such as books. Finally, the requirement for students to repeat a class due to academic deficiency may be related to their inability to utilize effective study strategies.

With respect to the F3 factor, which refers to the general attitude toward history, the elements of the class of attendance, the last grade classification, the possibility of choosing history (history orientation) as a main subject (regarding students who attend gymnasium and the first general high school class), the father's educational level, the mother's working conditions and the number of siblings positively affect the individual's general attitude toward history. Moreover, the father's working conditions and the mother's educational level have a negative impact on the F3 factor. The class of attendance is expected to be associated with an individual's maturity and cognitive development. The cognitive system rapidly develops during adolescence, acquiring the capacity for abstract and critical thinking (Eysenck and Brysbaert 2018; Schacter et al. 2020). Consequently, students in higher grades tend to demonstrate superior comprehension of contemporary conditions and everyday life. The latter does not mean that students are in favor of memorizing history texts but are willing to associate historical events with current developments that occur in the political and socioeconomical scene. This attitude is highly supported by the student's performance in the previous class (as captured by the last grade characterization), highlighting the fact that high performance is strongly linked with

5 The magnitude of the effect on boys is 0.449 compared to 1.353 on girls (Table C.2, column (2)).

the improvement of critical thinking. The positive attitude toward history is further justified by the personal interest that students might have because of their educational orientation (Dao 2024).

Moreover, our results reveal that the student's general attitude toward history is positively associated with the father's educational level but negatively associated with the father's working conditions.[6] However, it is observed that the effect of the mother's educational level and working condition is negative and positive, respectively, on the student's broad attitude toward history. The latter is contingent upon the extent to which maternal employment is aligned with the parenting style that is employed (Beyer 1995). Although parental work commitments can influence the quantity and quality of time spent on educational activities with children (Milkie et al. 2004), well-educated parents are more involved in their children's education as compared to less educated parents. Parental involvement in educational activities and encouraging the development of critical thinking skills lead to greater cognitive and analytical abilities in children (Xiong et al. 2021), implying that children become more independent of their parents' guidance. Instead of parents directly imparting their own attitude toward history, they may foster an environment where children are encouraged to form their own opinions. Indirect parental involvement, in the form of the provision of resources and learning opportunities, can be highly effective (Epstein 2001).

Some studies have demonstrated that parents' educational attainment is associated with the provision of a more stimulating home environment (physical, cognitive and emotional), as well as more accurate perceptions about their children's academic abilities (Davis-Kean 2005). These proximal processes are presumed to influence the developing child's achievement-related aspirations and subsequent achievement behavior.

On the basis of the results of our research, the number of siblings seemed to have a positive and significant effect on the student's attitude toward history. It is possible that peer influence and social networks are significant determinants of a child's educational attitude and performance (Carbonaro 2005). Children of more educated parents often have access to a wider variety of information sources, such as books, educational programs, the Internet and extracurricular activities. This diversity can dilute the direct influence any single source, including the mother's influence, has on the child's attitude. Furthermore, access to diverse educational resources significantly impacts a child's learning experiences and outcomes (Jeynes 2012).

6 However, Schildberg-Hoerisch (2011) provides evidence that parental employment does not substantially affect children's attitude toward school.

For factor F4, which reflects the use of the map as a learning tool, several variables influence its effectiveness. The factors of computer literacy, the classification of the last class grade and the educational level of the father have a positive effect, whereas educational orientation, the repetition of classes and the mother tongue, which indicate whether the individual is Greek or foreign, have a negative effect on the use of the map.

Computer literacy significantly influences the effective use of maps as educational tools. According to Lei (2009), students proficient in computer use are more likely to engage with digital learning resources, including interactive maps, thereby enhancing their learning experience (Taylor and Plewe 2006). The last grade characterization, reflecting previous academic performance, also positively correlates with effective map usage. High-performing students tend to adopt diverse learning strategies, including the use of maps, to maintain their academic achievements, as indicated by Zohar and Dori (2003), who reported that successful learners often use a variety of cognitive tools to sustain their performance.

The father's educational level plays a crucial role in the effective use of learning instruments. Higher parental education levels provide students with better academic support and access to educational resources, which can enhance their learning outcomes (Dubow et al. 2009). Conversely, certain factors negatively impact map usage. Educational orientation, such as a focus on vocational versus academic tracks, can influence the use of different learning tools. Compared with their peers in academic tracks, students in vocational tracks may have fewer opportunities to use tools such as maps (Alivernini and Lucidi 2011). Additionally, class repetition often reflects previous academic challenges, which can include difficulties in effectively utilizing educational tools. Jimerson et al. (2002) found that students who repeat classes often struggle with learning strategies, including the use of maps.

It seems that native Greek speakers are not confident in digital teaching and learning technologies related to the subject of history due to the school's curriculum construction. Instead, non-native Greek students, who might have the experience of another curriculum oriented with digital education tools, are more confident in using them effectively. Greek students tend to adopt a textbook focus during their learning pathway, aiming for higher grades in their assessment rather than accessing additional material. This practice contributes to students becoming mere listeners of the information taught in the textbook instead of deepening their knowledge with additional supplementary material such as maps (Bikos 2018), serving the purpose of preparing students for national examinations that are primarily based on the content of the book but not for the PISA international assessment (Anagnostopoulou et al. 2010, 2013). While students' computer literacy, previous academic performance, and parental education level positively influence their map usage, factors such as educational orientation, class repetition and language barriers can impede the effective use of this learning instrument.

14.5. Summary and conclusions

This study examines four subscales of the EDIS scale, namely, (i) the use of ICT on attitude toward history, (ii) strategies for studying a history course, (iii) broad attitude toward the subject of history and (iv) the use of a historical map in correlation with a variety of educational and socioeconomic variables. More specifically, we investigate the impact of the following educational variables: educational orientation, computer literacy, foreign language level, class repetition, last grade classification, type of school, class of attendance and history orientation. Additionally, we explore the effects of the following socioeconomic variables: gender, parents' educational level, parents' working conditions, number of siblings and students' nationality captured by the mother tongue.

Educational orientation positively affects the study strategies of a history course and negatively affects the use of a historical map. Computer literacy has a positive effect on the use of ICT on attitude toward history and on the use of historical maps, whereas it has a negative effect on study strategies. The foreign language level affects only the study strategies (positively), whereas class repetition has a negative effect on the use of ICT on attitude toward history, study strategies and the use of historical maps. Furthermore, the last grade classification positively affects all four EDIS subscales. School type has a negative impact on the use of ICT on attitude toward history, whereas class attendance and history orientation positively affect the broad attitude toward the subject of history.

Moreover, gender does not seem to have differentiation in signs in the study strategies, although females seem to be more flexible in using a variety of study strategies for the history course than males. The father's educational level positively affects almost all EDIS subscales apart from the use of ICT on attitude toward history. An examination of data derived from multiple extensive developmental studies conducted by Brooks-Gunn and Duncan (1997) revealed a statistically significant correlation between maternal education and children's intellectual achievements. However, in our study, the mother's educational level negatively affected the student's broad attitude toward history. The latter is affected negatively by the father's working conditions and positively by the mother's working conditions and the number of siblings in the family.

Finally, students' nationality (Greek or foreign) negatively affects the use of historical maps. One can posit that the limited map use among students is attributable to the fact that students typically engage with historical material in a superficial manner without undertaking a rigorous examination of the cartographic information at hand. This phenomenon can be attributed, at least in part, to the fact that the Greek educational system does not provide students with sufficient guidance regarding the utility of employing cartographical tools.

Our findings can be utilized in a multitude of ways. It can be employed for the evaluation of the teaching of the subject in general or for the recording of the learning progress of each student in particular. The above may serve to highlight aspects of teaching that require improvement, with a view to modification in the future. Alternatively, it may identify techniques that have yielded positive learning outcomes, with a view to adoption and extension. Individualized assessment enables the identification of potential learning difficulties and shortcomings in students, thereby facilitating the provision of targeted teaching support and overcoming learning difficulties. It can be concluded that the more interested students are in a subject, the more engaged they are and the greater their effort. This ultimately leads to higher performance (Harackiewicz et al. 2008; Tella et al. 2009; Lee et al. 2014).

The results of our research are considered very important, as they can contribute to the targeted use of the EDIS scale. In particular, the EDIS scale can be used as a self-referential tool for assessing students' personal interest and attitude toward the subject of history and the methods and strategies students use for its study. Furthermore, our findings can be employed for diagnostic assessment by teachers so that effective interventions and learning activities can be designed. At the level of the curriculum, decisions regarding restructuring the history course could be made based on factors affecting students' attitude. In light of the current redefinition of historical education objectives and pedagogies, this is an important consideration.

14.6. Appendices

14.6.1. Appendix A: the initial full questionnaire for the attitude survey toward history (EDIS)

Student code: ....Age: .... Class in school: ....Date: ....

Instructions

The following statements indicate what students do or feel when they are taught or when they study history. Five numbers follow each statement (1, 2, 3, 4, 5), and each number means the following:

☐ 1 means "I never or rarely do this".

☐ 2 means "I do this only occasionally".

☐ 3 means "Sometimes I do this" (approximately half the time).

☐ 4 means "I often do this".

☐ 5 means "I always or almost always do this".

After each sentence is read, circle the number (1, 2, 3, 4 or 5) that applies to you using the scale given. There are no right or wrong answers to the statements of this scale.

Item	Statement	Scale				
Q01	I attend the history lesson at school with interest.	1	2	3	4	5
Q02	I take notes during the lesson to help me understand what I hear from the teacher.	1	2	3	4	5
Q03	During the lesson, I associate what the teacher mentions with the textbook map.	1	2	3	4	5
Q04	When I study at home, I use a map to understand historical events better.	1	2	3	4	5
Q05	I like to read history in extracurricular books in my free time.	1	2	3	4	5
Q06	I believe that history contributes to the development of critical skills.	1	2	3	4	5
Q07	I learn more easily when I watch historical documentaries.	1	2	3	4	5
Q08	I believe that history is essential for students regardless of their further studies field.	1	2	3	4	5
Q09	In case I lose my train of thought, I go back to that point and reread.	1	2	3	4	5
Q10	I underline or circle information in the text and list it to help me remember it.	1	2	3	4	5
Q11	When I have difficulty, I study the material at a slower pace to help me understand it.	1	2	3	4	5
Q12	I study explanatory texts (e.g. historical terms) to better understand what I'm reading.	1	2	3	4	5
Q13	I understand the lesson better when the teacher uses a historical map to explain some points.	1	2	3	4	5
Q14	During my study, I use relevant tables, statistics and pictures.	1	2	3	4	5
Q15	I like the history lesson more when new technologies are used.	1	2	3	4	5
Q16	When I have questions during the lesson, I express them to my teacher.	1	2	3	4	5
Q17	I attend the lesson more pleasantly when the teacher makes a dialog during the lesson.	1	2	3	4	5
Q18	I would like to learn to create digital applications using new technologies.	1	2	3	4	5
Q19	I think that using new technologies could make me study more for the history lesson.	1	2	3	4	5
Q20	When I do digital work on a topic, I learn more things than when just studying the same topic from the book.	1	2	3	4	5
Q21	I am more interested in the history lesson when the teacher uses new technologies.	1	2	3	4	5
Q22	I find the study of local history – as a part of the national culture – interesting.	1	2	3	4	5
Q23	In the context of globalized modern society, I regard the study of world history as essential.	1	2	3	4	5

14.6.2. Appendix B: the final questionnaire for the attitude survey toward history (EDIS)

Mavrogianni Aristea© 2021

Student code: ....Age: .... Class in school: ....Date: ....

Instructions

The following statements indicate what students do or feel when they are taught or when they study history. Five numbers follow each statement (1, 2, 3, 4, 5), and each number means the following:

- ☐ 1 means "I never or rarely do this".
- ☐ 2 means "I do this only occasionally".
- ☐ 3 means "Sometimes I do this" (approximately half the time).
- ☐ 4 means "I often do this".
- ☐ 5 means "I always or almost always do this".

After each sentence is read, circle the number (1, 2, 3, 4 or 5) that applies to you using the scale given. There are no right or wrong answers to the statements of this scale.

Type	Item	Statement	Scale				
4	Q03	During the lesson, I associate what the teacher mentions with the textbook map.	1	2	3	4	5
4	Q04	When I study at home, I use a map to understand historical events better.	1	2	3	4	5
3	Q06	I believe that history contributes to the development of critical skills.	1	2	3	4	5
3	Q08	I believe that history is essential for students regardless of their further studies field.	1	2	3	4	5
2	Q09	In case I lose my train of thought, I go back to that point and reread.	1	2	3	4	5
2	Q10	I underline or circle information in the text and list it to help me remember it.	1	2	3	4	5
2	Q11	When I have difficulty, I study the material at a slower pace to help me understand it.	1	2	3	4	5
1	Q15	I like the history lesson more when new technologies are used.	1	2	3	4	5
1	Q19	I think that using new technologies could make me study more for the history lesson.	1	2	3	4	5
1	Q21	I am more interested in the history lesson when the teacher uses new technologies.	1	2	3	4	5
3	Q23	In the context of globalized modern society, I regard the study of world history as essential.	1	2	3	4	5

14.6.3. *Appendix C*

	(1)	(2)	(3)	(4)
Variables	F1WAVER	F2WAVER	F3WAVER	F4WAVER
School type	–0.356**			
	(0.160)			
Class of attendance			0.277***	
			(0.0590)	
Last grade classification	0.476**	0.706***	0.848***	0.205**
	(0.188)	(0.175)	(0.166)	(0.102)
Educational orientation		0.382***		–0.156**
		(0.118)		(0.0727)
History orientation			0.531***	
			(0.146)	
Class repetition	–1.051*			–1.397***
	(0.583)			(0.391)
PC usage level	0.482**	–0.308*		0.252**
	(0.217)	(0.163)		(0.123)
Language skills level		0.627***		
		(0.231)		
Gender		0.994***		
		(0.233)		
Mother tongue (Greek)				–1.284**
				(0.514)
Number of siblings	–0.352*		0.278*	
	(0.195)		(0.143)	
Father's educational level		0.204**	0.278***	0.171***
		(0.0818)	(0.0856)	(0.0620)
Mother's educational level			–0.256***	
			(0.0971)	
Father's work conditions			–0.595***	
			(0.162)	
Mother's work conditions			0.225**	
			(0.0920)	
Constant	7.277***	2.743***	3.423***	2.413***
	(1.157)	(0.730)	(1.008)	(0.657)
Observations	246	246	246	246
R-squared	0.095	0.345	0.284	0.132
Breusch–Pagan test of independence	chi-square-stat = 79.752		*p* value = 0.0000	

Table 14.3. *Effects on EDIS factors – weighted averages. F1WAVER,…,F4WAVER correspond to weighted averages of the components of factors 1,…4 considering the specific loading factors for each component (Mavrogianni et al. 2021). The Breusch–Pagan test of independence shows that the four equations (columns (1)–(4)) are correlated with each other (high values of the chi-square statistic and small p values), implying that the equations should be estimated as a system and not individually. Robust standard errors in parentheses: ***p < 0.01, **p < 0.05, *p < 0.1*

14.7. References

Acharya, N. and Joshi, S. (2009). Influence of parents' education on achievement motivation of adolescents. *Indian Journal Social Science Researches*, 6(1), 72–79.

Addi-Raccah, A. (2019). Private tutoring in a high socio-economic secondary school in Israel and pupils' attitudes towards school learning: A double-edged sword phenomenon. *British Educational Research Journal*, 45(5), 938–960. doi: 10.1002/berj.3545.

Ahmed, U. and Maryam, S. (2016). Secondary school students' attitude towards the Social Science studies in Sargodha. *International Journal of Academic Research in Progressive Education and Development*, 5(2), 67–76. doi: 10.6007/IJARPED/v5-i2/2093.

Ainley, M., Hidi, S., Berndorff, D. (2002). Interest, learning, and the psychological processes that mediate their relationship. *Journal of Educational Psychology*, 94(3), 545–561. doi: 10.1037/0022-0663.94.3.545.

Alivernini, F. and Lucidi, F. (2011). Relationship between social context, self-efficacy, motivation, academic achievement, and intention to drop out of high school: A longitudinal study. *Journal of Educational Research*, 104(4), 241–252. doi: 10.1080/00220671003728062.

Amengor, A. and Fredrick, P. (2007). *The Attitude of Senior Secondary Students Towards the Study of History*. Grin Verlag Publishers, Munich.

Anagnostopoulou, K., Hatzinikita, V., Christidou, V. (2010). Assessed students' competencies in the Greek school framework and the PISA survey. *Review of Science, Mathematics and ICT Education*, 4(2), 43–61. doi: 10.26220/rev.138.

Anagnostopoulou, K., Hatzinikita, V., Christidou, V., Dimopoulos, K. (2013). PISA test items and school-based examinations in Greece: Exploring the relationship between global and local assessment discourses. *International Journal of Science Education*, 35(4), 636–662. doi: 10.1080/09500693.2011.604801.

Anderson, C.A. and Huesmann, L.R. (2007). Human aggression: A social-cognitive view. In *The Sage Handbook of Social Psychology*, Hogg, M.A. and Cooper, J. (eds). Sage Publications, Thousand Oaks, CA.

Anil, D. and Ozer, Y. (2012). The effect of the aim and frequency of computer usage on student achievement according to PISA 2006. *Procedia – Social and Behavioral Sciences*, 46, 5484–5488. doi: 10.1016/j.sbspro.2012.06.462.

Artino, Jr, A.R., La Rochelle, J.S., Dezee, K.J., Gehlbach, H. (2014). Developing questionnaires for educational research: AMEE Guide no. 87. *Medical Teacher*, 36(6), 463–474. doi: 10.3109/0142159X.2014.889814.

Augustine, J.M., Cavanagh, S.E., Crosnoe, R. (2009). Maternal education, early child care and the reproduction of advantage. *Social Forces; a Scientific Medium of Social Study and Interpretation*, 88(1), 1–29. doi: 10.1353/sof.0.0233.

Baker, D.P., Akiba, M., LeTendre, G.K., Wiseman, A.W. (2001). Worldwide shadow education: Outside-school learning, institutional quality of schooling, and cross-national mathematic achievement. *Educational Evaluation and Policy Analysis*, 23(1), 1–17. doi: 10.3102/01623737023001001.

Bandura, A. (1986). *Social Foundations of Thought and Action*. Englewood Cliffs, NJ.

Barton, K. and Levstik, L. (2004). *Teaching History for the Common Good*. Lawrence Erlbaum, Malhwah-London.

Beyer, S. (1995). Maternal employment and children's academic achievement: Parenting styles as mediating variable. *Developmental Review*, 15(2), 212–253. doi: 10.1006/drev.1995.1009.

Bikos, G. (2018). The educational outcomes of the relationship between schoolbooks and teachers. *International Journal of Innovation and Research in Educational Sciences*, 5(4), 2349–5219.

Boadu, G. (2015). Effective teaching in history: The perspectives of history student teachers. *International Journal of Humanities and Social Science*, 3(1), 38–51.

Boadu, G. (2016). Teachers' perception of the problems faced in the teaching of history in senior high school. *Journal of Arts and Humanities*, 5(7), 38–48. doi: 10.18533/journal.v5i7.967.

Bourdieu, P. and Passeron, J.C. (1977). *Reproduction in Education, Society and Culture*. Sage Publications, London.

Breen, R. and Goldthorpe, J.H. (1997). Explaining educational differentials: Towards a formal rational action theory. *Rationality and Society*, 9(3), 275–305. doi: 10.1177/104346397009003002.

Brooks-Gunn, J. and Duncan, G.J. (1997). The effects of poverty on children. *Future of Children*, 7, 55–71. doi: 10.2307/1602387.

Bulgren, J., Deshler, D.D., Lenz, B.K. (2007). Engaging adolescents with LD in higher order thinking about history concepts using integrated content enhancement routines. *Journal of Learning Disabilities*, 40, 121–133. doi: 10.1177/00222194070400020301.

Carbonaro, W.J. (2005). Tracking, students' effort, and academic achievement. *Sociology of Education*, 78(1), 27–49. doi: 10.1177/003804070507800102.

Carneiro, P., Meghir, C., Parey, M. (2013). Maternal education, home environments and the development of children and adolescents. *Journal of the European Economic Association*, 11(1), 123–160. doi: 10.1111/j.1542-4774.2012.01096.x.

Cercadillo, L. (2001). Significance in history: Students' ideas in England and Spain. In *Raising Standards in History Education*, Dickinson, A.K., Gordon, P., Lee, P.J. (eds). Woburn Press, Portland, OR.

Cobbold, C. and Oppong, A.C. (2010). Re-echoing the place of history in the curriculum. *International Journal of Educational Leadership*, 3(3), 89–96.

Cronbach, L.J. (1990). *Essentials of Psychological Testing*. Harper & Row, New York.

Dan, Y. and Todd, R. (2014). Examining the mediating effect of learning strategies on the relationship between students' history interest and achievement. *Educational Psychology*, 34(7), 799–817. doi: 10.1080/01443410.2013.792331.

Dao, T.T.N. (2024). The attitude towards the subject of history in general education in Vietnam through a survey from the student's perspective. *VNU Journal of Science. Education and Research*, 40(1). doi: 10.25073/2588-1159/vnuer.4884.

Davis-Kean, P.E. (2005). The influence of parent education and family income on child achievement: The indirect role of parental expectations and the home environment. *Journal of Family Psychology*, 19(2), 294–304. doi: 10.1037/0893-3200.19.2.294.

Dawson, W. (2010). Private tutoring and mass schooling in East Asia: Reflections of inequality in Japan, South Korea, and Cambodia. *Asia Pacific Education Review*, 11(1), 14–24. doi: 10.1007/s12564-009-9058-4.

Dearing, E., McCartney, K., Weiss, H.B., Kreider, H., Simpkins, S. (2004). The promotive effects of family educational involvement for low-income children's literacy. *Journal of School Psychology*, 42(6), 445–460. doi: 10.1016/j.jsp.2004.07.002.

Dubow, E.F., Boxer, P., Huesmann, L.R. (2009). Long-term effects of parents' education on children's educational and occupational success: Mediation by family interactions, child aggression, and teenage aspirations. *Merrill-Palmer Quarterly*, 55(3), 224–249.

Dwarko, D.A. (2007). History – The ailing subject: The need for revival in the 21st century. In *Challenges of Education in Ghana in the 21st Century*, Amenumey, D.E.K. (ed.). Woeli Publishing Services, Accra.

Eccles, J.S., Vida, M.N., Barber, B. (2004). The relation of early adolescents' college plans and both academic ability and task-value beliefs to subsequent college enrollment. *Journal of Early Adolescence*, 24(1), 63–77. doi: 10.1177/0272431603260919.

Epstein, J.L. (2001). *School, Family, and Community Partnerships: Preparing Educators and Improving Schools*. Westview Press, Boulder, CO.

Eysenck, M.W. and Brysbaert, M. (2018). Fundamentals of cognition. In *Psychology Press Book*, Vasilaki, E. and Lipourli, E. (eds). Psychology Press, Hove.

Faize, F. and Dahar, M. (2011). Effect of mother's level of education on secondary grade science students in Pakistan. *Research Journal of International Studies*, 19, 13–19.

Gottfried, A.E. and Gottfried, A.W. (1991). Parents' reward strategies and children's academic intrinsic motivation and school performance. *Biennial Meeting of the Society for Research in Child Development*, 18–20 April, Seattle, WA.

Hansen, M.N. and Strømme, T.B. (2021). Historical change in an elite profession – Class origins and grades among law graduates over 200 years. *British Journal of Sociology*, 72(3), 651–671. doi: 10.1111/1468-4446.12852.

Harackiewicz, J.M., Durik, A.M., Barron, K.E., Linnenbrink-Garcia, L., Tauer, J.M. (2008). The role of achievement goals in the development of interest: Reciprocal relations between achievement goals, interest, and performance. *Journal of Educational Psychology*, 100(1), 105–122. doi: 10.1037/0022-0663.100.1.105.

Hattie, J. (2008). *Visible Learning: A Synthesis of Over 800 Meta-Analyses Relating to Achievement*. Routledge, London.

Henz, U. and Maas, I. (1995). Chancengleichheit durch die Bildungsexpansion? *Kölner Zeitschrift für Soziologie und Sozialpsychologie*, 47, 605–633.

Hidi, S. and Renninger, K.A. (2006). The four-phase model of interest development. *Educational Psychologist*, 41, 111–127. doi: 10.1207/s15326985ep4102_4.

Hill, N.E. and Tyson, D.F. (2009). Parental involvement in middle school: A meta-analytic assessment of the strategies that promote achievement. *Developmental Psychology*, 45(3), 740–763. doi: 10.1037/a0015362.

Hoffmann, M.M. and Ramirez, A.Y. (2018). Students' attitudes toward teacher use of technology in classrooms. *Multicultural Education*, 25(2), 51–56.

Hu, X., Gong, Y., Lai, C., Leung, F.K.S. (2018). The relationship between ICT and student literacy in mathematics, reading, and science across 44 countries: A multilevel analysis. *Computers and Education*, 125, 1–13. doi: 10.1016/j.compedu.2018.05.021.

Islam, M.N. and Chakrabarty, S. (2020). A study of the relationship between familial factors and academic motivation and achievement in high school students. *Psychological Studies*, 65, 87–96. doi: 10.1007/s12646-019-00500-7.

Issar, K. (2021). Students' attitude towards studying history and teaching practices. *Education Quarterly Reviews*, 4(3) [Online]. Available at: https://ssrn.com/abstract=3879925.

Izadpanah, S. and Alavi, M. (2016). The perception of EFL high school students in using of computer technology in the process of learning: Merits and demerits. *Advances in Language and Literary Studies*, 7(3), 146–156.

Janssen, N. and Lazonder, A.W. (2015). Implementing innovative technologies through lesson plans: What kind of support do teachers prefer? *Journal of Science Education and Technology*, 24, 910–920. doi: 10.1007/s10956-015-9573-5.

Jeynes, W. (2012). A meta-analysis of the efficacy of different types of parental involvement programs for urban students. *Urban Education*, 47(4), 706–742. doi: 10.1177/00420859 12445643.

Jimerson, S.R., Anderson, G.E., Whipple, A.D. (2002). Winning the battle and losing the war: Examining the relation between grade retention and dropping out of high school. *Psychology in the Schools*, 39(4), 441–457. doi: 10.1002/pits.10046.

Krapp, A., Hidi, S., Renninger, K.A. (1992). Interest, learning, and development. In *The Role of Interest in Learning and Development*, Renninger, K.A., Hidi, S., Krapp, A. (eds). Lawrence Erlbaum Associates, Hillsade, NJ.

La Placa, V. and Corlyon, J. (2016). Unpacking the relationship between parenting and poverty: Theory, evidence and policy. *Social Policy and Society*, 15(1), 11–28. doi: 10.1017/S1474746415000111.

Lareau, A. (2011). *Unequal Childhoods. Class, Race and Family Life. With an Update a Decade Later*, 2nd edition. University of California Press, Berkeley, CA.

Lareau, A. and Weininger, E.B. (2008). Class and the transition to adulthood. In *Social Class: How Does It Work?*, Lareau, A. and Conley, D. (eds). Russell Sage Foundation, New York.

Lee, P. and Ashby, R. (2000). Progression in historical understanding ages 7–14. In *Knowing, Teaching, and Learning History: National and International Perspectives*, Stearns, P., Seixas, P., Wineburg, S. (eds). New York University Press, New York.

Lee, J.S. and Bowen, N.K. (2006). Parent involvement, cultural capital, and the achievement gap among elementary school children. *American Educational Research Journal*, 43(2), 193–218. doi: 10.3102/00028312043002193.

Lee, P. and Shemilt, D. (2004). "I just wish we could go back in the past and find out what really happened": Progression in understanding about historical accounts. *Teaching History*, 117, 25–31.

Lee, C.D. and Spratley, A. (2010). *Reading in the Disciplines: The Challenges of Adolescent Literacy*. Carnegie Corporation of New York, New York.

Lee, P., Dickinson, A., Ashby, R. (2001). Children's ideas about historical explanation. In *Raising Standards in History Education*, Dickinson, A., Gordon, P., Lee, P. (eds). Woburn Press, London.

Lee, W., Lee, M.J., Bong, M. (2014). Testing interest and self-efficacy as predictors of academic self-regulation and achievement. *Contemporary Educational Psychology*, 39(2), 86–99. doi: 10.1016/j.cedpsych.2014.02.002.

Lei, J. (2009). Digital natives as preservice teachers: What technology preparation is needed? *Journal of Computing in Teacher Education*, 25(3), 87–97.

Levin, T. and Wadmany, R. (2006). Teachers' beliefs and practices in technology-based classrooms: A developmental view. *Journal of Research on Technology in Education*, 39, 157–182. doi: 10.1080/15391523.2006.10782478.

Levstik, L.S. (2011). Learning history. In *Handbook of Research on Learning and Instruction*, Mayer, R.E. and Alexander, P.A. (eds). Taylor & Francis, New York.

Li, D. and Guo, X. (2023). The effect of the time parents spend with children on children's well-being. *Frontiers in Psychology*, 14, 1096128. doi: 10.3389/fpsyg.2023.1096128.

Lo, J.J., Chang, C.J., Tu, H.H., Yeh, S.W. (2009). Applying GIS to develop a web-based spatial-person-temporal history educational system. *Computers and Education*, 53(1), 155–168. doi: 10.1016/j.compedu.2009.01.016.

Magnuson, K. (2007). Maternal education and children's academic achievement during middle childhood. *Developmental Psychology*, 43(6), 1497–1512. doi: 10.1037/0012-1649.43.6.1497.

Matsaggouras, I. (2019). Annual report of students' assessment in primary and secondary education. Greek Authority of Quality Assurance in Primary and Secondary Education.

Mavrogianni, A. (2021). Construction and psychometric testing of a scale to investigate students' attitude towards history. *Preschool and Primary Education*, 9(2) (in Greek). doi: 10.12681/ppej.25991.

Milkie, M.A., Mattingly, M.J., Nomaguchi, K.M., Bianchi, S.M., Robinson, J.P. (2004). The time squeeze: Parental statuses and feelings about time with children. *Journal of Marriage and Family*, 66(3), 739–761. doi: 10.1111/j.0022-2445.2004.00050.x.

Mulholland, R. (2006). A technology snapshot: Teacher preparation program and the local public schools. *Contemporary Issues in Technology and Teacher Education*, 6, 284–292.

Mustafina, A. (2016). Teachers' attitudes towards technology integration in a Kazakhstani secondary school. *International Journal of Research in Education and Science*, 2(2), 322–332. doi: 10.21890/ijres.67928.

Nyamwembe, E.O., Ondigi, S., Kiio, M. (2013). Attitudes of students toward studying history and government in some selected secondary schools in Mosocho division, Kisii County, Kenya. *Journal of Education and Practice*, 4, 17–26.

Obeidat, H.H., Abdelrahman, M.S.B., Ateyat, K., AL-Arood, M. (2011). The effect of students' reluctance of studying history on their level of historical culture. *Asian Social Science*, 7(2), 119–129. doi: 10.5539/ass.v7n2p119.

Osman, N. and Hamzah, M.I. (2020). Impact of implementing blended learning on students' interest and motivation. *Universal Journal of Educational Research*, 8(4), 1483–1490. doi: 10.13189/ujer.2020.080442.

Park, H., Buchmann, C., Choi, J., Merry, J.J. (2016). Learning beyond the school walls: Trends and implications. *Annual Review of Sociology*, 42, 231–252. doi: 10.1146/annurev-soc-081715-074341.

Paulus, W. and Blossfeld, H.P. (2007). Schichtspezifische Präferenzen oder sozioökonomisches Entscheidungskalkül? *Zeitschrift für Pädagogik*, 53, 491–508.

Reay, D., David, M.E., Ball, S. (2005). *Degrees of Choice: Social Class, Race and Gender in Higher Education*. Trentham Book Company, Sterling, VA.

Renninger, K.A., Hoffman, L., Krapp, A. (1998). Interest and gender: Issues of development and learning. In *Interest and Learning: Proceedings of the Seeon Conference on Interest and Gender*, Hoffmann, L., Krapp, A., Renninger, K.A., Baumert, J. (eds). IPN, Kiel.

Schacter, D., Daniel Gilbert, D., Wegner, D., Nock, M. (2020). *Introduction to Psychology*. Gutenberg, San Francisco, CA.

Schiefele, U. (2009). Situational and individual interest. In *Handbook of Motivation in School*, Wentzel, K.R. and Wigfield, A. (eds). Taylor & Francis, New York.

Schildberg-Hoerisch, H. (2011). Does parental employment affect children's educational attainment? *Economics of Education Review*, 30(6), 1456–1467. doi: 10.1016/j.econedurev.2011.07.013.

Schraw, G. and Lehman, S. (2001). Situational interest: A review of the literature and directions for future research. *Educational Psychology Review*, 13(1), 23–52. doi: 10.1023/A:1009004801455.

Seginer, R. (2006) Parents' educational involvement: A developmental ecology perspective. *Parenting*, 6(1), 1–48. doi: 10.1207/s15327922par0601_1.

Snow, C.E., Porche, M.V., Tabors, P.O., Harris, S.R. (2007). *Is Literacy Enough? Pathways to Academic Success for Adolescents*. Paul H. Brookes Publishing, Baltimore, MD.

Stalikas, A., Triliva, S., Roussi, P. (2012). *The Psychometric Tools in Greece*. Pedio Publications, Athens (in Greek).

Taylor, W. and Plewe, B. (2006). The effectiveness of interactive maps in secondary historical geography education. *Cartographic Perspectives*, 55, 16–33. doi: 10.14714/CP55.325.

Tella, A., Tella, A., Adeniyi, O. (2009). Locus of control, interest in schooling, self-efficacy and academic achievement. *Cypriot Journal of Educational Sciences*, 4(3), 168–182.

Tong, Y., Li, J.X., Shu, B. (2021). Is children's academic performance valuable to parents? Linking children's effort vs. results and fathers' vs. mothers' subjective well-being. *Child Indicators Research*, 14, 583–605. doi: 10.1007/s12187-020-09763-3.

VanSledright, B.A. (2004). What does it mean to think historically and how do you teach it? *Social Education*, 68, 230–233.

Wang, W., Dong, Y., Liu, X., Bai, Y., Zhang, L. (2020). The effect of parents' education on the academic and non-cognitive outcomes of their children: Evidence from China. *Children and Youth Services Review*, 117, 105307. doi: 10.1016/j.childyouth.2020.105307.

Wineburg, S. (2001). *Historical Thinking and Other Unnatural Acts. Charting the Future of Teaching the Past*. Temple University Press, Philadelphia, PA.

Wölfel, O. and Heineck, G. (2012). Parental risk attitudes and children's secondary school track choice. *Economics of Education Review*, 31(5), 727–743. doi: 10.1016/j.econedurev.2012.05.004.

Xiong, Y., Qin, X., Wang, Q., Ren, P. (2021). Parental involvement in adolescents' learning and academic achievement: Cross-lagged effect and mediation of academic engagement. *Journal of Youth and Adolescence*, 50(9), 1811–1823. doi: 10.1007/s10964-021-01460-w.

Yilmaz, K. (2008). A vision of history teaching and learning: Thoughts on history education in secondary schools. *High School Journal*, 92, 37–46. doi: 10.1353/hsj.0.0017.

Zellner, A. (1962). An efficient method of estimating seemingly unrelated regressions and tests for aggregation bias. *Journal of the American Statistical Association*, 57(298), 348–368. doi: 10.1080/01621459.1962.10480664.

Zohar, A. and Dori, Y.J. (2003). Higher order thinking skills and low-achieving students: Are they mutually exclusive? *Journal of the Learning Sciences*, 12(2), 145–181. doi: 10.1207/S15327809JLS1202_1.

Zusho, A., Pintrich, P.R., Cortina, K.S. (2005). Motives, goals, and adaptive patterns of performance in Asian American and Anglo American students. *Learning and Individual Differences*, 15(2), 141–158. doi: 10.1016/j.lindif.2004.11.003.

15

Methodological Procedures for Assessing the Quality of Death Certificates Due to Unknown Causes

Quality is a recurring problem when using death statistics from the civil or health registry information systems of a country or region, particularly with regard to causes of death. This problem is usually more acute in less developed regions. When the causes of death are unknown or not declared on death certificates, this can seriously restrict evaluations and analyses for population health planning purposes. The aim of this study was to outline a methodological approach to assessing the quality of declarations of causes of death applicable to any region. Mortality from unknown causes results from the combination of two factors: unregistered deaths (underregistration), whose causes of death are not known, and registered deaths, but those whose underlying causes are poorly defined and/or classified as garbage codes (GCs). A mathematical model is shown on how the percentage of unknown causes of death can be measured through these factors (underreporting, ill-defined and GCs). Various procedures available in the literature to estimate or measure each of these factors are presented. The proposed model can be applied to any group or cause of death, region, sex or age group. An illustrative example is provided for a region with high COVID-19 mortality in Brazil.

15.1. Introduction

Vital statistics are essential for establishing goals and evaluating health intervention plans for different segments of the population through the construction of extremely useful indicators, such as demographic estimates. However, to produce reliable indicators, the data must be of high quality or, even in the presence of errors,

---

Chapter written by Neir Antunes PAES.

be able to detect and correct them. When these statistics are used, many of the problems faced by demographers, public sector managers and health researchers are devoted to analyzing their quality, even in countries and regions known for their high quality. This concern is exacerbated in those with more compromised levels of socioeconomic development.

Bearing in mind that the available mortality information systems can generate uncertainties and questions regarding the quality and reliability of death records, with vital statistics being the raw material for important indicators in demography and health in general, two main types of errors are noted: coverage and completeness of statements.

Even though in recent decades, the quality of information in many countries, specifically related to death coverage, has significantly advanced, large regional variations persist. There are problems with the systematization of approaches to record coverage and the lack of studies related to specific aspects of population groups or territories – mainly small areas – which are still extremely limited (Hill 2000).

The problems of incomplete coverage and completeness of information in death certificates can also be found in birth certificates. However, these do not present the additional problem inherent to deaths: the causes of death.

High-quality data on causes of death are a source of evidence for implementing certain policies and decision-making to improve population health. A major problem with the use of these data is the practices applicable to the certification of these causes, which results in codes that provide little or no information about the true underlying cause of death.

With respect to the declaration and accuracy of death records, major challenges are still encountered, such as high levels of ill-defined causes (IDCs) and GCs in mortality statistics, with great variability between countries and regions (Paes 2007, 2018; Naghavi et al. 2010; United Nations 2014).

Therefore, when investigating the quality of death records, three steps must be considered, as illustrated in Figure 15.1.

Given this context and the need to elucidate the types of problems found in death records originating from information systems in many countries and regions, the aim of this study was to present a systematized methodology for evaluating the quality of death records, focusing on coverage and completeness, which can be applied to any geographic and temporal segment.

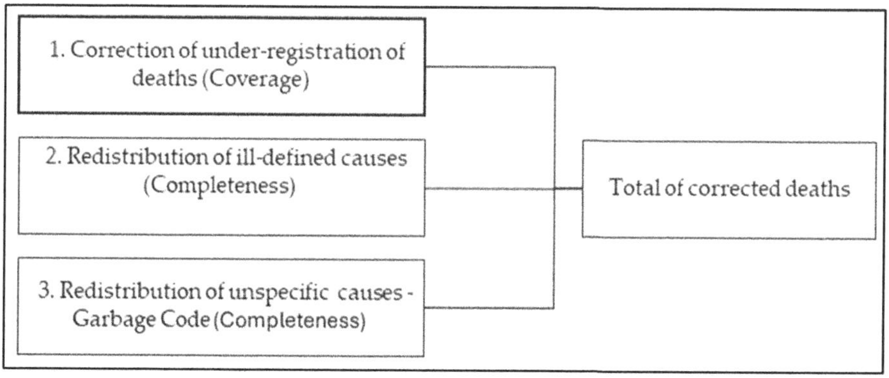

Figure 15.1. *Steps for correction of deaths*

15.2. Methods

When seeking to evaluate the quality of death records, the first step concerns the identification of the National Mortality Information System or Civil Registration System, usually responsible for the production and dissemination of death statistics for the country or region of interest.

In the database of these systems, variables can be found that allow us, based on the cause of death certified by the doctor, to construct indicators and carry out epidemiological analyses that contribute to the efficiency of health management.

Clearly, the way forward for improving the knowledge of the levels and trends of mortality risks in populations is to proceed with direct evaluation studies at the national and subnational levels that can directly quantify the completeness of death registration (Murray et al. 2010).

According to Paes (2018), to investigate the quality of deaths, considering both the completeness of records and the causes of death, three steps must be considered: (1) correction of underregistration of deaths; (2) redistribution of deaths due to non-specific causes (GCs); and (3) redistribution of deaths due to IDCs, which will make it possible to measure the magnitude of the total corrected deaths.

Mortality due to "unknown causes" is the result of a combination of two factors: unregistered deaths, whose causes of death are therefore unknown (underregistration), and registered deaths, whose underlying causes are poorly defined (including GC) and are also unknown (Paes 2018). By knowing this information, it is possible to determine the total number of deaths with unknown underlying causes, as described below:

The total expected number of deaths (D_{esp}) is given by the following expression:

$$D_{esp} = f * D_{obs} \qquad [15.1]$$

For a particular case of cause j, the calculation for the expected number of deaths from a group of underlying causes or unknown underlying causes is obtained using the following equation:

$$D^{j}_{esp} = f * D^{j}_{obs} + IDC_{j} + GC_{j} \qquad [15.2]$$

where:

– D^{j}_{esp} = total number of expected deaths from cause j;

– f = correction factor for underreporting of observed general deaths;

– D_{obs} = total number of observed deaths;

– D^{j}_{obs} = total number of observed deaths from the underlying cause j;

– IDC_{j} = ill-defined causes redistributed to the underlying cause j;

– CG_{j} = garbage code redistributed to the underlying cause j.

15.2.1. *First step: correction of underregistration of deaths (f)*

For studies at the national and subnational levels, child and adult deaths are often subject to different degrees of coverage. Therefore, it is necessary to identify methods that apply to the infant or child population and to adults. The reason for this is that underregistration is much greater at the earliest ages, resulting in lower coverage than at other ages.

There are various proposals available in the literature, both for early-aged patients and for adults (Brass 1975; Bennett and Horiuchi 1981; United Nations 1983; Preston et al. 2001; Hill et al. 2009).

The correction factor (f) can be obtained through the expression f = 1/C, where C is the death coverage.

15.2.1.1. *Coverage of infant deaths*

A method (Paes 2018) based on fertility rates can provide coverage, where coverage of deaths under one year of age (${}_1C_0$) can be estimated as:

$${}_1C_0 = \frac{Deaths_{obs}}{Deaths_{esp}} \cdot 100$$

The observed deaths ($Deaths_{obs}$) are taken from vital records or surveys. With knowledge of the total number of estimated live births (LB_{est}) and the infant mortality rate (*IMR*), it is possible to find the expected number of deaths ($Deaths_{esp}$). Thus,

$$Deaths_{esp} = LB_{est} \cdot IMR$$

where

$$LB_{est} = \sum_{x=15}^{49} {}_5SFR_x \cdot {}_5M_x$$

where:

- ${}_5SFR_x$ is the specific fertility rate in the five-year age group *x, x + 5*;
- ${}_5M_x$ is the total number of women in the 5-year age group *x, x + 5*.

The demographic practice of considering five-year age groups is fundamentally due to an attempt to reduce the errors that are made in age declarations, as well as the greater ease of interpretation of this indicator when presented in aggregate form.

The ${}_5SFR_x$ are usually obtained through indirect techniques referring to the study population or are taken from the fertility experience of another population assumed to be valid for the population of the study region. If the assumption does not seem appropriate, alternatively, a region can be considered in which there is evidence that its pattern is similar to that of the study area. To do this, it is always useful to check the pattern of the fertility curve in the reference area and compare it with that of the study area, using a measure of discrepancy to see how similar it is, such as the mean square error. As this is an indirect method, it is always important to be aware of the quality of the data of interest (births and population by age), as well as the fertility pattern of the reference source.

In the absence of complete and accurate prospective systems of data collection, the main methods of collection of child death information are based on questions in surveys and censuses about recent deaths in the household or on complete and summary birth histories (Mathers and Boerma 2010).

15.2.1.2. *Coverage of adult death records*

For many developing countries, the mainstay for adult mortality measurement remains civil registration systems.

Various methods have been proposed to measure the degree of coverage of adult deaths. However, these methods differ in their assumptions, requirements and degrees of precision. There is no mechanical way of using them to capture the sensitivity and types of errors present in the data. The principles and methodology for traditional methods can be found, for example, in the compilations made in Manual X, prepared by the United Nations (1983) (Vallin et al. 1985; Preston et al. 2001).

Death distribution methods are used to assess the completeness of reporting. They involve, in one form or another, comparisons of the number of deaths across age groups with population estimates. Unfortunately, all of these methods depend on assumptions (stable age structure of population, zero migration, no misreporting of ages in deaths or population) that are violated in practice and are known from direct experience to produce results that can be quite uncertain or unreliable (Murray et al. 2010).

In an attempt to summarize, the methods proposed can be allocated into three categories: (1) methods that require the assumption of population stability, such as the one proposed by Brass (1975); (2) methods that relax the assumption of population stability (Hill et al. 2009); and (3) methods that do not require population stability, such as that of Courbage and Fargues (1979).

Several other methods have been proposed, but most of them are considerably more complex than the original methods, involving extensive smoothing and using data from highly developed countries to fill gaps or requiring the estimation of several parameters, which are hardly applicable for countries whose vital statistics are deficient.

As an illustration of traditional methods for determining the underreporting of deaths (f) for adults, the Brass growth balance method (GBM) (Brass 1975) is presented. It is the first of what later became known as the death distribution methods for estimating the completeness of the reporting of deaths, relative to an estimate of the population. This method assumes that the population is stable (i.e. a population with an unchanging age structure over time – at least for the adult ages – growing at a constant rate, r, each year), closed to migration and has accurately reported data.

The first method, by allowing flexibility in its assumptions and requirements regarding basic data, underwent several adaptations and triggered, in turn, other methods, such as the well-known generalized growth balance (GGB) (Hill 2000). The basic equation is as follows:

$$\frac{N(a)}{N(a+)} = r + k \cdot \frac{D'(a+)}{N(a+)} \qquad [15.3]$$

where:

- $N(a)$ is the population at the exact age a;
- $N(a+)$ is the sum of people who are at the exact age up to any age limit w;
- $D'(a+)$ are deaths registered and affected by errors in age a e +;
- r is the stable population growth rate;
- k is the correction factor for deaths.

15.2.2. *Second step: redistribution of deaths due to ill-defined causes*

The group of IDCs is part of the GCs and refers to “symptoms, signs and abnormal findings of clinical and laboratory examinations, not classified elsewhere” (ICD-10) in Chapter XVIII (R00–R99) (ICD 2010). A major problem with IDCs is the lack of cause-of-death certification practices which result in codes that provide little or no information about the true underlying cause of death.

If the proportion of IDCs is high, this indicates that mortality from other causes is underestimated, which can seriously compromise evaluations and analyses of mortality by cause of death. In other words, it is likely that it will not be possible to draw reliable conclusions about the accuracy of the estimates.

An immediate solution to this problem would be the proportional redistribution of deaths by IDC in each of the chapters, with well-defined causes. However, this does not seem to be a fair solution unless the percentage of IDCs is very small (< 5%), since it would have little impact on the pattern of mortality by cause of death.

Alternatives have been used to recover these causes through methods such as “information retrieval”, which consists of visits to homes, hospitals, forensic medicine institutes and health units. One of the ways of recovering ill-defined deaths is through the method known as “verbal autopsy” (VA) (Mathers et al. 2005).

VA analysis is supposed to identify the sequence of events that lead to an individual's death when the underlying cause is not identified by the doctor or authorized person on the death certificate.

For the World Health Organization (2007), VA is an interview conducted with family members and/or caregivers of the deceased via a structured questionnaire to elicit signs and symptoms and other information that can be used later to assign a probable underlying cause of death. VA is an essential public health tool for obtaining a reasonable direct estimate of the structure of the cause of mortality at the community or population level, although it may not be an accurate method for attributing causes of death at the individual level.

To obtain the IDCs reallocated to cause j, one possibility is to use the method for estimating the redistributive factor proposed by Ledermann (1955). Ledermann's method assumes that the proportion of a cause among all deaths is underestimated, given that some of the deaths are attributed to IDCs; as the proportion of defined deaths increases, the proportion of ill-defined deaths decreases. Ledermann used simple linear regression between the proportions of each of the well-defined causes of death (Y_j, $j = 0,..., r$) and the proportion of ill-defined deaths, X (which represents the independent variable of the regression model), to obtain the observations (Y_j, $j = 0,..., r$) for each area of interest, for example, i ($i = 1,2,..., n$), a total of n areas. Thus, for each defined cause of death, a regression is performed.

Ledermann interpreted the slope of the regression line of Y_i (proportion of deaths attributed to well-defined cause Y_i) on X (proportion of ill-defined deaths) as an estimate of the proportion of ill-defined deaths attributed to cause j.

Therefore, by having r defined causes, it becomes possible to estimate the number of ill-defined deaths that should be among the r causes of death. Ledermann's interpretation is a consequence of a property of the simple linear regression line. In formal terms, it follows that:

$$Y_i = \alpha + \beta X_i + e_i$$

By the least squares method, it is estimated that:

$$\hat{\beta} = \frac{\sum_{i=1}^{n} X_i Y_i - n\overline{X}\overline{Y}}{\sum_{i=1}^{n} X_i^2 - n\overline{X}^2} \qquad \hat{\alpha} = \bar{Y} - \hat{\beta}\bar{X}$$

Considering r defined causes, each regression equation will assume the following relationship:

$$Y_{ij} = \alpha_j + \beta_j X_i + e_{ij}$$

where:

- Y_{ij} are deaths from cause *j* in area *i*;
- α_j is the straight line coefficient of cause *j*;
- β_j is the redistribution coefficient for cause *j*;
- X_i are the observed deaths from IDCs in area i;
- e_{ij} refers to the "error" or "residue";
- n represents the total number of deaths in area i.

It is demonstrated that:

$$\sum_{j=1}^{r} \beta_j = -1$$

where *r* represents the total number of causes of death.

The equation for the redistribution of deaths from IDCs for a given area is given by:

$$O_j = Y_j - 1 \cdot (X \cdot \beta_j)$$

where O_j represents the number of deaths redistributed by cause *j*; Y_j represents the number of observed deaths from cause *j*; β_j represents the redistribution factor for cause *j*; and X represents the number of deaths from IDCs.

Thus, taking COVID-19 deaths as an example, we have the dependent variable and the proportion of IDC deaths, disaggregated by sex, as the independent variable.

To use this estimation method, it is necessary to have a statistically reasonable number of subareas related to the area of interest (≥ 30 is desirable).

15.2.3. *Third step: redistribution of deaths due to non-specific causes (garbage codes)*

The GC definition was introduced in the Global Burden of Disease Study in 1990, which was published in 1996 (Murray and Alan 1996). The occurrence of deaths whose underlying cause is not specified is referred to as GCs. GCs consist of codes from the International Statistical Classification of Diseases and Related Health Problems – Tenth Revision (ICD-10) for underlying causes of death with ill-defined or incomplete diagnoses that do not allow for proper identification (Naghavi et al. 2010; Athern et al. 2011).

For example, causes such as septicemia, malignant neoplasm without a specific location, cerebral palsy, heart failure and kidney failure do not define the disease that caused death.

A high proportion of causes of death, such as GC, can compromise the quality of information on causes of death and, consequently, make it difficult to identify priority causes and adequately plan the actions to be taken by competent bodies.

For this reason, the World Health Organization (WHO) and analysts suggest reassigning deaths coded to GCs to other causes by adopting some valid method (Naghavi et al. 2010; Athern et al. 2011). A conceptual approach described in detail by Naghavi et al. (2010) has been widely used and has not changed since the Global Burden of Diseases (GBD) study (Ministry of Health of Brazil n.d.). This redistribution can be performed proportionally. In turn, the algorithms follow a classification that is usually grouped into two categories: GC-R codes: GC from chapter XVIII of the ICD-10; and GC-non-R codes: GC from chapters other than chapter XVIII. These include sepsis (ICD-10, A40–A41), hypertensive diseases (I10) and heart failure (I50).

For example, for the redistribution of GCs for COVID-19 cases, the algorithm can follow three steps: identification of GCs related to COVID-19; identification of target causes in which deaths attributed to a GC should, in principle, be reassigned to COVID-19 (based on pathophysiology); and redistribution of GCs.

There are no GCs specified for COVID-19, as this disease is relatively new, with newly opened ICD-10 rubrics, and is still under observation/investigation in terms of pathogenesis, systems involved in the pathology and specific reasons for deaths. The GCs for investigation were chosen on the basis of scientific knowledge about primary damage to the respiratory system by COVID-19 and its widespread complications, such as sepsis.

For the redistribution of GCs, two groups of target causes were established considering the ICD-10: Chapter I, "Certain Infectious Diseases" (A00–B99), and

Chapter X, "Diseases of the Respiratory System" (J00–J99). In addition to identifying a specific list of GCs and mapping them onto the two large established groups, the four-level typology of GCs was used in relation to the redistribution proposed in the GBD hierarchical list, as shown in Table 15.1.

GCs typology	Especific GCs
Level 1 (very high)	A41.9; (J80-J80.9); (J85-J85.3); (J86-J86.9); (J96-J96.9); (J98.1-J98.3)
Level 2 (high)	J81; J90; J94.1; (J94.8-J94.9)
Level 3 (medium)	(J71-J79); J83, J85.9; (J87-J89); J90.9; J93.6; (J97-J98.0); (J98.4-J99.8)
Level 4 (low)	(J17-J17.1); J18; J18.8; J18.9; J22

Table 15.1. *List of garbage codes (GCs) chosen for redistribution to COVID-19 according to the hierarchical typology and target groups (infectious diseases and diseases of the respiratory system) of deaths. Source: International Statistical Classification of Diseases and Related Health Problems 10th Revision* (ICD 2010)

The GCs were distributed by sex (male and female), and their proportions were calculated. In turn, the numbers of GCs according to their typology and two major groups were also extracted from Line A (diseases or conditions that led directly to death) for all COVID-19 deaths recorded for the geographical unit of study. The proportional redistribution method was used to reallocate GCs to cause j.

15.3. Illustrative example

To illustrate the above procedures, an example was taken of a state in Brazil, as well as spatial breakdowns of the state. The state of Paraíba was selected (4,039,277 estimated inhabitants and HDI of 0.714 in 2020), João Pessoa (capital) and all of the other municipalities in the state (not including the municipality of Campina Grande) (Brazilian Institute of Geography and Statistics n.d.). The underlying cause was COVID-19 death disaggregated by sex in 2020 (Ministry of Health of Brazil, n.d.; Ferreira et al. 2021).

The coverage of deaths was estimated according to the GBM proposal (Brass 1975) by sex for Paraíba, João Pessoa and the other municipalities in the state, as shown in Table 15.2. The coverage of deaths was greater for men in all of the geographical units analyzed.

The method of choice used to determine the coverage of deaths does not always work. This was the case for Paraíba's other municipalities for females. The following method was used: the ratio between the proportion of deaths among women and men in the state (0.9539) was obtained and applied to the coverage of men (90.7%), resulting in 86.5% coverage for women.

The values obtained by redistributing the IDCs (Ledermann 1955) and redistributing the GCs (Athern et al. 2011) related to the number of COVID-19 deaths are shown in Table 15.3 for both sexes.

Local	Males		Females	
	Correction factor	Coverage (%)	Correction factor	Coverage (%)
Paraíba	1.0475	95.5	1.0981	91.1
João Pessoa	1.0383	96.3	1.0665	93.8
Other municipalities	1.1023	90.7	1.1555	86.5

Table 15.2. *Correction factor and coverage of total deaths over 19 years of age, by sex, according to geographic areas of the state of Paraíba, Brazil, 2020. Source: Ministry of Health of Brazil. Mortality Information System (MIS) (Ferreira et al. 2021). Other municipalities do not include the municipality of Campina Grande/Paraíba*

Local	Registered deaths COVID-19	IDC redistributed COVID-19 n (%)	GC redistributed COVID-19 n (%)	Corrected deaths COVID-19
	Males			
Paraíba	1,929	228 (11.8)	281 (14.6)	2,438
João Pessoa	616	81 (13.2)	26 (4.2)	723
Other municipalities	1,081	125 (11.6)	157 (14.5)	1,363
	Females			
Paraíba	1,497	228 (15.2)	305 (20.4)	2,030
João Pessoa	478	81 (17.0)	174 (36.4)	733
Other municipalities	826	126 (15.3)	157 (19.0)	1,109

Table 15.3. *Redistribution of ill-defined causes (IDC) and garbage codes (GCs) related to COVID-19 with correction of registered deaths by sex, according to geographic areas of the state of Paraíba, Brazil, 2020. IDC: Ill-defined causes; GC: garbage code. Source: Ministry of Health of Brazil. Mortality Information System (MIS) (Ferreira et al. 2021)*

Table 15.4 illustrates the steps for applying the proposed methodology with the results of the redistribution of deaths caused by COVID-19, considering the total

IDCs and GCs for Paraíba, João Pessoa and the other municipalities in the state for both sexes.

The starting point was the correction factor (f_i) calculated using the GBM method, which was then applied to the number of registered deaths (O^j_{obs}). This resulted in the number of deaths corrected for underregistration ($f_j*O^j_{obs}$). With the inclusion of IDC_j and GC_j related to the cause under study, it was possible to determine the total number of deaths expected by COVID-19 for the state of Paraíba and the geographic units analyzed. As a result, the number of deaths increased in the order of 1,281 (37.4%), 418 (38.2%) and 804 (42.2) for Paraíba, João Pessoa and the other municipalities, respectively, as shown in Table 15.5.

Local	Correction factor	Registered deaths by COVID-19	Correction by underregistration	Ill-defined causes	Garbage Code (GC_j)	Expected deaths COVID-19
	f_j	O^j_{obs}	$f_j*O^j_{obs}$	IDC_j	GC_j	$(O^j_{esp} = f_j*O^j_{obs} + IDC_j + GC_j)$
Paraíba	1.0728	3,426	3,665	456	586	4,707
João Pessoa	1.0524	1,094	1,150	162	200	1,512
Other municipalities	1.1289	1,907	2,146	251	314	2,711

Table 15.4. *Redistribution of deaths from COVID-19 considering correction factors, ill-defined causes and garbage codes, according to geographic areas of the state of Paraíba, Brazil, 2020. Legend:* f_j *= Correction factor;* O^j_{obs} *= Registered deaths by COVID-19;* $f_j*O^j_{obs}$ *= Corrected deaths;* CMD_j *= Ill-defined causes by COVID-19;* GC_j *= Garbage code by COVID-19. Source: Ministry of Health of Brazil. Mortality Information System (MIS) (Ferreira et al. 2021)*

	Males			Females			Total		
	PB	JP	OM	PB	JP	OM	PB	JP	OM
Registered	1,929	616	1,081	1,497	478	826	3,426	1,094	1,907
Expected	2,530	747	1,474	2,177	765	1,237	4,707	1,512	2,711
Difference	601	131	393	680	287	411	1,281	418	804
(%)	31.2	21.3	36.4	45.4	60.0	49.8	37.4	38.2	42.2

Table 15.5. *Total and sex-adjusted expected deaths from COVID-19 according to geographic areas of the state of Paraíba, Brazil, 2020. PB: Paraíba; JP: João Pessoa; OM: other municipalities. Source: Ministry of Health of Brazil. Mortality Information System (MIS) (Ferreira et al. 2021)*

15.4. Conclusions

The methodological proposal for evaluating the quality of death data is applicable to any country or region in the world and for any underlying cause or group of causes of death if the data required by this proposal are available, such as the number of deaths disaggregated by sex, age and cause of death.

The inclusion of IDCs and GCs related to COVID-19 allowed the definition of a strategy for measuring the expected number of deaths due to COVID-19.

It is necessary to consider that the expected values are estimates subject to multiple errors, whether caused by incorrect counting of deaths and the population by age group and sex, violation of assumptions in the application of death correction techniques or errors that are intrinsic to any data estimation technique. In addition, estimates depend on the data source used. Therefore, the estimates obtained from such analyses may contain biases.

The procedures proposed here require low operating costs and are relatively simple for managers and technicians of vital statistics information systems to apply, which strengthens, for example, health surveillance actions and decision-making to address this and other epidemics that may affect the population.

15.5. References

Athern, R.M., Lozano, R., Naghavi, M., Foreman, K., Gakidou, E., Muray, C.J. (2011). Improving the public heath utility of global cardiovascular mortality data: The rise of ischemic heart disease. *Population Health Metrics*, 9(8), 1–11.

Bennett, N.G. and Horiuchi, S. (1981). Estimating the completeness of death registration in a closed population. *Population Index*, 47(2), 207–221.

Brass, W. (1975). *Methods for Estimating Fertility and Mortality from Limited and Defective Data*. International Program of Laboratories for Population Statistics, Chapel Hill, NC.

Brazilian Institute of Geography and Statistics. (n.d.). Demographic census [Online]. Available at: https://www.ibge.gov.br/cidades-e-estados/pb/ [Accessed 21 April, 2024].

Courbage, Y. and Fargues, P. (1979). A method for deriving mortality estimates from incomplete vital statistics. *Population Studies*, 33(1), 165–180.

Ferreira, A.M.S., Moura, L.A., Paes, N.A. (2021). Characteristics of deaths from COVID-19 in Paraíba and Brazil according to different data sources. *Conjecturas*, 21(2), 294–313.

Hill, K. (2000). Methods for measuring adult mortality in developing countries: A comparative review. Research Report, Harvard Burden of Disease Unit, Center for Population and Development Studies, Cambridge, MA.

Hill, K., You, D.Z., Choi, Y.J. (2009). Death distribution methods for estimating adult mortality: Sensitivity analysis with simulated data errors. *Demographic Research*, 21, 235–254.

ICD (2010). International Statistical Classification of Diseases and Related Health Problems, 10th revision (ICD-10) [Online]. Available at: https://icd.who.int/browse10/2010/en.

Ledermann, S. (1955). La répartition des décès de cause indéterminée. *Revue de l'Institut International de Statistique*, 23(1/3), 47–57.

Mathers, C.D. and Boerma, T. (2010). Mortality measurement matters: Improving data collection and estimation methods for child and adult mortality. *PLOS Medicine*, 7(4), e1000265. doi: 10.1371/journal.pmed.1000265.

Mathers, C.D., Fat, D.M., Inoue, M., Rao, C., Lopez, A.D. (2005). Counting the dead and what they died from: An assessment of the global status of cause of death data. *Bulletin of the World Health Organization*, 83(3), 171–177.

Ministry of Health of Brazil (n.d.). Mortality information system – MIS [Online]. Available at: https://www.gov.br/saude/pt-br/composicao/svs/sistemas-de-informacao/sistema-de-informacoes-sobre-mortalidade-sim. [Accessed 21 April, 2024].

Murray, C.J.L. and Alan, D.L. (1996). *The Global Burden of Diseases: A Comprehensive Assessment on Mortality and Disability from Diseases, Injuries and Risk Factors in 1990 and Projected Do 2020*. Harvard University Press, Cambridge, MA.

Murray, C.J.L., Rajaratnam, J.K., Marcus, J., Laakso, T., Lopez, A.D. (2010). What can we conclude from death registration? Improved methods for evaluating completeness. *PLOS Medicine*, 7(4), e1000262. doi: 10.1371/journal.pmed.1000262.

Naghavi, M., Makela, S., Foreman, K., O'Brien, J., Pourmalek, F., Lozano, R. (2010). Algorithms for enhancing public health utility of national causes-of-death data. *Population Health Metrics*, 8(9), 1–14.

Paes, N.A. (2007). Quality of death statistics by unknown causes in Brazilian states. *Revista de Saúde Pública*, 41(3), 436–445.

Paes, N.A. (2018). *Statistical Demographics of Vital Events*, 2nd edition. Ed CCTA, João Pessoa-Paraíba.

Preston, S.H., Heuveline, P., Guillot, M. (2001). *Demography: Measuring and Modeling Population Process*. Wiley-Blackwell Publisher Limited, Massachusetts.

United Nations. (1983). *Manual X: Indirect Techniques for Demographic Estimation*. United Nations, New York.

United Nations (2014). *Principles and Recommendations for a Vital Statistics System*. United Nations, New York.

Vallin, J., Pollard, J.H., Heligman, L. (eds) (1985). *Methodologies for the Collection and Analysis of Mortality Data*. Ordina, Liege.

World Health Organization (2007). *Verbal Autopsy Standards: Ascertaining and Attributing Cause of Death*. Work Health Organization, Geneva.

16

Health Status, Cancer and Pneumonia Death Rates in Europe: 2019–2022

This chapter follows previous research: "Analysis of Health Status in the Czech Republic: 2019–2022 Trends". It introduces the health profiles of EU-27 countries from 2019 to 2022. The aims are as follows: first, to construct a health profile scale for EU-27 member states in relation to pneumonia and cancer deaths; second, to analyze regional similarities and differences. The health profile scoring of EU-27 countries is enumerated. The main data sources are the Eurostat Database and the OECD. EU-27 countries are divided by final score into several groups: from the best score to the worst. The health statuses of pneumonia and cancer patients are mostly the same. The group with the best results belongs to Sweden and German. The groups with the worst results are Croatia, Poland, the Czech Republic, Bulgaria, Latvia, Slovakia and Romania. The major differences are in the following measures: outpatient care and inpatient care, long-term care and less, but also health expenditure per capita. Measurement results could be used for recommendations toward the social and health sectors. This chapter could be considered in future research by analyzing further aspects of the health status of the population.

16.1. Introduction

Czech Republic, together with other European countries, faced the COVID-19 pandemic in recent years, and together with pandemic tasks, it has solved questions related to other diseases, such as cancer and pneumonia. Therefore, we decided to extend our study to other diseases, such as cancer and pneumonia. Consequently, the observation period of our research was 2019–2022. The pandemic and economic crisis have led to emergency health needs, mental illnesses and high rates of stress, depression and anxiety. The current situation in the Czech Republic is as

Chapter written by Elena ŘÍHOVÁ and Kornélia SVAČINOVÁ.

For a color version of all figures in this chapter, see www.iste.co.uk/dimotikalis/data5.zip.

follows: the Czech population includes 10.5 million inhabitants. The total number of confirmed cases of COVID-19 (including reinfections) was 4.6 million on May 2, 2023. The number of confirmed cases in the population of seniors aged 65+ (including reinfections) is 623,000. With such a large number of COVID-19 cases, states must also treat other diseases (Komenda et al. 2020).

For instance, life expectancy at birth in Czechia in 2022 (79.1 years) was approximately 1.5 years below the European Union (EU) average (80.7 years). While it increased by more than 4 years in the two decades before the pandemic, it fell by more than 2 years in 2020 and 2021, before rebounding close to its pre-pandemic level in 2022. Circulatory diseases, cancer and COVID-19 were the leading causes of death in 2021 (OECD 2021c). Expenditures on the health system are below the EU average (7.8% of GDP in Czech Republic compared with 9.9% in the EU).

The following risk factors for death have been established: diabetes, cancer, alcohol consumption (one of the highest in Europe), smoking and obesity (OECD 2021c).

The aim of this chapter is to present the selected indicators of health status and highlight selected health trends in the period 2019–2022 in the EU-27. The 14 selected indicators are as follows: life expectancy, life expectancy reduction in 2020; gender gap in life expectancy; mortality rate from pneumonia; and mortality rate from cancer, alcohol consumption, tobacco smoking, dietary risk, air pollution, low physical activity, health expenditure per capita, outpatient care, inpatient care, pharmaceuticals, long-term care and prevention. For the research, data from the following sources were used: Eurostat, OECD and the State of Health in the EU: Country Health Profiles. The State of Health in the EU country profiles provide a relevant dataset of health and health systems in EU countries (including life expectancy, pneumonia and cancer mortality, behavioral risk factors, effectiveness and performance of healthcare systems).

16.2. Background

In recent years, awareness of health inequalities across Europe has increased, and pandemics have helped highlight these inequalities. The spot question was "What are the causes of these differences?". As reported in a previous study, health policies differ across EU countries.

Classifying EU health policies is a rational way to label what is complex, allows an international comparison and enables policy assessments and recommendations to be made within each group (Ferreira et al. 2018).

The EU strengthened national health policies by assisting local EU governments in achieving shared objectives and providing necessary resources. The Health 2020 framework addresses common challenges and promotes overall health and well-being. The EU's assistance to health systems acknowledges that member states hold the primary responsibility for their own healthcare. Unsurprisingly, many studies have confirmed a positive correlation between life expectancy and real per capita income across different countries. Therefore, countries with higher GDP per capita tend to enjoy significantly better life expectancy. In the EU, this elevated life expectancy has beautifully translated into more vibrant, healthy years. However, the widespread challenges of alcohol consumption and obesity remain pressing issues in most European countries. These problems not only diminish quality of life, but also contribute to the onset of various diseases or, at the very least, increase the risk of developing numerous health conditions.

From a European policy perspective, grouping countries with similar characteristics harmonizes with our proposed framework for classifying EU health policies. For instance, our selected indicators reveal that greater per capita health expenditure is intricately linked to reduced rates of preventable mortality. In our forthcoming work, we aspire to develop a groundbreaking health indicator to vividly monitor population health across diverse EU regions and delve into the necessity of multifaceted health policies.

16.3. Methods

The unified EU response to COVID-19 aims to standardize health assessments and measures across member states. We are trying to implement the same assessments for cancer and pneumonia. A central research question in this chapter is to examine the similarities and differences in life expectancy, health systems and mortality from cancer and pneumonia within the EU. The selection of indicators began with a comprehensive review of the literature addressing various determinants of population health (Ferreira et al. 2018). This chapter performs a comparable analysis for the EU-27 countries by selecting quantified measures. We will subsequently develop a unique scale to evaluate the health profiles of these countries from 2019 to 2022.

Creating such a scale is challenging and fraught with obstacles. It is likely impractical, if not impossible, to encompass all the factors influencing health profiles due to the difficulty in obtaining reliable and comparable data across the EU-27 countries (Karlsson and Österberg 2007). Therefore, we acknowledge certain limitations as follows: (1) the health and demographic measures included in the scale and (2) the time period of 2019–2022, for which data are collected and compared (Moskalewicz et al. 2016). The scale focuses on objective measures of health profiles (life expectancy, cancer and pneumonia mortality, behavioral risk factors and health system characteristics) within EU countries. The data were sourced from the OECD's "State of Health in the EU: Country Health Profiles", with the latest report available for 2022. The methodology and data from this source are relevant, transparent and designed around countries' health systems, making them highly suitable for our analysis. Conducting interviews with experts from individual countries was beyond the scope of this research and could be considered for future studies. The scale used in this paper was constructed to be simple and clear to prevent misinterpretations and ensure appropriate comparability, utilizing both quantitative and qualitative data. The cancer and pneumonia mortality rates were standardized. The questions and scale used in this chapter are presented in Table 16.1. The questionnaire consists of 14 questions, with a maximum possible score of 14 points (for pneumonia) and a maximum possible score of 13 points (for cancer).

Life expectancy (max. 3 points)

1. Life expectancy is above the EU average (Yes 1 p. / The same 0.5 p./ No 0 p.)
2. Life expectancy reduction in 2023 (Yes 0 p. /No 1 p.)
3. Gender gap in life expectancy is under the EU average (Yes 1 p. / The same 0.5 p./ No 0 p.)

Behavioral risk factors (max. 5 points)

4. Alcohol consumption is under the EU average (Yes 1 p. / The same 0.5 p. / No 0 p.)
5. Tobacco smoking is under the EU average (Yes 1 p. / The same 0.5 p. / No 0 p.)
6. Dietary risks as cause of death is under the EU average (Yes 1 p. / No 0 p.)
7. Air pollution as cause of death is under the EU average (Yes 1 p. / The same 0.5 p./ No 0 p.)
8. Low physical activity as cause of death is under the EU average (Yes 1 p. / The same 0.5 p. / No 0 p.)

Health system (max. 6 points)

9. Health expenditure per capita (Yes 1 p. / No 0 p.)
10. Outpatient care (Yes 1 p. / No 0 p.)
11. Inpatient care (Yes 1 p. / No 0 p.)
12. Pharmaceuticals and medical devices (Yes 1p. / No 0 p.)
13. Long-term care (Yes 1p. / No 0 p.)
14. Prevention (Yes 1p. / No 0 p.)

Table 16.1. *Pneumonia and cancer health profile framework and scoring used in the article. Source: State of Health in the EU: Country Health Profiles (2021); authors' modification*

The following four main research questions were formulated:

– *Research question 1*: Which areas of health and health systems are already harmonized for EU-27 countries and where are the disparities between regions?

– *Research question 2*: Which countries could be taken as an example for highlighting healthcare system?

– *Research question 3*: Could a reduction in the mortality rate of pneumonia be achieved due to improvements in the healthcare system?

– *Research question 4*: Is the mortality rate of cancer influenced by the healthcare system?

16.4. Results and discussion

The questionnaire was divided into three areas, namely, health profiles, such as life expectancy, behavioral risk factors and the health system (selected individually according to available data and information, as in previous research), and the other two areas included cancer and pneumonia deaths.

The main source of information was the OECD's *State of Health in the EU: Country Health Profiles*. For each question, the following values system was used: yes, 1 point; the same, 0.5 points; and no, 0 points. When information was not found, the NA was used. No weights were used in this case. Hence, the values for each question were between zero and one. The total number of achieved points is presented in the columns.

In the column "Total" in Table 16.2, the sum of all the achieved points was calculated.

States with the highest values are shown in green, and those with the lowest values are shown in red (Tables 16.2 and 16.3). The main differences between countries were for the last area: health system.

According to the results, EU-27 countries may be divided into six categories (Table 16.4).

Sweden and Germany had the best performance (score above 10.0 points). Czech Republic has the worst position in the ranking (together with Croatia, Poland, Bulgaria, Latvia, Slovakia and Romania with less than 2.0 points).

Country (EU-27)	1.	2.	3.	4.	5.	6.	7.	8.	9.	10.	11.	12.	13.	14.	Total
Austria	1	0	1	0.5	1	1	1	0	1	1	1	1	0	0	**9.5**
Belgium	1	0	1	0.5	0	1	1	0.5	1	0	1	0	1	0	**8**
Bulgaria	0	0	0	0	0	0	0	0.5	0	0	0	0	NA	0	**0.5**
Croatia	0	0	0	0.5	0	0	0	0.5	0	0	0	0	0	0	**1**
Cyprus	1	0	1	1	0	1	0	0.5	0	0	0	0	0	0	**4.5**
Czechia	0	0	0	0.5	0	0	0	0	0	0	0	0	0	0	**0.5**
Denmark	1	1	1	0.5	0	1	1	0.5	1	1	0	0	1	0	**9**
Estonia	0	0	0	0	1	0	1	0.5	0	0	0	0	0	0	**2.5**
Finland	1	1	0.5	1	1	0	1	0	0	1	0	0	0	1	**7.5**
France	1	0	NA	0	1	1	1	0.5	1	0	1	1	0	0	**7.5**
Germany	1	0	1	0	1	1	1	0.5	1	1	1	1	1	1	11.5
Greece	1	0	1	1	0	1	0	0.5	0	0	0	0	0	0	**4.5**
Hungary	0	0	0	0	0	0	0	0.5	0	0	1	1	0	1	**3.5**
Ireland	1	0	1	1	0	1	1	0	0	0	1	0	1	0	**7**
Italy	1	0	1	1	1	1	0.5	0	0	0	0	0	0	1	**6.5**
Latvia	0	0	0	0.5	1	0	0.5	0	0	0	0	0	0	0	**2**
Lithuania	0	0	0	0.5	1	0	1	0	0	0	0	0	0	0	**2.5**
Luxembourg	1	0	1	0	0.5	1	1	0.5	1	1	1	0	1	0	**9**
Malta	1	0	1	1	1	0	0.5	0	0	0	0	0	0	0	**4.5**
Netherlands	1	0	1	1	0	1	1	1	1	1	0	0	1	1	**10**
Poland	0	0	0	0.5	0	0	0	0.5	0	0	0	0	0	0	**1**
Portugal	1	0	0	0.5	1	1	1	0	0	1	0	0	0	0	**5.5**
Romania	1	0	0	0	0.5	0	0	0.5	0	0	0	0	0	0	**2**
Slovakia	1	0	0	0.5	0	0	0	0.5	0	0	0	0	0	0	**2**
Slovenia	0.5	0	0	1	1	1	0	1	0	0	0	0	0	0	**4.5**
Spain	1	0	0	1	1	1	1	0.5	0	0	0	0	0	0	**5.5**
Sweden	1	0	1	1	1	1	1	1	1	1	1	1	1	1	13
Total	18.5	2.0	12.5	15.0	14.0	15.0	15.5	10.5	8.0	8.0	8.0	5.0	7.0	6.0	

Table 16.2. *Scoring of the EU-27 countries (pneumonia). For a color version of this table, see www.iste.co.uk/dimotikalis/data5.zip*

Country (EU-27)	1.	2.	3.	4.	5.	6.	7.	8.	9.	10.	11.	12.	13.	Total
Austria	1	0	1	0.5	1	1	1	0	1	1	1	1	0	**9.5**
Belgium	1	0	1	0.5	0	1	1	0.5	1	0	1	0	1	**8**
Bulgaria	0	0	0	0	0	0	0	0.5	0	0	0	0	NA	**0.5**
Croatia	0	0	0	0.5	0	0	0	0.5	0	0	0	0	0	**1**
Cyprus	1	0	1	1	0	1	0	0.5	0	0	0	0	0	**4.5**
Czechia	0	0	0	0.5	0	0	0	0	0	0	0	0	0	**0.5**
Denmark	1	1	1	0.5	0	1	1	0.5	1	1	0	0	1	**9**
Estonia	0	0	0	0	1	0	1	0.5	0	0	0	0	0	**2.5**
Finland	1	1	0.5	1	1	0	1	0	0	1	0	0	0	**6.5**
France	1	0	NA	0	1	1	1	0.5	1	0	1	1	0	**7.5**
Germany	1	0	1	0	1	1	1	0.5	1	1	1	1	1	11.5
Greece	1	0	1	1	0	1	0	0.5	0	0	0	0	0	**4.5**
Hungary	0	0	0	0	0	0	0	0.5	0	0	1	1	0	**2.5**
Ireland	1	0	1	1	0	1	1	0	0	0	1	0	1	**7**
Italy	1	0	1	1	1	1	0.5	0	0	0	0	0	0	**6.5**
Latvia	0	0	0	0.5	1	0	0.5	0	0	0	0	0	0	**2**
Lithuania	0	0	0	0.5	1	0	1	0	0	0	0	0	0	**2.5**
Luxembourg	1	0	1	0	0.5	1	1	0.5	1	1	1	0	1	**9**
Malta	1	0	1	1	1	0	0.5	0	0	0	0	0	0	**4.5**
Netherlands	1	0	1	1	0	1	1	1	1	1	0	0	1	**9**
Poland	0	0	0	0.5	0	0	0	0.5	0	0	0	0	0	**1**
Portugal	1	0	0	0.5	1	1	1	0	0	1	0	0	0	**5.5**
Romania	1	0	0	0	0.5	0	0	0.5	0	0	0	0	0	**2**
Slovakia	1	0	0	0.5	0	0	0	0.5	0	0	0	0	0	**2**
Slovenia	0.5	0	0	1	1	1	0	1	0	0	0	0	0	**4.5**
Spain	1	0	0	1	1	1	1	0.5	0	0	0	0	0	**5.5**
Sweden	1	0	1	1	1	1	1	1	1	1	1	1	1	12
Total	18.5	2.0	12.5	15.0	14.0	15.0	15.5	10.5	8.0	8.0	8.0	5.0	7.0	

Table 16.3. *Scoring of the EU-27 countries (cancer). For a color version of this table, see www.iste.co.uk/dimotikalis/data5.zip*

1.	Sweden, Germany.	**score: > 10.0**
2.	Denmark, Luxembourg, Ireland, Austria, Netherlands.	**score: 10.0–8.0**
3.	France, Italy, Finland, Belgium, Portugal, Spain.	**score: 8.0–5.0**
4.	Slovenia, Hungary, Malta, Cyprus, Greece.	**score: 5.0–3.0**
5.	Lithuania, Estonia.	**score: 3.0–2.0**
6.	Croatia, Poland, Czechia, Bulgaria, Latvia, Slovakia, Romania.	**score: < 2.0**

Table 16.4. *Ranking of the EU-27 countries (for both pneumonia and cancer). Source: authors' calculation*

Healthcare profiles were made for each of the six groups (Figures 16.1–16.6).

Inside groups (see Table 16.4) the healthcare profiles were more similar, but the differences between groups are more significant.

Notable disparities were uncovered in critical metrics: health expenditure per capita, outpatient services, inpatient services, long-term care and preventive measures. These findings suggest that these particular elements of countries' pneumonia and cancer health profiles require substantial reinforcement and harmonization across EU regions to enhance overall resilience and response efficacy.

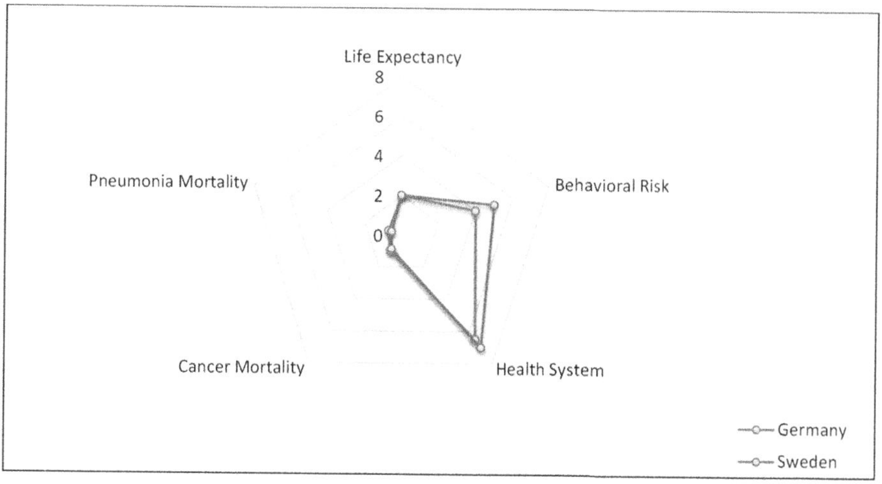

Figure 16.1. *Matches and differences in countries' health profiles (the first group)*

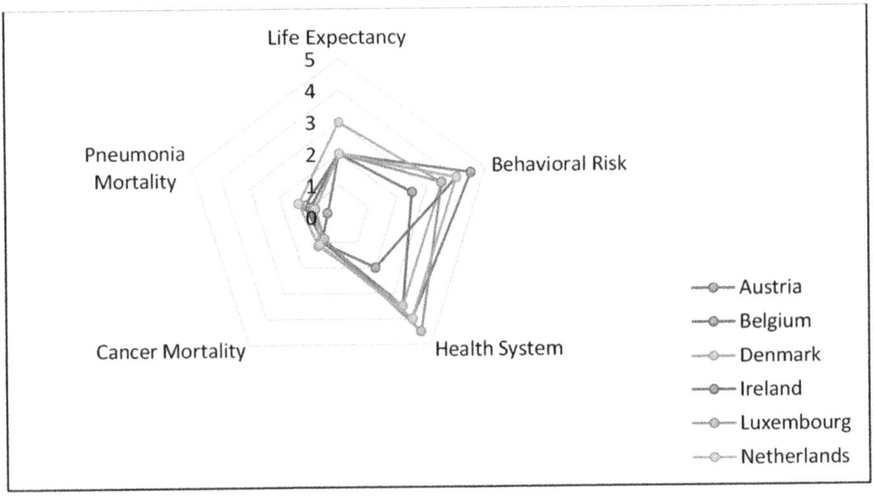

Figure 16.2. *Matches and differences in countries' health profiles (the second group)*

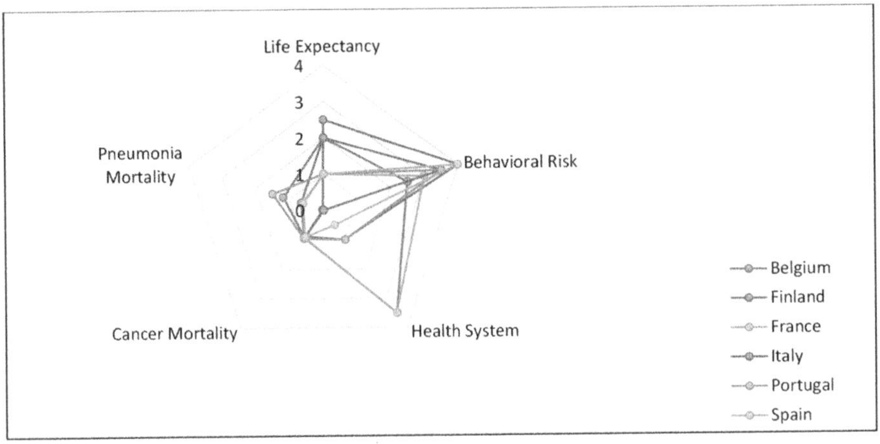

Figure 16.3. *Matches and differences in countries' health profiles (the third group)*

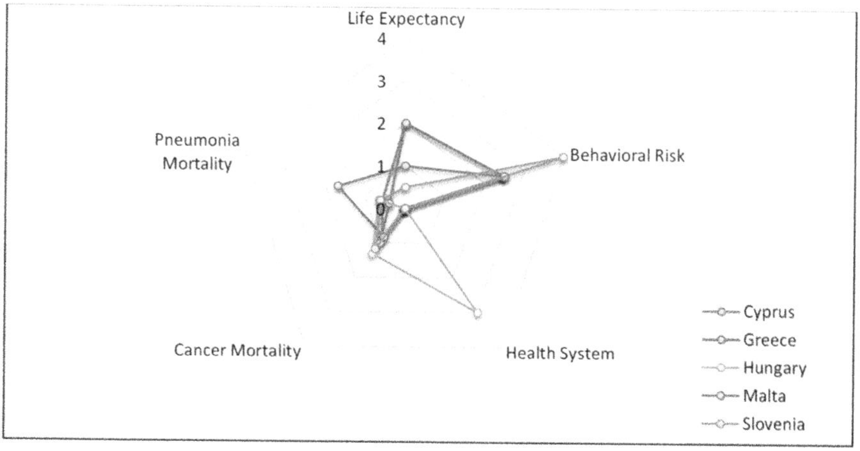

Figure 16.4. *Matches and differences in countries' health profiles (the fourth group)*

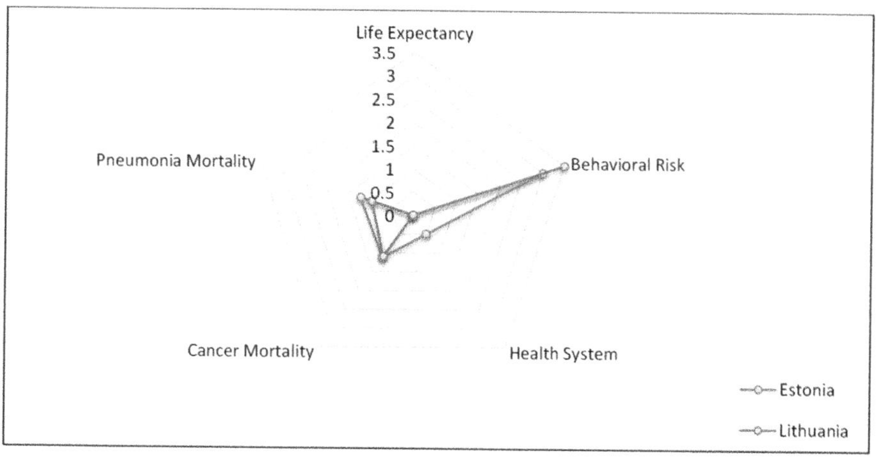

Figure 16.5. *Matches and differences in countries' health profiles (the fifth group)*

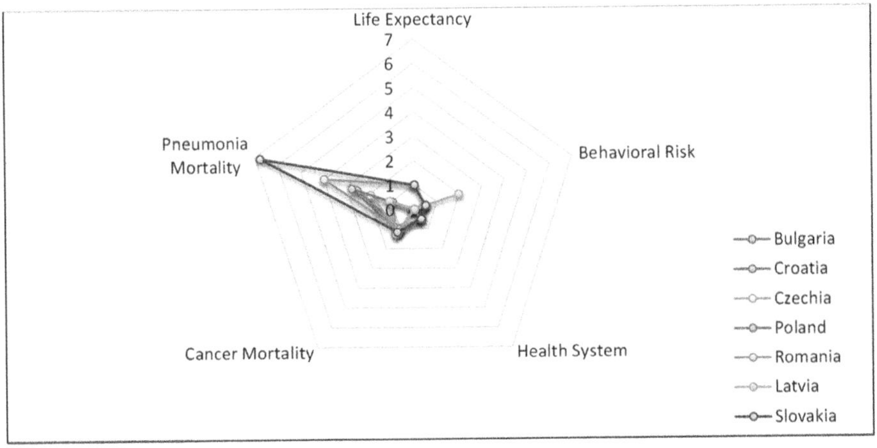

Figure 16.6. *Matches and differences in countries' health profiles (the sixth group)*

These findings led us to consider the statistical significance of these disparities. Specifically, we questioned whether these factors (health system, life expectancy and behavioral risk) have a statistically significant impact on mortality rates from cancer and pneumonia.

To assess the statistical significance of the observed disparities, we employed single-factor analysis of variance (ANOVA) (Meloun and Melitky 2006). This method allows us to determine whether there are any statistically significant differences between the means of various groups. By applying ANOVA, we can rigorously evaluate whether the identified factors – such as health expenditure per capita, outpatient care, inpatient care, long-term care and preventive measures – contribute to variations in mortality rates from cancer and pneumonia across different regions. This analysis is crucial for understanding the underlying determinants and guiding targeted policy interventions. The significance level for both tests was 0.05.

The following hypotheses were determined: H_0: $\mu_1 = \ldots = \mu_6$; H_1: non-H_0, where μ_i is the mean mortality rate of the group. In other words, the null hypothesis told us that there were no differences in the mortality rate between the groups; hence, the mortality rate was not significantly affected by the current healthcare system. The results are presented in Table 16.5.

According to the p value of 0.06579936, the healthcare ranking did not influence the cancer mortality rate. Instead, other aspects of the healthcare system that were not covered in the questionnaire could affect it. According to the p value 0.00602521, the null hypothesis for the pneumonia mortality rate could be rejected;

hence, the alternative hypothesis could be accepted at the significance level. In other words, the pneumonia mortality rate is affected by the healthcare system.

ANOVA single factor	p-value
Cancer mortality rate	0.06579936
Pneumonia mortality rate	0.00602521

Table 16.5. *ANOVA results. Source: authors' calculation*

To research the differences between group means identified by ANOVA, we utilized Scheffé's individual test. This post hoc analysis is particularly robust for multiple comparisons, allowing us to identify which specific group differences are statistically significant. By applying Scheffé's test, we can more accurately determine the relationships between healthcare factors and pneumonia mortality rates, providing a comprehensive understanding of the variables at play. The results are shown in Figure 16.7. The statistically significant results are shown in red.

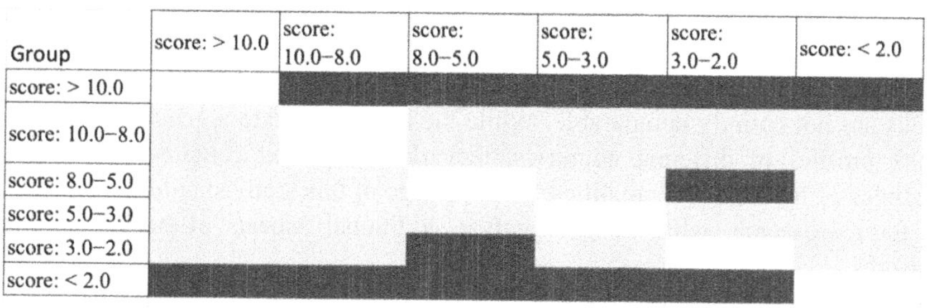

Figure 16.7. *Scheff's test results. Source: authors' calculation*

The pneumonia mortality rate is influenced by the healthcare score. The most significant influence is on the states in the last group (Croatia, Poland, Czechia, Bulgaria, Latvia, Slovakia and Romania). Weaker differences, however significant, are between states: France, Italy, Finland, Belgium, Portugal, Spain, Lithuania and Estonia.

The proposed typology contributes to the discussion about how to classify health policies; the typology of EU health policy allows comparisons of characteristics and health system performance across groups, and policy assessment and policy recommendation within each group (Ferreira et al. 2018). The analysis of selected health areas in this chapter confirmed that the unification of rules within the EU is missing. Utter harmonization of EU states is needed.

16.4. Conclusions

The health profile of the EU-27 countries primarily provides a comprehensive analysis of life expectancy, mortality rates, behavioral risk factors and the effectiveness of the health system, encompassing health expenditures, pharmaceuticals, long-term care and preventive measures. According to the results of this study, the EU-27 region can be stratified into six distinct clusters. The innovative health profile scale has validated the most advanced and sophisticated health systems in four EU regions: Sweden and Germany achieved the highest score values (exceeding 10.0 points); Nordic and Western European nations present a stringent and precise health profile. Conversely, the Czech Republic, along with Poland, Croatia and Bulgaria, have been categorized in the lowest tier (scores below 2.0 points). There are major differences in the following measures: outpatient care and inpatient care, long-term care and less, as well as health expenditure per capita.

Strengthening public health and preventive measures is a central objective of the Czech health strategy for 2021–2030. This chapter has confirmed the existence of disparities, while also highlighting the progressive harmonization of health profiles among EU countries. It is imperative to exercise caution and avoid making overly broad conclusions based solely on the results and evaluations of this or any other scale. Owing to substantial social and cultural differences among countries, the results are not entirely comparable. While the scores indicate a general trend in the health profiles of different countries, they do not permit conclusions about the dynamics of healthcare regulations. The findings of this study should be considered for future research, which could analyze additional aspects of health condition measures.

16.5. References

Eurostat (n.d.). Database – EU policies: Health [Online]. Available at: https://ec.europa.eu/eurostat/web/main/data/database.

Ferreira, P.L., Tavares, A.I., Quintal, C., Santana, P. (2018). EU health systems classification: A new proposal from EURO-HEALTHY. *BMC Health Services Research*, 18, 511. doi: 10.1186/s12913-018-3323-3.

Forster, T., Kentikelenis, A., Bambra, C. (2018). *Health Inequalities in Europe: Setting the Stage for Progressive Policy Action*. FEPS/TASC, Belgium/Dublin [Online]. Available at: https://www.tasc.ie/assets/files/pdf/18456_health_inequalities_finalweb.pdf.

Karlsson, T. and Österberg, E. (2007). Scaling alcohol control policies across Europe. *Drugs: Education, Prevention and Policy*, 14, 499–511. doi: 10.1080/09687630701392032.

Komenda, M., Panoška, P., Bulhart, V., Žofka, J., Brauner, T., Hak, J., Jarkovský, J., Mužík, J., Blaha, M., Kubát, J. et al. (2020). COVID-19: Overview of the current situation in the Czech Republic. The current diseases. Ministry of Health, Czech Republic [Online]. Available at: https://onemocneni-aktualne.mzcr.cz/covid-19.

Meloun, M. and Militky, J. (2006). *Kompendium Statistického Zpracování Dat*, 2nd edition. Academia, Prague.

Moskalewicz, J., Room, R., Thom, B. (2016). Comparative monitoring of alcohol epidemiology across the EU. Baseline assessment and suggestions for future action. Synthesis Report, RARHA (Reducing Alcohol Related Harm).

OECD (2021a). Country health profiles [Online]. Available at: https://www.oecd.org/health/country-health-profiles-eu.htm.

OECD (2021b). *Slovakia: Country Health Profile 2022: State of Health in the EU*. OECD Publishing, Paris.

OECD (2021c). *Czechia: Country Health Profile 2022: State of Health in the EU*. OECD Publishing, Paris.

OECD (2022). *Health at a Glance: Europe 2022: State of Health in the EU Cycle*. OECD Publishing, Paris. doi: 10.1787/82129230-en.

Sawyer, S.F. (2009). Analysis of variance: The fundamental concepts. *Journal of Manual & Manipulative Therapy*, 17, 27E–38E. doi: 10.1179/jmt.2009.17.2.27E.

Turcinovic, M., Singson, R., Harrigan, M., Ardito, S., Ilyas, A., Sinvani, L., Hajzadeh, N., Burns, E. (2021). Physical therapy for hospitalized patients with COVID-19 in isolation: Feasibility and pilot implementation of telehealth for delivering individualized therapy. *Quality Improvement Report*, 3(2) [Online]. Available at: https://www.archives-rrct.org/article/S2590-1095(21)00013-6/fulltext.

17

A Bayesian Asymmetric Approach to Modeling Volatility on Portfolios with Many Assets

A Bayesian approach for estimating and forecasting asymmetric GARCH models with Student's t-distributed errors is proposed for modeling the dynamic principal components (DPCs) of a hedge fund portfolio. The case study used is a hedge fund portfolio with 106 assets from various European exchanges. MCMC methods simulate the posterior distribution of the model parameters, and depending on the number of DPCs used in the reconstruction, the resulting predictive distributions allow us to obtain a measure for the predictive ability of the models and forecast risk. The current study follows a similar published study by the same authors where a Bayesian GARCH(1,1) approach with t-distributed errors is used instead; thus, potential asymmetry in volatility was not accounted for. Asymmetry in GARCH models can be an important inclusion in modeling financial volatility because of its ability to capture leverage effect scenarios where negative shocks have a stronger impact on volatility than positive shocks. The Student's t GJR(1,1) approach is used to address asymmetry, and the predictive performance of the proposed method is evaluated using an extended time horizon of the case study as a test period. We compare the predictive performance of multiple models with the formerly proposed Bayesian GARCH(1,1) approach using the same number of DPCs and show that models that cater to asymmetry tend to have better predictive ability, with a lower number of principal components. Risk measures are also evaluated for the different models.

17.1. Introduction

In this chapter, the problem originally addressed in Bonello et al. (2024) is revisited, which is that of modeling and forecasting the risk of portfolios with many assets, where the use of multivariate approaches becomes infeasible due to the curse of dimensionality. In a previous study, the problem was analyzed by performing

Chapter written by David SUDA, Monique Borg INGUANEZ and Matthew CAMILLERI.

dimension reduction with dynamic principal component analysis (DPCA) on the assets and subsequently modeling the extracted DPCs, which are uncorrelated, using the Bayesian GARCH(1,1) model in Ardia and Hoogerheide (2010). Forecasts on these DPCs were obtained and then used to forecast the individual assets/value of the portfolio through DPCA reconstructions. The use of DPCA is important because cross-correlations in a time series need to be considered, which will also concentrate the variance explained in lower order DPCs. In this chapter, the Brillinger approach for DPCA (see, for example, Brillinger 1981 and Shumway and Stoffer 2017), which adopts a frequency domain approach, is applied. However, regression-based approaches by Peña and Yohai (2016) and Peña et al. (2019, 2021) are also available.

One aspect not considered in Bonello et al. (2024) is the asymmetric nature of asset volatility, where rising markets tend to display low volatility and declining markets tend to display high volatility. It will thus be useful to determine whether accounting for this asymmetry in volatility when modeling DPCs can enhance the model's predictive ability. To address this, the Bayesian GARCH(1,1) model will be replaced with the Bayesian Student-t GJR(1,1) model in Ardia (2008), which caters to potential asymmetry in the DPCs obtained.

17.2. Dynamic principal component analysis

In this section, DPCA is revisited. Let $\mathbf{X}_t = \left(X_{1,t}, X_{2,t}, \dots, X_{p,t}\right)'$ denote a p-variate asset vector at time t belonging to a stationary multivariate time series with mean vector $\mathbf{0}$ and covariance matrix function $\mathbf{P}_{\mathbf{XX}}(\cdot)$. The function $f_{mn}(\omega) = \sum_{h=-\infty}^{\infty} \rho_{mn}(h)e^{-i2\pi\omega h}, -\frac{1}{2} \leq \omega \leq \frac{1}{2}$ is called the cross spectrum of the time series $X_{m,t}$ and $X_{n,t}$, where $m, n \in \{1,2, \dots, p\}$ and $m \neq n$, and $\rho_{mn}(h)$ refers to the covariance between the series $X_{m,t}$ and $X_{n,t}$ at lag h. Hence, the definition of the $p \times p$ spectral density matrix of $\mathbf{X}_t$ at frequency ω is as follows:

$$\mathbf{F}_{\mathbf{XX}}(\omega) = \sum_{h=-\infty}^{\infty} \mathbf{P}_{\mathbf{XX}}(h)e^{-i2\pi\omega h} = \begin{bmatrix} f_{11}(\omega) & f_{12}(\omega) & \dots & f_{1n}(\omega) & \dots & f_{1p}(\omega) \\ f_{21}(\omega) & f_{22}(\omega) & & f_{2n}(\omega) & \dots & f_{2p}(\omega) \\ \vdots & \vdots & \ddots & \vdots & \ddots & \vdots \\ f_{m1}(\omega) & f_{m2}(\omega) & \dots & f_{mn}(\omega) & \dots & f_{mp}(\omega) \\ \vdots & \vdots & \ddots & \vdots & \ddots & \vdots \\ f_{p1}(\omega) & f_{p2}(\omega) & \dots & f_{pn}(\omega) & \dots & f_{pp}(\omega) \end{bmatrix}$$

In Brillinger's approach to DPCA (see Brillinger 1981), the aim is to find a complex vector $\mathbf{c}(\omega)$ of unit length such that:

$$\max_{\mathbf{c}(\omega)\neq\mathbf{0}} \mathbf{c}(\omega)'\mathbf{F}_{\mathbf{XX}}(\omega)\mathbf{c}(\omega). \qquad [17.1]$$

The proposed method uses the discrete Fourier transform to transition from the time domain to the frequency domain and the inverse discrete Fourier transform to revert back. The solution to equation [17.1] is $\mathbf{c}(\omega) = \mathbf{e}_1(\omega)$, which maximizes the objective function, giving $\lambda_1(\omega)$. The first PC series is then defined as $Y_{1,t} = \sum_{h=-\infty}^{\infty} \mathbf{e}_{1,h}{}'\mathbf{X}_{t-h}$, where $\mathbf{e}_1(\omega) = \sum_{h=-\infty}^{\infty} \mathbf{e}'_{1,h} e^{-i2\pi h\omega}$. This process can be repeated for the q series such that $q \leq p$, where the kth dynamic PC series ($k \leq q$) is formulated as follows:

$$Y_{k,t} = \sum_{h=-\infty}^{\infty} \mathbf{e}_{k,h}{}'\mathbf{X}_{t-h} \qquad [17.2]$$

and the coherency between $Y_{i,t}$ and $Y_{k,t}$ for $i \neq k$ is zero. The resulting eigenvalue–eigenvector pairs are $\{(\lambda_1(\omega), \mathbf{e}_1(\omega)), \dots, (\lambda_q(\omega), \mathbf{e}_q(\omega))\}$, and $\mathbf{Y}_t = (Y_{1,t}, \dots, Y_{q,t})'$ has a spectral density of $\mathbf{F}_{\mathbf{YY}}(\omega) = diag(\lambda_1(\omega), \dots, \lambda_q(\omega))$.

Given observations $\mathbf{X}_t = (X_{1,t}, \dots, X_{p,t})'$, equation [17.3] determines the empirical lagged covariances between $x_{m,t}$ and $x_{n,t}$. More precisely, it determines $\hat{\rho}_{mn}(h)$ for h lags. For a sample of size v, set $\hat{\mu}_m = \frac{1}{v}\sum_{t=1}^{v} x_{m,t}$ and $\hat{\mu}_n = \frac{1}{v}\sum_{t=1}^{v} x_{n,t}$ such that

$$\hat{\rho}_{mn}(h) = \frac{1}{v}\sum_{t=1}^{v-h}(x_{m,t+h} - \hat{\mu}_m)(x_{n,t} - \hat{\mu}_n)' \qquad [17.3]$$

The spectral density f is often estimated by a function of the form:

$$\hat{f}_{mn}(\omega) = \frac{1}{2\pi}\sum_{|h|<q} K\left(\frac{h}{q}\right)\hat{\rho}_{mn}(h)e^{-i2\pi h\omega} \qquad [17.4]$$

for all $m, n \in \{1,2,\dots,p\}$, where $\hat{\rho}(\cdot)$ is the sample autocovariance function, and $K(x)$ is a kernel smoother with window size q. $K(x)$ is taken to be the Bartlett kernel. The $p \times p$ cross-spectral matrix, $\hat{\mathbf{F}}_{\mathbf{XX}}(\omega)$, consequently follows. Equation [17.4] is repeated for all $\omega_j = \frac{j}{n}, j = 1, \dots, n$.. Next, we can obtain the dynamic eigenvectors and eigenvalues of $\hat{\mathbf{F}}_{\mathbf{xx}}(\omega)$ for each ω_j. Denote the estimated dynamic eigenvectors as $\hat{\mathbf{e}}_1(\omega), \dots, \hat{\mathbf{e}}_q(\omega)$, and via the Fourier inverse, we have:

$$\hat{\mathbf{e}}_{l,h} = \frac{1}{2\pi}\int_{-\pi}^{\pi} \hat{\mathbf{e}}_l(\omega)e^{ih\omega}d\omega \qquad [17.5]$$

for $|h| \leq d$ and $1 \leq l \leq q$. To reduce the dimensions, take $q < p$ PCs and calculate [17.5] for $1 \leq l \leq q$. The estimated scores $\hat{Y}_{1,t}, \dots, \hat{Y}_{p,t}$ are computed using [17.2] with $\hat{Y}_{l,t} = \sum_{h=-d}^{d} \hat{\mathbf{e}}_{l,h}{}'\mathbf{X}_{t-h}, l = 1, \dots q$.. Furthermore, the reconstruction of $\mathbf{X}_t$ is performed using the dynamic Karhunen–Loève expansion:

$$\hat{\mathbf{X}}_t = \sum_{l=1}^{q}\sum_{h=-d}^{d} \hat{Y}_{l,t+h}\,\hat{\mathbf{e}}_{l,h} \qquad [17.6]$$

17.3. Bayesian Student-t GJR(1,1) model

In this section, we introduce the Student-t GJR(1,1) model, which is formulated as:

$$Y_t = \tilde{Z}_t \sigma_t$$

$$\sigma_t^2 = \alpha_0 + \left(\alpha_1 1_{\{Y_{t-1} \geq 0\}} + \alpha_2 1_{\{Y_{t-1} < 0\}}\right) Y_{t-1}^2 + \beta_1 \sigma_{t-1}^2$$

$$\tilde{Z}_t \overset{iid}{\sim} S(0,1,\nu) \qquad [17.7]$$

where $S(0,1,\nu)$ refers to a scaled t-distribution with mean zero, unit variance and ν degrees of freedom; $1_{\{Y_{t-1} \geq 0\}}$ denotes an indicator function; and $\alpha_0 > 0$, $\alpha_1, \alpha_2, \beta \geq 0$ and $\nu > 2$. The term $\alpha_1 1_{\{Y_{t-1} \geq 0\}} + \alpha_2 1_{\{Y_{t-1} < 0\}}$ in [17.7] applies an asymmetric effect based on the sign of the Y_t. This parameterization is not suitable for Bayesian inference; thus, the following reparameterization in Ardia (2008) is used:

$$Y_t = Z_t \left(\frac{v-2}{v} \omega_t \sigma_t^2\right)^{\frac{1}{2}} ; t = 1, \ldots, T$$

$$\sigma_t^2 = \alpha_0 + \left(\alpha_1 1_{\{Y_{t-1} \geq 0\}} + \alpha_2 1_{\{Y_{t-1} < 0\}}\right) Y_{t-1}^2 + \beta_1 \sigma_{t-1}^2$$

$$Z_t \overset{iid}{\sim} N(0,1)$$

$$\omega_t \overset{iid}{\sim} IG\left(\frac{\nu}{2}, \frac{\nu}{2}\right) \qquad [17.8]$$

In [17.8], $N(0,1)$ refers to the standard normal distribution, and $IG\left(\frac{\nu}{2}, \frac{\nu}{2}\right)$ refers to the inverted gamma distribution with a shape and scale parameter equal to $\frac{\nu}{2}$. Defining the observed values as $\boldsymbol{y} := (y_1, \ldots, y_T)'$ and the vectors to be estimated, which are missing here $\boldsymbol{\omega} := (\omega_1, \ldots, \omega_T)'$ and $\boldsymbol{\alpha} := (\alpha_0, \alpha_1, \alpha_2)'$, the parameters of interest are grouped as follows: $\boldsymbol{\theta} := (\boldsymbol{\alpha}', \beta, \nu)'$. By Bayes' formula, we have this here as the posterior I introduce the prior first and then say that, using Bayes' theorem, the joint posterior distribution is given by:

$$P(\boldsymbol{\theta}, \boldsymbol{\omega} \mid \boldsymbol{y}) = \frac{\mathcal{L}(\boldsymbol{\theta}, \boldsymbol{\omega} \mid \boldsymbol{y}).P(\boldsymbol{\theta}, \boldsymbol{\omega})}{\int \mathcal{L}(\boldsymbol{\theta}, \boldsymbol{\omega} \mid \boldsymbol{y}).P(\boldsymbol{\theta}, \boldsymbol{\omega})\, d\boldsymbol{\theta}\, d\boldsymbol{\omega}} \qquad [17.9]$$

where $\mathcal{L}(\boldsymbol{\theta}, \boldsymbol{\omega} \mid \boldsymbol{y})$ refers to the likelihood of the reparameterized GJR model. Given the d-dimensional truncated normal density $\tilde{\phi}_{N_d}$, the priors suggested by Ardia (2008) are as follows:

– $P(\boldsymbol{\alpha}) \propto \phi_{N_3}(\boldsymbol{\alpha} \mid \boldsymbol{\mu}_\alpha, \boldsymbol{\Sigma}_\alpha); \boldsymbol{\alpha} \in R_+^3$;

– $P(\beta) \propto \phi_{N_1}(\beta \mid \mu_\beta, \Sigma_\beta); \beta \in R_+$;

– $P(\boldsymbol{\omega} \mid \nu) = \left(\frac{\nu}{2}\right)^{\frac{T\nu}{2}} \left[\Gamma\left(\frac{\nu}{2}\right)\right]^{-T} (\prod_{t=1}^{T} \omega_t)^{-\frac{\nu}{2}-1} \times \exp\left[-\frac{1}{2}\sum_{t=1}^{T} \frac{\nu}{\omega_t}\right]$;

– $P(\nu) = \lambda \exp[-\lambda(\nu - \delta)] 1_{\{\nu>\delta\}}$; $\nu > \delta$.

In [17.9], $P(\boldsymbol{\theta}, \boldsymbol{\omega}) = P(\boldsymbol{\alpha}).P(\beta).P(\boldsymbol{\omega} \mid \nu).P(\nu)$ is the joint prior distribution. Refer to Ardia (2008) for information about the MH algorithm used to estimate the posterior distribution.

In the next section, the extraction of uncorrelated DPCs and the use of Bayesian Student-*t* GJR(1,1) to model them are discussed. The uncorrelatedness of the DPCs allows us to model the DPCs univariately and independently.

17.4. Asymmetric modeling of a portfolio with many assets

The dataset used in this study is the same as the one analyzed in Bonello et al. (2024), comprising 106 assets traded on various European exchanges based on a typical hedge fund portfolio. The dataset consists of daily adjusted closing prices of each asset for five years between September 10, 2015 and September 19, 2020, all of which were downloaded from Yahoo Finance. The included assets are traded in multiple different currencies (EUR, GBX, SEK, NOK, CHF and DKK) but have all been converted to EUR using the relevant daily exchange rates. Let $(\boldsymbol{P}_t)$ represent the prices and let $(\boldsymbol{X}_t)$ be the corresponding derived log returns. Bonello et al. (2024) reported that $k = 4$, where the elbow in the scree plot is attained, whereas $k = 11$ and $k = 36$, where a minimum of 70% and 90% explanation, respectively, of the total variation in the original dataset is attained. For comparability, the approach shall be tested on models based on these number of DPCs (i.e. $k = 4, 11, 36$) from $(\boldsymbol{X}_t)$. We implement the Bayesian Student-t GJR(1,1) model on all the first 36 dynamic PCs and present the results for k= 1,4,11,36. We run two chains of length 35,000 with a burn-in period of 25,000 and use the average of the two chains to estimate the empirical probability density function and other characteristics.

The parameter α_0 is an intercept term that ensures that the volatility is never equal to zero. Table 17.1 shows that the posterior mean for this parameter decreases for principal components of larger order, although for the 36th DPC, it is greater than that for the 11th DPC. The role of α_1 and α_2, on the other hand, is to cater to asymmetry in the principal components. We see that for the first PC, the posterior mean for α_2 is greater than the posterior mean for α_1, which indicates that for low-order DPCs, the behavior is similar to what is expected of equities in financial markets (i.e. higher volatility for negative shocks and lower volatility for positive shocks). This asymmetry changes for higher-order DPCs, where α_1 tends to have a higher posterior mean. However, the effects of both α_1 and α_2 decrease with increasing order. When α_1 or α_2 is greater than 0.1, then the volatility is said to be sensitive to market events. This finding indicates that the 11th and 36th PC are not sensitive to market events. This contrasts with the Bayesian GARCH(1,1) approach in Bonello et al. (2024), where the 11th PC was still sensitive to market events when no distinction was made between positive and negative shocks in the PCs. Notably, the credibility upper bound of α_1 does still include 0.1 in this order.

		1st PC	4th PC	11th PC	36th PC
α_0	**Mean**	0.00041	0.00013	0.00004	0.00006
	St. Dev.	0.00013	0.00004	0.00001	0.00002
	95% HPD l.b.	0.00019	0.00006	0.00001	0.00002
	95% HPD u.b.	0.00068	0.00021	0.00007	0.07677
α_1	**Mean**	0.04067	0.13907	0.08019	0.03355
	St. Dev.	0.02167	0.02753	0.02852	0.02412
	95% HPD l.b.	0.00331	0.08615	0.02559	0.00001
	95% HPD u.b.	0.08148	0.19145	0.13335	0.07677
α_2	**Mean**	0.16421	0.03073	0.04431	0.02182
	St. Dev.	0.04016	0.02547	0.02927	0.02132
	95% HPD l.b.	0.08534	0.00010	0.00026	0.00010
	95% HPD u.b.	0.23884	0.08032	0.09772	0.06420
β	**Mean**	0.85687	0.77897	0.83933	0.37952
	St. Dev.	0.02766	0.03718	0.04228	0.17193
	95% HPD l.b.	0.80396	0.70774	0.75481	0.09480
	95% HPD u.b.	0.90869	0.84919	0.91342	0.70914
ν	**Mean**	7.22590	12.24717	27.78274	20.03333
	St. Dev.	1.36019	4.50229	17.80120	11.62087
	95% HPD l.b.	5.08865	6.26119	7.76005	6.92529
	95% HPD u.b.	9.97231	21.08901	66.97885	44.72216

Table 17.1. *Posterior mean, standard deviation, and HPD interval for the 10,000 realizations generated from the posterior distribution of $\alpha_0, \alpha_1, \alpha_1, \beta$ and ν for the PCs $\hat{Y}_{1,t}$ $\hat{Y}_{4,t}$, $\hat{Y}_{11,t}$ and $\hat{Y}_{36,t}$*

Here, β represents the degree to which the volatility of the last period affects the next period's volatility. As we can see from Table 17.1, the HPD intervals for $k = 1$, 4 and 11 are similar, with relatively high numbers. The parameter ν is responsible for the heavy tails of the distribution and is a crucial component in accounting for the leptokurtosis that is present in financial data. In our model, the role of the degrees of freedom parameter ν is to magnify the effect of the conditional variance. Table 17.1 shows that for larger k values, the HPD intervals become elongated, indicating more dispersion in the chains (due to convergence issues) for larger k values.

17.5. Forecasting, predictive ability and risk estimation

This section presents the procedure for obtaining a predictive distribution for each DPC introduced. The DPCs are then used to obtain forecasts of the log returns of each asset via reconstruction. The conversion of these log returns to asset prices, and ultimately, the value of the portfolio is then straightforward, and consequently, their empirical predictive distribution can be derived. We can then use these empirical predictive distributions to measure the predictive ability of the models and apply a direct approach for estimating the value at risk (VaR) and expected shortfall (ES) n.

Given G estimated MCMC realizations $\alpha_0^{(g)}$, $\alpha_1^{(g)}$, $\alpha_2^{(g)}$, $\beta^{(g)}$, and $\nu^{(g)}$ for $g = 1, \dots, G$, the following equations yield future simulations for the DPCs:

$$\hat{Y}_{i,T+1}^{(g)} = Z_{i,T+1}^{(g)} \left(\frac{\hat{\nu}_{(i)}^{(g)} - 2}{\hat{\nu}_{(i)}^{(g)}} \omega_{i,T+1}^{(g)} \hat{\sigma}_{i,T+1}^{2\ (g)} \right)^{\frac{1}{2}}, Z_{i,T+1}^{(g)} \overset{iid}{\sim} N(0,1), \omega_{i,T+1}^{(g)} \overset{iid}{\sim} IG\left(\frac{\hat{\nu}_{(i)}^{(g)}}{2}, \frac{\hat{\nu}_{(i)}^{(g)}}{2} \right),$$

$$\hat{\sigma}_{i,T+1}^{2\ (g)} = \hat{\alpha}_{0(i)}^{(g)} + \left(\hat{\alpha}_{1(i)}^{(g)} 1_{\{Y_{i,T} \geq 0\}} + \hat{\alpha}_{2(i)}^{(g)} 1_{\{Y_{i,T} < 0\}} \right) Y_{i,T}^2 + \hat{\beta}_{(i)}^{(g)} \hat{\sigma}_{i,T}^{2\ (g)};$$

$$\hat{Y}_{i,T+m}^{(g)} = Z_{i,T+m}^{(g)} \left(\frac{\hat{\nu}_{(i)}^{(g)} - 2}{\hat{\nu}_{(i)}^{(g)}} \omega_{i,T+m}^{(g)} \hat{\sigma}_{i,T+m}^{2\ (g)} \right)^{\frac{1}{2}}, Z_{i,T+m}^{(g)} \overset{iid}{\sim} N(0,1), \omega_{i,T+m}^{(g)} \overset{iid}{\sim} IG\left(\frac{\hat{\nu}_{(i)}^{(g)}}{2}, \frac{\hat{\nu}_{(i)}^{(g)}}{2} \right),$$

$$\hat{\sigma}_{i,T+m}^{2\ (g)} = \hat{\alpha}_{0(i)}^{(g)} + \left(\hat{\alpha}_{1(i)}^{(g)} 1_{\{\hat{Y}_{i,T+m-1}^{(g)} \geq 0\}} + \hat{\alpha}_{2(i)}^{(g)} 1_{\{\hat{Y}_{i,T+m-1}^{(g)} < 0\}} \right) \hat{Y}_{i,T+m-1}^{(g)\ 2} + \hat{\beta}_{(i)}^{(g)} \hat{\sigma}_{i,T+m-1}^{2\ (g)} \quad [17.10]$$

for $m = 2, \dots, M$. In [17.10], T refers to the time index of the final observed value. Future simulations of $\hat{X}_{i,T+m}^{(g)}, m = 1, \dots, M$ of the log returns of the original assets are reconstructed from a specified number of dynamic PCs using the Karhunen–Loève expansion. Consequently, from these, the forecasts of the prices

$\hat{P}^{(g)}_{i,T+m}, m = 1, \ldots, M$ are easily recovered, and furthermore, the portfolio values are retrieved by assigning the relevant weightings, $\tau_1, \ldots, \tau_p$, to each asset as follows: $\hat{V}^{(g)}_{T+m} = \tau_1 \hat{P}^{(g)}_{1,T+m} + \tau_2 \hat{P}^{(g)}_{2,T+m} + \cdots + \tau_p \hat{P}^{(g)}_{p,T+m}\,; m = 1, \ldots, M$. The simulated sample of size G of our portfolio's value at time $T+m$ is combined into a vector, that is, $\hat{\boldsymbol{V}}_{T+m} := \left(\hat{V}^{(1)}_{T+m}, \hat{V}^{(2)}_{T+m}, \ldots, \hat{V}^{(G)}_{T+m}\right)'$, for $m = 1, \ldots, M$.

Cross-validation was performed to evaluate the predictive ability of the models. As a validation dataset, the dates September 11, 2020 to May 4, 2021 were taken, where all assets in the portfolio were simultaneously observed for a total of 135 days. Forward testing will be performed, and the models with reconstructions based on $k = 4, k = 11$, and $k = 36$, respectively, will be compared. Let $\hat{\mathbb{V}} = \{\hat{\boldsymbol{V}}_{1186+1}, \ldots, \hat{\boldsymbol{V}}_{1186+135}\}$ denote the simulated paths for values of the portfolio, and let $\boldsymbol{V} = \{V_{1186+1}, \ldots, V_{1186+135}\}$ be the validation dataset. The pseudomarginal likelihood, as suggested by Congdon (2007), $\hat{p}(\boldsymbol{V}) = \prod_{m=1}^{135} p\left(V_{1186+m} \middle| \hat{\boldsymbol{V}}_{1186+m}\right)$ (or, alternatively, its log), is used to assess the predictive ability of the entire model with the validation dataset. The components $p\left(V_{1186+m} \middle| \hat{\boldsymbol{V}}_{1186+m}\right)$ in the product are called the conditional predictive ordinates and can be estimated empirically from the simulated paths.

	4 DPCs	11 DPCs	36 DPCs
log PsML	-2081,052	-2247,589	-2210,835

Table 17.2. *Displaying the log PsML for the model when taking $k = 4, k = 11$ and $k = 36$ dynamic PCs for reconstruction.*

Table 17.2 displays the log PsML for the different models when modeling the DPCs using the Bayesian asymmetric GJR(1,1) model. The log PsML is lowest (worst) when we take 11 DPCs and only marginally better with 36 DPCs. The success of the asymmetric approach lies in the fact that the largest log PsML was achieved when dealing with four DPCs. This is in stark contrast to the results obtained in Bonello et al. (2024), where the best log PsML was obtained for the 11DPC reconstruction (–2,210.67) and the worst log PsML was obtained for the 4DPC reconstruction. This is a very important result for the asymmetric approach, as dealing with fewer DPCs is easier because this becomes less computationally intensive (timewise) and easier to handle (memorywise).

This conclusion is restricted to this particular validation set; however, it is encouraging to obtain the best results for a low-dimensional model.

To obtain the m-step ahead Bayesian estimation of the VaR and ES, we can use the direct approach of Hoogerheide and van Dijk (2010). This approach involves obtaining the forecasted loss at time $T+m$. To do this, we may simply calculate $\hat{L}_{T+m}^{(g)} = \hat{V}_{T+m}^{(g)} - V_T$ for all $g = 1, \ldots G$. Thus, at confidence level $\alpha \in (0,1)$, the m-step ahead estimate for the VaR of the portfolio will be obtained through the sample α-quantile q_α obtained from $\hat{\boldsymbol{L}}_{T+m} = \left(\hat{L}_{T+m}^{(1)}, \hat{L}_{T+m}^{(2)}, \ldots, \hat{L}_{T+m}^{(G)}\right)'$, where $\widehat{VaR}_\alpha(\boldsymbol{L}_{T+m}) = -q_\alpha(\hat{\boldsymbol{L}}_{T+m})$. The m-step ahead estimate for the ES of the portfolio will be obtained using:

$$\widehat{ES}_\alpha(\boldsymbol{L}_{T+m}) = -\frac{1}{\alpha}\left\{\frac{\sum_{g=1}^{G} \hat{L}_{T+m}^{(g)} 1_{\left\{\hat{L}_{T+m}^{(g)} \leq \hat{q}_\alpha(\boldsymbol{L}_{T+m})\right\}}}{\sum_{g=1}^{G} 1_{\left\{L_{T+m}^{(g)} \leq \hat{q}_\alpha(\boldsymbol{L}_{T+m})\right\}}}\right\}$$

	k	$VaR_{0.01}$	$ES_{0.01}$	$VaR_{0.05}$	$ES_{0.05}$	$VaR_{0.1}$	$ES_{0.1}$
1-day ahead	4	–4.84%	–4.99%	–4.63%	–4.77%	–4.51%	–4.66%
	11	–5.97%	–6.12%	–5.82%	–5.82%	–5.42%	–5.66%
	36	–7.05%	–7.40%	–6.44%	–6.80%	–6.13%	–6.53%
5-day ahead	4	–6.07%	–6.50%	–5.27%	–5.76%	–4.87%	–5.42%
	11	–8.39%	–8.99%	–7.26%	–7.98%	–6.88%	–7.48%
	36	–10.57%	–11.13%	–8.92%	–9.87%	–8.12%	–9.59%
10-day ahead	4	–7.09%	–7.92%	–5.88%	–6.64%	–5.27%	–6.09%
	11	–10.86%	–12.07%	–8.94%	–10.16%	–7.98%	–9.34%
	36	–13.21%	–14.58%	–10.78%	–12.32%	–9.51%	–11.16%
50-day ahead	4	–12.73%	–14.6%	–9.75%	–11.59%	–8.35%	–10.28%
	11	–19.76%	–22.11%	–15.10%	–18.02%	–12.78%	–15.90%
	36	–24.70%	–27.43%	–19.09%	–22.37%	–16.16%	–20.01%
100-day ahead	4	–16.32%	–18.05%	–12.58%	–15.01%	–10.51%	–13.25%
	11	–25.56%	–29.17%	–19.24%	–23.42%	–16.03%	–20.60%
	36	–31.99%	–35.46%	–24.40%	–20.32%	–20.33%	–25.84%

Table 17.3. *Estimated 1-, 5-, 10-, 50- and 100-day ahead $VaR_{0.01}$, $VaR_{0.05}$, $VaR_{0.1}$, $ES_{0.01}$, $ES_{0.05}$ and $ES_{0.1}$ when $k=4, k=11$ and $k=36$ dynamic PCs are taken. The percentages reflect the estimated fluctuations from the last observed value of the portfolio, that is, V_{1186}.*

In Table 17.3, measures of risk at different time horizons and different α values are estimated. To do this, the losses/gains experienced for each MCMC realization compared to V_{1186} are extracted, and $\widehat{VaR}_\alpha(\mathbf{L}_{T+m})$ and $\widehat{ES}_\alpha(\mathbf{L}_{T+m})$ are evaluated and converted as percentages. When analyzing Table 17.3, a clear discrepancy between the estimations using different k values is noted; however, this is not surprising. Models with a higher number of dynamic PCs account for more variation in the original portfolio, which consequently increases the VaR and ES. In Bonello et al. (2024), the same was extracted for $\alpha = 0.05$ when the Bayesian Student-t GARCH(1,1) approach was used, which provides less conservative estimates of the estimated value at risk and expected shortfall.

17.6. Conclusion

In this chapter, we extend the Bayesian approach to modeling portfolios with many assets introduced in Bonello et al. (2024) by replacing the model component for DPCs with the asymmetric Bayesian Student-t GJR(1,1) instead of the Bayesian Student-t GARCH(1,1). Swapping the modeling approach has improved the predictive ability of the models considerably with a lower number of DPCs. The estimated risk measures are also more pessimistic for a larger number of DPCs, but the asymmetric approach yields less pessimistic risk measures than the other approaches do. Despite the fact that the predictive ability of the models based on a lower number of DPCs is improved when catering for asymmetry, it must be noted that the pseudomaximum likelihood values in the validation set are close to the mode of a distribution but do not necessarily indicate how well a distribution explains the extremes, which is what is most important when we are estimating risk measures.

For this purpose, in future work, Bayesian approaches for historic backtesting hypothesis tests using values at risk and expected shortfall should be determined. In the frequentist contest, we already have tests by Kupiec (1995) and Christoffersen (1998) for value at risk, and McNeil and Frey (2000) for expected shortfall. Furthermore, it will also be worthwhile to look into dynamic factor models as opposed to DPC reconstructions (see, for example, Peña and Poncela 2006) and consider quantile regression approaches for conditional heteroscedastic models.

17.7. References

Ardia, D. (2008). *Financial Risk Management with Bayesian Estimation of GARCH Models: Theory and Applications*. Springer-Verlag, Berlin.

Ardia, D. and Hoogerheide, L. (2010). Bayesian estimation of the GARCH(1,1) model with Student-t innovations. *The R Journal*, 2(10-045/4), 41–47.

Bonello, S., Suda, D., Inguanez, M.B. (2024). A Bayesian approach to measuring risk on portfolios with many assets. In *Data Analysis and Related Applications: Theory and Practice – New Approaches*, Yiannis, D. and Christos, H.S. (eds). ISTE Ltd, London and John Wiley and Sons, New York.

Brillinger, D.R. (1981). *Time Series: Data Analysis and Theory*, expanded edition. Holden-Day, San Francisco.

Christoffersen, P.F. (1998). Evaluating interval forecasts. *International Economic Review*, 39(4), 841–862.

Congdon, P. (2007). *Bayesian Statistical Modelling*. Wiley and Sons, New York.

Hoogerheide, L. and van Dijk, H.K. (2010). Bayesian forecasting of value at risk and expected shortfall using adaptive importance sampling. *International Journal of Forecasting*, 26(2), 231–247.

Kupiec, P.H. (1995). Techniques for verifying the accuracy of risk measurement models. *Journal of Derivatives*, 3(2), 73–84.

McNeil, A.J. and Frey, R. (2000). Estimation of tail-related risk measures for heteroscedastic financial time series: An extreme value approach. *Journal of Empirical Finance*, 7(3–4), 271–300.

Peña, D. and Poncela, P. (2006). Nonstationary dynamic factor analysis. *Journal of Statistical Planning and Inference*, 136(4), 1237–1257.

Peña, D. and Yohai, V.J. (2016). Generalized dynamic principal components. *Journal of the American Statistical Association*, 111, 1121–1131.

Peña, D., Smucler, E., Yohai, V.J. (2019). Forecasting multiple time series with one-sided dynamic principal components. *Journal of the American Statistical Association*, 114, 1683–1694.

Peña, D., Smucler, E., Yohai, V.J. (2021). Sparse estimation of dynamic principal components for forecasting high-dimensional time series. *International Journal of Forecasting*, 37(4), 1498–1508.

Shumway, R.H. and Stoffer, D.S. (2017). *Time Series Analysis and Its Applications: With R Examples*. Springer, Berlin.

18

Pandemic-Driven Innovations: Utilizing Online Learning and Big Data Analysis for Decision-Making in Educational Environments

The COVID-19 era marked a crucial moment for the global education system, necessitating rapid and substantial adaptations toward online learning. This transition highlighted the need for effective strategies and tools for remote learning. Technologies such as learning management systems (LMSs), virtual reality (VR), artificial intelligence (AI) and the Internet of Things (IoT) have emerged as key supports for online teaching and learning. Concurrently, the pandemic underscored the importance of big data analysis in understanding student needs, engagement and performance in a digital learning environment. Data analysis offered unique opportunities for improving and customizing teaching methods and practices, recognizing challenges faced by students and teachers, and providing solutions. Online learning has become an integral part of modern educational settings, emphasizing the need for flexible and accessible learning opportunities. Incorporating big data analysis in educational program design and execution allows for more targeted and personalized learning experiences.

This study emphasizes the importance of integrating online learning and big data analysis in contemporary educational frameworks. The pandemic not only expedited this transition but also revealed the need for further research, development and innovation in technology and pedagogy to enhance the quality and effectiveness of education. The findings underscore the importance of integrating technology and data-driven strategies to create resilient and effective educational frameworks for the future.

Chapter written by Leonidas THEODORAKOPOULOS, Ioanna KALLIAMPAKOU, Alexandra THEODOROPOULOU and Gerasimos KALOGERATOS.

18.1. Introduction

The COVID-19 pandemic has caused irreversible changes in many areas of our society, and perhaps nowhere are these changes more evident than in the field of education. The forced transition to online learning, in response to the need for social distance and a reduction in the spread of the virus, has caused a fundamental reordering of educational methods and practices. This study addresses the evaluation of online learning in the COVID-19 era for the education system, with a particular focus on big data analysis.

The challenges presented to education during the pandemic were multidimensional. From the need to adapt quickly to online platforms to the development of new pedagogical approaches, teachers, students and parents faced a number of unexpected challenges. Moreover, the forced transition to online learning led to issues such as Internet access, the digital divide and educational equity. In this context, big data analysis is a critical factor in understanding and addressing the challenges of online learning. Through data collection and analysis, it is possible to better understand how students interact with online content, what their needs are, what the gaps in learning are and how teaching methods can be improved. In addition, data analysis can provide valuable information for evaluating the efficiency and effectiveness of online learning.

This chapter seeks to evaluate online learning in the COVID-19 era, with a focus on big data analysis. In conclusion, the challenges, opportunities and prospects arising from this unprecedented period in education should be considered, with a focus on both current practices and possible directions for the future.

18.2. Literature review

18.2.1. *Difficulties during the COVID-19 period*

During the COVID-19 pandemic, the education system faced multiple difficulties in testing both students and teachers:

1) Difficulties in teacher adjustment: many teachers faced challenges in transitioning from traditional physical classroom instruction to online methods. A lack of experience or training in new technologies, as well as difficulty in maintaining student interaction and engagement, were significant challenges.

2) Inequalities in access to education: the unequal distribution of technological resources and lack of access to reliable Internet for many students reinforced educational inequalities. Students in remote or economically disadvantaged areas were at a distinct disadvantage relative to their peers in more advantaged areas.

3) Maintaining the quality of education: maintaining the quality of education was another challenge. The need for rapid transition to online platforms and the lack of prior preparation or resources often led to reduced teaching effectiveness and difficulties in assessing student performance.

4) Psychological burden and well-being: the absence of the physical teaching process and the need for self-regulation and self-management of learning added considerable psychological stress on the students. The stress, isolation and uncertainty that resulted from this period affected overall well-being and academic performance.

5) Technical and management challenges: reliance on technology creates technical challenges such as connectivity outages, software compatibility and data security issues. In addition, teachers face the challenge of managing the classroom and maintaining student engagement in an entirely online environment.

The analysis of these challenges revealed the significant differences and needs that emerged in the educational field during the pandemic period, as well as the need for rapid and effective adaptations.

18.2.2. *Effects of COVID-19 on education*

The COVID-19 pandemic has had a significant impact on education at all levels, from preschool to higher education (Bazimaziki 2020; Malik et al. 2020; Jalongo 2021). Schools and universities suspended their in-service operations, and students, teachers, staff and administrators faced multiple challenges to continue education effectively while maintaining safety (Hallett and De 2020). The pandemic has led to the transition from face-to-face instruction to e-learning, creating a large gap in learning and knowledge for students worldwide (Malik et al. 2020).

The challenges of online teaching include limited or non-existent IT equipment and skills, making online learning during lockdowns inadequate and non-inclusive (Bazimaziki 2020). Additionally, the pandemic has had a transformative effect on medical education, with academic health systems adapting to the new reality (Halkiopoulos et al. 2023). For the most part, the pandemic disrupted education and created significant challenges for students, teachers and educational institutions.

In this context, the need for the digital transformation of education has become more urgent than ever. Online platforms and tools not only enabled the continuation of teaching but also created new opportunities for adaptation and innovation in education. Teachers have been forced to rethink their pedagogical methods and integrate new technologies into their teaching practices, while students have developed new skills of self-regulation and digital interaction.

This period also highlighted the need for more comprehensive policies and strategies aimed at reducing the digital divide and promoting equality of access to education, ensuring that every student had the necessary resources and support to succeed in this new educational environment.

18.2.3. *Big data analysis in educational research*

Big data analysis has grown significantly in the field of educational research, with the aim of improving the quality of teaching, developing learning methods and enhancing educational technology. Many studies have explored the application of big data analytics in educational research, focusing on areas such as exam data analysis, vocational education, curriculum design, and ideological and political education.

One study proposed a method for analyzing and evaluating educational exam data based on an improved linear mixed-efficient model, aiming to improve the efficiency of exam data acquisition and storage, reduce the computational burden and increase the computational speed (Zhao and Wang 2021). Other research focused on the "dual system" educational culture in Germany and its applications in China, using big data analysis to investigate vocational education and the role of information technology in curriculum design and graduate quality supervision (Bai and Jiang 2021). In addition, the process analysis study of educational big data based on Hive data storage technology, using Hive and Spark for data analysis and statistics, visualizing the analysis results through facade and back-end separation technology (Lv et al. 2023).

In addition, big data has been used to leverage its role and contribute to educational technology research, particularly in the transformation of face-to-face teaching to online learning during the COVID-19 pandemic. The use of big data in educational technology research can contribute to the study of education in general and educational technology in particular, facilitating the development of learning strategies and the monitoring and evaluation of students, teachers, materials and learners (Lutfiani and Meria 2022).

In addition, big data analysis has been applied to accurate ideological and political education strategies, where an algorithm based on collaborative filtering for ideological and political education resource recommendations and suggestions was presented. This accurate recommendation system can identify users' needs by studying how they use the website, leading to more useful information recommendations. Teachers can use big data technology to collect students' data information scattered in cyberspace, understand students' situations in real time and provide accurate educational materials according to students' various situations and needs (Wang and Ma 2022).

In conclusion, big data analysis in educational research has shown tremendous potential in improving teaching quality, developing learning methods, and enhancing educational technology, with applications in exam data analysis, vocational education, curriculum design, and ideological and political education. These studies demonstrate the growing importance of big data in its formative role in the future of education.

18.2.4. *Related work*

Recent studies have examined the impact of the COVID-19 pandemic on online learning and the education system. One study investigated students' perceptions of online learning as a digital tool for educational sustainability during the COVID-19 pandemic, using the technology acceptance model (TAM) and information systems (IS) performance models to assess the relationship between system quality, service quality, quality of life, perceived ease of use, perceived usefulness, behavioral intention to use and actual use of an e-learning system (Alqahtani et al. 2022).

Another study analyzed public sentiment toward e-learning during the COVID-19 pandemic using Twitter data and reported that public sentiment tends to be neutral, indicating that people neither fully support nor react to e-learning during the pandemic (Candrayani et al. 2023).

A third study investigated students' level of engagement in online courses using a dedicated school platform in the Saudi Arabian region and reported a high level of engagement among students studying English as a foreign language (EFL) (Oraif and Elyas 2021).

A fourth study sought to capture primary and secondary school teachers' views on online learning during the COVID-19 pandemic in Indonesia and reported that teachers believed that their online learning was ineffective during the pandemic, mainly because of their inability to adapt to a new online teaching culture (Karras et al. 2023).

Finally, a fifth study investigated higher education students' use of an LMS during the COVID-19 pandemic on student engagement and reported that students' desire to use the LMS had beneficial effects and outcomes on learning, such as sustained engagement (Alturki and Aldraiweesh 2021). These studies suggest that the COVID-19 pandemic has transformed the education system and that online learning has become common in every education system on the planet. However, there are still challenges and barriers to overcome, such as the ability of teachers to adapt to the new culture of online teaching and the need for appropriate curriculum design for online learning.

In summary, these studies highlight the importance of the continuous adaptation and evolution of teaching methods to meet new challenges. They also highlight the need for a deeper understanding of the perceptions and attitudes of students, teachers and administrators toward e-learning. This requires the integration of innovative technological solutions and pedagogical approaches which will enhance teaching effectiveness and promote an interactive and enriched learning environment.

18.3. Methodology

This study employs a comprehensive dataset to analyze the impact of COVID-19 on digital learning across various environments and states in the United States. Using exploratory data analysis (EDA), the study visualizes trends in digital learning access and engagement through time series and comparative graphs across different states and environments (urban, rural, suburban and small towns).

Analytical techniques involve setting a visualization environment, calculating value frequencies and defining color palettes to create clear and informative visualizations. Time series analyses focus on metrics such as percentage access to digital learning and the Engagement in Digital Education Index to illustrate the pandemic's impact on educational engagement patterns. This approach allows for a detailed understanding of the variations in digital learning adoption and engagement influenced by COVID-19.

18.4. Research questions

The research questions are as follows:

– RQ1: How did the percentage of access to digital learning vary across states, and how did COVID-19 impact these trends?

– RQ2: What variations in the Engagement in Digital Education Index were observed across different states, and how did COVID-19 influence these engagement patterns?

– RQ3: How did the percentage of access to digital learning differ among urban, rural, suburban and small town environments, and what trends in digital participation emerged during the COVID-19 pandemic?

– RQ4: What trends in the Digital Learning Course Start Index were observed across cities, rural areas, suburbs and small towns, and how did the COVID-19 pandemic influence participation in these contexts?

18.4.1. *Dataset presentation*

The dataset used for this analysis consists of two main files, districts_info.csv and products_info.csv, which provide important information on various aspects of the education sector.

1) Education districts information (districts_info.csv): this file contains detailed information on various school districts, with data from the National Center for Education Statistics (NCES) for the 2018–2019 academic year, the Federal Communications Commission (FCC) as of December 2018, and the Edunomics Lab. To ensure privacy and confidentiality:

– information identifying school districts was removed;

– the ARX tool (Prasser et al. 2004) was used to anonymize several data fields, reducing the risk of reidentification;

– for data generalization purposes, some data points are given with ranges where the actual value is included, and there are several data points marked as "NaN", indicating that the data were tabulated to maximize anonymization of the dataset.

2) Product information (products_info.csv): this file contains information on the top 372 educational products by number of users in 2020. Products are ranked according to LearnPlatform's product classification and include the following:

– LP ID: the unique identifier for each product;

– URL: the web link for that product;

– product name: the name of the product;

– provider/company name: the name of the company or entity providing the product;

– domains: the educational domains where the product is used;

– main essential function: categorizes the primary function of each product. Products are initially classified into one of three categories: learning and curriculum (LC), classroom management (CM), and school and district operations (SDO). Each category has further subcategories for more detailed classification. Some products may not have labels due to duplicates, inaccurate URLs or other reasons.

Additionally, engagement data are aggregated at the school district level, and each file in the engagement_data folder represents data from one school district. The four-digit file name represents the district_id, which can be used to link to the district information in district_info.csv. The lp_id can be used to link to the product information in product_info.csv. This dataset is a rich resource for analyzing trends and characteristics in educational technology use at both the district and product levels, providing valuable information and comprehensive analysis for stakeholders in the education sector.

18.4.1.1. *Analytical techniques and tools*

At this point, we carry out EDA. For this purpose, we will need to perform the following steps:

The methodology and process involved in the initialization and application of data visualization in EDA are illustrated as follows:

– First, we set the visualization environment: the sns.set_context() function is used to set the visualization environment with a specific font scale and line thickness, which is ideal for notes in a notebook.

– Create function for WandB bar visualization (plot_wb_bar): this function opens a connection to WandB (Weights & Biases) for data visualization, creates a table from the data and plots a bar chart in WandB.

– Create a function for calculating the frequency of values (count_values): this function creates a DataFrame containing the frequencies of occurrence of different values in a column of the DataFrame df. It may also return only the first 10 values.

– Create function for creating an intermediate DataFrame (intermediate_df): this function creates a new DataFrame from two lists, one for labels and one for values.

– Define color palettes: five different color palettes (pal1, pal2, pal3, pal4, pal5) are defined, each containing different shades.

Once these functions and parameters are defined, we begin EDA analysis by applying these functions to process and then visualize the data in a way that makes it easier to understand and analyze.

18.4.1.2. *Data analysis and findings*

Continuing the EDA analysis, we want to print the distribution of areas by state in the United States since our dataset contains data from each state. This will allow us to see which state contains more data, which contains less data, etc.

This is accomplished with the following command that generates our graph.

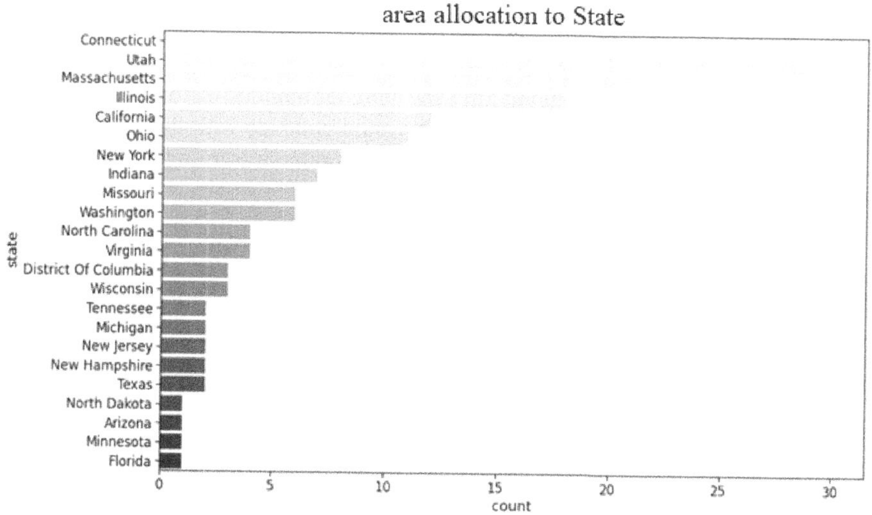

Figure 18.1. *Graph of the distribution of districts by state in the US based on data from districts_df*

18.4.1.3. *Big data analysis*

To perform big data analysis, we generate time series that will show us the impact of COVID-19 on digital education.

The graph above depicts a series of time series for various states, illustrating the metric noted as Pct_Access (percentage of access to digital education) in the time period from January 2020 to November 2020. According to the graph, COVID-19 may have impacted digital learning based on the trends visible in the graphs:

1) Increase in digital learning access: for most states, there is a noticeable increase in "Pct_Access" beginning around March 2020, which coincides with the widespread implementation of closure measures and the transition to online education due to COVID-19. This suggests that there has been an increase in the use of digital learning platforms as schools have transitioned to distance learning.

2) Differential impact by state: the degree of increase and patterns of access varied by state. For example, Arizona shows a high and somewhat unstable level of access, which may indicate an ongoing and potentially changing interaction with digital learning tools. In contrast, North Dakota shows a sharp but brief increase, suggesting a rapid adjustment followed by a decline in digital learning access.

3) Effect of summer vacation: as illustrated, there is a decrease around June, July and August, likely due to summer vacation when students are typically away from

school. This suggests a seasonal pattern where access to digital learning decreases when a school is not in a session.

4) Possible re-launch in autumn: after the summer months, there is evidence that access levels begin to increase again, which would coincide with the start of a new school year and, likely, a resumption or increase in remote learning due to ongoing pandemic restrictions.

5) Differences in sustained participation: some states, such as New York, show a relatively consistent level of access throughout the period after the initial surge, which may indicate a more consistent and sustained interaction with digital learning.

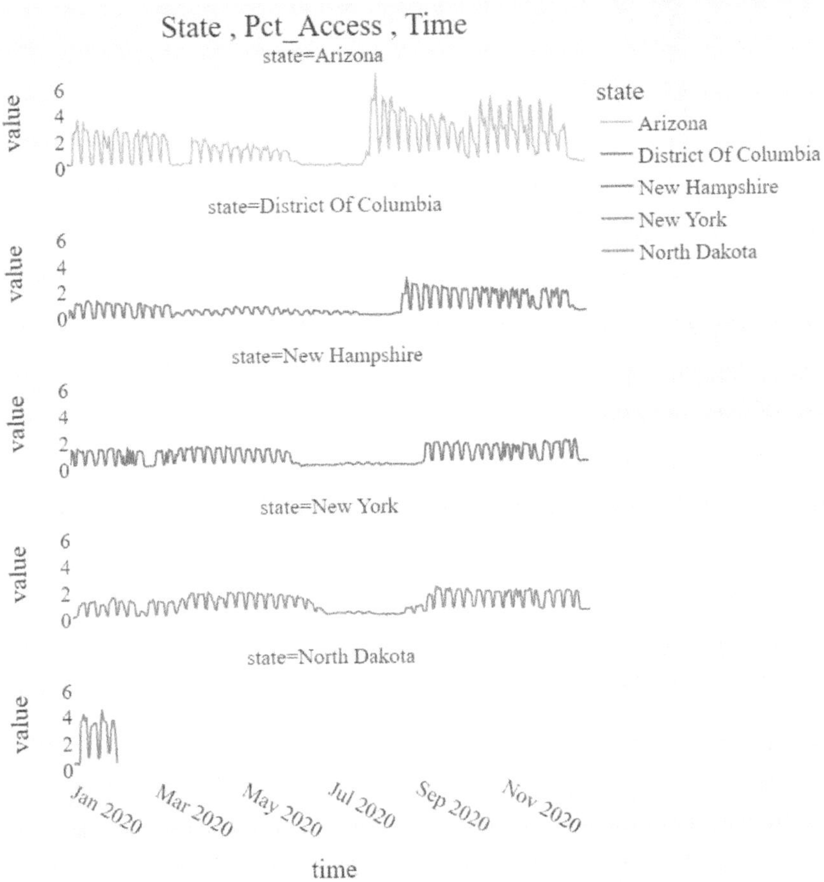

Figure 18.2. *Time series from various states, illustrating trends in the percentage of access to digital learning (Pct_Access) from January to November 2020, with the impact of COVID-19 on education. For a color version of this figure, see www.iste.co.uk/dimotikalis/data5.zip*

The graph suggests that COVID-19 led to a significant shift toward digital learning, with a significant increase in access during the months when traditional schools were closed. The subsequent decline during the summer holidays and the varying degrees of replication reflect both the seasonal patterns of schooling and the evolving response to the challenges of pandemic education.

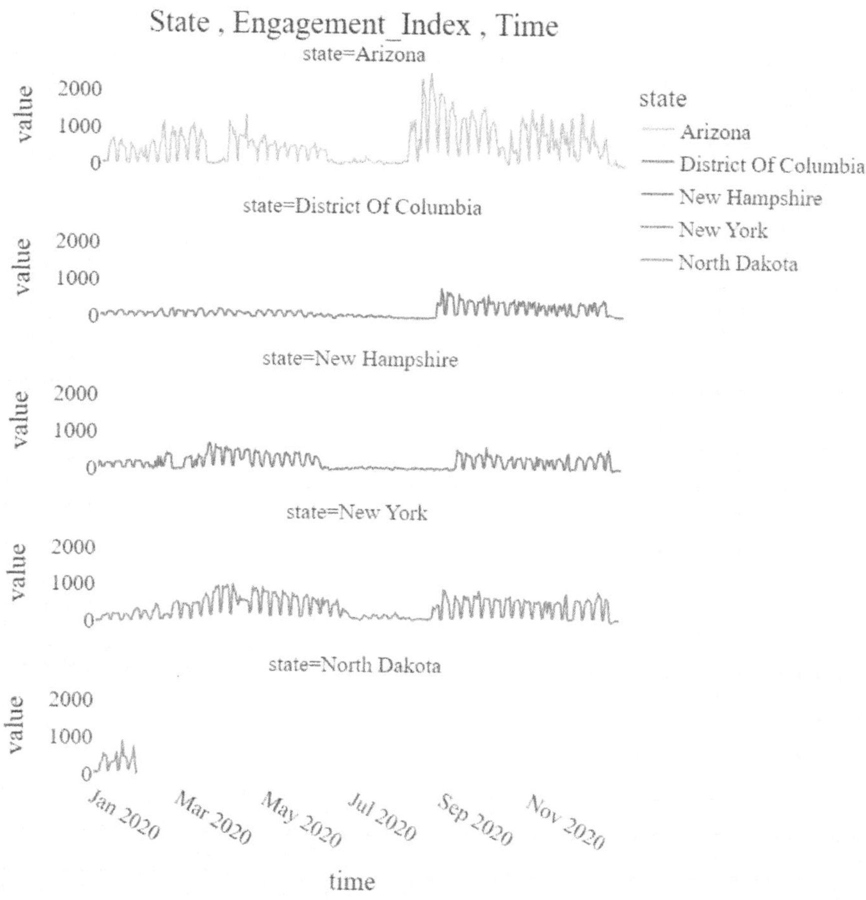

Figure 18.3. *Time series of different states for the Engagement in Digital Education Index from January to November 2020, showing the impact of COVID-19 on different engagement patterns. For a color version of this figure, see www.iste.co.uk/dimotikalis/data5.zip*

The graph above shows time series for various states in terms of the Engagement Index (how many students started online education) over time from January 2020 to

November 2020. The following is a breakdown of how it appears that COVID-19 affected digital learning in each state, based on the graphs:

1) Arizona: there is significant volatility in the Engagement Index, with peaks as high as 2,000 points. This may indicate a high degree of interaction with digital learning, with a strong influence from the pandemic.

2) Federal District of Columbia: the Course Initiation Index (engagement) is relatively stable and lower, indicating a mild reaction to the transition to digital learning.

3) New Hampshire: the Engagement Index appears to be stable, with a slight increase over the year, likely reflecting a gradual increase in digital engagement due to COVID-19.

4) New York: there is an increase at the beginning, likely due to the initial transition to digital learning, with the Engagement Index remaining relatively high but stable throughout the rest of the year.

5) North Dakota: it shows a sudden increase early in the year, possibly in response to the pandemic, after which the Engagement Index returns to lower levels.

The period identified with low activity likely corresponds to summer vacation, when digital engagement declines due to students being out of school. The variations and trends observed in these graphs provide insight into how the pandemic may have affected digital education in different geographic areas.

The graph above shows the percentage access (Pct_Access) to digital learning by different locale – city, rural, suburb and town – during 2020, from January to November. Each graph shows trends in digital engagement for each type of locale during the COVID-19 pandemic.

A breakdown for each region is as follows:

1) City: the graph shows stable peaks and valleys, which may represent regular periods of learning and rest, such as school schedules and weekends.

2) Rural: the observed variability is similar to that of cities, but the pattern appears less pronounced, possibly due to different school schedules or Internet access.

3) Suburb: here, we observe smoother peaks, which may indicate more consistent and regular digital engagement, which may be related to more uniform access to technological resources.

4) Small towns: the graph for small towns shows some consistency in digital engagement with smaller peaks, possibly reflecting different school habits or challenges.

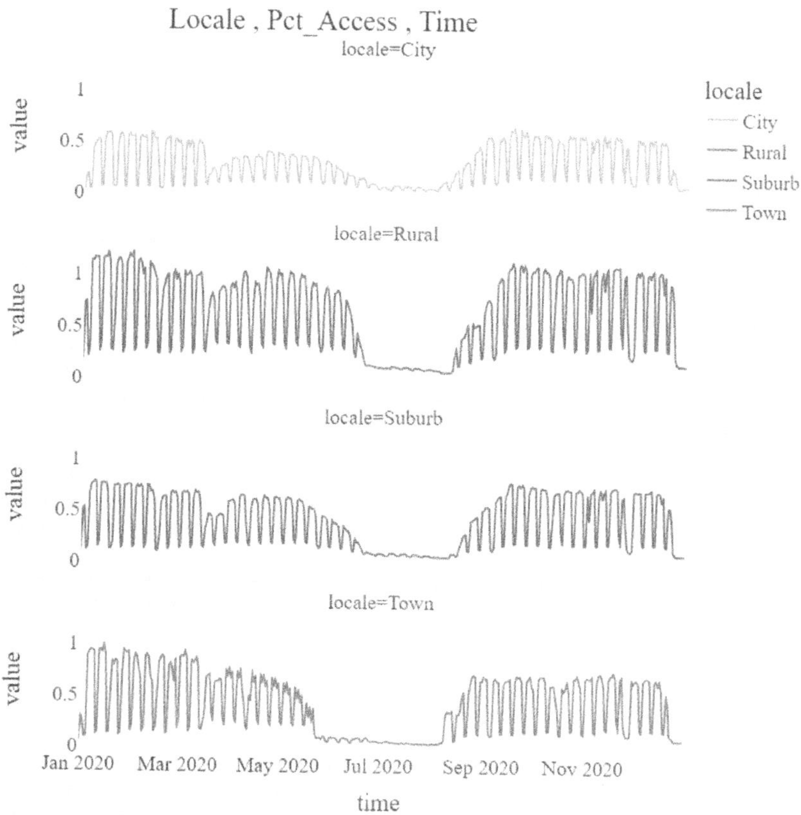

Figure 18.4. *Graph of percentage access to digital learning (Pct_Access) for different environments – urban, rural, suburban and small towns – in 2020, highlighting digital participation trends during the COVID-19 pandemic. For a color version of this figure, see www.iste.co.uk/dimotikalis/data5.zip*

All of the graphs show a general decrease in engagement during the summer months, which may correspond to summer vacation, as we have already mentioned. This decline is consistent with the reduced use of digital learning when schools are closed. The overall trend and variation by district type provides evidence of how different environmental conditions may have affected educational interaction during the COVID-19 pandemic.

Finally, the graph above shows the Digital Learning Course Start Index for different localities – cities (City), rural areas (Rural), suburbs (Suburb) and small towns (Town) – throughout the year 2020, from January to November. Each graph shows trends in access to digital education during the COVID-19 pandemic.

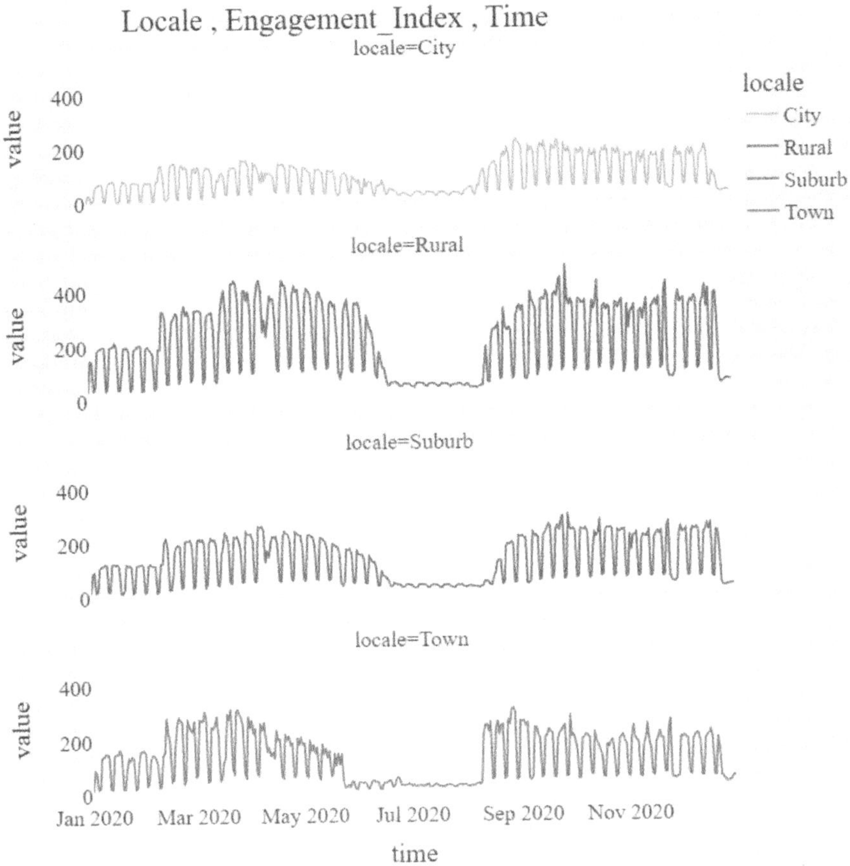

Figure 18.5. *Graph of the Digital Learning Course Start Index for different local contexts (cities, rural areas, suburbs and small towns) in 2020, illustrating trends in participation during the COVID-19 pandemic. For a color version of this figure, see www.iste.co.uk/dimotikalis/data5.zip*

For each category, the breakdown is as follows:

1) Cities (City): the graph shows a steady activity with frequent peaks and valleys, which may represent regular periods of learning and rest, such as school trips and weekends.

2) Rural: the pattern is similar to that of urban areas, but there appears to be a relatively higher frequency of peaks and valleys, which may indicate different rates of digital engagement.

3) Suburbs (Suburb): compared with cities and rural areas, the Engagement Index shows greater stability with less variability. This may suggest a more homogeneous digital learning routine in suburbs.

4) Small Towns (Town): this activity is similar to that of suburbs, with peaks that are less frequent and less intense, which may reflect different school habits or challenges in digital engagement.

As in the previous graphs, there is a general decrease in activity during the summer months, which may be related to summer holidays. The overall analysis of these data reveals how the local environment may have influenced students' interaction with digital learning during the COVID-19 pandemic.

18.5. Conclusion

The COVID-19 pandemic was an unexpected catalyst for the forced transition to digital learning globally, causing significant changes in the education system. Assessing the impact of this transition through big data analysis has revealed valuable insights into the needs, challenges and opportunities that have emerged.

Through the use of time series from different regions, the analysis revealed significant differences in access to (and engagement of) digital learning across urban, suburban, rural and peri-urban areas. For example, urban centers showed a high rate of engagement and participation, whereas rural areas presented more difficulties in terms of access, possibly due to limited network infrastructure.

The time series study also showed a seasonality in digital engagement, with a decrease in the summer months, probably due to the summer holidays. This observation suggests the need for more flexible and tailored approaches to digital learning that take into account the learning cycle.

The use of big data to analyze the impact of COVID-19 on digital learning has allowed researchers and educators to better understand the needs of students and identify where improvements are needed, such as strengthening network infrastructure in rural areas or providing additional resources to support remote education. In addition, time series have revealed the need for more flexible education models that can adapt to unexpected situations, such as a pandemic.

The findings of this study provide critical insights for educational policymakers and stakeholders in making informed decisions regarding the future of digital learning. The clear trends identified in digital learning access and engagement across various states and environments highlight the need for targeted interventions to bridge the digital divide. For urban areas, sustaining high levels of engagement can be achieved through continuous technological support and infrastructure enhancement. In contrast, rural and small-town settings require significant investments in Internet access and digital resources to ensure equitable learning opportunities. The seasonality of digital engagement, particularly the decrease during the summer months, suggests a need for flexible and adaptive educational models that can maintain student engagement year-round. Furthermore, the integration of big data analysis into educational strategies allows for the personalization of learning experiences, addressing specific student needs, and improving overall educational outcomes. By leveraging these insights, educational leaders can develop more resilient, inclusive and effective digital learning ecosystems that are better prepared to handle future disruptions and continuously enhance the quality of education.

In conclusion, the evaluation of digital learning in the COVID-19 era through the analysis of large-scale data has provided a clear picture of the challenges and opportunities that have emerged, as well as the importance of technology as a key tool for continuing learning in times of crisis.

18.6. Suggestions for further research

In this context, future research should focus on solving the challenges that emerged during the pandemic and consider strategies to respond to the developments of the future educational landscape. The integration of technology in education is not just a temporary solution but an opportunity to substantially improve and renew learning processes. The continuous evolution and constant enrichment of digital learning are essential for the development of a resilient and interactive educational environment that can meet the demands of the 21st century.

18.7. References

Alamri, H., Lowell, V., Watson, W., Watson, S.L. (2020). Using personalized learning as an instructional approach to motivate learners in online higher education: Learner self-determination and intrinsic motivation. *Journal of Research on Technology in Education*, 52, 322–352. doi: 10.1080/15391523.2020.1728449.

Alqahtani, M.A., Alamri, M.M., Sayaf, A.M., Al-Rahmi, W.M. (2022). Investigating students' perceptions of online learning use as a digital tool for educational sustainability during the COVID-19 pandemic. *Frontiers in Psychology*, 13, 886272. doi: 10.3389/fpsyg.2022.886272.

Alturki, U. and Aldraiweesh, A. (2021). Application of learning management system (LMS) during the COVID-19 pandemic: A sustainable acceptance model of the expansion technology approach. *Sustainability*, 13(19), 10991. doi: 10.3390/su131910991.

Antonopoulou, H., Giannoulis, A., Theodorakopoulos, L., Halkiopoulos, C. (2022). Socio-cognitive awareness of inmates through an encrypted innovative educational platform. *International Journal of Learning, Teaching and Educational Research*, 21(9), 52–75. doi: 10.26803/ijlter.21.9.4.

Anwar, N., Ismail, M.S., Lissyari, M.S. (2022). The development of offline learning to online learning in the era of the Covid 19 pandemic and emerging impacts on Indonesian students. *Jurnal Islam Dan Masyarakat Kontemporari*, 23, 164–171. doi: 10.37231/jimk.2022.23.1.658.

Bai, L. and Jiang, L. (2021). Research on 'dual system' educational culture in German based on big data analysis. In *International Conference on Education, Information Management and Service Science (EIMSS)*, Xi'an. doi: 10.1109/EIMSS53851.2021.00009.

Bazimaziki, G. (2020). Challenges in using ICT gadgets to cope with effects of COVID-19 on education: A short survey of online teaching literature in English. *International Journal of Humanities and Education Development (IJHED)*, 2, 299–307.

Candrayani, K.M.A., Made, I., Suarjaya, D., Agung Cahyawan, A.A.K. (2023). Analisis Sentimen Pembelajaran Daring Era Pandemi COVID-19 Menggunakan Naive Bayes Dan SVM. *TEMATIK*, 10, 47–53. doi: 10.38204/tematik.v10i1.1274.

Chau, K.Y., Law, K.M.Y., Tang, Y.M. (2021). Impact of self-directed learning and educational technology readiness on synchronous E-learning. *Journal of Organizational and End User Computing*, 33(6), 1–20. doi: 10.4018/JOEUC.20211101.oa26.

Chen, V., Sandford, A., LaGrone, M., Charbonneau, K., Kong, J., Ragavaloo, S. (2022). An exploration of instructors' and students' perspectives on remote delivery of courses during the COVID-19 pandemic. *British Journal of Educational Technology*, 53(3), 512–533. doi: 10.1111/bjet.13205.

Chiablaem, P. (2021). Enhancing English communication skills of Thai university students through Google Apps for Education (GAFE) in a digital era during Covid-19 pandemic. *Shanlax International Journal of Education*, 9, 91–98. doi: 10.34293/education.v9i3.3921.

Chowdhury, M.J.M., Ferdous, M.S., Biswas, K., Chowdhury, N., Muthukkumarasamy, V. (2020). COVID-19 contact tracing: Challenges and future directions. *IEEE Access*, 8, 225703–225729. doi: 10.1109/ACCESS.2020.3036718.

Coleman, E. and Mtshazi, S. (2017). Factors affecting the use and non-use of Learning Management Systems (LMS) by academic staff. *South African Computer Journal*, 29(3). doi: 10.18489/sacj.v29i3.459.

Costa, Y., Cunha, M., Oliveira, A.F., Rivero, L., Priscila, A., Meireles, A., Viana, D. (2022). Improving accessibility in virtual learning environments and educational resources: A practical case and future challenges. In *14th International Conference on Computer Supported Education*. doi: 10.5220/0011092400003182.

Dhawan, S. (2020). Online learning: A panacea in the time of COVID-19 crisis. *Journal of Educational Technology Systems*, 49(1), 5–22. doi: 10.1177/0047239520934018.

Dinh, L.P. and Nguyen, T.T. (2022). Convenient and comfortable, yet limited in many ways: Advantages and disadvantages of online learning during the COVID-19 pandemic from perspectives of social work students in Vietnam. *Asia-Pacific Journal of Social Work and Development*, 33, 193–201.

Elgrably, I.S. and Oliveira, S.R.B. (2022). Using flipped classroom to promote active learning and engagement in a software testing subject remotely during the COVID-19 pandemic. In *IEEE Frontiers in Education Conference (FIE)*, Nashville. doi: 10.1109/FIE56618.2022.9962379.

Firmansyah, R., Putri, D.M., Wicaksono, M.G.S., Putri, S.F., Widianto, A.A. (2021). *The University Students' Perspectives on the Advantages and Disadvantages of Online Learning Due to COVID-19*. Atlantis Press, Dordrecht. doi: 10.2991/aebmr.k.210717.025.

Gareev, I., Gallyametdinov, A., Beylerli, O., Valitov, E., Alyshov, A., Pavlov, V., Izmailov, A., Zhao, S. (2021). The opportunities and challenges of telemedicine during COVID-19 pandemic. *Frontiers in Bioscience*, 13, 291–298. doi: 10.52586/E885.

Gkintoni, E., Dimakos, I., Halkiopoulos, C., Antonopoulou, H. (2023). Contributions of neuroscience to educational praxis: A systematic review. *Emerging Science Journal*, 7, 146–158. doi: 10.28991/ESJ-2023-SIED2-012.

Günther, S.A. (2021). The impact of social norms on students' online learning behavior: Insights from two randomized controlled trials. In *11th International Learning Analytics and Knowledge Conference*, Newport Beach, CA. doi: 10.1145/3448139.3448141.

Haji, S.A. (2020). Exploring the frequent use of the learning management systems (LMS) features and learners' interactions in higher education. *European Journal of Open Education and E-Learning Studies*, 5. doi: 10.46827/ejoe.v5i2.3477.

Halkiopoulos, C., Antonopoulou, H., Giotopoulos, K. (2023). Implementation of digital marketing techniques in smart tourism. In *Tourism, Travel, and Hospitality in a Smart and Sustainable World. IACuDiT 2022*, Katsoni, V. (ed.). Springer, Cham. doi: 10.1007/978-3-031-26829-8_24.

Hallett, J. and De, S. (2020). Effects of COVID-19 on education in healthcare and STEM. Preprint, AIJR. doi: 10.13140/RG.2.2.36137.21607.

Helgesson, M., Marklund, S., Gustafsson, K., Aronsson, G., Leineweber, C. (2020). Interaction effects of physical and psychosocial working conditions on risk for sickness absence: A prospective study of nurses and care assistants in Sweden. *International Journal of Environmental Research and Public Health*, 17(20), 7427. doi: 10.3390/ijerph17207427.

Hollister, B., Nair, P., Hill-Lindsay, S., Chukoskie, L. (2022). Engagement in online learning: Student attitudes and behavior during COVID-19. *Frontiers in Education*, 7. doi: 10.3389/feduc.2022.851019.

Jalongo, M.R. (2021). The effects of COVID-19 on early childhood education and care: Research and resources for children, families, teachers, and teacher educators. *Early Childhood Education Journal*, 49(5), 763–774. doi: 10.1007/s10643-021-01208-y.

Kalogeratos, G., Alexandropoulou, A., Pierrakeas, C. (2023). Digital and socio emotional benefits of the students and the teachers from the implementation of a STEAM education project. In *14th International Conference on Information, Intelligence, Systems & Applications (IISA)*. IEEE. doi: 10.1109/IISA59645.2023.10345899.

Karras, A., Giannaros, A., Theodorakopoulos, L., Krimpas, G.A., Kalogeratos, G., Karras, C., Sioutas, S. (2023). FLIBD: A federated learning-based IoT big data management approach for privacy-preserving over Apache Spark with FATE. *Electronics*, 12(22), 4633. doi: 10.3390/electronics12224633.

Karras, A., Giannaros, A., Karras, C., Theodorakopoulos, L., Mammassis, C.S., Krimpas, G.A., Sioutas, S. (2024). TinyML algorithms for big data management in large-scale IoT systems. *Future Internet*, 16(2), 42. doi: 10.3390/fi16020042.

Khargonkar, N., Desai, K., Prabhakaran, B., Annaswamy, T.M. (2022). Virtepex: Virtual remote tele-physical examination system. In *Designing Interactive Systems Conference.* doi: 10.1145/3532106.3533486.

Kruger, D., Inman, S., Ding, Z., Kang, Y., Kuna, P., Liu, Y., Lu, X., Oro, S., Wang, Y. (2015). Improving teacher effectiveness: Designing better assessment tools in learning management systems. *Future Internet*, 7(4), 484–499. doi: 10.3390/fi7040484.

Leoste, J., Lavicza, Z., Fenyvesi, K., Tuul, M., Õun, T. (2022). Enhancing digital skills of early childhood teachers through online science, technology, engineering, art, math training programs in Estonia. *Frontiers in Education*, 7. doi: 10.3389/feduc.2022.894142.

Ling, N.H., Chen, C.J., Teh, C.S., John, D.S., Ch'ng, L.C., Lay, Y.F. (2023). Global trends of educational data mining in online learning. *International Journal of Technology in Education*, 6(4), 656–680. doi: 10.46328/ijte.558.

Listiyanti, E. and Indrawati, D. (2022). The impact of Covid-19 on the implementation of online learning at SDN Jenggot for the 2020 academic year. *Buana Pendidikan*, 18(1), 135–142. doi: 10.36456/bp.vol18.no1.a5240.

Liu, Y. and Shirley, T. (2021). Without crossing a border: Exploring the impact of shifting study abroad online on students' learning and intercultural competence development during the COVID-19 pandemic. *Online Learning*, 25(1). doi: 10.24059/olj.v25i1.2471.

Lutfiani, N. and Meria, L. (2022). Utilization of big data in educational technology research. *International Transactions on Education Technology*, 1(1), 73–83. doi: 10.33050/itee.v1i1.198.

Lv, T., Zou, Y., Tang, P. (2023). Research on educational big data analysis based on Hive and Spark. In *8th International Conference on Information Systems Engineering (ICISE).* IEEE Computer Society, Los Alamitos, CA. doi: 10.1109/ICISE60366.2023.00076.

Malik, F., Ajmal, F., Jumani, Z. (2020). The effects of COVID-19 on education in Pakistan: Students' perspective. *International Journal of Distance Education and E-Learning*, 6(1), 217–234.

Md Salleh, N., Sarina, N., Hamid, R., Abdul Rahman, K., Zainal Abidin, I.F., Zawawi, A.S. (2022). Learning flexibility and environmental changes with the advent of online learning during COVID-19 pandemic. *Jurnal Intelek*, 17(1), 116. doi: 10.24191/ji.v17i1.15901.

Means, B. (2022). Making insights from educational psychology and educational technology research more useful for practice. *Educational Psychologist*, 57(3), 226–230. doi: 10.1080/00461520.2022.2061974.

Muntu, D.F., Yuliana, O.Y., Tarigan, Z.J.H. (2023). The influence of digital literacy on learning effectiveness through classroom management: Moderating effect of IT infrastructure. *Petra International Journal of Business Studies*, 6(1), 42–52. doi: 10.9744/petraijbs.6.1.42-52.

Nandlall, N., Hawke, L.D., Hayes, E., Darnay, K., Daley, M., Relihan, J., Henderson, J. (2022). Learning through a pandemic: Youth experiences with remote learning during the COVID-19 pandemic. *Sage Open*, 12(3), 215824402211241. doi: 10.1177/215824402211 24122.

Oraif, I. and Elyas, T. (2021). The impact of COVID-19 on learning: Investigating EFL learners' engagement in online courses in Saudi Arabia. *Education Sciences*, 11(3), 99. doi: 10.3390/educsci11030099.

Ovionita, V. and Saridewi, S. (2022). The impact of online and offline learning on social development of early childhood in the Covid-19 pandemic. *EduBasic Journal: Jurnal Pendidikan Dasar*, 4, 23–30. doi: 10.17509/ebj.v4i1.38196.

Pathare, A.V. (2023). Medical interventions and their poor scientific backup: A threat to evidence-based medicine. *International Journal of Advanced Research in Medicine*, 5(2), 117–120. doi: 10.22271/27069567.2023.v5.i2b.488.

Peng, P. and Fu, W. (2022). A pattern recognition method of personalized adaptive learning in online education. *Mobile Networks and Applications*, 27, 1186–1198. doi: 10.1007/s11036-022-01942-6.

Presser, S., Couper, M.P., Lessler, J.T., Martin, E., Martin, J., Rothgeb, J.M., Singer, E. (2004). *Public Opinion Quarterly*, 68 (1), 109–130. doi: 10.1093/poq/nfh008.

Rasheed Hasan, L. (2020). Is it possible to use Facebook instead of Moodle learning management systems (LMS) to support the learning process? In *The 4th International Conference on E-Society, E-Education and E-Technology*, Taipei. doi: 10.1145/3421682.3421695.

Restrepo, E., Ko, N., Warner, E.T. (2024). An evaluation of readability and understandability of online education materials for breast cancer survivors. *Journal of Cancer Survivorship: Research and Practice*, 18, 457–465. doi: 10.1007/s11764-022-01240-w.

Sedon, M.F., Zulkifli, C.Z., Khairani, M.Z., Sabran, A.B., Zalay, A.A. (2021). Covid-19: Disadvantages of online learning towards visual arts practiced-based nature. *IJEBD International Journal of Entrepreneurship and Business Development*, 4(1), 25–30. doi: 10.29138/ijebd.v4i1.1123.

See, A.R. and Advincula, W.D. (2021). Creating tactile educational materials for the visually impaired and blind students using AI cloud computing. *Applied Sciences*, 11(16), 7552. doi: 10.3390/app11167552.

Thamri, T., Hasan, D.C., Rina, N., Gani, M.H., Gani, M.H., Miranda, A.M. (2022). Advantages and disadvantages of online learning during the COVID-19 pandemic: The perceptions of students at Bung Hatta University. *KnE Social Sciences*, Dubai. doi: 10.18502/kss.v7i6.10636.

Theodorakopoulos, L., Antonopoulou, H., Mamalougou, V., Giotopoulos, K. (2022). The drivers of volume volatility: A big data analysis based on economic uncertainty measures for the Greek banking system. *Banks and Bank Systems*, 17, 49–57.

Verma, D., Sharma, D., Khapre, M. (2021). Content analysis of educational videos on hand hygiene during COVID-19 pandemic. *Journal of Education and Health Promotion*, 10, 278. doi: 10.4103/jehp.jehp_1024_20.

Vlachou, E., Karras, A., Karras, C., Theodorakopoulos, L., Halkiopoulos, C., Sioutas, S. (2023). Distributed Bayesian inference for large-scale IoT systems. *Big Data and Cognitive Computing*, 8(1), 1. doi: 10.3390/bdcc8010001.

Wang, Y. and Ma, C. (2022). Precision strategy of ideological and political education using big data analysis in online behavior monitoring environment. *Journal of Environmental and Public Health*, 2394668. doi: 10.1155/2022/2394668.

Weißenfels, M., Benick, M., Perels, F. (2022). Teachers' prerequisites for online teaching and learning: Individual differences and relations to well-being during the COVID-19 pandemic. *Educational Psychology*, 42, 1283–1300. doi: 10.1080/01443410.2022.2034747.

Wilson-Menzfeld, G., Gates, J.R., Moreland, M., Raw, H., Johnson, A. (2023). Learning digital skills online: Empowering older adults through one-to-one, online digital training provision. *Frontiers in Psychology*, 14, 1122277. doi: 10.3389/fpsyg.2023.1122277.

Wu, W., Hu, R., Tan, R., Liu, H. (2022). Exploring factors of middle school teachers' satisfaction with online training for sustainable professional development under the impact of COVID-19. *Sustainability*, 14(20), 13244. doi: 10.3390/su142013244.

Yu, Z. (2021). The effects of gender, educational level, and personality on online learning outcomes during the COVID-19 pandemic. *International Journal of Educational Technology in Higher Education*, 18(1), 14. doi: 10.1186/s41239-021-00252-3.

Zhang, L., Carter, R.A., Qian, X., Yang, S., Rujimora, J., Wen, S. (2022). Academia's responses to crisis: A bibliometric analysis of literature on online learning in higher education during COVID-19. *British Journal of Educational Technology*, 53, 620–646. doi: 10.1111/bjet.13191.

Zhao, J. and Wang, Y. (2021). A novel massive big data analysis of educational examination research using a linear mixed-effects model. *Complexity*, 2021(1), 1–14. doi: 10.1155/2021/3752598.

19

Credit Card Fraud Detection with Machine Learning and Big Data Analytics: A PySpark Framework Implementation

This chapter presents a comprehensive study on applying machine learning (ML) techniques for real-time credit card fraud detection. With the increasing prevalence of credit card fraud, financial institutions face the challenge of detecting fraudulent transactions promptly and accurately. This research evaluates various ML models, including logistic regression, decision trees, random forests, XGBoost (eXtreme gradient boosting) and deep convolutional neural networks for their effectiveness in identifying fraudulent activities. The use of PySpark for processing large-scale transaction data highlights the importance of real-time analysis, adaptive learning and handling imbalanced datasets. Key findings reveal that XGBoost, with its balance of accuracy and complexity, emerged as the most promising model, achieving an accuracy rate of 98% in detecting fraudulent transactions. This chapter further discusses the potential of ensemble methods, graph-powered systems and intelligent sampling in enhancing fraud detection capabilities. Challenges such as overfitting, data access and the need for real-time analysis are addressed. Future research directions include implementing models in live transaction environments, expanding model applicability across financial platforms and developing advanced anomaly detection methodologies. This study underscores the pivotal role of ML in safeguarding financial transactions against fraud, offering significant implications for consumers, financial institutions and the broader financial ecosystem.

19.1. Introduction

Machine learning (ML) has demonstrated its ability to significantly revolutionize decision-making processes in various domains, particularly in tasks that require high

Chapter written by Leonidas THEODORAKOPOULOS, Ioanna KALLIAMPAKOU, Alexandra THEODOROPOULOU and Fotini ZAKKA.

levels of precision, effectiveness and adaptability, such as detecting fraud in transactions, diagnosing healthcare conditions and enhancing customer experiences.

Traditional decision-making typically relies on empirical methods, the expertise of a specialist, or rigid, outdated algorithms that cannot adapt to new information or intricate patterns found in modern data. Although the methods above may yield positive results in specific domains, they are often constrained by inherent human cognitive biases and the sheer impossibility or difficulty of analyzing such immense volumes of incoming data. Consequently, decisions made using conventional methods instead of ML techniques may experience delays in response, considerably higher rates of errors and a general inability to handle large datasets to uncover accurate and valuable information.

ML algorithms are being used to automate the analysis of large and complex datasets, enabling the discovery of patterns and relationships that human analysts or experts may not notice. By continuously learning and adapting, ML algorithms greatly increase decision-making accuracy. They accomplish this by iteratively improving their models' use of data, thereby minimizing errors in tasks such as fraud detection. This improves the quality of decisions and accelerates the decision-making process, allowing for immediate analysis and responses.

The prevalence of credit card fraud is increasing in modern economies, paralleling advancements in digital transactions. With the advent of artificial intelligence, ML and big data, innovative tools are being developed to combat fraud. According to the literature (Boutaher et al. 2020), a machine learning algorithm can use past transactions to develop highly intricate features that detect fraud in real time. This algorithm has the potential to outperform even the most skilled human investigators.

Nevertheless, despite technological advancements, the progress of fraud detection algorithms has encountered substantial impediments (Minastireanu and Mesnita 2019). Significant challenges arise from the imbalanced nature of fraud-related data, the requirement for benchmarks and standards to assess classifiers and the complexity of obtaining confidential transaction data for research purposes.

Researchers have proposed several ML methods to address this issue, including employing genetic algorithms to select features, integrating the spatiotemporal attention mechanism with graphical neural networks and utilizing Apache Spark with ML to analyze extensive data (Alnafessah and Casale 2020). Nevertheless, detecting credit card fraud remains a significant challenge because of the constantly evolving characteristics of fraudulent patterns and behaviors and the imbalanced nature of the datasets.

This research contributes significantly by introducing a novel framework for detecting fraud using ML methods tailored to handle large datasets. It aims to introduce novel methodologies or enhancements to existing methods to address the challenges associated with detecting fraud in extensive datasets. The research study also offers guidance for implementing algorithms in real-time settings, enabling banking and financial institutions to respond promptly to fraudulent activities. Moreover, it explains the difficulties and possibilities of using ML to identify credit card fraud. Finally, the study enhances the development of payment security technologies, resulting in a more secure and reliable consumer environment.

19.2. Literature review

19.2.1. *Introduction to credit card fraud detection*

Currently, financial institutions face significant problems with digital transactions, especially fraud detection, specifically fraud detection regarding credit cards. While the digitization of financial services is increasing daily, so are online transactions, thus increasing the risk of fraudulent activities.

Recent research (Kasa et al. 2019; Priscilla and Prabha 2020; Shirodkar et al. 2020) has underscored the rise in credit card fraud, necessitating the use of ML methods to swiftly identify suspicious transactions. Financial organizations and businesses are investing heavily in the development of advanced fraud detection systems, demonstrating their commitment to safeguarding customers and their personal interests. Their primary goal is to identify and halt potentially fraudulent activities, ensuring the security of all parties involved.

One of the main problems that needs to be addressed in detecting credit card fraud is the imbalance discerned in the datasets. Legitimate transactions seem to outnumber fraudulent transactions, which limits the ability of experts to detect fraud. For this reason, generative adversarial networks (GANs) have emerged. They are used as a powerful solution, generating synthetic data to balance the datasets and improve the accuracy of detection rates (Fiore et al. 2019). ML techniques provide a plethora of algorithms suitable for such tasks. Techniques such as logistic regression, decision trees, random forests, and the XGBoost algorithm are some of the most commonly applied algorithms (Abdulghani et al. 2021). The deep convolutional neural network (DCNN) design has improved detection accuracy, especially when handling large volumes of data (Karthika and Senthilselvi 2023).

19.2.2. *The importance of detecting credit card fraud*

Detecting credit card fraud is crucial not only for safeguarding consumer financial assets and maintaining trust in payment systems, but also for ensuring data security, enhancing decision-making processes, and leveraging advanced machine learning techniques to identify suspicious activities with greater accuracy and efficiency. The detection of credit card fraud serves several important purposes. It protects consumers by shielding them from fake transactions, identity theft and financial harm. Additionally, it helps protect financial institutions from losses caused by suspicious or fraudulent behavior, thereby supporting the stability of the broader financial system. Detecting and preventing fraud in time can also potentially lower the costs linked to the investigation and resolution of such incidents. Ensuring legal compliance ensures that the right regulations and standards are followed, depending on the market or the country. Efficient fraud detection helps consumers trust more in the credit card system, promoting more frequent usage of credit cards. Finally, successful fraud detection offers a significant boost to the reputation of organizations that issue credit cards and provide payment services by showcasing their dedication to security and customer safety.

Fraud detection systems utilize various techniques to detect and prevent fake transactions in time (Darwish 2020). These are ML algorithms, anomaly detection algorithms and various behavioral analysis techniques. These techniques and systems remain involved in the rise and further complexity of the different forms that fraudulent activities can take. Big data and AI have played equally important roles in improving fraud detection systems since they allow real-time analysis of vast volumes of data with great precision (Tyagi et al. 2022). If we want to prevent fraudulent activities and protect the interests of customers and financial institutions, we need to continue upgrading and evolving detection algorithms and methods.

19.2.3. *Role of machine learning in improving decision-making processes in fraud detection*

ML has revolutionized the methods used by organizations to detect, analyze and combat fraudulent behaviors (Velasco et al. 2021). Consequently, this directly affects organizations' decision-making processes, particularly in the area of fraud detection, leading to substantial improvements. They can implement and utilize advanced ML algorithms to analyze the constant influx of extensive datasets, uncover concealed patterns and predict potential fraudulent transactions with exceptional precision and speed. Below, we examine the concept of ML and its importance in facilitating efficient decision-making in the context of fraud detection.

19.2.4. *Automated pattern recognition*

In regard to the identification of fraudulent activities, ML's unique ability to recognize patterns automatically is unmatched and of the utmost importance. ML algorithms, especially unsupervised learning models, seem to perform exceptionally well in identifying complicated patterns within vast datasets, which could lead to fraud detection of any kind. This capability of ML becomes a very important asset in this war of the detection and interception of fraud, especially when fake operations formulate some kind of anomaly or divergence from what is considered normal behavior patterns within the data (Kannagi et al. 2023). Furthermore, the process of continuous learning further enhances the ability of ML models to adapt and change, which are both important in identifying new fraud patterns.

19.2.5. *Predictive modeling*

ML algorithms also support predictive modeling, which can significantly improve an organization's decision-making processes. This can be achieved through the use of historical data to predict future fraudulent transactions or other similar activities. In addition, supervised learning models also have the ability to develop predictive qualities by being trained on existing fraudulent and legitimate datasets; thus, they can be applied to invisible data to effectively estimate the probability rates of fraud (Patil et al. 2018) . Through this predictive power of ML, organizations can detect, even at a proactive level, possible fraud, which allows them to set appropriate measures in place and prevent fraud altogether. By using predictive models, the accuracy of decision-making processes is considerably improved, and a proactive approach to fraud detection and management is promoted within the organization (Karthik et al. 2022).

19.2.6. *Dynamic risk scoring*

Decision-making can also be improved by ML algorithms using a tool called the risk scoring system. Unlike traditional static risk assessment models, these systems work by updating the risk scores for transactions on the basis of available data, patterns and behaviors of detected fraud (Vanini et al. 2023). Thus, decision-making can become diverse and take context into consideration through real-time evaluation. This can make distinguishing between high-risk and low-risk activities much easier (Nascimento et al. 2019). Having detailed risk scoring is vital for resource allocation and minimizing the impact on legitimate transactions as much as possible.

19.2.7. *Anomaly detection*

Anomaly detection, a specialized application of ML, plays a very important role in identifying outliers that may indicate fraudulent activity. By establishing a normative baseline from historical data, ML algorithms can flag transactions that deviate significantly from established patterns (Alazizi et al. 2019). This capability is particularly useful in detecting novel or sophisticated fraud schemes that do not match known fraud signatures. Anomaly detection through ML thus contributes to a more adaptable and resilient fraud detection system.

19.2.8. *Natural language processing (NLP)*

Natural language processing, powered by ML, improves decision-making skills by examining textual information to detect fraudulent activities. NLP can assess customer interactions, feedback and complaints to pinpoint possible signs of fraud (Sood et al. 2023). Through this procedure, NLP can extend the reach of fraud detection beyond just numbers, integrating qualitative observations into decision-making processes. The capacity to swiftly process and evaluate textual information in real time enhances the complexity of the tactics used in fraud detection.

19.2.9. *Integration with existing systems*

ML techniques do not need to be used solely as standalone methods. They can work equally well when integrated into existing business information systems and decision-making frameworks, thus increasing their overall effectiveness (Xu et al. 2023). This integration of traditional fraud detection techniques and ML algorithms can result in a more robust and detailed fraud detection strategy.

19.2.10. *Credit card fraud detection: machine learning applications*

Currently, technology has permeated even the most superficial aspects of our lives, making credit card fraud detection a critical area for both consumers and financial institutions. Fraud can have severe financial and psychological effects on consumers. A closer look at the ML methods predominantly used in this field reveals two primary techniques. Logistic regression is a statistical method valued for its simplicity and effectiveness in predicting categorical outcomes such as the likelihood of a transaction being fraudulent. Decision trees simplify decision-making by dividing data into subsets on the basis of their characteristics, creating a hierarchical structure that helps determine the type of transaction. These methods exemplify the application of ML in enhancing the security and reliability of financial transactions.

The problem of credit card fraud prevention has become a matter of concern in the domain of online transactions. ML models are necessary for detecting and preventing this type of activity. Several ML approaches, such as neural networks, decision trees, support vector machines and deep learning models, have been used to identify credit card fraud through the assessment and evaluation of different data patterns (Esenogho et al. 2022). Most fraud detection systems suffer from this problem, as imbalanced datasets are quite common (Ludera 2021). Various resampling techniques can balance the data to mitigate the problem and increase the accuracy of fraud detection (Abd El-Naby et al. 2023). The most effective algorithms can be gauged using AUC, recall and F1 index.

In this regard, the best performance was obtained from the AllKNN-CatBoost model, with an AUC of 97.94%, a recall of 95.91%, and an F1 index of 87.40% (Alfaiz and Fati 2022). Recently, a new method has been proposed to address the problem of credit card fraud detection. This technique combines the swarm technique with ML in a firefly cluster search algorithm. This technique involves tuning support vector machines, extreme learning machines and extreme gradient-boosting machine-learning models.

19.2.11. *Credit card fraud detection using Apache Spark*

One of the almost optimal solutions for more efficient and far-reaching fraud detection based on credit cards is to make use of Apache Spark in data analysis. With the high processing speeds offered by Spark, the tool works well with large datasets and provides a fast way of identifying probable fraud transactions. Spark incorporates ML algorithms that provide real-time data analysis, making the detection of fraud rather timely and accurate. Besides, Spark supports integration with all kinds of data sources, from banking systems to online chalks – such as those needed for representing a fuller view of transactional behaviors. This ability of cross-platform detection proves to be of paramount importance for the effective prevention of fraud; therefore, it becomes very instrumental for most financial institutions and charge card companies to deter digital fraudulent activities.

Severe threats to the financial sector are from credit card fraud. Some solutions have been proposed in which rigid analysis of data and complex ML algorithms are used for fraud detection in real time. Apache Spark has emerged as a tool in this domain, and numerous studies have investigated its effectiveness in detecting credit card fraud (Chouiekh and Ibn El Haj 2022). These studies have employed diverse ML algorithms, such as the K-means, C5.0 decision tree, naive Bayes, random forest, and multilayer perceptron algorithms, showcasing accuracy rates in identifying fraudulent activities. The proposed models are assessed using authentic and fraudulent credit card datasets, which demonstrate enhanced classification accuracy compared with existing methodologies. The utilization of Apache Spark has proven to be more efficient in deploying fraud detection systems than other methods.

19.2.12. *How can machine learning algorithms enhance decision quality in detecting fraud?*

ML has proven to be an invaluable tool in the identification of online fraudulent activities, making a significant contribution to the fields of financial integrity and security. These algorithms have the ability to learn and anticipate outcomes on the basis of vast datasets, which is impossible when traditional analysis methods are used. This is why we can accept the fact that there is an increase in the quality of the decisions being made by organizations (El Hajjami et al. 2021). Below, we investigate the various ways in which decision quality is improved with respect to fraud detection by utilizing ML algorithms.

19.2.13. *Improved detection accuracy*

ML algorithms enhance detection accuracy by utilizing complex data patterns and relationships that cannot be tracked through manual analysis or traditional computational techniques (Vlachou et al. 2023; Karras et al. 2024). By using techniques such as supervised learning (Khalid et al. 2024), ML models can be trained on historical data that are made of both fraudulent and legitimate transactions. This kind of training enables models to identify subtle and complex indicators of fraud, thereby significantly reducing the instances of false negatives (missed fraud) and false positives (legitimate transactions being flagged as fraudulent). The ability to learn from new data ensures that the models' accuracy improves over time, adapting to new fraud tactics and patterns.

19.2.14. *Real-time processing and analysis*

The ability of ML algorithms to process data in real time plays a vital role in detecting frauds promptly. Unlike approaches that involve processing data in batches, which can cause delays in spotting and addressing fraudulent behavior, ML algorithms can swiftly analyze transactions as they occur, quickly identifying suspicious activities. This feature not only improves decision quality by minimizing the time for fraudulent transactions to slip through unnoticed transactions, but also enables immediate intervention to prevent potential financial losses (Li et al. 2024).

19.2.15. *Handling big data and complex variables*

In regard to detecting fraudulent activity, the emergence of big data has led to both new obstacles and possibilities. The algorithms that are used in ML are designed in such a way that they are able to deal with large numbers of datasets that contain many variables (Singh et al. 2024). They have the ability to collect and evaluate data from a wide variety of sources, including transaction histories, consumer behavior patterns and external databases, to reach well-structured conclusions. With such extensive analytical capabilities, ML algorithms are able to examine a wider variety of elements that influence fraud, which ultimately results in decision-making that is more complex and accurate.

19.2.16. *Adaptive learning for evolving threats*

Fraudulent schemes are continuously evolving and require adaptive mechanisms for effective detection. ML algorithms excel in this respect through their ability to learn from new data perpetually. As they are exposed to the latest fraudulent techniques, ML models adjust their parameters and improve their predictive capabilities (Chen et al. 2024). This ongoing learning process ensures that the decision-making process remains robust against evolving threats, maintaining high detection rates over time.

19.2.17. *Cost efficiency through automation*

Using ML models to automate fraud detection processes results in cost efficiency for organizations (Aburbeian and Fernández-Veiga 2024). Businesses can now better allocate their resources for more critical tasks by implementing automation techniques for data analysis and fraud detection, at least during their initial stages, where a first general screening is needed. This task reallocation reduces operational costs and improves the overall quality of decision-making processes by redirecting human expertise to other key areas within the organization.

19.2.18. *Enhanced scalability*

Traditional fraud detection systems may find it challenging to increase their scaling abilities without an equivalent increase in costs and computational resources.

ML algorithms offer such scaling capabilities, which have been proven essential in the growing volumes of digital transactions and data management (Koutras et al. 2023; Zhao et al. 2023). By using these ML models, organizations can maintain consistent decision quality without the burden of increasing costs or resources (Antonopoulou et al. 2007).

ML algorithms improve accuracy, real-time analysis, adaptation to new threats and cost effectiveness, significantly changing the quality of decision-making processes regarding fraud detection (Zehra et al. 2023). The ability of ML to absorb and learn from enormous datasets, recognize intricate patterns and adapt to ever-evolving fraud schemes places it at the forefront of contemporary fraud detection strategies (Antonopoulou et al. 2023). It is anticipated that these algorithms' role in improving decision quality regarding fraud detection will become increasingly prominent as they continue to develop. This will signal the beginning of a new era in the overall battle against financial fraud.

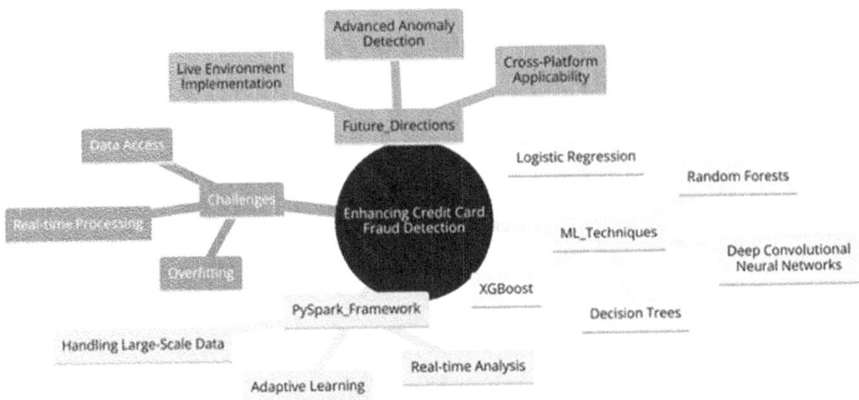

Figure 19.1. *Credit card fraud detection mindmap. For a color version of this figure, see www.iste.co.uk/dimotikalis/data5.zip*

19.3. Materials and methods

In this section, we will present the methods and techniques used to predict credit card fraud. We used the dataset "Credit Card Fraud Detection" from kaggle.com, which contains anonymized data from credit card transactions with a size of more than 200 MB. We will create four training and prediction models: logistic regression, decision trees, random forests and the complex XGBoost method.

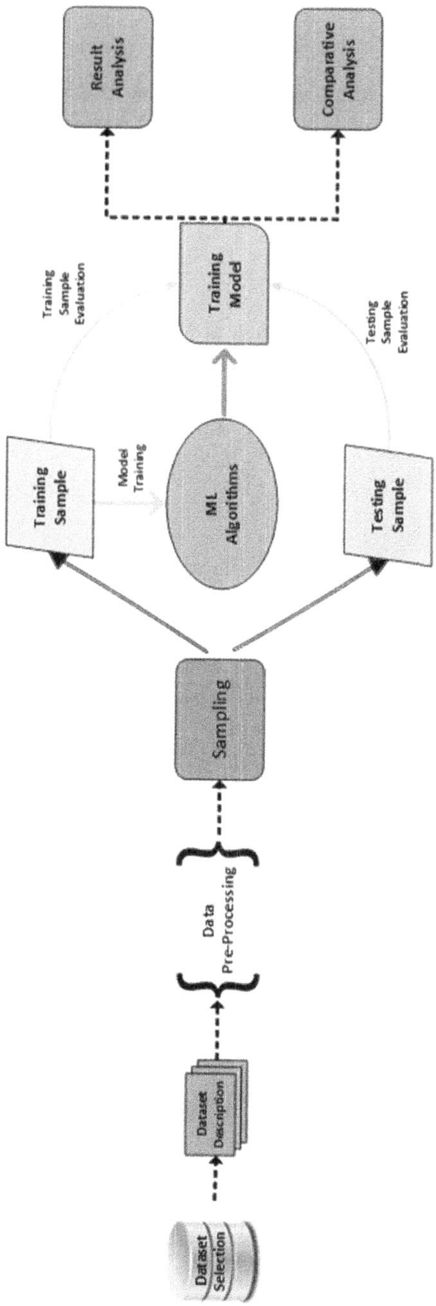

Figure 19.2. *Methodological framework. For a color version of this figure, see www.iste.co.uk/dimotikalis/data5.zip*

19.3.1. *Performance evaluation*

19.3.1.1. *Logistic regression*

Logistic regression is a statistical model often used for classification. Instead of predicting the exact value of a variable, as in linear regression, logistic regression estimates the probability of an outcome on the basis of one or more independent variables. It is ideal for binary classification, such as predicting whether a transaction is fraudulent.

19.3.1.2. *Decision trees*

Decision trees are widely used algorithms in ML that utilize a tree-like structure for decision-making. Each node in the tree represents a question or property, and each branch is a possible answer to that question. Decision trees are easy to understand and interpret but can be sensitive or perform poorly in training with new, unseen data.

19.3.1.3. *Random forest*

The random forest algorithm is an ML algorithm that utilizes predictions from multiple ML algorithms, most notably decision trees, to improve performance and reduce overfitting. Each tree in the forest is trained on a random subset of the data, and the predictions from all the trees are combined to give one final result. This method is very effective in classification and regression.

19.3.1.4. *XGBoost*

XGBoost is an optimized machine learning algorithm that boosts decision trees. It uses a series of models built sequentially, each new model focusing on correcting errors found in the previous models. XGBoost is known for its high performance, ability to handle large datasets effectively and flexibility in parameter tuning.

19.3.1.5. *Dataset description*

To describe the dataset, we first need to study some of the data from it. Specifically, we import the dataset with the following command:

– data=pd.read_csv('creditcard_2023_dataset.csv')

This command imports the dataset into our project and creates a data frame called "data". Then, with data.head() we print some information about the dataset that we will need later. The result of running the above command is shown in Table 19.1.

id	V1	V2	V3	V4	V5	V6	V7	V8	V9	V10	V11	V12	V13	V14
0	-0.260648	-0.469648	2.496266	-0.083724	0.129681	0.732898	0.519014	-0.130006	0.727159	0.637735	-0.987020	0.293438	-0.941386	0.549020
1	0.985100	-0.356045	0.558056	-0.429654	0.277140	0.428605	0.406466	-0.133118	0.347452	0.529808	0.140107	1.564246	0.574074	0.627719
2	-0.260272	-0.949385	1.728538	-0.457986	0.074062	1.419481	0.743511	-0.095576	-0.261297	0.690708	-0.272985	0.659021	0.805173	0.616874
3	-0.152152	-0.508959	1.746840	-1.090178	0.249486	1.143312	0.518269	-0.065130	-0.205698	0.575231	-0.752581	0.737483	0.592994	0.559535
4	-0.206820	-0.165280	1.527053	-0.448293	0.106125	0.530549	0.658849	-0.212660	1.049921	0.968045	-1.203171	1.029577	1.439310	0.241454

Table 19.1. *Printing the first rows of the dataset with data.head() in Python*

V15	V16	V17	V18	V19	V20	V21	V22	V23	V24	V25	V26	V27	V28	Amount
1.804879	0.215598	0.512307	0.333644	0.124270	0.091202	-0.110552	0.217606	-0.134794	0.165999	0.126280	-0.434824	-0.081230	-0.151045	17982.10
0.706121	0.789188	0.403810	0.201799	-0.340687	-0.233984	-0.231984	-0.194936	-0.605761	0.073469	-0.577395	0.296503	-0.248052	-0.064512	6531.37
3.060253	-0.577514	0.885536	0.239442	-2.366079	0.361652	-0.005020	0.702906	0.945045	-1.154666	-0.605564	-0.312895	-0.300258	-0.244718	2513.54
-0.697664	-0.030669	0.242629	2.178616	-1.345060	-0.378223	-0.378223	-0.146927	-0.038212	-1.893131	1.003963	-0.511950	-0.165316	0.048324	5384.44
0.153008	0.224358	0.366466	0.291782	0.445317	0.247237	-0.106984	0.729727	-0.161666	0.312561	-0.141416	1.071126	0.023712	0.419117	14278.97

Table 19.2. *Display the data classes and transaction amount in the dataset*

As shown above, we have the classes of data (v1,v2,v3, etc.) and other classes, such as the number of transactions, as shown in Table 19.2.

The classes, as mentioned earlier, have been anonymized for privacy reasons. The goal here is to identify class correlations to predict the potential for fraud in electronic credit card transactions. Next, by running data.info(), we print the class types contained in our dataset. The results are shown in Table 19.3.

<class ‘pandas.core.frame.DataFrame’>				
RangeIndex: 568,630 entries, 0 to 568,629				
Data columns (total 31 columns):				
#	Column	Non-null	Count	Dtype
0	Id	568,630	nonnull	int64
1	V1	568,630	nonnull	float64
2	V2	568,630	nonnull	float64
3	V3	568,630	nonnull	float64
4	V4	568,630	nonnull	float64
5	V5	568,630	nonnull	float64
6	V6	568,630	nonnull	float64
7	V7	568,630	nonnull	float64
8	V8	568,630	nonnull	float64

Table 19.3. *Presentation of class types in the credit card dataset with the data.info() command*

As shown in Table 19.3, we have the classes and their types. The type – float64 – indicates that this class contains elements with decimal numbers, whereas the ID, which is the odd number of each transaction, is an integer. By running data.describe(), we can see more details about our data and, in particular, some important statistics (Table 19.4).

As shown above, we have the sum (number of numbers) via count for each feature of our dataset, the mean, the standard deviation, the minimum number, the maximum and other important statistics. From the above analysis, we can conclude that we have 568,630 rows of observations with 31 columns. The class row is our output attribute that indicates whether the transaction is fraudulent (1) or not (0) and that no missing data are observed in our dataset. Finally, the data types of all the attributes seem quite satisfactory.

	id	V1	V2	V3	V4	V5	V6	V7	V8	V9
count	568630.000000	5.686300E+05	5.686300E+05	5.686300E+05	5.686300E+05	5.686300E+05	5.686300E+05	5.686300E+05	5.686300E+05	5.686300E+05
mean	284314.500000	-5.638058E-17	-1.319545E-16	-3.518788E-17	-2.879008E-17	7.997245E-18	-3.958636E-17	-3.198898E-17	2.109273E-17	3.998623E-17
std	164149.486122	1.000001E+00	1.000001E+00	1.000001E+00	1.000001E+00	1.000001E+00	1.000001E+00	1.000001E+00	1.000001E+00	1.000001E+00
min	0.000000	-3.495584E+00	-4.099666E+01	-3.183760E+00	-4.951222E+00	-9.952786E+00	-2.111111E+01	-4.351839E+00	-1.075634E+01	-3.751919E+00
25%	142157.500000	-5.652859E-01	-4.866777E-01	-6.492987E-01	-6.560203E-01	-2.934955E-01	-4.458712E-01	-2.835329E-01	-1.922572E-01	-5.687446E-01
50%	284314.500000	-9.363846E-02	-1.358939E-01	3.528579E-04	-7.376152E-02	8.108788E-02	7.871758E-02	2.333659E-01	-1.145242E-01	9.252647E-02
75%	426471.750000	8.326582E-01	3.435552E-01	6.285380E-01	7.070074E-01	4.397368E-01	4.977881E-01	5.259548E-01	4.729905E-02	5.592621E-01
max	568629.000000	2.229046E+00	4.361865E+00	1.412583E+01	3.201536E+00	4.271689E+00	2.616840E+01	2.178730E+02	5.958040E+00	2.027006E+01

Table 19.4. *Presentation of credit card dataset statistics*

19.3.1.6. *Dataset preprocessing*

We continue with the preprocessing of our data. First, it is important to check if there are any missing values for each feature in our dataset. We do this by running data.isna().sum(). The results are shown in Table 19.5.

As you can see from the table, no feature contains any missing values. Therefore, we can continue with the preprocessing of our data. It is also important to check if there are duplicate entries. This is achieved by using the following command: da-ta.duplicated().any(). The result of the execution is False, which means that there are no duplicate records, as shown below.

- In 12 data.duplicated().any()

- Out 12 False

Next, we want to investigate the correlation of classes with each other. We do this by running a command to create a heatmap graph. Specifically, the following command is executed:

- heatmap = plt.figure(figsize=[20,10])

- sns.heatmap(data.corr(), cmap='crest',annot=True)

- plt.show()

The result of the command is the heatmap shown in Figure 19.3.

The information deduced from the heatmap indicates that there are several notable correlations among different characteristics. V17 and V18 display high correlations with each other, as do V16 and V17. V14 is negatively correlated with V4, whereas V12 is negatively correlated with both V10 and V11. Additionally, V11 is negatively correlated with V10 but positively correlated with V4. V3 is positively correlated with both V10 and V12, and V9 and V10 also have positive correlations.

Next, we want to investigate the transaction amounts to be able to draw conclusions. By executing data['Amount'].plot.box(), we can print a box plot type graph that shows us roughly where the transactions are moving in terms of amount. The result of running the above command is shown in the graph in Figure 19.4.

Id	V1	V2	V3	V4	V5	V6	V7	V8	V9	V10	V11	V12	V13	V14	V15	V16	V17	V18	V19	V20	V21	V22	V23	V24	V25	V26	V27	V28	Amount	Class
Data	0	0	0	0	0	0	0	0	0	0	0	0	0	0	0	0	0	0	0	0	0	0	0	0	0	0	0	0	0	0

Table 19.5. *Verification of the presence of missing values in the dataset with data.isna().sum()*

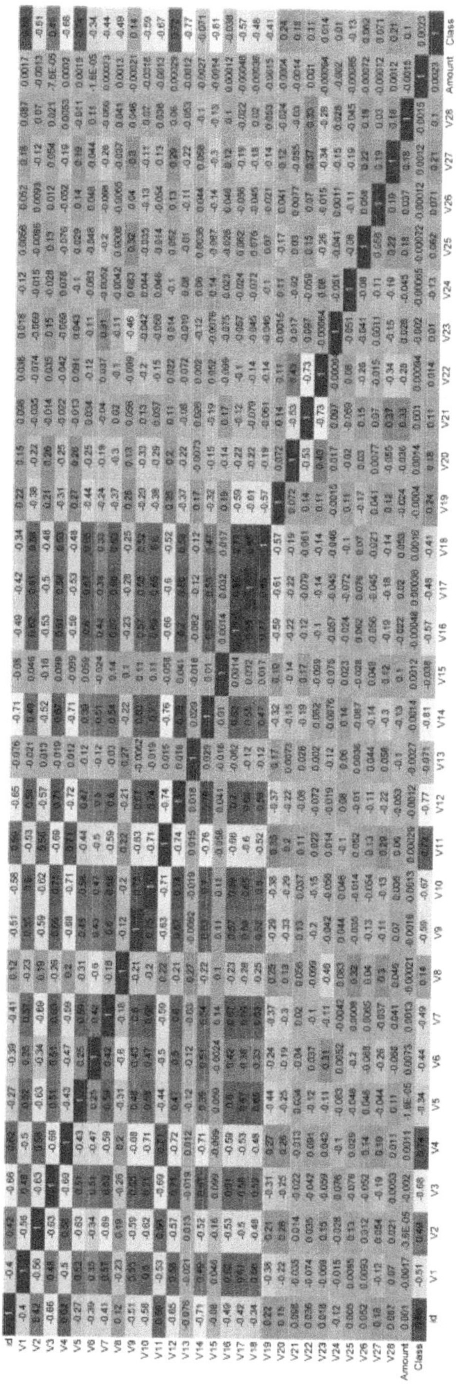

Figure 19.3. *Generation of a heatmap to examine the correlations between classes. For a color version of this figure, see www.iste.co.uk/dimotikalis/data5.zip*

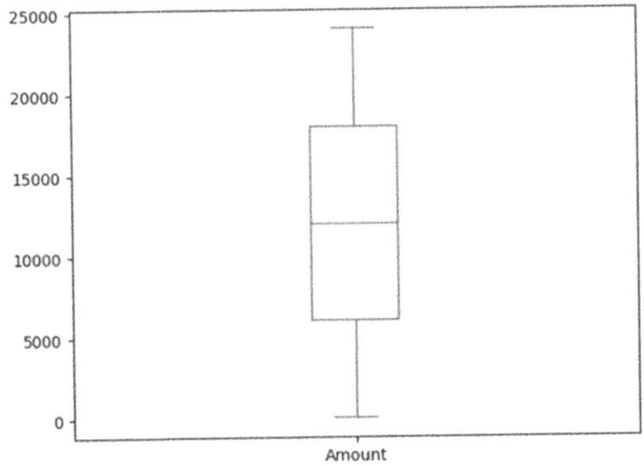

Figure 19.4. *Amount of transactions*

Next, we want to check the distribution of the feature amount to determine whether the distribution of our feature amount data is normal. By executing the following command, we can create a graph, known as kdeplot, which shows the curvature of the data:

– sns.kdeplot(data=data['Amount'], shade=True)

– plt.show()

The result of running the above command is shown in the graph in Figure 19.5.

As the graph shows, our data is fairly well distributed. Next, we want to study some features, which, as shown by the heatmap in Figure 19.3, illustrate high correlation. These features are V1, V10, V12 and V23. To see the correlation of the above features, we will need to create histograms. This is achieved by using the following command:

– paper, axes = plt.subplots(2, 2, figsize=(10,6))

– data['V1'].plot(kind='hist', ax=axes[0,0], title='Distribution of V1')

– data['V10'].plot(kind='hist', ax=axes[0,1], title='Distribution of V10')

– data['V12'].plot(kind='hist', ax=axes[1,0], title='Distribution of V12')

– data['V23'].plot(kind='hist', ax=axes[1,1], title='Distribution of V23')

– plt.suptitle('Distribution of V1,V10,V12 and V23', size=14)

– plt.tight_layout()

– plt.show()

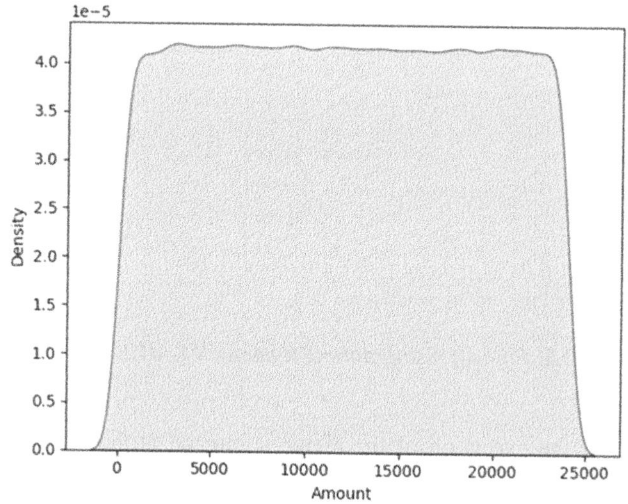

Figure 19.5. *Kdeplot of transaction amount distribution to examine data curvature and normality*

The result of running the above command is different histograms showing features V1, V10, V12 and V23 (Figure 19.6).

As shown in Figure 19.6, we successfully printed the features that are highly correlated with each other, particularly the distribution of data. On the basis of these features, we want to study what percentage of our data constitutes credit card fraud (class 1) or not (class 0). To achieve the above, we execute the command:

– data['Class'].value_counts().plot.pie(explode=[0,1,0],autopct='%3.1f%%', shadow=True, legend= True, startangle=45)

– plt.title('Distribution of Class', size=14)

– plt.show()

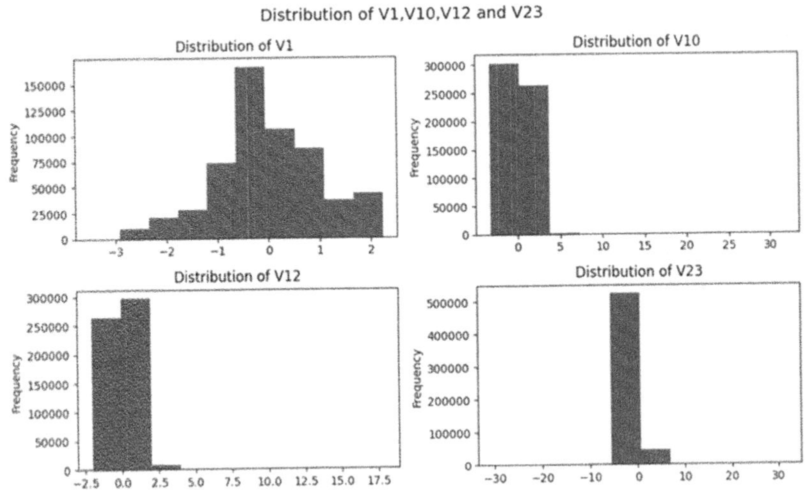

Figure 19.6. *Printing histograms of features V1, V10, V12, and V23*

The result of the execution of the above command is the following pie chart, which shows that 50% of the transactions are fraudulent, whereas the other 50% are not fraudulent (Figure 19.7).

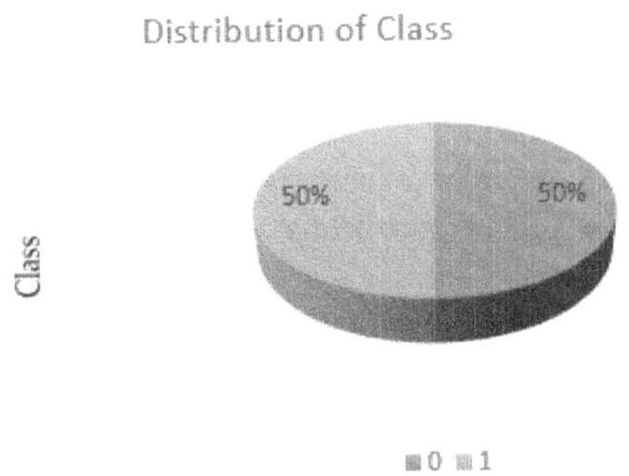

Figure 19.7. *Data pie chart representing the fraud rate in credit card transactions*

Next, we need to divide our data into dependent and independent data. Therefore, we run the following command:

– x=data.drop(['id','Class'],axis=1)

– y=data. Class

	V1	V2	V3	V4	V5	V6	V7	V8	V9	V10	V11	V12	V13	V14	V15
0	-0.260648	-0.469648	2.496266	-0.083724	0.129681	0.732898	0.519014	-0.130006	0.727159	0.637735	-0.987020	0.293438	-0.941386	0.549020	1.804879
1	0.985100	-0.356045	0.558056	-0.429654	0.277140	0.428605	0.406466	-0.133118	0.347452	0.529808	0.140107	1.564246	0.574074	0.627719	0.706121
2	-0.260272	-0.949385	1.728538	-0.457986	0.074062	1.419481	0.743511	-0.095576	-0.261297	0.690708	-0.272985	0.659021	0.805173	0.616874	3.060253
3	-0.152152	-0.508959	1.746840	-1.090178	0.249486	1.143312	0.518269	-0.065130	-0.205698	0.575231	-0.752581	0.737483	0.592994	0.559535	-0.697664
4	-0.206820	-0.165280	1.527053	-0.448293	0.106125	0.530549	0.658849	-0.212660	1.049921	0.968045	-1.203171	1.029577	1.439310	0.241454	0.153008

Table 19.6. *Removing the "class" class from the dataset to create an independent dataset X*

The above command removes the class “class”, which indicates whether the transaction is valid or fraudulent. At this point, we should note that this class is the specific class we are trying to predict, which is why we “drop” it.

Next, we print the head (representation) of the X dataframe we created. This dataset does not contain the fraud class. The results are shown in Table 19.6.

Next, we want to study the number of numbers contained in our X and Y datasets. Note that our data must be equally distributed.

– print(‘Shape of x’, x.shape)

– print(‘Shape of y’, y.shape)

– Shape of x (568,630, 29)

– Shape of y (568630)

As shown above, the data are equally distributed for the two subsets of the dataset. Next, we will need, in order to train our model on prediction, to scale the data, a useful step for correct prediction. We accomplish this by running the following commands:

– sc = StandardScaler()

– x_scaled = sc.fit_transform(x)

– x_scaled_df = pd.DataFrame(x_scaled, colomns=x.colomuns)

We then study our data again to see if the transformation has been successful. This is accomplished with x_scaled_df.head(). The result is shown in Table 19.7.

As the graph shows, our data seem to have been converted correctly. We then split our data into training/testing subsets. This is accomplished with the following command:

– x_train,x_test,y_train,y_test =

– train_test_split(x_scaled_df,y,test_size=0.25,random_state=15,stratify=y)

	V1	V2	V3	V4	V5	V6	V7	V8	V9	V10	V11	V12	V13	V14	V15
0	-0.260648	-0.469648	2.496266	-0.083724	0.129681	0.732898	0.519014	-0.130006	0.727159	0.637735	-0.987020	0.293438	-0.941386	0.549020	1.804879
1	0.985100	-0.356045	0.558056	-0.429654	0.277140	0.428605	0.406466	-0.133118	0.347452	0.529808	0.140107	1.564246	0.574074	0.627719	0.706121
2	-0.260272	-0.949385	1.728538	-0.457986	0.074062	1.419481	0.743511	-0.095576	-0.261297	0.690708	-0.272985	0.659021	0.805173	0.616874	3.060253
3	-0.152152	-0.508959	1.746840	-1.090178	0.249486	1.143312	0.518269	-0.065130	-0.205698	0.575231	-0.752581	0.737483	0.592994	0.559535	-0.697664
4	-0.206820	-0.165280	1.527053	-0.448293	0.106125	0.530549	0.658849	-0.212660	1.049921	0.968045	-1.203171	1.029577	1.439310	0.241454	0.153008

Table 19.7. *Checking transformed data after scaling application*

Next, we want to examine whether the subset splitting has been done successfully and the subset shapes are correct. This is achieved with the following commands:

- print(x_train.shape)
- print(x_test.shape)
- print(y_train.shape)
- print(y_test.shape)

The result is the elements contained in each subset:

- (426472, 29)
- (142158, 29)
- (426472,)
- (142158,)

On the basis of these subsets, we start training our first model, namely, logistic regression. We execute the command:

- 1r=LogisticRegression()

Next, we run the command:

- 1r.fit(x_train,y_train)

Our two commands above are responsible for loading the appropriate libraries and making our data fit. Next, we need to create a function that is subservient to perform a quality evaluation of the prediction model we are building.

- def model_eval(actual,predicted):
- acc_score = accuract_score(actual, predicted)
- conf_matrix = confusion_matrix(actual, predicted)
- clas_rep = classification_report(actual, predicted)
- print('Model Acurracy is: ', round(acc_score, 2))
- print(conf_matrix)

With the above function, we evaluate the model. Specifically, we want to predict the actual values on the basis of what we have predicted. The classification report class shows the actual values with the predicted values, whereas the accuracy score reflects how well our model was able to predict transactions and classify them as either normal or fraudulent. Finally, we print the confusion matrix and the prediction class.

19.4. Results

For the logistic regression model, and specifically for the training subset, the results are shown in Table 19.8.

Training Accuracy				
Model Accuracy is:	0.97			
[[208643 4593]				
[10330 202906]]				
	precision	recall	f1-score	support
0	0.95	0.98	0.97	213236
1	0.98	0.95	0.96	213236
accuracy			0.97	426472
macro avg	0.97	0.97	0.97	426472
weighted avg	0.97	0.97	0.97	426472

Table 19.8. *Prediction model accuracy by comparing actual and predicted values, presenting an analytical classification reference, and displaying a confusion matrix*

Specifically, as shown above, the prediction accuracy is 0.97 or 97%. The evaluation metrics are detailed further as follows: precision is a measure that reflects the percentage of correct positive predictions relative to the total number of positive predictions made by the model. Recall indicates the percentage of correct positive predictions relative to the total number of true positive cases in the data. The F1 score is a combination of accuracy and recall and is used to assess model performance overall, particularly when there is a class imbalance in the data. Support refers to the number of observations in the data for each class considered in the model, essentially representing the sample size for each class. These metrics were used to evaluate the performance of a ranking or classification model in ML and statistical analysis.

For the same model and for the subset of tests (test), the results are presented in Table 19.9.

Training Accuracy				
Model Accuracy is:	0.96			
[[69545 1534]				
[3520 67559]]				
	precision	recall	f1-score	support
0	0.95	0.98	0.96	71079
1	0.98	0.95	0.96	71079
accuracy			0.96	142158
macro avg	0.96	0.96	0.96	142158
weighted avg	0.96	0.96	0.96	142158

Table 19.9. *Analytical evaluation of prediction model performance using the precision, recall, F1 score and support methods for the test subset*

For decision trees, we create a similar training model once the dataset has been partitioned and investigate the performance again. Specifically, for the training subset, the results are shown in Table 19.10.

Training Accuracy				
Model Accuracy is:	1.0			
[[213236 0]				
[0 213236]]				
	precision	recall	f1-score	support
0	1.0	1.0	1.0	213236
1	1.0	1.0	1.0	213236
accuracy			1.0	426472
macro avg	1.0	1.0	1.0	426472
weighted avg	1.0	1.0	1.0	426472

Table 19.10. *Evaluation of a decision tree training model for the training subset*

As shown in Table 19.10, the accuracy of this model is 100% or 1.00. For the test subset, the results are shown in Table 19.11.

Training Accuracy				
Model Accuracy is:	1.0			
[[70864 215]				
[92 70987]]				
	precision	recall	f1-score	support
0	1.00	1.00	1.00	71079
1	1.00	1.00	1.00	71079
accuracy			1.00	142158
macro avg	1.00	1.00	1.00	142158
weighted avg	1.00	1.00	1.00	142158

Table 19.11. *Decision tree model performance results for the test subset*

In this case, the model also performs better than the regression model, achieving 100% performance on all evaluation metrics. Therefore, this model is much better at detecting and predicting credit card fraud. We then proceed with the creation of a random forest model. For subset creation and training, we use the same procedure as before.

We insert the following library:

– from sklearn.ensemble import RandomForestClassifier

Training Accuracy				
Model Accuracy is:	1.0			
[[213236 0]				
[0 213236]]				
	precision	recall	f1-score	support
0	1.00	1.00	1.00	213236
1	1.00	1.00	1.00	213236
accuracy			1.00	426472
macro avg	1.00	1.00	1.00	426472
weighted avg	1.00	1.00	1.00	426472

Table 19.12. *Performance results of the random forest model for the training subset*

We set a variable → rf = RandomForestClassifier() and fit our data → rf.fit(x_train, y_train). For the predictions, we use the following:

– preds_rf_train =rf.predict(x_train)m preds_rf_test = rf.predict(x_test)

The performance of the training subset is shown in Table 19.12.

The performance of the test subset is shown in Table 19.13.

Training Accuracy				
Model Accuracy is:	1.0			
[[71060 19]				
[0 71079]]				
	precision	recall	f1-score	support
0	1.00	1.00	1.00	71079
1	1.00	1.00	1.00	71079
accuracy			1.00	142158
macro avg	1.00	1.00	1.00	142158
weighted avg	1.00	1.00	1.00	142158

Table 19.13. *Performance results of the random forest model for the test subset*

We then create another ML model for prediction called XgBoost. This model is complex compared with the others, and we want to see if it performs better than the previous models do.

We run the model import again. This time, our model is as follows: import xgboost as xgb. We set up the model loading as follows:

– xgclf = xgb. XGBRFClassifier()

– xgclf.fit(x train, y train)

We initiate the prediction with the following commands:

– preds_xgb_train =xgclf.predict(x_train)

– preds_xgb_test = xgclf.predict(x_test)

The result in the training subset is as shown in Table 19.14.

Training Accuracy				
Model Accuracy is:	0.97			
[[209470 3766]				
[9686 203550]]				
	precision	recall	f1-score	support
0	0.96	0.98	0.97	213236
1	0.98	0.95	0.97	213236
accuracy			0.97	426472
macro avg	0.97	0.97	0.97	426472
weighted avg	0.97	0.97	0.97	426472

Table 19.14. *Performance results of the XgBoost model for the training subset*

The result in the test subset is as shown in Table 19.15.

Training Accuracy				
Model Accuracy is:	0.97			
[[69837 1242]				
[3280 67799]]				
	precision	recall	f1-score	support
0	0.96	0.98	0.97	71079
1	0.98	0.95	0.97	71079
accuracy			0.97	142158
macro avg	0.97	0.97	0.97	142158
weighted avg	0.97	0.97	0.97	142158

Table 19.15. *Performance results of the XgBoost model for the test subset*

As seen from the classification reports above, this model, although more complex, showed lower performance than the previous models did. Therefore, we will attempt to improve its performance further. We enter the following command:

– from sklearn.model_selection import RandomizedSearchCV

We go through the parameters we want to improve:

– param_dist_xgb = {

'n_estimators': [50,100,150,200,300,400],

'learning_rate': [0.01, 0.1, 0.2, 0.3],

'max_depth': [3, 4, 5, 6}

}

We import our model with the following command:

– xgb_clf.fit(x_train,y_train)

The training of the model with improved parameters begins. The result is shown in Table 19.16.

[CV]	END	..learning_rate=0.01	max_depth=4	n_estimators=400	total time=	8.1s
[CV]	END	..learning_rate=0.01	max_depth=4	n_estimators=400	total time=	7.9s
[CV]	END	..learning_rate=0.01	max_depth=4	n_estimators=400	total time=	8.2s
[CV]	END	..learning_rate=0.01	max_depth=4	n_estimators=400	total time=	7.9s
[CV]	END	..learning_rate=0.01	max_depth=5	n_estimators=300	total time=	6.5s
[CV]	END	..learning_rate=0.01	max_depth=5	n_estimators=300	total time=	6.9s
[CV]	END	..learning_rate=0.01	max_depth=5	n_estimators=300	total time=	7.0s
[CV]	END	..learning_rate=0.01	max_depth=5	n_estimators=300	total time=	6.6s
[CV]	END	..learning_rate=0.01	max_depth=5	n_estimators=300	total time=	6.8s
[CV]	END	...learning_rate=0.1	max_depth=5	n_estimators=300	total time=	6.8s
[CV]	END	...learning_rate=0.1	max_depth=5	n_estimators=300	total time=	7.2s
[CV]	END	...learning_rate=0.1	max_depth=5	n_estimators=300	total time=	6.7s
[CV]	END	...learning_rate=0.1	max_depth=5	n_estimators=300	total time=	6.5s
[CV]	END	...learning_rate=0.1	max_depth=5	n_estimators=300	total time=	6.5s

Table 19.16. *Improved XgBoost model trained with custom parameters for better performance*

The goal here is to find the best parameters for this model. By printing the best parameters for the XgBoost model, we can achieve better prediction performance. Specifically, the result is as follows:

Best Parameters for XG Boost:

– {'n_estimators': 400, 'max_depth': 6, 'learning_rate': 0.1}

On the basis of the improved parameters, we retrain our model and print the results again. The results for the training subset are shown in Table 19.17.

Training Accuracy				
Model Accuracy is:	0.97			
[[209366 3870]				
[9538 203698]]				
	precision	recall	f1-score	support
0	0.96	0.98	0.97	213236
1	0.98	0.96	0.97	213236
accuracy			0.97	426472
macro avg	0.97	0.97	0.97	426472
weighted avg	0.97	0.97	0.97	426472

Table 19.17. *Training the XgBoost model with improved parameters and printing the results for the training subset*

The results for the test subset are shown in Table 19.18.

Training Accuracy				
Model Accuracy is:	0.97			
[[69810 1269]				
[3214 67869]]				
	precision	recall	f1-score	support
0	0.96	0.98	0.97	71079
1	0.98	0.95	0.97	71079
accuracy			0.97	142158
macro avg	0.97	0.97	0.97	142158
weighted avg	0.97	0.97	0.97	142158

Table 19.18. *Training the XgBoost model with improved parameters and printing the results for the test subset*

As shown in Table 19.18, there was an improvement in the model using the new parameters but not a significant improvement. Overall, the model reached 98% prediction, whereas before the improvement, it was still 98%. The only noticeable difference is in class 1, which is credit card fraud. Therefore, the improvement here is in the second class of data and not in the data that are normal transactions.

19.4.1. *Comparative analysis*

Training Sample for 4 algorithms				
	Log. Regression	Decision Trees	RF	XGBoost
Accuracy	0.97	1.00	1.00	0.97
Testing Sample for 4 algorithms				
Accuracy	0.96	1.00	1.00	0.97

Table 19.19. *Accuracy results of the models used in this research*

As shown in Table 19.19, for the training samples, the accuracies of logistic regression, decision trees, random forest and XGBoost are 0.97, 1.00, 1.00 and 0.97, respectively. For the testing sample, the accuracies of logistic regression, decision tree, random forest and XGBoost are 0.96, 1.00, 1.00 and 0.97, respectively. The accuracy of the logistic regression changes in the testing sample by +1%, whereas the remaining three algorithms retain an unchanged percentage of accuracy.

	Log. Regression	Decision Trees	RF	XGBoost
Precision	0.97	1.00	1.00	0.97
Recall	0.97	1.00	1.00	0.97
F1-Score	0.97	1.00	1.00	0.97

Table 19.20. *Precision, recall and F1 score for all 4 models for training*

As we can see in Table 19.20, in the training dataset, the precision–recall–F1-score for the logistic regression and XGBoost algorithms is 97%. The algorithms of decision trees and random forest, however, demonstrated 100% precision, recall and F1 score.

Finally, as we can see in Table 19.21, in the testing dataset, the precision, recall and F1 score for the logistic regression are 96%, and those for XGBoost are 97%. The algorithms of decision trees and random forest demonstrated 100% precision, recall and F1 score, as they did in the training sample.

	Log. Regression	Decision Trees	RF	XGBoost
Precision	0.96	1.00	1.00	0.97
Recall	0.96	1.00	1.00	0.97
F1-Score	0.96	1.00	1.00	0.97

Table 19.21. *Precision, recall and F1 score for all 4 models for the testing samples*

19.5. Conclusions

The logistic regression model showed significant efficiency, with an accuracy of 97%, demonstrating its usefulness in scenarios where simplicity and interpretability are key. However, these flawless 100% accuracy scores attained by both the decision tree and random forest models have sparked concerns about overfitting, considering the ever-changing nature of real-world economic data. XGBoost, on the other hand, while maintaining a balance between efficiency and predictive capability, demonstrated a commendable 98% accuracy, highlighting its proficiency in tackling complex classification challenges.

This research methodology drew much support from PySpark, which was of great help in managing computational requirements to be met for large-scale transaction data processing. The models used here, from the simplest logistic regression to most complex ensemble methods such as XGBoost, provide insight into the different approaches and methodologies applicable to fraud detection.

These summaries also support collective research efforts on the role of ML in credit card fraud detection and prevention. These modernization researchers implement advanced algorithms relevant to logistic regression, decision trees, random forest and XGBoost to ensure greater accuracy and efficiency than traditional techniques in fraud detection systems. These algorithms are further complemented by tools such as Apache Spark and Python libraries that allow the handling of vast datasets involved in fraud transaction detection in real time.

Although high accuracy rates have been realized and the high benefits of ML in this domain have been observed, some challenges, such as data imbalance, model overfitting and real-time processing capability, remain. These present future research topics on how to develop models that will dynamically learn to adapt to new patterns of fraud and techniques.

Future research should promote the collaborative efforts and sharing of insights across the financial sector. A network of fraud patterns and strategies shared among them will further fortify this collective defense against credit card fraud, thereby increasing the strength of any single ML model. Future improvements in ML models engaged in fighting credit card fraud are accomplished through continued research and collaboration. In the future, real-time detection, scalability and continuous improvement of algorithms to stay at the very top in securing financial transactions against fraudulent activities will be the focus.

Other emerging smart city platforms can also be related to security and privacy issues in credit card fraud detection, where advanced technologies are embedded to enhance all aspects related to citizens' security and privacy (Stamatiou et al. 2023). In the same way, sophisticated ML methods and data security measures are applied in credit card fraud detection over sensitive financial information in such a way that complete compliance is maintained with privacy laws such as the GDPR.

The individual research efforts summarized here underscore the important role of ML in credit card fraud detection and prevention. Advanced algorithms that include logistic regression, decision trees, random forest and XGBoost have gone a long way in improving the accuracy and efficiency of fraud detection systems over traditional methods. These are then supported by tools such as Spark Apache and Python libraries, which can manipulate huge data sets – clearly vital in finding, in real time, fraudulent transactions.

Although high rates of accuracy have been hit and the large benefits of machines in this particular domain are already being procured, some of the other challenges still exist, especially in the areas of data imbalance, model overfitting and real-time processing capabilities. These challenges pose opportunities for future research, especially in building models that can adapt dynamically to new patterns and techniques of fraud.

Moreover, how important collaborative efforts and intelligence exchanges are across the financial industry cannot be emphasized enough. Building a system to share such patterns and approaches will strengthen the collective defense of credit card fraud, hence positive amplification of the effectiveness of disparate ML models.

On the other hand, ML has shown itself to be a powerful tool against credit card fraud today; however, further research and collaboration must be conducted toward its model development. Bounds in real-time detection, scalability of models and improvement in algorithms will truly stand for the continuous sustenance of ML at the very forefront in securing financial transactions from fraud.

19.6. Future work

This research comprehensively investigates ML applications in detecting credit card fraud. This approach has the potential to improve the accuracy and adaptability of fraud detection systems. In future work, it is essential to integrate models into live financial transaction systems in real time to evaluate their feasibility and efficiency under real-world operating conditions. This involves improving ML models to ensure their ability to adapt to the ever-changing nature of fraudulent tactics and integrating advanced anomaly detection techniques that encompass the analysis of user behavior, potentially providing a more sophisticated capability to detect anomalies beyond just transactional ones. In addition, investigating the potential of emerging technologies, such as blockchain for secure data sharing and quantum computing for processing capabilities, could lead to significant advancements in fraud detection methodologies. Implementing this would bolster consumers' confidence in digital financial transactions and conform to worldwide movements toward heightened financial security and transparency, akin to the progress examined by researchers (Karras et al. 2022, 2023; Gousteris et al. 2023) in cloud storage.

Furthermore, it is imperative to comprehend and anticipate consumer behavior in the context of credit card fraud detection to identify anomalies that could signify fraudulent actions. Fraud detection systems can enhance their understanding of typical versus unusual user behaviors by using social signal processing techniques, which involve analyzing transactional behavior patterns and contextual data (Gkintoni et al. 2023). This can result in the creation of more sophisticated and flexible models, such as Kolmogorov complexity, which can identify and forecast possible instances of fraud by analyzing deviations from established patterns of behavior (Antonopoulou 2020).

19.7. Limitations

Research has focused mainly on credit card transactions. However, its scope should be broadened to include other financial platforms, such as digital wallets and online banking systems. This will create a more comprehensive framework for detecting fraud. One limitation of this research is its narrow focus on specific ML models and technologies, such as PySpark and XGBoost. This limited scope may only partially represent the capabilities of other emerging or established technologies and algorithms. The difficulties of integrating in real time, such as dealing with delays and the ability to handle large amounts of data while also protecting user privacy and managing the complexities of global data collaboration for the purpose of detecting fraud, are essential aspects that require thoughtful analysis and strategic preparation. Addressing these constraints and exploring the identified areas for future research could significantly enhance the efficiency, dependability and range of fraud detection systems, rendering them more adaptable and potent in countering the ever-changing realm of financial fraud.

19.8. References

Abd El-Naby, A., Hemdan, E.E.D., El-Sayed, A. (2023). An efficient fraud detection framework with credit card imbalanced data in financial services. *Multimedia Tools and Applications*, 82, 4139–4160. doi: 10.1007/s11042-022-13434-6.

Abdulghani, A.Q., Uçan, O.N., Alheeti, K.M.A. (2021). Credit card fraud detection using XGBoost algorithm. In *14th International Conference on Developments in eSystems Engineering (DeSE)*. IEEE, Sharjah, 487–492. doi: 10.1109/DeSE54285.2021.9719580.

Aburbeian, A.M. and Fernández-Veiga, M. (2024). Secure internet financial transactions: A framework integrating multi-factor authentication and machine learning. *AI*, 5(1), 177–194. doi: 10.3390/ai5010010.

Alazizi, A., Habrard, A., Jacquenet, F., He-Guelton, L., Oblé, F., Siblini, W. (2019). Anomaly detection, consider your dataset first an illustration on fraud detection. In *31st International Conference on Tools with Artificial Intelligence (ICTAI)*, Portland, OR, 1351–1355. doi: 10.1109/ICTAI.2019.00188.

Alfaiz, N.S. and Fati, S.M. (2022). Enhanced credit card fraud detection model using machine learning. *Electronics*, 11(4), 662. doi: 10.3390/electronics11040662.

Alnafessah, A. and Casale, G. (2020). Artificial neural networks based techniques for anomaly detection in Apache Spark. *Cluster Computing*, 23(2), 1345–1360. doi: 10.1007/s10586-019-02998-y.

Antonopoulou, H. (2020). Kolmogorov complexity based upper bounds for the unsatisfiability threshold of random k-SAT. *Journal of Discrete Mathematical Sciences and Cryptography*, 23(7), 1431–1438. doi: 10.1080/09720529.2020.1711602.

Antonopoulou, S., Stamatiou, Y.C., Vamvakari, M. (2007). An asymptotic expansion for the q-binomial series using singularity analysis for generating functions. *Journal of Discrete Mathematical Sciences and Cryptography*, 10(3), 313–328. doi: 10.1080/09720529.2007.10698122.

Antonopoulou, H., Theodorakopoulos, L., Halkiopoulos, C., Mamalougkou, V. (2023). Utilizing machine learning to reassess the predictability of bank stocks. *Emerging Science Journal*, 7(3), 724–732. doi: 10.28991/ESJ-2023-07-03-04.

Boutaher, N., Elomri, A., Abghour, N., Moussaid, K., Rida, M. (2020). A review of credit card fraud detection using machine learning techniques. In *5th International Conference on Cloud Computing and Artificial Intelligence: Technologies and applications (CloudTech)*. IEEE, Marrakesh, 1–5. doi: 10.1109/CloudTech49835.2020.9365916.

Chen, C.T., Lee, C., Huang, S.H., Peng, W.C. (2024). Credit card fraud detection via intelligent sampling and self-supervised learning. *ACM Transactions on Intelligent Systems and Technology*, 15, 1–29. doi: 10.1145/3641283.

Chouiekh, A. and Ibn El Haj, E.H. (2022). Towards spark-based deep learning approach for fraud detection analysis. In *Proceedings of the Sixth International Congress on Information and Communication Technology: ICICT 2021*. Springer, Singapore. doi: 10.1007/978-981-16-1781-2_2.

Darwish, S.M. (2020). A bio-inspired credit card fraud detection model based on user behavior analysis suitable for business management in electronic banking. *Journal of Ambient Intelligence and Humanized Computing*, 11(11), 4873–4887. doi: 10.1007/s12652-020-01759-9.

El Hajjami, S., Malki, J., Berrada, M., Mostafa, H., Bouju, A. (2021). Machine learning system for fraud detection. A methodological approach for a development platform. In *International Conference on Digital Technologies and Applications*. Springer, Cham. doi: 10.1007/978-3-030-73882-2_10.

Esenogho, E., Mienye, I.D., Swart, T.G., Aruleba, K., Obaido, G. (2022). A neural network ensemble with feature engineering for improved credit card fraud detection. *IEEE Access*, 10, 16400–16407. doi: 10.1109/ACCESS.2022.3148298.

Fiore, U., De Santis, A., Perla, F., Zanetti, P., Palmieri, F. (2019). Using generative adversarial networks for improving classification effectiveness in credit card fraud detection. *Information Sciences*, 479, 448–455. doi: 10.1016/j.ins.2017.12.030.

Gkintoni, E., Kakoleres, G., Telonis, G., Halkiopoulos, C., Boutsinas, B. (2023). A conceptual framework for applying social signal processing to neuro-tourism. In *Springer Proceedings in Business and Economics*. doi: 10.1007/978-3-031-26829-8_20.

Gousteris, S., Stamatiou, Y.C., Halkiopoulos, C., Antonopoulou, H., Kostopoulos, N. (2023). Secure distributed cloud storage based on the blockchain technology and smart contracts. *Emerging Science Journal*, 7(2), 469–479. doi: 10.28991/ESJ-2023-07-02-012.

Kannagi, A., Gori Mohammed, J., Sabari Giri Murugan, S., Varsha, M. (2023). Intelligent mechanical systems and its applications on online fraud detection analysis using pattern recognition K-nearest neighbor algorithm for cloud security applications. *Materials Today: Proceedings*, 81, 745–749. doi: 10.1016/j.matpr.2021.04.228.

Karras, A., Karras, C., Bompotas, A., Bouras, P., Theodorakopoulos, L., Sioutas, S. (2022). SparkReact: A novel and user-friendly graphical interface for the apache spark MLlib library. In *Proceedings of the 26th Pan-Hellenic Conference on Informatics*. ACM, New York. doi: 10.1145/3575879.3575998.

Karras, A., Giannaros, A., Theodorakopoulos, L., Krimpas, G.A., Kalogeratos, G., Karras, C., Sioutas, S. (2023). FLIBD: A federated learning-based IoT big data management approach for privacy-preserving over Apache Spark with FATE. *Electronics*, 12(22), 4633. doi: 10.3390/electronics12224633.

Karras, A., Giannaros, A., Karras, C., Theodorakopoulos, L., Mammassis, C.S., Krimpas, G.A., Sioutas, S. (2024). TinyML algorithms for big data management in large-scale IoT systems. *Future Internet*, 16, 42. doi: 10.3390/fi16020042.

Karthik, V.S.S., Mishra, A., Reddy, U.S. (2022). Credit card fraud detection by modelling behaviour pattern using hybrid ensemble model. *Arabian Journal for Science and Engineering*, 47, 1987–1997. doi: 10.1007/s13369-021-06147-9.

Karthika, J. and Senthilselvi, A. (2023). Smart credit card fraud detection system based on dilated convolutional neural network with sampling technique. *Multimedia Tools and Applications*, 82, 31691–31708. doi: 10.1007/s11042-023-15730-1.

Kasa, N., Dahbura, A., Ravoori, C., Adams, S. (2019). Improving credit card fraud detection by profiling and clustering accounts. In *Systems and Information Engineering Design Symposium (SIEDS)*. IEEE, Charlottesville, VA, 1–6. doi: 10.1109/SIEDS.2019.8735623.

Khalid, A.R., Owoh, N., Uthmani, O., Ashawa, M., Osamor, J., Adejoh, J. (2024). Enhancing credit card fraud detection: An ensemble machine learning approach. *Big Data and Cognitive Computing*, 8(1), 6. doi: 10.3390/bdcc8010006.

Koutras, K., Bompotas, A., Halkiopoulos, C., Kalogeras, A., Alexakos, C. (2023). Dimensionality reduction on IoT monitoring data of smart building for energy consumption forecasting. In *IEEE International Smart Cities Conference (ISC2)*. doi: 10.1109/ISC257844.2023.10293689.

Krishna Rao, N.V., Harika Devi, Y., Shalini, N., Harika, A., Divyavani, V., Mangathayaru, N. (2021). Credit card fraud detection using spark and machine learning techniques. In *Machine Learning Technologies and Applications: Proceedings of ICACECS 2020*. Springer, Singapore. doi: 10.1007/978-981-33-4046-6_16.

Li, Z., Wang, B., Huang, J., Jin, Y., Xu, Z., Zhang, J., Gao, J. (2024). A graph-powered large-scale fraud detection system. *International Journal of Machine Learning and Cybernetics*, 15(1), 115–128. doi: 10.1007/s13042-023-01786-w.

Ludera, D.T. (2021). Credit card fraud detection by combining synthetic minority oversampling and edited nearest neigh-bours. In *Advances in Information and Communication. Proceedings of the 2021 Future of Information and Communication Conference (FICC)*. Springer, Cham. doi: 10.1007/978-3-030-73103-8_52.

Madhavi, A. and Sivaramireddy, T. (2021). Real-time credit card fraud detection using spark framework. In *Machine Learning Technologies and Applications: Proceedings of ICACECS 2020*. Springer, Singapore.

Minastireanu, E.A. and Mesnita, G. (2019). An analysis of the most used machine learning algorithms for online fraud detection. *Informatica Economica*, 23(1), 5–16. doi: 10.12948/issn14531305/23.1.2019.01.

Nascimento, D.C., Barbosa, B., Perez, A.M., Caires, D.O., Hirama, E., Ramos, P.L., Louzada, F. (2019). Risk management in e-commerce–A fraud study case using acoustic analysis through its complexity. *Entropy*, 21(11), 1087. doi: 10.3390/e21111087.

Patil, S., Nemade, V., Soni, P.K. (2018). Predictive modelling for credit card fraud detection using data analytics. *Procedia Computer Science*, 132, 385–395. doi: 10.1016/j.procs.2018.05.199.

Priscilla, C.V. and Prabha, D.P. (2020). Credit card fraud detection: A systematic review. In *Intelligent Computing Paradigm and Cutting-edge Technologies. Proceedings of the First International Conference on Innovative Computing and Cutting-edge Technologies (ICICCT 2019)*. Springer, Cham. doi: 10.1007/978-3-030-38501-9_29.

Sadgali, I., Sael, N., Benabbou, F. (2018). Detection of credit card fraud: State of art. *International Journal of Computer Science and Network Security*, 18(11), 76–83.

Shirodkar, N., Mandrekar, P., Mandrekar, R.S., Sakhalkar, R., Chaman Kumar, K.M., Aswale, S. (2020). Credit card fraud detection techniques–A survey. In *International Conference on Emerging Trends in Information Technology and Engineering (ic-ETITE)*. IEEE, Vellore, 1–7. doi: 10.1109/ic-ETITE47903.2020.112.

Singh, A. and Jain, A. (2022). An efficient credit card fraud detection approach using cost-sensitive weak learner with imbalanced dataset. *Computational Intelligence*, 38(6), 2035–2055. doi: 10.1111/coin.12555.

Singh, K., Kolar, P., Abraham, R., Seetharam, V., Nanduri, S., Kumar, D. (2024). Automated secure computing for fraud detection in financial transactions. In *Automated Secure Computing for Next-Generation Systems*, Tyagi, A.K. (ed.). John Wiley & Sons, Hoboken, NJ. doi: 10.1002/9781394213948.ch9.

Sood, P., Sharma, C., Nijjer, S., Sakhuja, S. (2023). Review the role of artificial intelligence in detecting and preventing financial fraud using natural language processing. *International Journal of System Assurance Engineering and Management*, 14(6), 2120–2135. doi: 10.1007/s13198-023-02043-7.

Stamatiou, Y., Halkiopoulos, C., Antonopoulou, H. (2023). A generic, flexible smart city platform focused on citizen security and privacy. In *Proceedings of the 27th Pan-Hellenic Conference on Progress in Computing and Informatics*. ACM, New York. doi: 10.1145/3635059.3635095.

Tyagi, N., Rana, A., Awasthi, S., Tyagi, L.K. (2022). Data science: Concern for credit card scam with artificial intelligence. In *Cyber Security in Intelligent Computing and Communications*. Springer, Singapore. doi: 10.1007/978-981-16-8012-0_10.

Vanini, P., Rossi, S., Zvizdic, E., Domenig, T. (2023). Online payment fraud: From anomaly detection to risk management. *Financial Innovation*, 9(1), 1–25. doi: 10.1186/s40854-023-00470-w.

Velasco, R.B., Carpanese, I., Interian, R., Paulo Neto, O.C.G., Ribeiro, C.C. (2021). A decision support system for fraud detection in public procurement. *International Transactions in Operational Research*, 28(1), 27–47. doi: 10.1111/itor.12811.

Vlachou, E., Karras, A., Karras, C., Theodorakopoulos, L., Halkiopoulos, C., Sioutas, S. (2023). Distributed Bayesian inference for large-scale IoT systems. *Big Data and Cognitive Computing*, 8(1), 1. doi: 10.3390/bdcc8010001.

Xu, X., Xiong, F., An, Z. (2023). Using machine learning to predict corporate fraud: Evidence based on the gone framework. *Journal of Business Ethics*, 186(1), 137–158. doi: 10.1007/s10551-022-05120-2.

Zehra, S., Faseeha, U., Syed, H.J., Samad, F., Ibrahim, A.O., Abulfaraj, A.W., Nagmeldin, W. (2023). Machine learning-based anomaly detection in NFV: A comprehensive survey. *Sensors*, 23(11), 5340. doi: 10.3390/s23115340.

Zhao, Y., Zheng, G., Mukherjee, S., McCann, R., Awadallah, A. (2023). ADMoE: Anomaly detection with mixture-of-experts from noisy labels. *Proceedings of the AAAI Conference on Artificial Intelligence*, 37(4), 4937–4945. doi: 10.1609/aaai.v37i4.25620.

Zhou, H., Sun, G., Fu, S., Wang, L., Hu, J., Gao, Y. (2021). Internet financial fraud detection based on a distributed big data approach with node2vec. *IEEE Access*, 9, 43378–43386.

20

Quantitative Modeling of the Demographic Aging Process

With the development of medical technology and improvements in healthy lifestyles, human life expectancy is increasing. Consequently, the number of elderly people is also growing. The growth rate of the elderly population in Korea is the highest in the world. The aim of this chapter is to attempt to describe the changes in the boundaries initiating an individual's old age. An indication of the structural changes taking place in the senior group, including double ageing in Europe and Poland. The study undertook the task of describing the current trends in structural change in the senior group. Additionally, in this study, we use multiple regression analysis to indicate changes in the structure of age groups in the senior group. The analyses were conducted for selected European countries.

20.1. Introduction

A study used demographic data to explore current and projected population changes around the world. We can observe that Europe and Asia are shrinking, while Africa is still growing. For the first time in history, people aged 65+ outnumber children younger than five years old. Underpopulation will cause serious challenges for sustainability. Globally, people above 65 years of age are the fastest growing segments of the population and in 2019, for the first time in human history, they outnumbered children younger than five years old. In 2020, 9% of the global population was above 65 years old, accounting for 728 million people. This population is projected to increase more than twofold, reaching 1.55 billion in 2050 and accounting to 16% of global population, at medium fertility rates. These changes will not spread evenly across the globe. By 2050, the regions set to see the

Chapter written by Grażyna TRZPIOT.

biggest increases in elderly populations include Europe, Asia and North America, while most nations in Africa will continue to have a relatively young population.

My research of the demographic aging process started with the first publication about the nature of longevity risk (Trzpiot 2017). In Majewska and Trzpiot (2019), we studied the problem of the transition in health in a population aged 65 years and over in Europe. Then, we studied Trzpiot (2020, 2022) for additional details.

The aim of this chapter is to attempt to describe the changes in the boundaries initiating an individual's old age. An indication of the structural changes taking place in the senior group, including double ageing in Europe and Poland. For the attempt to describe the changes in structures of senior population, we propose the double aging index and the multivariate regression model for the double aging index.

20.2. Literature review

The age classification in the senior's group has varied between countries and over time, reflecting, in many cases, differences in functional capacity related to the workforce, but more often a reflection of the current political and economic situation. Many times, the definition is tied to the retirement age, which in some cases was lower for women than men. This transition in livelihood became the basis for defining old age. Although there are different ways to classify this population, some studies have classified elderly adults between the ages of 65 and 74 years as youngest, those between ages 75 and 84 years as middle and those aged over 85 years as oldest (Lee et al. 2018).

When we say today that 75 is the new 65, we are stating that 75-year-olds now have an analogous remaining life expectancy compared to 65-year-olds in the past. Adjusting the age description for changes in remaining life expectancy is called adjusting for "age inflation". It is like adjusting the value of a currency to changes in purchasing power (Sanderson and Scherbov 2019).

The new measure of aging was introduced by IIASA and VID researchers based on observations of remaining life expectancy. The proposed indicator is the prospective old-age dependency ratio (Sanderson and Scherbov 2015). The old-age threshold is no longer fixed, but changes as life expectancy changes, and is based on constant remaining life expectancy. It assumes that people are old when the average life expectancy of their age group is below 15 years.

People have a chronological age and a prospective age. People who have the same chronological age have the same number of years. People who have the same prospective age are in age groups where they have the same remaining life expectancy. Calculating prospective age is similar to calculating accounting for inflation in economics. Economists typically adjust volumes for inflation using price indices. Prospective age is similar to inflation-adjusted volumes, except it uses life expectancy tables instead of price indices. Informally, prospective age can be thought of as an adjustment for "age inflation" caused by changes in life expectancy (Sanderson and Scherbov 2015).

20.3. Methodology

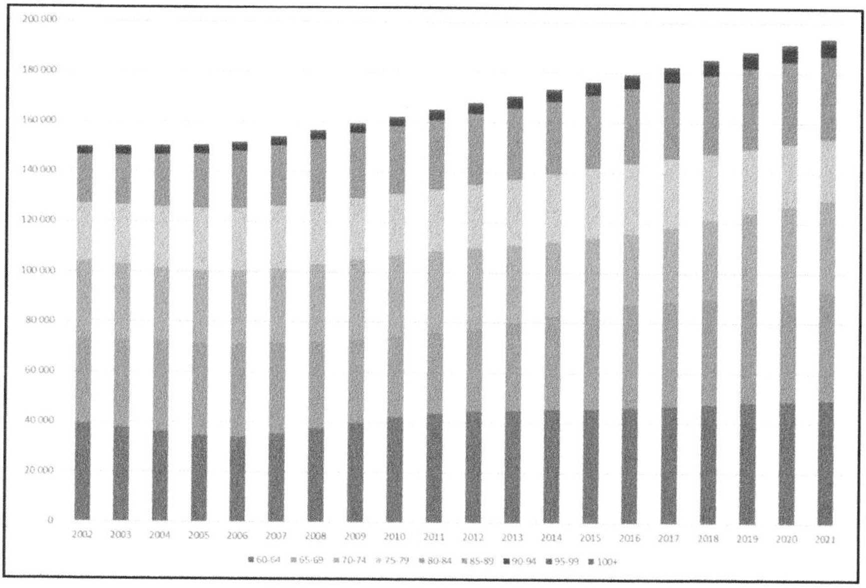

Figure 20.1. *Size of the senior population in Europe from 2002 to 2021 (in thousands). For a color version of this figure, see www.iste.co.uk/dimotikalis/data5.zip*

In an attempt to describe the changes in structures of senior population, we propose the double aging index and the multivariate regression model for the double aging index. We use, in official statistics, many measures for describing elderly dependency ratios. The original uses of the dependency ratio were as approximations to the ratios of nonworkers to workers. The old-age dependency ratio could be used as an approximation to the effects of population aging on pension costs. In most OECD countries, normal retirement ages and pension eligibility rules are in the process of changing (OECD 2013). Some OECD countries have introduced explicit demographic indexation of pensions (OECD 2013).

To describe the changes in structure of senior population, we can start from the data shown in Figure 20.1.

The elderly population is defined as people aged 65 and over. The comparability of elderly population data is affected by differences, both within and across countries, in how regions and the geography of rural and urban communities are defined. We compared the aggregate data for the chosen countries (Figure 20.2) and we observed the big difference between them (e.g. 23.67% for Italy in 2021 but 18.52% for Canada in the same year).

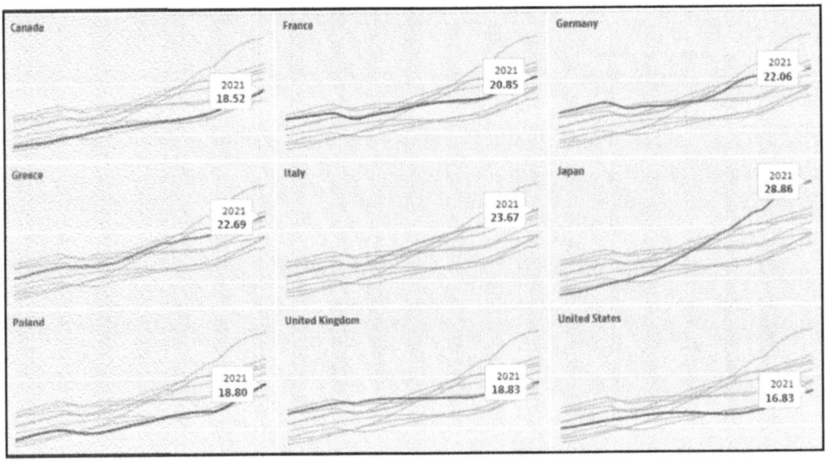

Figure 20.2. *Elderly population (total percentage of the population, 1970–2021). Source: Labour Statistics. For a color version of this figure, see www.iste.co.uk/dimotikalis/data5.zip*

The old-age to working-age demographic ratio is defined as the number of individuals aged 65 and over per 100 people of working age defined as those at age of 20–64 years. The evolution of old-age to working-age ratios depends on mortality rates, fertility rates and migration. OECD countries have seen prolonged increases in life expectancy that most analysts project to continue, implying an increasing number of older people and most likely of pensioners too. This indicator is measured as a percentage (Figure 20.3).

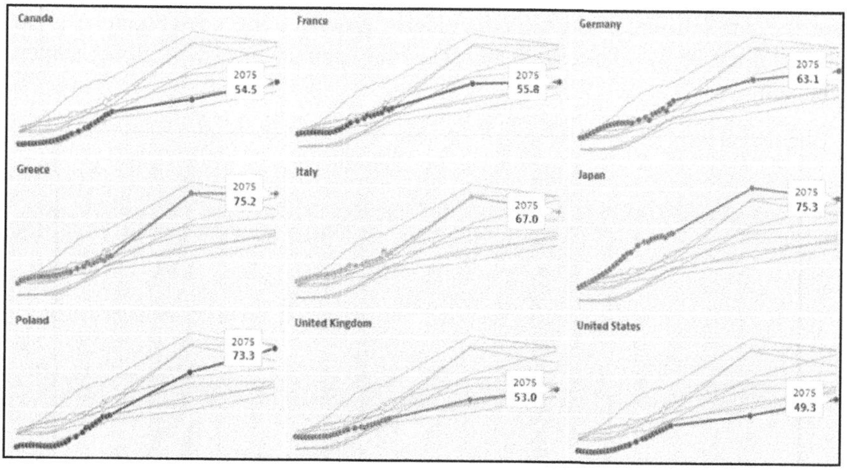

Figure 20.3. *Old dependency ratio, total and percentage, 2000–2075. Source: Labour Statistics. For a color version of this figure, see www.iste.co.uk/dimotikalis/data5.zip*

20.3.1. *Dependency ratios – double aging index*

In the present day, in official statistics, such as EUROSTAT[1], we use many measures for describing elderly dependency ratios. In the general statistics, we have classic measures:

1) share of population aged 65 and over in total population;

2) support ratio of the oldest:

– population aged 85 and over per 100 people aged 50–64;

3) elderly dependency ratio (ODR):

– population aged 65 and over per 100 people aged 15–64;

4) old age index:

– population aged 65 and over per 100 people aged 0–14.

Each of these measures describes the structure of the study population in a different way and provides different information. The research question concerns what the tendency of the rate of change of structures is in the senior group. So, we

1 See: https://ec.europa.eu/eurostat/web/population-demography/demography-population-stock-balance.

count the three different ratios in the elderly group for Europe (Figure 20.4) and Poland (Figure 20.5). The results are remarkably similar in case of global tendency of changing.

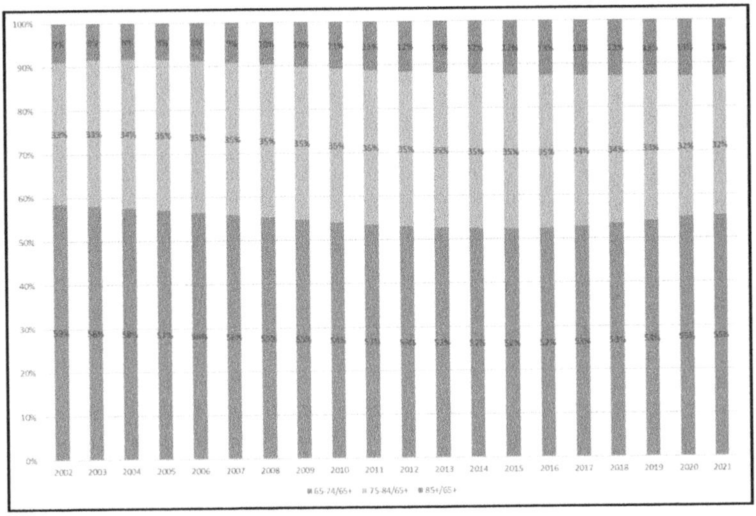

Figure 20.4. *Changes in senior group shares in Europe between 2002 and 2021. For a color version of this figure, see www.iste.co.uk/dimotikalis/data5.zip*

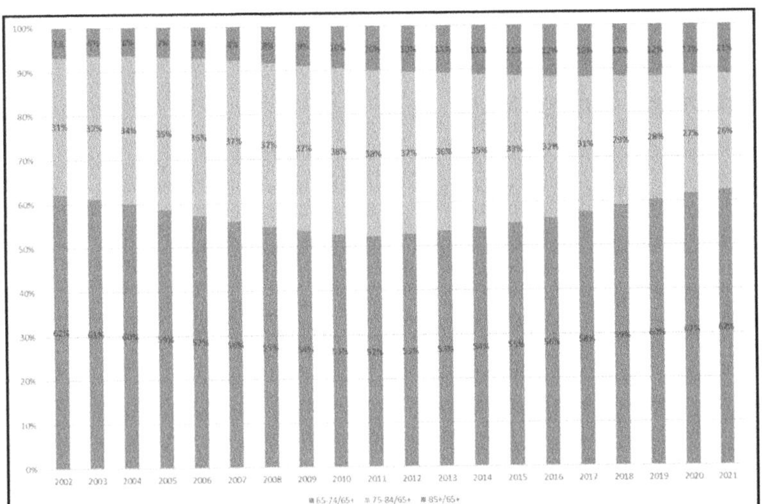

Figure 20.5. *Changes in senior group shares in Poland between 2002 and 2021. For a color version of this figure, see www.iste.co.uk/dimotikalis/data5.zip*

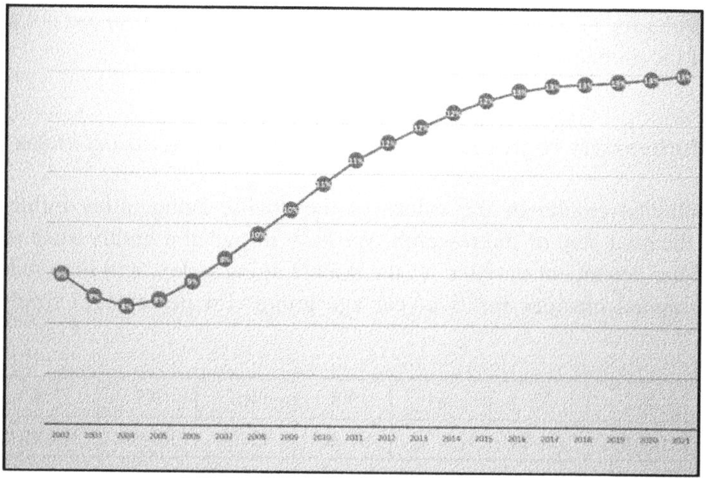

Figure 20.6. *Double aging index for Europe in 2002–2021*

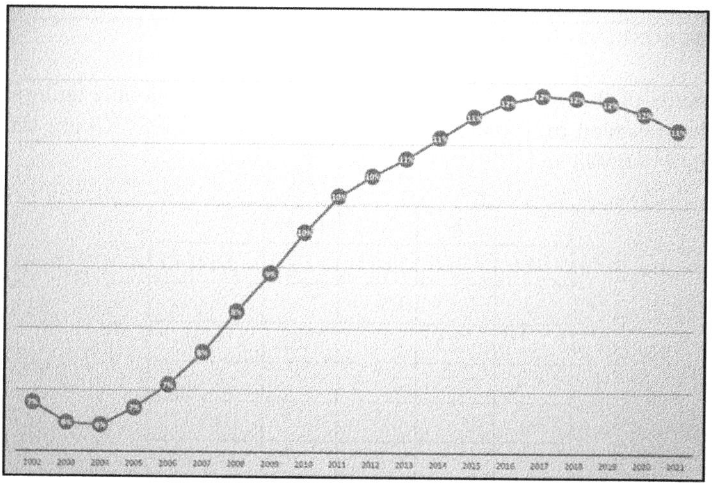

Figure 20.7. *Double aging index for Poland in 2002–2021*

For our own proposition of new measures for describing an old population, we defined the double aging index[2] (Trzpiot in press) that is:

– population aged 85+ years and over per 100 people aged 65+ years.

2 LIX Conference of Statisticians, Econometricians and Mathematicians of Southern Poland, Krakow 2023.

The results for Europe (Figure 20.6) and Poland (Figure 20.7) are not similar in the case of the global tendency of change.

20.3.2. *Multivariate regression model for the double aging index*

The obtained results of the values of the double aging index influenced the choice of the next step of the research. We have designed a multivariate regression model for the dependent variable Y: the double aging index; and nine independent variables: annual changes for five-year age groups (in percentage) from 2002 to 2021.

X1	X2	X3	X4	X5	X6	X7	X8	X9
60–64	65–69	70–74	75–79	80–84	85–89	90–94	95–99	100+

Table 20.1. *Independent variables: annual changes for five-year age groups (in percentage)*

20.4. Research results and discussion

The results of the model for dependent variables for the double aging index for Europe are presented in Table 20.2. The variables from X1 to X8 are statistically significant, $R^2 = 0.998$ and F(9,10) = 375 with $p < 0.000$.

	b	S(b)	t(10)	p
slope	–1.06	0.25	–4.21	0.0017
X1	0.21	0.027	7.64	0.00001
X2	0.33	0.037	8.81	0.000005
X3	0.53	0.068	7.75	0.000015
X4	0.31	0.099	3.15	0.0102
X5	–0.34	0.047	–7.28	0.00002
X6	–0.08	0.24	–3.53	0.00537
X7	0.096	0.018	5.08	0.0047
X8	0.10	0.016	6.14	0.0001
X9	0.012	0.012	0.96	0.355

Table 20.2. *Parameters of the multivariate regression model for dependent variables for the double aging index (in percentage) for Europe. For a color version of this table, see www.iste.co.uk/dimotikalis/data5.zip*

The results of the model for dependent variables for the double aging index for Poland are presented in Table 20.3. The variables X1, X5 and X7 are statistically significant, $R^2 = 0{,}996$ and $F(9,10) = 116.65$ with $p < 0.000$.

	b	S(b)	t(10)	p
slope	0.07	0.29	0.25	0.80
X1	0.08	0.036	2.37	0.039
X2	0.06	0.037	1.79	0.103
X3	0.11	0.05	2.13	0.058
X4	–0.01	0.106	–0.13	0.89
X5	–0.31	0.037	–8.15	0.00001
X6	–0.05	0.028	–1.77	0.105
X7	0.09	0.03	3.08	0.011
X8	0.03	0.018	1.62	0.136
X9	0.002	0.016	0.16	0.87

Table 20.3. *Parameters of the multivariate regression model for dependent variables for the double aging index (in percentage) for Poland. For a color version of this table, see www.iste.co.uk/dimotikalis/data5.zip*

The double aging index rate for Europe depends on changes in all age groups from 2002 to 2021. The double aging rate for Poland in period from 2002 to 2021 depends on changes in the following age groups: 60–64, 80–84 and 90–94.

The model for the index rate of double aging for each country should be determined individually due to different age structures in the senior group. An additional task is to consider the age limit for retirement, which varies in different countries.

20.5. Conclusions

Elderly people tend to be concentrated in a few areas within each country, which means that a small number of regions will have to face a number of specific social and economic challenges due to population ageing. These demographic trends have a number of implications for government and private spending on pensions, health care and education and, more generally, for economic growth and welfare. This indicator is measured as a percentage of population.

20.6. References

Lee, S.B., Oh, J.H., Park, J.H., Choi, S.P., Wee, J.H. (2018). Differences in youngest-old, middle-old, and oldest-old patients who visit the emergency department. *Clinical and Experimental Emergency Medicine*, 5(4), 249–255. doi: 10.15441/ceem.17.261.

Majewska, J. and Trzpiot, G. (2019). The transition in health in a population aged 65 years and over in Europe. *Communications in Statistics: Case Studies, Data Analysis and Applications*, 6(1), 3–18. doi: 10.1080/23737484.2019.1613456.

OECD (2013). *Pensions at a Glance 2013: Retirement-Income Systems in OECD and G20 Countries*. OECD Pensions Outlook, Paris [Online]. Available at: https://ec.europa.eu/eurostat/web/population-demography/demography-population-stock-balance.

Sanderson, W.C. and Scherbov, S. (2015). Are we overly dependent on conventional dependency ratios? *Population and Development Review*, 41(4), 687–708. doi: 10.1111/j.1728-4457.2015.00091.x.

Sanderson, W.C. and Scherbov, S. (2019). *Prospective Longevity: A New Vision of Population Aging*. Harvard University Press, Cambridge, MA [Online]. Available at: www.jstor.org/stable/j.ctv24trd3k/.

Trzpiot, G. (2017). Global aging – The nature of longevity risk. *Acta Universitatis Lodziensis. Folia Oeconomica*, 5(325), 165–179.

Trzpiot, G. (2020). The impact of longevity on a valuation of long-term investments returns: The case of selected European countries. In *Classification and Data Analysis. SKAD 2019. Studies in Classification, Data Analysis, and Knowledge Organization*, Jajuga, K., Batóg, J., Walesiak, M. (eds). Springer, Cham. doi: 10.1007/978-3-030-52348-0_10.

Trzpiot, G. (2022). Longevity risk versus longevity dividend, modern classification and data analysis. Methodology and applications to micro- and macroeconomic problems. In *Studies in Classification, Data Analysis, and Knowledge Organization*, Jajuga, K., Dehnel, G., Walesiak, M. (eds). Springer, Cham. doi: 10.1007/978-3-031-10190-8_16.

21

Hotel Sales During COVID-19: Evidence from the United States

This chapter delves into the dynamics of hotel sales in the United States. Its analysis considers a number of factors that impact pricing, including location, number of rooms and a location analytics score (LARC). The chapter also incorporates various economic variables as control variables, using data from LW Hospitality Advisors and the St. Louis FED. Furthermore, the chapter investigates how COVID-19 has affected hotel sales. One notable finding is the robustness of the LARC variable in explaining hotel prices in the United States. The chapter's findings may particularly interest real estate and financial managers seeking to gain insights into the hotel industry.

21.1. Introduction

The hotel industry's corporate performance relies heavily on economic conditions (Jones et al. 2014). This is because high fixed costs make the hospitality industry very sensitive to the state of the economy. In periods of economic downturns, hotel companies cannot reduce costs as output falls in response to falling sales. Therefore, hotel profits are more susceptible to fluctuations in sales, as costs do not move to offset revenue variability. This means that even small swings in business conditions can profoundly affect hotel profitability (Chen 2010).

The growth of tourism also has a significant impact on the performance of hotel companies. As tourism expands, the hotel industry experiences a direct, albeit unproportionate increase in occupancy rates and revenue. Additionally, tourism

Chapter written by Dimitrios VORTELINOS, Christos FLOROS, Alexandros APOSTOLAKIS and Ioannis PASSAS.

development indirectly affects the business environment, which can improve hotels' overall corporate performance. Extensive research has been conducted on the relationship between the economy and tourism as well as tourism development by various scholars (Balaguer and Cantavella-Jordá 2002; Dritsakis 2004; Gunduz and Hatemi 2005; Kim 2006; Chen 2007; Fayissa et al. 2008; Lee and Chang 2008; Proença and Soukiazis 2008). The positive economic effects of tourism expansion can lead to increased corporate earnings and financial performance for hotel companies and other tourism-related firms.

This chapter utilizes the latest quarterly data to analyze hotel sales in the United States during the COVID-19 pandemic. We examine various factors, including sales price, number of rooms and a location score (LARC), to evaluate the impact of location and rooms on the price and its economic consequences. The findings are supported by policy suggestions for hotel industry real estate and financial managers.

21.2. Literature review

Chen (2010) evaluated the impact of economic conditions and tourism expansion on hotels' corporate performance, considering factors such as sales revenue, profitability, stock performance and overall financial performance. The empirical findings revealed that both GDP growth rate and tourism growth exert a statistically significant impact on occupancy rates, but only tourism growth strongly correlates with corporate performance through return on assets (ROA) and return on equity (ROE). However, neither GDP growth rate nor tourism growth has a significant influence on hotel stock performance. The study also found that GDP is slightly more crucial than the industry factor in describing the overall financial performance of the Taiwanese hotel industry.

O'Neill et al. (2008) argue that the number of hotel rooms (size indicator) positively correlates with the hotel's revenue, regardless of the hotel's star rating (quality indicator). Similarly, both Lee et al. (2016) and O'Neill and Mattila (2004) report that hotel size, measured in terms of number of guest rooms, significantly predicts a hotel's sale price in the United States. Roubi and Litteljohn (2004) reached the same conclusion when examining hotel sales in the UK. They have also found that hotel location is a significant predictor of sale price, with hotels closer to the city center commanding a higher price premium. Corgel and deRoos (1993) confirmed this finding for hotel sales in the United States. Bull (1998) and Mandić and Petrić (2021) maintain that place-sensitive products, such as hotels, are most likely to be affected by location variables when examining their selling price. This is because the hotel's location encapsulates a number of other factors that indirectly affect the selling price.

Chen (2012) reported that the effect of changes in monetary policy on hospitality index returns was influenced by the state of the economy. Specifically, the impact of changes in the discount rate was significant only during business cycle contractions. The same applied for the US hospitality index returns. The response of US hospitality index returns to changes in the federal funds rate was notably larger and more significant during periods of business cycle contractions. Additionally, the effect of changes in the discount rate and federal funds rate on hospitality index returns is affected by credit market conditions, particularly when the credit market is tight. According to Aratuo and Etienne's (2019) findings, investing in US tourism may yield fruitful results in the long term despite economic downturns. Yet, in the short term, the tourism industry could benefit from an economic expansion, and investment in this field should align with the overall economic climate.

21.3. Travel and tourism economic impact in 2022

This section presents the economic impact of travel and tourism in 2022, as reported by the World Travel & Tourism Council (WTTC). The data covers the global travel and tourism industry. This section is divided into three subsections: travel and tourism GDP, employment and forecasts.

21.3.1. *Travel and tourism GDP*

The report depicts a significant drop in the share of travel and tourism in GDP by almost half from 2019 to 2020. This decline is most likely attributed to the COVID-19 pandemic. Nonetheless, the graph shows an upward trend in 2021. It is important to note that the travel and tourism sector is far more susceptible to crises like the pandemic, as compared to other sectors of the economy (Gunter et al. 2024).

21.3.2. *Travel and tourism employment*

The tourism sector provided employment for 333 million people worldwide in 2019, which accounted for one in every 10 jobs globally. There was a 21.7% increase in the sector's contribution to the global economy in 2021, along with a rise in the number of travel and tourism jobs from 271.3 million in 2020 to 289.5 million in 2021, which is an increase of 18.2 million jobs (a 6.7% rise). As a result, the sector supported one in eleven jobs across the entire economy in 2021. The travel and tourism total contribution to jobs table of the report indicates that the sector's contribution to overall economic jobs corrected after the 2009 real estate crisis. Data unambiguously demonstrate that there has been a consistent upward trend in employment within the travel and tourism industry since 2000, except for one conspicuous dip in 2020 (due to the pandemic crisis). The change in the sector's contribution to employment is slower than its contribution to GDP since jobs are less elastic and, therefore, less volatile. This is because the process of laying off existing staff and hiring new employees takes time.

21.3.3. *Travel and tourism forecasts*

Based on 2022–2032 forecasts, the travel and tourism industry is expected to significantly increase employment opportunities from 2022 to 2032, with an estimated 126 million new jobs being created globally. During this time period, the WTTC predicts an average annual growth rate of 2.7% in the global GDP, while the sector's contribution to the economy's GDP is expected to grow at an average annual rate of 5.8%.

The data reveal a stark contrast in the volatility of the sector's GDP growth as compared to the overall economy. The WTTC projects that the sector's growth rate will not only mirror the overall economy's volatility but also be almost identical to it. On the employment front, an upward trend is expected from 2020 onward. The most significant increase in employment is anticipated to take place until 2024. Subsequently, the rate of increase will taper off from 2015 onwards.

21.4. Key developments in the hospitality sector in 2022

The key developments of the hospitality sector in the United States for the year 2022 include overall highlights, hotel room demand, occupancy, room revenue, workforce, state and local tax revenue and US hotel markets. The analysis in this section is based on the 2022 annual report of LW Hospitality Advisors, USA.

21.4.1. *Overall highlights*

The year 2022 saw a rise in leisure travel demand, which, combined with better-than-expected group business performance, led to significant performance gains for US hotels. By the end of the year, leisure travel revenue exceeded pre-pandemic levels by 14%, while business travel revenue adjusted to approximately 1% of its 2019 equivalent. The MICE (meetings, incentives, conferences and events) sector also performed better than expected, with activity recovering to 73.1% of its 2019 levels in 2022 and 106.4% in 2023.

However, some economic concerns overshadowed COVID-19 anxieties among Americans making travel decisions in 2022. A Morning Consultant poll conducted in October 2022 on behalf of AHLA revealed that 85% of Americans were considering gas prices and inflation when deciding whether to travel over the next three months, compared to 70% who said the same about COVID-19 infection rates. This is somewhat expected considering the fact that respondents perceived the pandemic as something of a temporary nature, whereas economic downturns are perceived as more serious, longer lasting and with more severe repercussions for consumers as compared to the pandemic crisis.

The post-pandemic period also increased leisure travel (Holleran 2022), with organizations adopting more flexible remote working policies. This has led to more digital nomads who work while exploring new destinations and leisure travelers who combine business and leisure during trips. The post-pandemic period also introduced us to the concept of "revenge travel" (Wang and Xia 2021). The global leisure tourism market rose to $497.5 billion by the end of 2022.

Despite some progress, labor shortages remain a persistent challenge for hotels in the United States and globally. According to a survey conducted by the AHLA (2023), 79% of hoteliers reported a staff shortage at their property. While this represents a modest improvement from the previous survey conducted in September 2022, where 87% of respondents cited a staffing shortage, a significant 36% of those surveyed indicated that their staffing shortage was severe and long lasting. This overall trend is observed throughout the world and is not confined to the United States alone (Morosan and Bowen 2022).

21.4.2. *Hotel room demand*

Demand for hotel rooms in the United States is projected to surpass pre-pandemic levels (Sanchez 2023). In 2023, the industry achieved the goal of 1.3 billion occupied room nights, which is slightly more than the total number in 2019. This projection represents a significant improvement of 56.9% over 2020's low point of 831.64 million occupied room nights. Furthermore, there has already been an 11.1% increase in hotel demand from 2021 to 2022.

21.4.3. *Occupancy*

It appears that the hospitality industry is slowly but surely bouncing back from the impact of the pandemic. A recent report (STR 2020) revealed that over 75% of hotel rooms in the United States were unoccupied. However, the situation has significantly improved almost 3 years later, with US hotel occupancy rates expected to continue upward in the coming years. Experts anticipate that the average occupancy rate for US hotels will reach 63.8% in 2024 (PwC 2024), which is quite close to 2019's level of 65.9%. This marks a considerable improvement as compared to the historic low of 43.9% in 2020. Notably, in 2022, US hotels made significant strides in occupancy, recording a 9% increase over the previous year, with an overall occupancy rate of 62.7%.

21.4.4. *Room revenue*

According to recent data (STR 2020), the COVID-19 pandemic caused a significant drop in US hotels' annual room revenue, from $170.35 billion in 2019 to $86.01 billion in 2020. However, the industry has been showing signs of recovery, with room revenue reaching $142.92 billion in 2021 and reaching a new high of $189.07 billion in 2022, surpassing the pre-pandemic levels. Fueled by the desire for more travel ("revenge travel"), as well as a generally more relaxed economic outlook after the crisis, hotels and the hospitality industry in general are experiencing a surge in demand. This positive trend is expected to continue in the coming years, with projected US hotel room revenue of $197.48 billion in 2024, representing a 4.4% increase over 2023 and a 15.9% increase since 2019. Although these figures do not factor in inflation, and the real revenue recovery may take a few more years, the industry is moving positively.

21.4.5. *Workforce*

Although the hotel industry's workforce is improving, staffing remains challenging. Due to the pandemic, the industry lost over 682,000 direct employees in 1 year, reducing employment from almost 2.4 million in 2019 to around 1.7 million in 2020. While the industry has been gradually recovering, its annual employment number has yet to reach pre-pandemic levels. As of 2022, US hotels directly employ almost 2 million people, over 400,000 fewer than in 2019.

21.4.6. *State and local tax revenue*

Hotels play an important role in their communities. The travel industry suffered a major setback in 2020 due to the decline in travel demand, which had a negative impact on community hotel services across the country. The industry incurred a loss of $13.2 billion in annual state and local tax revenue, and nearly 2.5 million jobs worldwide were affected as a result. However, as hotels continue to recover, the communities they serve are also benefitting. By 2024, US hotels are projected to generate $46.71 billion in state and local taxes and support more than 7.6 million jobs in the US economy.

21.4.7. *US hotel markets*

According to an analysis (STR 2020) for the AHLA, most US hotel markets have recovered their top-line performance in 2022, reaching or exceeding 2019 levels. However, when factoring in inflation, the percentage of the recovered market decreases and profitability dips further. Fortunately, the return of business travel in the fall of 2022 has helped push more major markets closer to their pre-pandemic levels in gross operating profit per available room (GOPPAR).

Of the 25 largest markets in the country, which are generally more reliant on business travel, 18 remained below pre-pandemic levels in GOPPAR until the fourth quarter of 2022. However, all seven of the major markets that exceeded their 2019 GOPPAR levels (as of October 2022) have one thing in common: sustainable leisure travel options. For example, Miami in Florida is leading the pack, exceeding its 2019 levels by 61% through the first 10 months of 2022. Other cities that made the list include Anaheim and San Diego in California, Tampa in Florida, Phoenix in Arizona, Nashville in Tennessee and Orlando in Florida.

Many markets experienced an increase in total revenue but also witnessed lower expenses due to a reduction in full-time staff and services earlier in the year. As service demand continued to rise throughout the year, traditional groups and business travelers returned. This resulted in more services being offered, and labor per available room (LPAR) also increased.

However, 15 major markets still had not reached 90% of their 2019 GOPPAR year-to-date through October. The most significant deficits were observed in San Francisco, California (43%); Oahu Island, Hawaii (66%); Minneapolis, Minnesota (68%); Atlanta, Georgia (74%); and New York (75%). While leisure components were present in some of these markets, most heavily relied on business travel, especially in San Francisco and Minneapolis. Fortunately, most of the major markets saw a gradual improvement in top-line performance and profitability toward the end of the year. New York is a prime example. Initially, leisure guests were the primary visitors to the market, but the post-summer months brought in groups and business travelers.

Profit margins for the year-to-date period had improved significantly in the fall months, bringing them in line with pre-pandemic trends. For the first 10 months of 2022, the top 25 market GOPPAR was $81, slightly lower than $89 during the same period in 2019. Moreover, the GOP (gross operating profit) percentage of revenues was 38% in 2022, while it was 39% in 2019. This margin improvement relative to GOPPAR can be attributed to the efficiencies developed during the pandemic. Although returning demand is crucial, efficient processes have played a significant role in improving profit margins. Profit margins were at their highest peak in April, reaching 42%. They then moderated during the summer season and were at 33% in August due to the slowing down of leisure travel. However, margins began to rise again in autumn as business demand increased, with September at 38% and October at 41%.

21.5. Data and methodology

21.5.1. *Data description*

Our dataset for the year 2022 includes information from two sources: LW Hospitality Advisors, USA, and the St. Louis FED. It comprises data related to hotel sales, number of rooms, the location of the hotel (LARC score) and various economic variables such as real GDP (RGDP), CPI, unemployment (UNEMP), interest rates and price indexes (IRPI), commercial real estate prices (CREP) and US average sales price of houses sold (ASPHS). The dataset includes 481 companies.

21.5.2. *Methodology*

An analysis was conducted to examine the correlation between hotel prices and different variables. The analysis was performed using a regression model with hotel sales as the dependent variable and other variables such as number of rooms (rooms) and LARC score (location), RGDP, US CPI (CPI), UNEMP, IRPI, CREP and ASPHS as the explanatory variables. The models were created using ordinary least squares (OLS), which used logarithmic values instead of actual values. This analysis was based on a sample size of 481 observations, representing hotel sales in the United States.

21.5.3. *LARC score*

The LARC score is one simple metric that objectively quantifies the quality of a given hotel location in terms of its proximity to demand generators relative to competitive supply. The LARC score enables a user to compare hotel locations across geographies in a purely objective and analytical way. LARC is a precise method of evaluating the excellence of a hotel's location. It considers the distance between the hotel and well-liked attractions and measures it against other nearby hotels. The score ranges from 0 to 100, with 50 being the average score across the United States. It is important to note that the score only reflects the quality of the location and not the quality of the hotel itself. For instance, Motel 6 and Four Seasons would have similar scores in the same area.

21.5.4. *Graphical analysis of variables*

Figure 21.1 reveals the break (rapid decline) in Q3 2009 in CREP. It then followed a sharp increase for the next 2 years. Thereafter, it remained more stable and always positive.

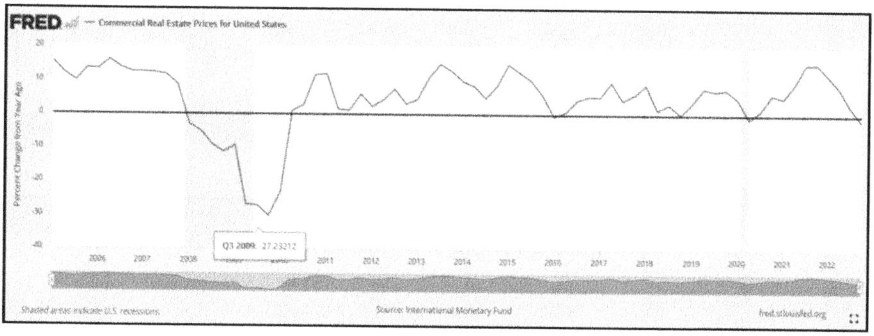

Figure 21.1. *Commercial real estate prices for the United States*

Figure 21.2. indicates the 2009 peak in the value of CREP. In 2010, there was an impressive decline, and the incline trend continued thereafter.

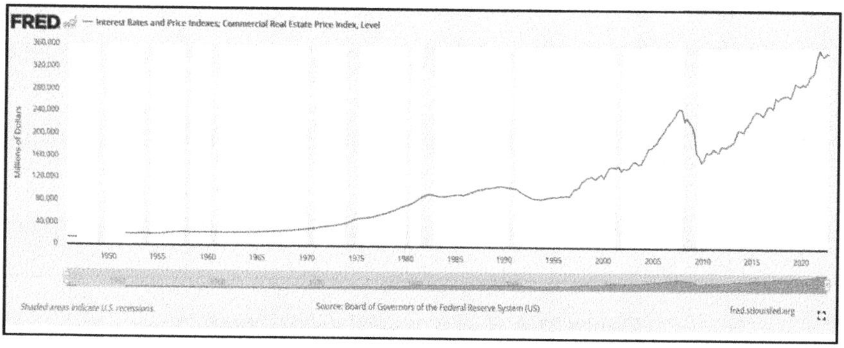

Figure 21.2. *Interest rates and price indexes: commercial real estate price index*

In terms of real gross domestic product, there was a correction in 2009 because of real estate. It seems quite volatile. We may also mention the COVID-19 impact in the last few years.

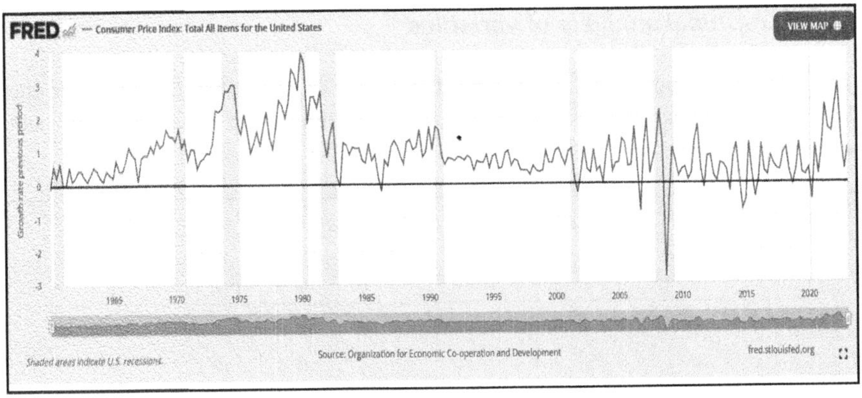

Figure 21.3. *Consumer price index*

The consumer price index (CPI) has always had an upward trend, except for 2009, when it suffered a huge decline. We may also see the impact of the 2007 financial crisis, which caused a similar decline, but lower magnitude than the real estate crisis.

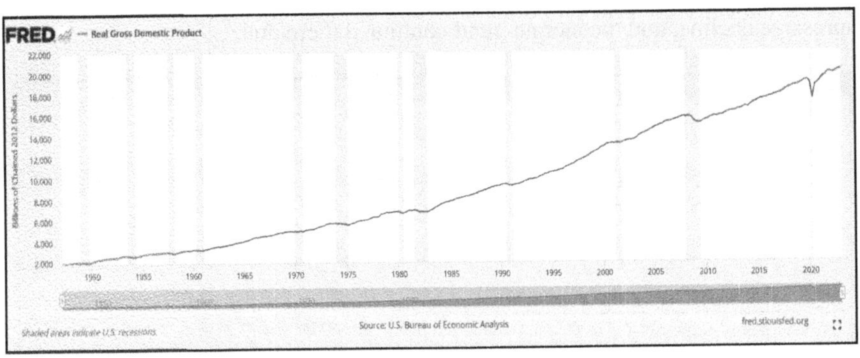

Figure 21.4. *Real gross domestic product*

The unemployment rate faces seasonalities, with the highest increase in years 2009 (real estate crisis) and 2019 (pandemic). We may also mention a periodicity, with a cycle lasting at around 10 years.

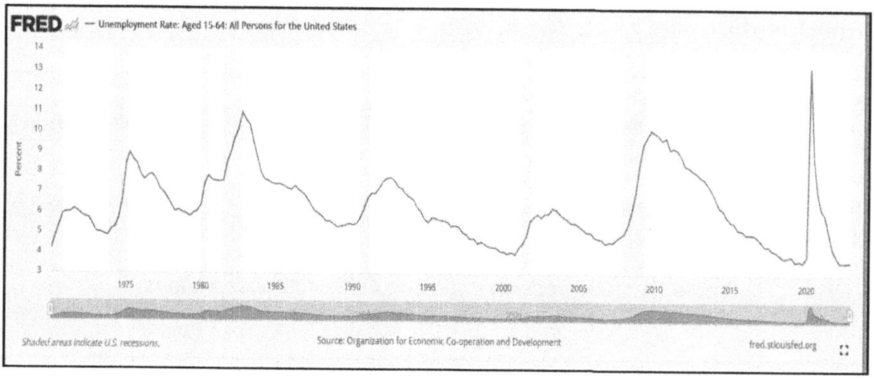

Figure 21.5. *Unemployment rate: ages 15–64: all persons for the United States*

The ASPHS in the United States declined in 2009, throughout the financial crisis that plagued the United States. It stayed stable until 2012 when it started and remained in an upward trend.

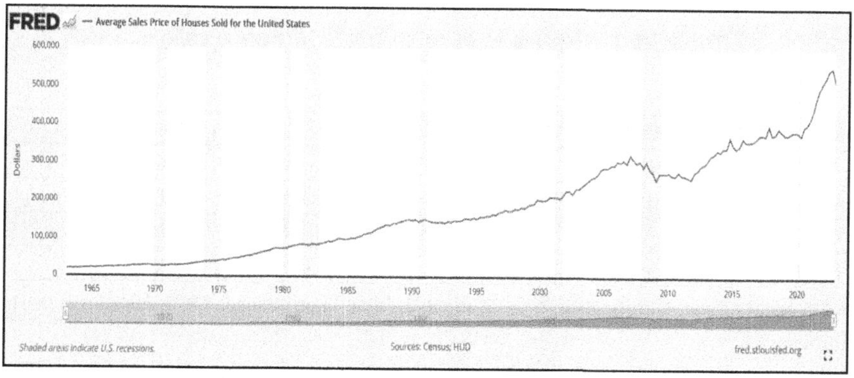

Figure 21.6. *Average sales of houses sold in the United States*

21.6. Results

Tables 21.1–21.4 reveal the explanatory power of house-related and macroeconomic condition variables.

Dependent vbl: l_sales				
	coeff.	**s.e.**	**t-stat**	***p*-value**
const	11.7106	0.542319	21.59	5.69e-11***
l_rooms	0.694546	0.0686932	10.11	3.18e-7***
l_larc	0.474139	0.0937175	5.059	0.0003***

* = 1% level of stat. significance, ** = 5% level of stat. significance, *** = 10% level of stat. significance.

Table 21.1. *Regression 1: pooled OLS, 480 observations*

Dependent vbl.: l_sales				
	coeff.	**s.e.**	**t-stat**	***p*-value**
const	280.412	113.287	2.475	0.0292**
l_RGDP	−17.8278	7.61139	−2.342	0.0372**
l_CPI	0.0530070	0.0252571	2.099	0.0577*
l_UNEMPL	−0.890325	1.13512	−0.7843	0.4480

* = 1% level of stat. significance, ** = 5% level of stat. significance, *** = 10% level of stat. significance.

Table 21.2. *Regression 2: pooled OLS, 481 observations*

Dependent vbl.: l_sales				
	coeff.	**s.e.**	**t-stat**	***p*-value**
const	80.0539	80.7404	0.9915	0.3448
l_CREP	0.0913516	0.0495853	1.842	0.0952*
l_IRPI	−4.94871	6.31757	−0.7833	0.4516

* = 1% level of stat. significance, ** = 5% level of stat. significance, *** = 10% level of stat. significance.

Table 21.3. *Regression 3: pooled OLS, 376 observations*

Dependent vbl.: l_sales				
	coeff.	**s.e.**	**t-stat**	***p*-value**
const	54.1829	6.12864	8.841	1.33e-6***
l_ASPHS	−2.81704	0.463658	−6.076	5.54e-5***

* = 1% level of stat. significance, ** = 5% level of stat. significance, *** = 10% level of stat. significance.

Table 21.4. *Regression 4: pooled OLS, 481 observations*

Most of variables significantly predict US hotel sales. In particular, number of rooms (rooms), LARC score (larc), CPI and CREP positively explain hotel sales. On the other hand, RGDP, IRPI, and ASPHS negatively predict hotel sales. There was no statistically significant explanatory power in the UNEMP and the IRPI.

The empirical results presented in Table 21.1 largely align with the empirical evidence in the literature. In particular, the spatial effect on hotels' sales price reported in this chapter confirms earlier results in Roubi and Litteljohn (2004), and updates findings by Corgel and deRoos (1993) and Valentin and O'Neill (2019) for hotels in the United States. Although more research is required in this respect, the hotel's location is however a very influential factor for either the hotel's REVPAR, or the selling price of the hotel itself. Hotel services are extremely place-sensitive products, and location appears to have a great influence on their selling price. In other words, spatial and geographical features of the hotel seem to influence hotels' RevPAR, as well as their selling price. The same applies to a hotel's size (in terms of number of rooms). Bigger hotels command a higher selling price. This finding also aligns with the literature in the field (O'Neill et al. 2008). What remains to be examined is the combined effect of the hotel's location and its size. In other words, it would be interesting to examine whether location and size exert a combined or diverging effect on hotels' selling price.

Of the remaining findings, one could take notice of the contrasting effect of CREP (positive) and ASPHS (negative) on hotels' selling price. Commercial property sales have a positive effect, whereas residential sales have a negative effect on hotels' selling prices. We attribute this finding to the fact that investors are more likely to search for and invest in hotels located close to dynamic and vibrant commercial centers. In addition to that, as the ability to travel has returned after the pandemic and people have started traveling again for business and leisure purposes, it is anticipated that hotels located near big urban and business centers will experience a surge in their popularity and their prices. On the other hand, hotels located close to residential areas (i.e. suburbs and places further away from commercial centers) may not command strong business and investment interest.

For policy makers, practitioners and investors, the empirical findings regarding the positive effect of location, commercial real estate sales prices and the negative effect of ASPHS provide a clear-cut direction. Thus, despite the recent turn in urban economics toward decentralized locations and moving away from city centers (Archer and Smith 2003), the empirical findings in this chapter advise against this move. Hotel centrality and proximity to commercial (and urban) centers is still one of the most significant factors determining their valuation (Mitsis 2024). Our results tend to suggest that spatial factors affect hotel sale prices both directly and indirectly. For policy makers, investors in the sector and practitioners, this is a very interesting finding since this could suggest a different business strategy in relation to other forms of hospitality accommodation available in the market (e.g. Airbnb units). The central locality of hotels could support different narratives, different experiences and a whole set of different business strategies as compared to competing hospitality accommodation types.

21.7. Concluding remarks and future research

This chapter provided a view of travel and tourism's economic impact, key developments in the hospitality sector in 2022 and a preliminary analysis of data. It also examined the relationships between US hotel sales with the number of rooms and LARC score, as well as economic variables (GDP, CPI and UNEMP) and other key variables (RPI, CREP and ASPHS) for the year 2022. The most important findings concern the statistically significant positive in-sign relations between hotel prices and rooms, LARC, CPI and CREP variables. Significant relations were also found between hotel prices and GDP, as well as hotel prices and ASPHS, both negative, however. Our future research plans include forecasting US hotel sales based on the present chapter's in-sample predictive results of the aforementioned variables.

21.8. Acknowledgments

The authors acknowledge LW Hospitality Advisors, USA, for providing us with LARC scores for the US.

21.9. References

AHLA (2023). A new era for U.S. hotels. American Hotel & Lodging Association: 2023 state of the hotel industry report [Online]. Available at: https://www.ahla.com/sites/default/files/AHLA.SOTI_.Report.2023.final_.002.pdf?inf_contact_key=b0761d7a09db3213fa8aa6ca34c764ff.

Aratuo, D.N. and Etienne, X.L. (2019). Industry level analysis of tourism-economic growth in the United States. *Tourism Management*, 70, 333–340. doi: 10.1016/j.tourman.2018.09.004.

Archer, W.R. and Smith, M.T. (2003). Explaining location patterns of suburban offices. *Real Estate Economics*, 31(2), 139–164.

Balaguer, J. and Cantavella-Jordá, M. (2002). Tourism as a long-run economic growth factor: The Spanish case. *Applied Economics*, 34(7), 877–884. doi: 10.1080/00036840110058923.

Bull, O.A. (1998). The effects of location and other attributes on the price of products which are place-sensitive in demand. PhD Thesis, Griffith University, Queensland.

Chen, F.F. (2007). Sensitivity of goodness of fit indexes to lack of measurement invariance. *Structural Equation Modeling: A Multidisciplinary Journal*, 14(3), 464–504. doi: 10.1080/10705510701301834.

Chen, M.H. (2010). The economy, tourism growth and corporate performance in the Taiwanese hotel industry. *Tourism Management*, 31(5), 665–675. doi: 10.1016/J.TOURMAN.2009.07.011.

Chen, M.H. (2012). State dependence in the influence of monetary policy regime shifts on hospitality index returns. *International Journal of Hospitality Management*, 31(4), 1203–1212. doi: 10.1016/J.IJHM.2012.02.008.

Corgel, J.B. and deRoos, J.A. (1993). The ADR rule-of-thumb as predictor of lodging property values. *International Journal of Hospitality Management*, 12(4), 353–365. doi: 10.1016/0278-4319(93)90051-A.

Dritsakis, N. (2004). Tourism as a long-run economic growth factor: An empirical investigation for Greece using causality analysis. *Tourism Economics*, 10(3), 305–316. doi: 10.5367/0000000041895094.

Fayissa, B., Nsiah, C., Tadasse, B. (2008). Impact of tourism on economic growth and development in Africa. *Tourism Economics*, 14(4), 807–818. doi: 10.5367/000000008786440229.

Gunduz, L. and Hatemi, J.A. (2005). Is the tourism-led growth hypothesis valid for Turkey? *Applied Economics Letters*, 12(8), 499–504. doi: 10.1080/13504850500109865.

Gunter, U., Smeral, E., Zekan, B. (2024). Forecasting tourism in the EU after the COVID-19 crisis. *Journal of Hospitality and Tourism Research*, 48(5), 909–919. doi: 10.1177/10963480221125130.

Holleran, M. (2022). Pandemics and geoarbitrage: Digital nomadism before and after COVID-19. *City*, 26(5–6), 831–847.

Jones, P., Hillier, D., Comfort, D. (2014). Sustainability in the global hotel industry. *International Journal of Contemporary Hospitality Management*, 26(1), 5–17. doi: 10.1108/IJCHM-10-2012-0180.

Kim, S. (2006). Public service motivation and organizational citizenship behavior in Korea. *International Journal of Manpower*, 27(8), 722–740. doi: 10.1108/01437720610713521.

Lee, C.C. and Chang, C.P. (2008). Energy consumption and economic growth in Asian economies: A more comprehensive analysis using panel data. *Resource and Energy Economics*, 30(1), 50–65. doi: 10.1016/J.RESENEECO.2007.03.003.

Lee, S., O'Neill, J.W., McGinley, S. (2016). Effects of economic conditions and other factors on hotel sale prices. *International Journal of Contemporary Hospitality Management*, 28(10), 2267–2284. doi: 10.1108/IJCHM-07-2014-0363.

Mandić, A. and Petrić, L. (2021). *Mediterranean Protected Areas in the Era of Overtourism: Challenges and Solutions*, Springer, Cham. doi: 10.1007/978-3-030-69193-6/COVER.

Mitsis, P. (2024). Selecting independent variables in the hedonic analysis of hotel rooms. *Journal of Vacation Marketing*, 30(3), 535–552.

Morosan, C. and Bowen, J.T. (2022). Labor shortage solution: Redefining hospitality through digitization. *International Journal of Contemporary Hospitality Management*, 34(12), 4674–4685.

O'Neill, J.W. and Mattila, A.S. (2004). Hotel branding strategy: Its relationship to guest satisfaction and room revenue. *Journal of Hospitality & Tourism Research*, 28(2), 156–165. doi: 10.1177/1096348004264081.

O'Neill, J.W., Hanson, B., Mattila, A.S. (2008). The relationship of sales and marketing expenses to hotel performance in the United States. *Cornell Hospitality Quarterly*, 49(4), 355–363. doi: 10.1177/1938965508324634.

Proença, S. and Soukiazis, E. (2008). Tourism as an economic growth factor: A case study for southern European countries. *Tourism Economics*, 14(4), 791–806. doi: 10.5367/0000000 08786440175.

PwC (2024). US hospitality directions: May 2024. PricewaterhouseCoopers [Online]. Available at: https://www.pwc.com/us/en/industries/consumer-markets/hospitality-leisure/us-hospitality-directions.html. [Accessed 5 July 2024].

Roubi, S. and Litteljohn, D. (2004). What makes hotel values in the UK? A hedonic valuation model. *International Journal of Contemporary Hospitality Management*, 16(3), 175–181. doi: 10.1108/09596110410531168.

Sanchez, R. (2023). Hospitality's major comeback. Matthew's real estate investment services [Online]. Available at: https://www.matthews.com/thought-leadership-hospitalitys-major-comeback/. [Accessed 16 July 2024].

STR (2020). STR: Europe hotel performance for 2020 [Online]. Available at: https://str.com/press-release/str-europe-hotel-performance-2020.

Valentin, M. and O'Neill, J.W. (2019). The value of location for urban hotels. *Cornell Hospitality Quarterly*, 60(1), 5–24. doi: 10.1177/1938965518777725.

Wang, J. and Xia, L. (2021). Revenge travel: Nostalgia and desire for leisure travel post COVID-19. *Journal of Travel and Tourism Marketing*, 38(9), 935–955.

22

Investigating the Mediating Role of Religious Services Attendance in the Relationship Between Religion Variables and Social Class Perceptions

In the literature, social class is considered important in all aspects of life. However, its relation to religion has not been adequately researched. In this respect, the purpose of this study is to explore the mediating role of attending religious services in the relationship between religious values, beliefs and practices and social class perceptions as measured in the World Values Survey (WVS) questionnaire, which classifies respondents into five class categories: upper, upper middle, lower middle, working and lower class. The analysis was based on the 2017–2020 7th wave WVS datasets for four countries: Germany, Greece, the Russian Federation and the United States. In all four countries, the separate path analysis models provided adequate model fit. In all countries, social class perceptions were positively predicted by religious services attendance, except in the case of Greece, where the reverse was true. However, weak total effect of religious services attendance on subjective social class was observed in all countries. The findings showed only in certain cases significant but weak mediation effects of religious values, beliefs and practices and subjective social class by religious services attendance. These results indicate that further research is necessary.

22.1. Introduction

In the literature, social class is considered important in all aspects of life. However, its relation to religion has not been adequately researched and the data that exists is considered to be often misleading (McKinnon 2017). As it is well known, Karl Marx pointed out that religion was the source of oppression and deceit in

---

Chapter written by Aggeliki YFANTI and Catherine MICHALOPOULOU.

society, benefiting the bourgeoisie by deceiving the working class into thinking that the social setup, built on their exploitation, is God's will. Max Weber argued that there is a connection between religiosity and poverty as it seems that religion appeals to working-class people because it offers support and comfort from the daily struggles and deprivation they suffer. According to McCloud,

> class has and still plays an important role in creating and sustaining social, cultural and religious distinctions. First, class has served as an externally ascribed marker placed upon particular groups by outsiders engaged in boundary demarcation. Second, class has historically been used as an aspect of individual and group identity. Third, I argue that class plays a role in determining religious preferences.

In the sociological literature, a distinction is made between religious belief and religiosity: religious belief is generally considered as referring to people's faith and whether they believe in a God and the dogmas of a certain religion, whereas, religiosity is considered as referring to an individual's involvement with religious practices, such as attending church. However, it should be kept in mind that religious practices, such as religious services' attendance, do not provide a reliable indicator of how religious a person is, as people may go to church for family or appearances sake. According to Thompson (2005), "the middle classes are, in general, more likely to attend church, but they are also less likely to believe in God and more likely to be atheists … The working classes are less likely to attend church, yet more likely to believe in God than the middle classes".

In the literature, attempts have been made to measure religious belief, church attendance and social class. In the WVS questionnaire, the measurements of religious belief and church attendance are presented as religious values. Social class is treated as one of the background variables and it is measured by a self-perceived question that serves as an encompassing measurement that classifies respondents into five class categories: upper class, upper middle class, lower middle class, working class and lower class.

In previous work by Yfanti and Michalopoulou (2024), we investigated how religious values, beliefs and practices were impacting social class perceptions. The purpose of this chapter is to explore the mediating role of attending religious services in the relationship between religious values, beliefs and practices and social class perceptions as measured in the WVS questionnaire. The analysis is based on the 2017–2020 7th wave WVS datasets (Haerpfer et al. 2020) for four countries: Germany, Greece, the Russian Federation and the United States. These countries were selected on the basis of their populations' diverse religious affiliations as reported by the 2017–2020 WVS:

– Germany: Roman Catholic (29.6%); Protestant (26.5%); do not belong to a denomination (34.9%);

– Greece: Orthodox (91.3%);

– Russian Federation: Orthodox (55.5%); do not belong to a denomination (29.4%);

– United States: Roman Catholic (22.6%); Protestant (19.5%); do not belong to a denomination (45.9%).

22.2. Method

22.2.1. *Procedure and participants*

The WVSs were designed to test the hypothesis that economic and technological changes are transforming the basic values and motivations of the publics of industrialized societies. The surveys build on the European Values Study (EVS) first carried out in 1981. The WVS is an international research program devoted to the scientific and academic study of social, political, economic, religious and cultural values of people in the world and 120 countries have participated. It is organized in waves conducted every five years and time-series data is available for free for 39 years (1981–2020). The 7th wave of the WVS was realized worldwide in 2017–2021. The first release comprised data for countries/territories surveyed from early 2017 to mid-2020. All countries employed stratified multi-stage probability samples of the resident (regardless of citizenship) population aged 18 years and older and have to achieve specified minimum sample sizes. The realized sample for each country under investigation and a summary of the participants' demographic and social characteristics are presented in Table 22.1.

		Men	Women	Age	Married	Educ	Empl.
Country	*N*	(%)	(%)	$\bar{X}$ (SD)	(%)	(%)	(%)
Germany	1,528	48.6	51.4	50.8 (18.086)	54.7	72.9	57.1
Greece	1,200	46.9	53.1	50.9 (17.819)	55.4	76.1	46.4
Russian Federation	1,810	45.1	54.9	45.3 (17.339)	47.9	66.6	59.7
United States	2,596	53.5	46.5	43.4 (16.307)	50.1	58.5	67.2

Educ = Secondary education or lower; Empl = employed.

Table 22.1. *The demographic and social characteristics of participants: World Values Survey, 2017–2020*

As shown, in Germany, Greece and the Russian Federation, women were more than men and the reverse holds true in the United States. Participants' mean age ranged from 43.4 (United States) to 50.9 (Greece). More than 47.9% (Russian Federation) of the participants were married, over 58.5% (United States) had completed secondary education or lower and at least 46.4% (Grece) were employed.

In the WVS, face-to-face interviewing is mainly used for data collection employing paper and pencil personal interviewing (PAPI) or computer-assisted personal interviewing (CAPI). The application of any alternative method of data collection such as computer-assisted web interviewing (CAWI) and computer-assisted telephone interviewing (CATI) is considered on a country basis and requires approval of the World Values Survey Association (WVSA) Scientific Committee (World Values Survey). In this respect, the following methods of data collection were used by each country: Germany (CAPI), Greece (PAPI), the Russian Federation (CAPI/PAPI), and the United States (CAWI/CATI). As different methods of data collection were used by each country, it should be pointed out that to ensure cross-national comparability, the same method of data collection needs to be applied by each survey (Kish 1994; Carey 2000).

The 7th wave of the WVS was launched in January 2017 and was completed in December 2021. The duration of fieldwork for the countries under consideration was as follows: Germany (October 25, 2017 to March 31, 2018); Greece (September 08, 2017 to October 16, 2017); the Russian Federation (November 07, 2017 to December 29, 2017); and the United States (April 28, 2017 to May 31, 2017). In this respect, we should bear in mind that for cross-national comparability fieldwork periods should not be diverse (Kish 1994; Carey 2000).

22.2.2. *Measures*

As mentioned before, the self-perceived question on social class is included in the WVS questionnaire as a background variable (Q287). It is worded as follows: "People sometimes describe themselves as belonging to the working class, the middle class, or the upper or lower class. Would you describe yourself as belonging to the upper class (1), upper-middle class (2), lower-middle class (3), working class (4) and lower class (5)".

The religious services attendance and the religious values and beliefs variables considered in the analyses were the following:

– Q164: "How important is God in your life? Please use this scale to indicate. 10 means 'very important' and 1 means 'not at all important'".

– Q165: "Do you believe in God? Yes (1); No (2)".

– Q166: "Do you believe in life after death? Yes (1); No (2)".

– Q167: "Do you believe in hell? Yes (1); No (2)".

– Q168: "Do you believe in heaven? Yes (1); No (2)".

– Q171: "Apart from weddings and funerals, about how often do you attend religious services these days? More than once a week (1); Once a week (2); Once a month (3); Only on special holy days (4); Once a year (5); Less often (6); Never, practically never (7)".

– Q174: "With which of the following statements do you agree most? The basic meaning of religion is: to follow religious norms and ceremonies (1); to do good to other people (2)".

– Q175: "And with which of the following statements do you agree most? The basic meaning of religion is: to make sense of life after death (1); to make sense of life in this world (2)".

Questions Q164–Q168 and Q174–Q175 were included in the "Religious values" section of the questionnaire.

22.2.3. *Statistical analyses*

22.2.3.1. *Preliminary decisions, tests and procedures*

Preliminary decisions, tests and procedures refer to the adequacy of the sample size for performing path analyses and how outliers and missing values are to be dealt with.

Kline (1998) proposed that a sample size of 10 times the number of parameters in a model is adequate for performing path analysis, and a sample size of 20 times the number of parameters in path analysis is best. However, it should be pointed out that path analysis is a large sample method (Tabachnick and Fidell 2007).

Data screening for outliers was based on the variables' boxplots. Cases were eliminated if they were shown in the boxplots as outliers (Tabachnick and Fidell 2007). Missing data analysis was performed, and the size and pattern of missing values for each variable was investigated. Missing data had to be replaced because complete data sets are required for SPSS Amos.

Initially, univariate statistics were computed for each measure, and their distributional properties were inspected (testing for normality) to decide on the appropriateness of the methods to be used. Bivariate analyses were performed and only statistically significant results at $p < 0.05$ are presented.

22.2.3.2. *The theoretical structure of the path analysis model*

The theoretical structure of the path analysis model under consideration was defined as follows (Figure 22.1): religious values and beliefs (Q164, Q165, Q166, Q167, Q168, Q174 and Q175) defined the independent variables (IV), the question on religious services attendance, the mediator and the self-perceived social class measurement the dependent variable (DV).

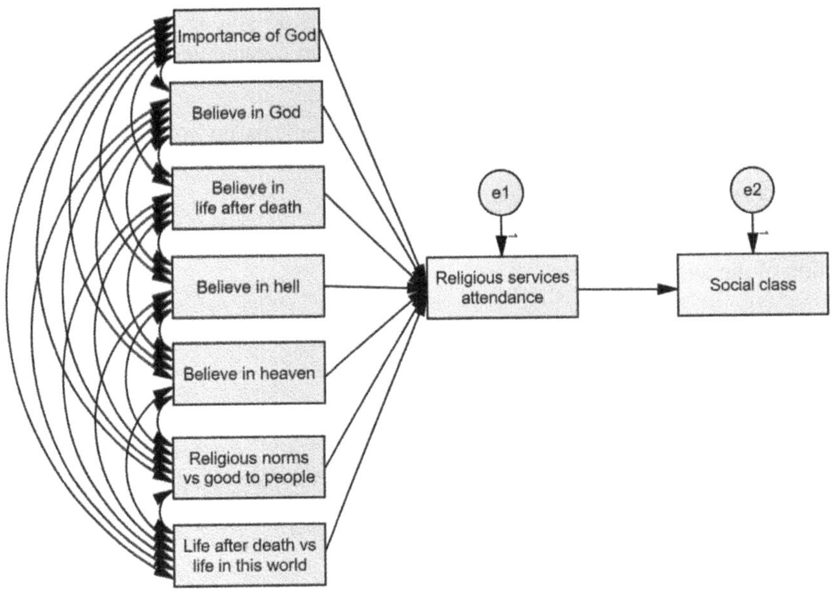

Figure 22.1. *The theoretical structure of the path analysis model*

The level of measurement of the DV and mediator variables is ordinal and pseudo-interval, respectively. All IVs are dichotomies except for the "importance of God" variable that is measured as pseudo-interval.

Based on the literature and our previous work (Yfanti and Michalopoulou 2024), the background variables measuring educational attainment (E274, pseudo-interval), employment status (Q280, recoded as a dichotomy – economically active/inactive) and income (Q288, interval) were used as controls.

22.2.3.3. *Path analysis*

Separate path analyses were performed with maximum likelihood for each country. Standardized indirect effects were considered as the "index of mediation" (Preacher and Hayes (2008, p. 38); see also Cheung (2009)) and tested with bootstrapping methods.

To generate bootstrap confidence intervals for the standardized indirect effects, 5,000 bootstrap samples were used (Cheung 2009; Preacher and Hayes 2008). A standardized indirect effect was considered statistically significant only if its 95% bootstrap confidence interval excluded zero (Hayes 2018).

Model fit was considered adequate if chi-square tests were not significant, comparative fit index (CFI) and Tucker–Lewis index (TLI) values were greater than or close to 0.95 and the root-mean-square error approximation (RMSEA) ≤ 0.06 with the 90% confidence interval (CI) upper limit ≤ 0.06 (Bollen 1989; Hu and Bentler 1999; Tabachnick and Fidell 2007). Model fit was considered acceptable if chi-square tests were not significant, CFI and TLI values were > 0.90 and RMSEA < 0.08 with the 90% CI upper limit < 0.08 (Hu and Bentler 1999; Marsh et al. 2004).

Statistical analyses and path analyses were performed using IBM SPSS Statistics Version 29 and IBM SPSS Amos Version 29, respectively.

22.3. Results

22.3.1. *Univariate analyses*

In Table 22.2, the frequency distribution and univariate statistics of the 2017–2020 7th wave WVS of self-perceived social class, religious services attendance, religious values and beliefs are presented for Germany, Greece, the Russian Federation and the United States.

As shown, respondents perceived themselves as belonging mainly to the lower middle class in the cases of Germany (41.0%) and the United States (35.8%). In the case of Greece and the Russian Federation, they considered themselves as belonging mainly to the working class of 40.8% and 34.7%, respectively. The percentages of the respondents perceiving themselves as belonging to the upper middle class ranged from 10.5% (Greece) to 36.0% (Germany).

The Greeks attend church mainly on special holy days, the Russians and Americans once a year and the Germans less often than most.

		Frequency (%) of response categories										
Country/variable	M	1	2	3	4	5	6	7	8	9	10	NA
Germany												
Social class	3	1.4	36.0	41.0	16.8	1.8						3.0
Religious services attendance	6	1.3	7.1	10.5	16.4	8.7	15.1	40.5				0.4
Importance of God	4.92	26.4	8.8	7.1	4.6	9.8	5.2	7.7	9.1	3.9	16.0	1.3
Believe in God	1	55.7	38.2									6.0
Believe in life after death	2	38.8	50.5									10.7
Believe in hell	2	14.7	78.9									6.4
Believe in heaven	2	30.6	62.3									7.2
Religious norms vs. good to people	1	51.7	40.9									7.4
Life after death vs life in this world	2	11.9	79.1									9.0
Greece												
Social class	4	0.3	10.5	33.0	40.8	12.5						2.8
Religious services attendance	4	3.6	18.1	22.8	34.9	4.0	10.4	5.2				0.9
Importance of God	8.12	3.9	2.1	1.9	1.9	6.2	4.2	7.1	14.0	13.1	44.7	1.1

Table 22.2. *The frequency distribution and mean/median/mode (M) of the 2017–2020 7th wave of the World Values Survey measurements of self-perceived social class, religious services attendance, religious values and beliefs for Germany, Greece, the Russian Federation and the United States*

		Frequency (%) of response categories										
Country/variable	M	1	2	3	4	5	6	7	8	9	10	NA
Greece												
Believe in God	1	91.7	6.2									2.1
Believe in life after death	1	47.7	41.2									11.0
Believe in hell	1	44.3	43.8									11.8
Believe in heaven	1	46.1	42.6									11.3
Religious norms vs. good to people	2	14.6	82.8									2.6
Life after death vs. life in this world	2	8.3	85.3									6.4
Russian Federation												
Social class	3	1.3	18.6	31.1	34.7	5.9						8.4
Religious services attendance	5	1.5	4.6	10.1	29.4	7.0	10.5	32.7				4.2
Importance of God	6.28	7.5	3.2	5.3	5.0	16.6	11.9	11.3	11.3	4.7	17.8	5.5
Believe in God	1	77.4	14.4									8.2
Believe in life after death	2	40.3	43.2									16.5
Believe in hell	2	36.8	45.8									17.3
Believe in heaven	2	38.3	44.4									17.2
Religious norms vs. good to people	2	18.9	71.1									9.9
Life after death vs. life in this world	2	16.1	71.2									12.7
United States												
Social class	3	1.3	29.4	35.8	24.8	7.3						1.4
Religious services attendance	5	9.2	20.0	9.7	8.4	5.0	14.1	33.3				0.3
Importance of God	7.05	12.8	3.5	4.1	3.3	9.0	4.6	5.8	7.7	5.3	43.2	0.7

Table 22.2. *(continued)*

		Frequency (%) of response categories										
Country/variable	M	1	2	3	4	5	6	7	8	9	10	NA
United States												
Believe in God	1	81.2	17.6									1.2
Believe in life after death	1	68.2	28.4									3.4
Believe in hell	1	66.7	29.8									3.5
Believe in heaven	1	66.9	30.6									2.5
Religious norms vs. good to people	2	20.6	77.7									1.6
Life after death vs. life in this world	2	22.9	74.6									2.5

Table 22.2. *(continued)*

The findings showed on average that the Greeks believe that God is very important in their lives (8.12) and the same applies to the Americans (7.05) and the Russians (6.28), albeit to a lesser extent, whereas the Germans (4.92) do not believe it so very much.

They all believe in God. The Greeks and the Americans mainly believe in life after death, in hell and in heaven but not the Germans and the Russians. The Greeks the Russians and the Americans primarily believe that the meaning of religion is to do good to other people but the Germans believe mostly that it is to follow religious norms and ceremonies. They all believe that the basic meaning of religion is to make sense of life in this world.

22.3.2. *Bivariate analyses: correlation analyses*

In Table 22.3, bivariate correlations of social class perceptions to religious values and beliefs and religious services attendance are presented for Germany, Greece, the Russian Federation and the United States.

	Social class perceptions			
Variable	**Germany**	**Greece**	**Russian Federation**	**United States**
Importance of God	–0.002**	0.216*	0.033**	0.059**
Believe in God	0.020**	–0.109*	0.032**	–0.040**
Believe in life after death	–0.006**	–0.112**	0.015**	–0.036**
Believe in hell	–0.097*	–0.168*	–0.021**	–0.082*
Believe in heaven	–0.056**	–0.156*	–0.027**	–0.052**
Religious norms vs.				
good to people	0.120*	–0.131*	0.000**	–0.021**
Life after death vs.				
life in this world	–0.035**	–0.093**	0.032**	0.003**
Attend religious services	0.076**	–0.195*	0.037**	0.097*

* $p < 0.001$. ** $p < 0.05$.

Table 22.3. *The relation of social class perceptions to religious values, beliefs and practices: Spearman's correlation coefficients*

As shown, the importance of God variable was significantly related to social class perceptions in all countries with the respective correlations ranging from –0.002 (Germany) to 0.216 (Greece).

The believe in God variable was significantly related to social class perceptions in all countries with the respective correlations ranging from –0.040 (United States) to 0.032 (Russian Federation).

The believe in life after death variable was significantly related to social class perceptions in all countries with the respective correlations ranging from –0.112 (Greece) to 0.015 (Russia).

The believe in hell variable was significantly related to social class perceptions in all countries with the respective correlations ranging from –0.168 (Greece) to –0.021 (Russia).

22.3.3. *Multivariate analyses: mediation analyses*

The sample sizes (Table 22.1) ranged from 1,200 (Greece) to 2,596 (United States) and were considered large enough for carrying out path analyses separately in each country. The screening of samples detected only a negligible number of outlying cases, and it was decided not to reject them from the analysis. All missing values were replaced by the mean values of each variable because complete data sets were required for SPSS Amos.

In Table 22.4, the path analyses results are presented.

			β			
Model			**DE**	**GR**	**RU**	**US**
Attend religious services	←	Importance of God	–0.437	–0.337	–0.232	–0.485
Attend religious services	←	Believe in God	0.135	0.076	0.179	0.001
Attend religious services	←	Believe in life after death	0.019	0.036	0.023	0.037
Attend religious services	←	Believe in hell	0.075	–0.067	0.121	0.035
Attend religious services	←	Believe in heaven	0.055	0.233	0.075	0.111
Attend religious services	←	Religious norms vs.				
		good to people	0.005	0.122	0.004	0.025
Attend religious services	←	Life after death vs.				
		life in this world	–0.020	0.029	–0.006	0.065
DV: Social class perceptions	←	Attend religious services	0.033	–0.063	0.004	0.034
		Variable	R^2			
		Attend religious services	0.406	0.364	0.256	0.363
		Social class perceptions	0.405	0.434	0.319	0.402

Table 22.4. *Path analyses performed with maximum likelihood: standardized coefficients and squared multiple correlations*

As shown, in all countries, social class perceptions were positively predicted by religious services attendance, except in the case of Greece where the reverse was true. In all countries, religious services attendance was positively affected by belief in God, in life after death, in hell (except for Greece), in heaven, religious norms versus good to people and life after death versus life in this world (except for Germany and Russia). In all countries, religious services attendance was negatively affected by the importance of God.

The squared multiple correlations for social class perceptions and religious services attendance models ranged from 0.319 (Russia) to 0.434 (Greece) and 0.256 (Russia) to 0.406 (Germany), respectively.

In Table 22.5, the goodness of fit indices for the path analyses models performed with maximum likelihood are presented for each country.

Country	χ^2 (*df*)	*p*	**CFI**	**TLI**	**RMSEA (90% CI)**
Germany	13.093 (7)	0.070	0.999	0.990	0.024 (0.000–0.044)
Greece	26.259 (7)	0.000	0.997	0.972	0.048 (0.029–0.068)
Russian Federation	4.871 (7)	0.676	1.000	1.003	0.000 (0.000–0.023)
United States	22.118 (7)	0.002	0.999	0.987	0.029 (0.016–0.043)

df = degrees of freedom; CFI = comparative fit index; TLI = Tucker–Lewis index; RMSEA = root-mean-square error of approximation; CI = confidence interval. Model fit is considered adequate if χ^2 is not significant, CFI and TLI values greater than or close to 0.95 and RMSEA ≤ 0.06 with the 90% CI upper limit ≤ 0.06. Model fit is considered acceptable if χ^2 is not significant, CFI > 0.90, TLI > 0.90 and RMSEA < 0.08 with the 90% CI upper limit < 0.08.

Table 22.5. *Path analyses performed with maximum likelihood: goodness-of-fit indices*

As shown, the models of Germany, the Russian Federation and the United States provided acceptable model fit, and the model of Greece provided adequate model fit.

In Table 22.6, the mediating effects are presented for each country. As shown, weak simple mediation effects of importance of God by religious services attendance were detected in the cases of Greece and the United States with significant standardized indirect effects: –0.021 and –0.017, respectively.

Furthermore, weak simple mediation effects of belief in heaven by religious services attendance were detected in the cases of Greece and the United States with significant standardized indirect effects: –0.015 and 0.004, respectively.

Moreover, weak simple mediation effects of belief in God and religious norms versus good to people by religious services attendance were detected in the case of Greece with significant standardized indirect effects: –0.005 and –0.008, respectively.

There were no mediating effects for any of the IVs by religious services attendance in the cases of Germany and the Russian Federation.

	Germany			Greece		
Variables	**SIE**	**95% CI**	***p*-value**	**SIE**	**95% CI**	***p*-value**
Importance of God	–0.014	–0.033, 0.002	0.090	–0.021	0.006, 0.040	0.009
Believe in God	0.004	0.000, 0.011	0.074	–0.005	–0.012, –0.001	0.041
Believe in life after death	0.001	–0.001, 0.004	0.306	–0.002	–0.008, 0.001	0.194
Believe in hell	0.002	0.000, 0.008	0.055	0.004	–0.008, 0.023	0.386
Believe in heaven	0.002	0.000, 0.007	0.085	–0.015	–0.039, –0.002	0.015
Religious norms vs.						
good to people	0.000	–0.001, 0.003	0.573	–0.008	–0.015, –0.002	0.006
Life after death vs.						
life in this world	–0.001	–0.004, 0.001	0.240	–0.002	–0.007, 0.001	0.162
	Russian Federation			**United States**		
Importance of God	–0.001	–0.011, 0.009	0.865	–0.017	–0.031, –0.002	0.026
Believe in God	0.001	–0.007, 0.008	0.862	0.000	–0.002, 0.002	0.890
Believe in life after death	0.000	–0.001, 0.002	0.658	0.001	0.000, 0.004	0.047
Believe in hell	0.000	–0.004, 0.008	0.695	0.001	0.000, 0.004	0.107
Believe in heaven	0.000	–0.003, 0.007	0.624	0.004	0.001, 0.008	0.017
Religious norms vs.						
good to people	0.000	–0.001, 0.001	0.799	0.001	0.000, 0.003	0.063
Life after death vs.						
life in this world	0.000	–0.001, 0.001	0.759	0.002	0.000, 0.005	0.018

Table 22.6. *Path analyses: standardized indirect effects (SIE), their 95% bootstrap confidence intervals (CI) and significance*

22.4. Conclusions

In this chapter, the relation of social class perceptions to religious values, beliefs and practices was investigated. Moreover, the mediating role of attending religious services in the relationship between religious values, beliefs and practices and social class perceptions as measured in the 7th wave WVS questionnaire was also explored. The analysis was based on the WVS datasets for four countries: Germany, Greece, the Russian Federation and the United States.

The findings showed that all the religious values and beliefs (IVs) and the religious services attendance variable (mediator) were significantly related to social class perceptions (DV) in all four countries.

The models of the separate path analyses provided acceptable model fit for Germany, the Russian Federation and the United States, and adequate model fit for Greece.

In all countries, social class perceptions were positively predicted by religious services attendance, except in the case of Greece. In all countries, religious services attendance was positively affected by belief in God, in life after death, in hell (except for Greece), in heaven, religious norms versus good to people and life after death versus life in this world (except for Germany and Russia). In all countries, religious services attendance was negatively affected by the importance of God.

The results showed weak simple mediation effects of importance of God by religious services attendance in the cases of Greece and the United States. Furthermore, weak simple mediation effects of belief in heaven by religious services attendance were detected in the cases of Greece and the United States. Moreover, weak simple mediation effects of belief in God and religious norms versus good to people by religious services attendance were detected in the case of Greece. There were no mediating effects for any of the religious values and beliefs (IVs) by religious services attendance in the cases of Germany and the Russian Federation.

Certainly, the resulting percentages of the total variation explained by the models with social class perceptions and religious services attendance as the dependent and mediating variables, respectively, indicate that in future research, additional social indicators should be considered to provide a more coherent interpretation.

22.5. References

Bollen, K.A. (1989). *Structural Equations with Latent Variables*. John Wiley and Sons, New York.

Carey, S. (ed.) (2000). *Measuring Adult Literacy: The International Adult Literacy Survey (IALS) in the European context*. Office for National Statistics, London.

Cheung, M.W.-L. (2009). Comparison of methods for constructing confidence intervals of standardized indirect effects. *Behavior Research Methods*, 41(2), 425–438. doi: 10.3758/BRM.41.2.425.

Haerpfer, C., Inglehart, R., Moreno, A., Welzel, C., Kizilova, K., Diez-Medrano, J., Lagos, M., Norris, P., Ponarin, E., Puranen, B. et al. (eds) (2020). *World Values Survey: Round Seven – Country-pooled Datafile*. JD Systems Institute & WVSA Secretariat, Madrid and Vienna. doi: 10.14281/18241.

Hayes, A.F. (2018). *Introduction to Mediation, Moderation, and Conditional Process Analysis: A Regression-based Approach*, 2nd edition. Guilford Press, New York.

Hu, L. and Bentler, P.M. (1999). Cutoff criteria for fit indexes in covariance structure analysis: Conventional criteria versus new alternatives, *Structural Equation Modeling*, 6(1), 1–55. doi: 10.1080/10705519909540118.

Kish, L. (1994). Multi-population survey designs: Five types with seven shared aspects, *International Statistical Review*, 62(2), 167–186.

Kline, R.B. (1998). *Principles and Practice of Structural Equation Modeling*. Guilford Press, New York.

Marsh, H.W., Hau, K.T., Wen, Z. (2004). In search of golden rules: Comment on hypotheses-testing approaches to setting cutoff values for fit indexes and dangers in overgeneralizing Hu and Bentler's (1999) findings. *Structural Equation Modeling*, 11(3), 320–341. doi: 10.1207/s15328007sem1103_2.

McCloud, S. (2007). Putting some class into religious studies: Resurrecting an important concept. *Journal of the American Academy of Religion*, 75(4), 840–862.

McKinnon, A. (2017). Religion and social class: Theory and method after Bourdieu. *Sociological Research Online*, 22(1), 1–13. doi: 10.5153/sro.4247.

Preacher, K.J. and Hayes, A.F. (2008). Contemporary approaches to assessing mediation in communication research. In *The Sage Sourcebook of Advanced Data Analysis Methods for Communication Research*, Hayes, A.F., Slater, M.D., Snyder, L.B. (eds). Sage, Thousand Oaks, CA, 13–54.

Tabachnick, B.G. and Fidell, L.S. (2007). *Using Multivariate Statistics*. Pearson Allyn & Bacon, Upper Saddle River, NJ.

Thompson, B. (2005). *Exploratory and Confirmatory Factor Analysis: Understanding Concepts and Applications*. American Psychological Association, Washington, D.C.

World Values Survey. (n.d.) WVS wave 7 [Online]. Available at: http://www.worldvaluessurvey.org/WVSContents.jsp.

Yfanti, A. and Michalopoulou, C. (2021). Investigating peoples' perceptions of their social class: Evidence from the 7th wave of the world values survey, 2017–2020. In *15th Conference of the European Sociological Association (ESA)*, Barcelona, 31 August – 3 September.

Yfanti, A. and Michalopoulou, C. (2022). Exploring factors impacting social class perceptions: Evidence from the 2017–2020 7th wave of the World Values Survey for Greece. In *European Sociological Association (ESA) RN21 Midterm Conference "Quantitative Methods and the Covid-19 Pandemic"*, Salamanca, 5–7 October.

Yfanti, A. and Michalopoulou, C. (2024). Modeling religion variables on self-perceived social class: Evidence from the 7th wave of the world values survey, 2017–2020. In *Quantitative Methods and Data Analysis in Applied Demography – Volume 2: Models, Risk and Surveys*. Skiadas, C.H. and Skiadas, C. (eds). Springer, Berlin.

23

New Methods of Constructing Confidence Intervals of a Sensitive Proportion in Survey Statistics

Dealing with sensitive features is an important problem in survey statistics. To elicit truthful responses from respondents, several methods of indirect questioning have been devised, such as Item Count/Sum Technique (ICT/IST) (Raghavarao and Federer 1979; Miller 1994; Trappmann et al. 2014). For a binary sensitive feature, the target of a survey is the population proportion. Estimators of this proportion are accompanied by standard confidence intervals (CIs) based on normal approximation. However, in practice, the actual coverage probability of such CIs is not sufficiently close to the nominal level of confidence. We propose two new methods of constructing CIs for a sensitive proportion in ICT/IST surveys. One of these methods uses a parametric bootstrap and the expectation-maximization (EM) algorithm as in Kowalczyk et al. (2023). The other one is based on a completely different idea, namely, on computing an exact CI in a parametric model and then substituting a method-of-moments estimate in place of the nuisance parameter (Jaworski and Zieliński 2023). We use a Poisson distribution to model the answers to the masking neutral question, following Tian et al. (2017).

23.1. Introduction

In various fields of economy, sociology, health care, psychology and criminology, information about sensitive behaviors and characteristics is required. Eliciting truthful responses via direct questioning is usually either very hard or impossible to achieve when dealing with questions about stigmatizing, socially unaccepted, highly personal or illegal features. Analogous applies to preferable, norm-conforming and universally acclaimed attributes. In the direct questioning people tend to under-report undesirable, stigmatizing, illegal features and

---

Chapter written by Marta ZALEWSKA and Wojciech NIEMIRO.

over-report the preferable and socially desirable ones (Silver et al. 1986; Blair and Imai 2012; Krumpal 2013).

Item count technique (ICT), proposed by Raghavarao and Federer (1979) and Miller (1994) is one of the methods designed to overcome these difficulties. ICT is useful for large-scale sample surveys, is easy for implementation, can be adopted in internet and telephone surveys, does not require any randomizing device to be handled by the respondents and allows respondents to understand how their privacy is being protected. Therefore, ICT has attracted much attention among applied researchers (Kuklinski et al. 1997; Holbrook and Krosnick 2010; Comsa and Postelnicu 2013; Kuha and Jackson 2014).

In this chapter, we consider a version of ICT recently proposed by Kowalczyk et al. (2022) based on two different treatment groups (in contrast with the classical ICT, where we have one treatment end one control group). Respondents are randomly assigned to either a first treatment group of n_1 elements or to a second treatment group of n_2 elements, where $n_1 + n_2 = n$. Every respondent is presented with a simple two item questionnaire. The first question is a neutral, masking question and the second one is the sensitive question we are really interested in. Let us denote the answer to the neutral question by X (where X is a count variable with positive integer values) and the answer to the sensitive question by Z (where Z is a binary variable with values 0 or 1). Respondents in the first group are asked to report the difference of the two answers while respondents in the second group report the sum of the two answers. Thus, we observe variable Y, where:

$$Y = \begin{cases} X - Z & \text{in the first group} \\ X + Z & \text{in the second group} \end{cases}$$

We assume that X and Z are independent, Y is observed, and X and Z are hidden (missing) variables. Let $P(Z = 1) = \pi$, $P(Z = 0) = 1 - \pi$, that is:

$$Z \sim Bernoulli(\pi)$$

We focus on the case when:

$$X \sim Poisson(\psi)$$

We are interested in estimating the sensitive proportion π while ψ plays the role of nuisance parameter. The data consist of answers of $n_1 + n_2$ respondents, assumed to be independent:

$$\begin{cases} Y_1, \dots, Y_{n_1} : \text{ in group 1; } Y_i = X_i - Z_i \\ Y_{n_1+1}, \dots, Y_{n_1+n_2} : \text{ in group 2; } Y_i = X_i + Z_i \end{cases}$$

An exemplary questionnaire for the first treatment group could be the following:

A) *How many times did you shop last week? Remember your number. But do not reveal it.*

B) *Have you ever bribed an official? Assign number 1 if your answer is "yes" and number 0 if your answer is "not". Remember your number. But do not reveal it.*

We do not want to invade your privacy. So please report only the difference between your two answers. From your answer to question A subtract your answer to question B. The resulting difference is…

The questionnaire for the second group consists of the same questions (A) and (B), but the respondent is asked to give the *sum* of the two answers.

23.2. Method of moments (MM) for ICT data

A straightforward method of estimating π is based on a simple observation that $EY = \psi - \pi$ in the first group and $EY = \psi + \pi$ in the second. If we denote:

$$\overline{Y_1} = \frac{1}{n_1}\sum_{i=1}^{n_1} Y_i\,,\ \overline{Y_2} = \frac{1}{n_2}\sum_{i=n_1+1}^{n_1+n_2} Y_i$$

then

$$\hat{\pi} = (\overline{Y_2} - \overline{Y_1})/2$$

is an unbiased estimator of π (and $\hat{\psi} = (\overline{Y_2} + \overline{Y_1})/2$ is an unbiased estimator of the nuisance parameter ψ). MM estimators are usually accompanied by asymptotic CIs based on normal approximation. Approximate 0.95 CI for π is given as:

$$[\hat{\pi} - 2\widehat{\sigma_{MM}}, \hat{\pi} + 2\widehat{\sigma_{MM}}]$$

where

$$\widehat{\sigma^2_{MM}} = \frac{1}{4}[\hat{\psi} + \hat{\pi}(1 - \hat{\pi})]\frac{n_1+n_2}{n_1 n_2}$$

23.3. EM estimation for ICT data and parametric bootstrap

We consider the maximum likelihood (ML) estimators because they are statistically efficient and allow for generalization to regression models.

If $f_\psi(x)$ is a PDF of X, then the PDF of observed variable Y is simply a mixture, namely:

$$f_{\pi,\psi}(y) = \begin{cases} \pi f_\psi(y+1) + (1-\pi) f_\psi(y) & \textit{if y belongs to the first group} \\ \pi f_\psi(y-1) + (1-\pi) f_\psi(y) & \textit{if y belongs to the second group} \end{cases}$$

23.3.1. *Maximum likelihood via the EM algorithm*

Log-likelihood functions for mixtures are usually optimized via some iterative algorithm. Analogously as in the two seminal papers for earlier ICTs (Imai 2011; Tian et al. 2017), we apply the EM algorithm pioneered by Dempster et al. (1977). Our interest lies of course in estimation of π, while ψ is just a nuisance parameter.

In our model, the complete data are $(\mathbf{y},\mathbf{z})$, where $\mathbf{y}$ is a vector of observed data and $\mathbf{z}$ is a vector of hidden (missing) data. The complete data log-likelihood function is:

$$\ln L_c(\pi, \psi; \mathbf{y}, \mathbf{z}) = \left(\sum_{i=1}^{n_1+n_2} z_i\right)\ln\pi + \left(\sum_{i=1}^{n_1+n_2}(1-z_i)\right)\ln(1-\pi)$$

$$+\sum_{i=1}^{n_1+n_2} z_i \ln f_\psi(y_i \pm 1) + \sum_{i=1}^{n_1+n_2}(1-z_i)\ln f_\psi(y_i)$$

In the notation "$\pm$", plus refers always to $i = 1, \dots, n_1$, and minus refers to $i = n_1+1, \dots, n_1+n_2$. This convention is used consistently throughout the paper. Additionally, we use the convention that $0\ln 0 = 0$.

In the M-step, the complete data ML estimators of all model parameters π,ψ are computed. In the E-step, the components of $\mathbf{z}$ are replaced by their conditional expectations:

$$\tilde{z}_i = E_{\pi,\psi}(Z_i | Y_i = y_i) = P_{\pi,\psi}(Z_i = 1 | Y_i = y_i) =$$

$$\frac{f_\psi(y_i \pm 1)\pi}{f_\psi(y_i \pm 1)\pi + f_\psi(y_i)(1-\pi)}$$

In this chapter, we consider $X \sim Poisson(\psi)$, so $f_\psi(x) = e^{-\psi}\psi^x/x!$. Explicit formulas for E and M steps in the EM algorithm are as follows:

– *M step*: it is easy to see that maximizers of the complete log-likelihood (we use symbols $\tilde{\pi}$ and $\tilde{\psi}$ to indicate that these quantities are updated at each step) are given as:

$$\tilde{\pi} = \frac{1}{n_1+n_2}\sum_{i=1}^{n_1+n_2} \tilde{z}_i \quad \tilde{\psi} = \frac{1}{n_1+n_2}\sum_{i=1}^{n_1+n_2}(y_i \pm \tilde{z}_i)$$

– *E step*: The updates of the z variables are given as:

$$\tilde{z}_i = \frac{\tilde{\psi}\tilde{\pi}}{\tilde{\psi}\tilde{\pi}+(y_i+1)(1-\tilde{\pi})} \text{ in the first group}$$

$$\tilde{z}_i = \frac{y_i\tilde{\pi}}{y_i\tilde{\pi}+\tilde{\psi}(1-\tilde{\pi})} \text{ in the second group}$$

23.3.2. *Percentile parametric bootstrap confidence intervals*

Having obtained ML estimators $(\hat{\pi}_{ML}, \hat{\psi}_{ML})$ of all model parameters by using the EM algorithm, we can construct a bootstrap CI for unknown sensitive proportion π. For this purpose, we should generate an iid sample $x_1, \dots, x_{n_1+n_2}$ from the probability distribution with the PDF $f_{\hat{\psi}_{ML}}(x)$ and an independent iid sample $z_1, \dots, z_{n_1+n_2}$ from the Bernoulli distribution with parameter $\hat{\pi}_{ML}$ to obtain a replication of the vector of observable data $y_1, \dots, y_{n_1}, y_{n_1+1}, \dots, y_{n_1+n_2}$, where $y_i = x_i - z_i$ for $i = 1, \dots, n_1$ and $y_j = x_j + z_j$ for $j = n_1 + 1, \dots, n_1 + n_2$. Next, having a replication of the vector of observable data, we should derive, based on ML estimation and the EM algorithm, a bootstrap replication $\hat{\pi}_{ML}^{\text{Bootstrap}}$. The whole procedure should be repeated independently B times to yield a set of bootstrap replications $\{\hat{\pi}_{ML}^{\text{Bootstrap}}(b): b = 1, \dots, B\}$. The lower and upper limits of bootstrap CI at the confidence level $(1-\alpha)$ are, respectively, the $\alpha/2$ and $(1-\alpha/2)$ percentiles of $\{\hat{\pi}_{ML}^{Bootstrap}(b): b = 1, \dots, B\}$.

23.4. "Almost exact" confidence intervals for ICT data

In this section, we present a method of computing "almost exact" CIs for the sensitive proportion π in the ICT model. Recall that the data consist of answers $Y_1, \dots, Y_{n_1}$ and $Y_{n_1+1}, \dots, Y_{n_1+n_2}$ to the questionnaires in the first and the second group, respectively. Let us shorten the notation and write:

$$\Sigma Y_1 = \sum_{i=1}^{n_1} Y_i, \ \Sigma Y_2 = \sum_{i=n_1+1}^{n_1+n_2} Y_i$$

and similarly for the Z and X variables. We thus have:

$$\Sigma Y_1 = \Sigma X_1 - \Sigma Z_1, \ \Sigma Y_2 = \Sigma X_2 + \Sigma Z_2$$

Under our assumptions, we have:

$$\Sigma X_1 \sim Poisson(n_1\psi), \ \Sigma X_2 \sim Poisson(n_2\psi) \ independent$$

The difference between two independent Poisson-distributed variables has a so-called Skellam distribution:

$$\sum X_2 - \sum X_1 \sim Skellam(n_2\psi\,, n_1\psi)$$

$$\sum Z_1 \sim Binomial(n_1, \pi),\ \sum Z_2 \sim Binomial(n_2, \pi)\ independent$$

All of these probability distributions are available in R (R Core Team 2016). The construction of the CIs is based on statistic V defined in the following:

$$V = \sum Y_2 - \sum Y_1 = (\sum X_2 - \sum X_1) + (\sum Z_1 + \sum Z_2) \sim Skellam(n_2\psi\,, n_1\psi) * Binomial(n_1 + n_2, \pi)$$

This probability distribution of this statistic (a convolution of a Skellam with a Binomial) is easy to compute numerically. We denote the cumulative distribution function by:

$$F_{\pi,\psi}(v) = P(V \leq v)\ (CDF\ of\ V)$$

Exact CI at level $1 - \alpha$ is $[\pi_{LOW}, \pi_{UP}]$, where:

$$\pi_{LOW}(v) = \inf\left\{\pi: F_{\pi,\psi}(v-1) \leq \frac{\alpha}{2}\right\}$$

$$\pi_{UP}(v) = \sup\left\{\pi: F_{\pi,\psi}(v) \geq 1 - \frac{\alpha}{2}\right\}$$

(essentially, these are quantiles of CDF; computation of each of these quantiles only requires solving a nonlinear equation with one unknown π).

$$\pi_{LOW}(v) = \begin{cases} 0\ if\ F_{0,\psi}(v-1) \leq \dfrac{\alpha}{2} \\ \text{solution to equation } F_{\pi,\psi}(v-1) = \dfrac{\alpha}{2} \text{ otherwise} \end{cases}$$

$$\pi_{LOW}(v) = \begin{cases} 1\ if\ F_{1,\psi}(v) \geq 1 - \dfrac{\alpha}{2} \\ \text{solution to equation } F_{\pi,\psi}(v) = 1 - \dfrac{\alpha}{2} \text{ otherwise} \end{cases}$$

By construction, we have:

$$P(\pi_{LOW}(V) \leq \pi \leq \pi_{UP}(V)) \geq 1 - \alpha$$

and this relation is exact, provided that the nuisance parameter ψ is known. In practice, we replace unknown ψ by its estimate $\hat{\psi}$. A MM estimator is given as:

$$\hat{\psi} = (\bar{Y}_1 + \bar{Y}_2)/2, \text{ where } \bar{Y}_1 = \frac{\sum Y_1}{n_1} \text{ and } \bar{Y}_2 = \frac{\sum Y_2}{n_2}$$

In this way, we obtain a CI which is no longer exact but "almost exact". Its actual coverage probability is very close to the nominal level of confidence. To support this claim, we performed several series of simulations.

23.5. Simulation results

In this section, we report the results of a series of simulations aimed at comparing three methods of computing Cis for ICT data: (1) the classical method based on MM estimators; (2) parametric bootstrap which uses EM algorithm in every replication; and (3) "almost exact" construction based on Skellam distribution. We decided to restrict our presentation to just one, relatively "big" and realistic scenario, described below.

The model parameters are chosen to be $\pi = 0.2, \psi = 10$. The rationale for these choices is the following. Usually, in real surveys, the sensitive feature of interest is rather rare, so probability π should be "small". On the other hand, the masking variable X should be bounded away from 0 with high probability, because otherwise the respondents' privacy may be compromised. For the Poisson model, this requirement translates to choosing sufficiently big ψ (e.g. if $\psi = 10$, then we have $P(X = 0) = e^{-10} = 0.000045$).

We repeated the simulated experiment 1,000 times. In each replication, computing the MM estimates with classical asymptotic CIs, and EM estimates with parametric bootstrap CIs and "almost exact" CIs. Let us begin with presenting comparison between MM and EM estimates (this slight digression from the main topic of this article is probably of independent interest).

The summary of estimates computed for 1,000 examples is as follows (recall that the "true" π is equal to 0.20). RMSE represents the root mean square error, which is defined as:

$$\text{RMSE} = \sqrt{\sum_{i=1}^{1,000} (\hat{\pi} - \pi)^2}$$

Estimates of the sensitive proportion π

	Min.	1st Qu.	Median	Mean	3rd Qu.	Max.
MM	0.0022	0.1497	0.1965	0.1971	0.2430	0.3972
EM	0.0192	0.1550	0.1965	0.1971	0.2389	0.3759

RMSE for MM 0.0669978

RMSE for EM 0.0635681

The boxplot given in Figure 23.1 illustrates graphically these results.

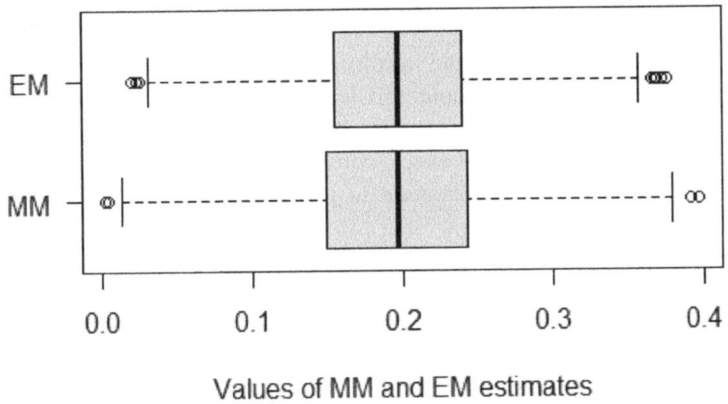

Figure 23.1. *Boxplots of MM and EM estimates in 1,000 experiments (with true value $\pi = 0.2$)*

It is clear (and not surprising) that in our model EM estimators outperform MM ones.

Now we turn to analyzing the performance of CIs. We first compare CIs computed by the classical method based on MM estimate combined with the normal approximation (referred to as MM) with the parametric bootstrap CIs (referred to as EM). The intervals obtained in 1,000 independent simulated experiments are shown in Figure 23.2. To get a readable picture, the experiments are sorted in the order of increasing MM estimates $\hat{\pi}$ (the values of these estimates are depicted by the black line). The CIs are vertical spans between blue lines (MM) and red lines (EM). The "bad" intervals (those which do not cover the green horizontal line) are concentrated at the left and right ends of the picture.

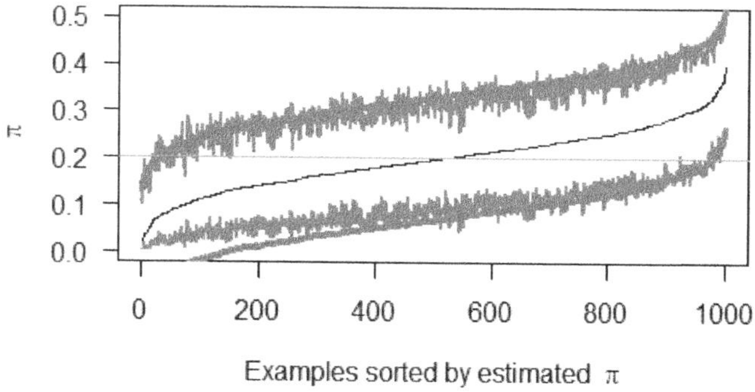

Figure 23.2. *CIs obtained by MM and EM methods in 1,000 experiments (with the same value $\pi = 0.2$). For a color version of this figure, see www.iste.co.uk/dimotikalis/data5.zip*

The actual coverage probabilities assessed from 1,000 repetitions are the following (the nominal level of confidence is 0.95):

```
coverage probability for method MM = 0.948
coverage probability for method EM = 0.924
```

The lengths of the CIs are summarized and shown in Figure 23.3.

	Min.	1st Qu.	Median	Mean	3rd Qu.	Max.
MM	0.2563	0.2595	0.2602	0.2602	0.2609	0.2633
EM	0.0969	0.2152	0.2261	0.2220	0.2351	0.2603

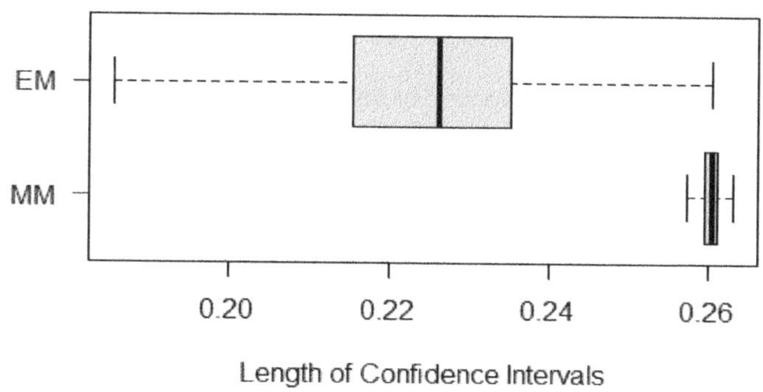

Figure 23.3. *Length of CIs computed by the classical method (MM) and bootstrap EM method (EM) methods in the same 1,000 experiments as in Figure 23.2. The actual coverage probability for EM intervals is lower than that for MM and lower than the nominal level of confidence 0.95. EM intervals are on the average shorter than MM intervals but their length is more variable*

In the next series of 1,000 experiments, we compared the behavior of the classical CIs (referred as MM) with exact CI based on Skellam distribution and their "almost exact" version, as described in section 23.4.

Figure 23.4 is constructed analogously to Figure 23.2. The values of estimates $\hat{\pi}$ are depicted by the black line. The CIs are vertical spans between light green lines (MM), blue lines (exact method) and green lines ("almost exact method").

The actual coverage probabilities assessed from 1,000 repetitions are as follows (the nominal level of confidence is 0.95).

```
coverage probability for method MM = 0.954
coverage probability for the exact method = 0.956
coverage probability for the "almost exact" method = 0.948
```

The lengths of the CIs are shown in Figure 23.5.

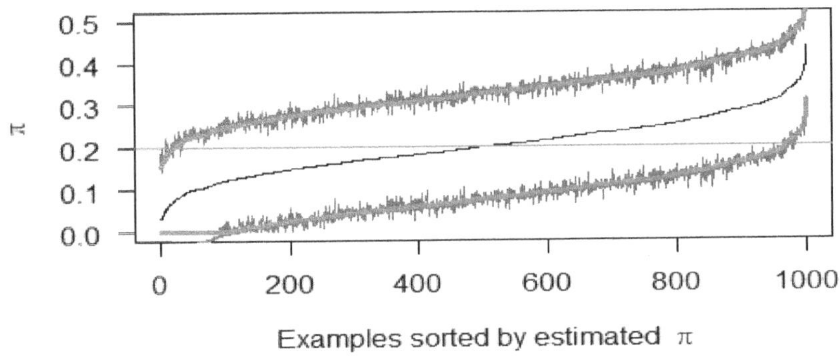

Figure 23.4. *CIs obtained by classical MM method (light green), the exact method (blue) and almost exact method (dark green) in 1,000 experiments (with the true value* $\pi = 0.2$*). For a color version of this figure, see www.iste.co.uk/dimotikalis/data5.zip*

The actual coverage probability for the exact and "almost exact" methods is very close to the nominal level of confidence 0.95. These both methods produce on the average shorter intervals than the classical method. It is worth mentioning that the exact and "almost exact" methods lead to quite similar results. This means that replacing the nuisance parameter ψ by its MM estimate does not significantly worsen the performance of the resulting CIs.

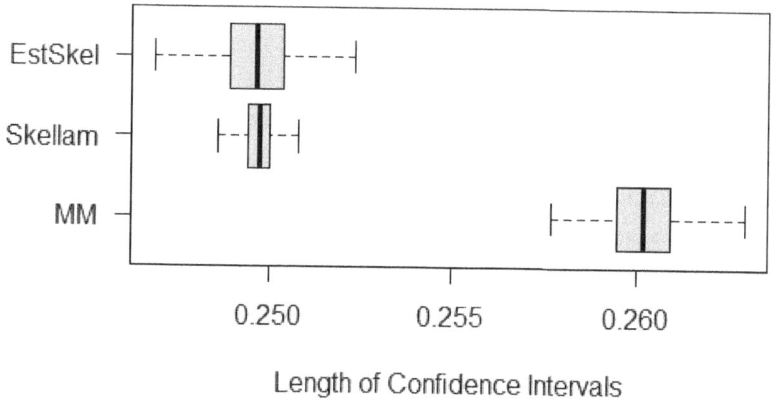

Figure 23.5. *Length of CIs obtained by the exact method (Skellam), almost exact method (EstSkellam) and the classical method (MM) in the same 1,000 experiments as in Figure 23.4*

23.6. Conclusions

We presented two new methods of constructing CIs for ICT data. Both methods have certain advantages over the classical CIs based on the MM estimators and normal approximation. They produce on average shorter intervals and thus improve the accuracy of inference. They produce intervals, which are always contained in the range from 0 to 1 (that obviously desirable property is not guaranteed for the classical method). The "almost exact" method turns out to have the actual coverage probability very close to the nominal level of confidence. The coverage probability of the bootstrap method is slightly lower than the nominal level, and the length of the intervals is more variable (probably due to additional variability introduced by the bootstrap sampling). On the other hand, the bootstrap method is more flexible and can be easily adapted to different parametric models, beyond the Poisson/Bernoulli model considered here. These issues go beyond the scope of this paper and will be subject to further studies.

23.7. References

Blair, G. and Imai, K. (2012). Statistical analysis of list experiments. *Political Analysis*, 20(1), 47–77.

Comsa, M. and Postelnicu, C. (2013). Measuring social desirability effects on self-reported turnout using the item-count technique. *International Journal of Public Opinion Research*, 25(2), 153–172.

Dempster, A.P., Laird, N.M., Rubin, D.B. (1977). Maximum-likelihood from incomplete data via the EM algorithm. *Journal of the Royal Statistical Society Series B*, 39(1), 1–22.

Holbrook, A.L. and Krosnick, J.A. (2010). Social desirability bias in voter turnout reports: Tests using the item count technique. *Public Opinion Quarterly*, 74(1), 37–67.

Imai, K. (2011). Multivariate regression analysis for the item count technique. *Journal of the American Statistical Association*, 106(494), 407–416.

Jaworski, S. and Zieliński, W. (2023). The optimal sample size in the crosswise model for sensitive questions. *Applicationes Mathematicae*, 50(1), 21–34.

Kowalczyk, B., Niemiro, W., Wieczorkowski, R. (2023). Item count technique with a continuous or count control variable for analyzing sensitive questions in surveys. *Journal of Survey Statistics and Methodology*, 11(4), 919–941.

Krumpal, I. (2013). Determinants of social desirability bias in sensitive surveys: A literature review. *Quality and Quantity*, 47, 2025–2047.

Kuha, J. and Jackson, J. (2014). The item count method for sensitive survey questions: Modeling criminal behavior. *Journal of the Royal Statistical Society Series C*, 63(2), 321–341.

Kuklinski, J.H., Cobb, M.D., Gilens, M. (1997). Racial attitudes and the 'new south'. *Journal of Politics*, 59, 323–349.

Lewis, J., Brown, P., Tsagris, M. (2024). Densities and sampling for the Skellam distribution. R package version 0.2.3 [Online]. Available at: https://r-forge.r-project.org/projects/healthqueues/.

Miller, J.D. (1994). A new survey technique for studying deviant behavior. PhD Thesis, The George Washington University, Washington, D.C.

R Core Team (2016). *R: A Language and Environment for Statistical Computing*. R Foundation for Statistical Computing, Vienna [Online]. Available at: https://www.r-project.org/.

Raghavarao, D. and Federer, W.T. (1979). Block total response as an alternative to the randomized response method in surveys. *Journal of the Royal Statistical Society Series B*, 41(1), 40–45.

Silver, B.D., Anderson, B.A., Abramson, P.R. (1986). Who overreports voting? *American Political Science Review*, 80(2), 613–624.

Tian, G.L., Tang, M.L., Wu, Q., Liu, Y. (2017). Poisson and negative binomial item count techniques for surveys with sensitive question. *Statistical Methods in Medical Research*, 26(2), 931–947.

Trappmann, M., Krumpal, I., Kirchner, A., Jann, B. (2014). Item sum: A new technique for asking quantitative sensitive questions. *Journal of Survey Statistics and Methodology*, 2(1), 58–77.

24

Spreading Diseases Models Under Vaccination

To understand how an epidemic spreads, it becomes necessary to analyze and test epidemiological models. Mathematical epidemiological models can contribute to disease reduction and control, thereby aiding real-time decision-making during an epidemic. In this work, a series of epidemiological models were analyzed in order to control the spread of infectious diseases in a population. The analysis of the models SEIVR and SIRV that take vaccination into account aims to investigate the effectiveness of vaccination in the population.

The results of this analysis showed us that as the number of vulnerable people decreases, the number of recovered people increases. The population of the exposed shows mobility similar to that of the infected, showing a slowdown in the population of the latter. The addition of the vaccinated compartment led to a decrease in the number of infected as the number of vaccinated individuals increased.

24.1. Introduction

An outbreak of disease that is characterized as an epidemic appears in one population of people in a given period of time to such an extent that it exceeds "expected" or "predicted" limits. An epidemic occurs when host immunity to either a known pathogen or a new pathogen suddenly decreases below the endemic equilibrium and crosses the threshold transmission.

A term that is linked to the epidemic is the term pandemic. A pandemic is essentially a type of infectious disease (epidemic), but it spreads rapidly over a large area or on a global scale, thus threatening almost the entire population.

Chapter written by S. ZIMERAS and D. VASILEIOU.

In general, modeling an epidemic consists of three components (Abbey 1952; Ackerman et al. 1984; Allen and Allen 2003; Thieme 2003):

– understanding the mechanisms of propagation as well as how different parameters have the potential to influence its development epidemic;

– the ability to predict the evolution of the epidemic;

– understanding the mechanisms to deal with the epidemic to prevent its possible spread and avoid the risk of conversion into a pandemic.

The mechanisms of spread are responsible for how the virus is transmitted which, depending on the species, has the ability to spread in a different way (Thieme 2003).

24.2. Modeling epidemic disease

Epidemic models aim to predict the evolution of epidemics. Mathematical models play an important role in comparison, planning, implementation, evaluation and optimization of various methods of detection, prevention, treatment and control programs and these contribute significantly to the fight against spread and control of infectious diseases. Due to the uncertainty and often unreliability of clinical data, the prediction of the actual evolution of the epidemic is rather difficult, if not impossible (Thieme 2003; Hikmah et al. 2023)

The accuracy of epidemiological model predictions is highly dependent on the quality of the parameters input to the model. If the data quality is good, the model can accurately describe the situation.

The *infectious period of a virus* is characterized mainly by its capacity of being transmitted to the community. As is known, the behavior of each virus is different with the result that some diseases are more contagious than others, and with a different duration.

Contact probability is defined as the average probability that an infected person will come in contact with a healthy person.

The *medium of transmission* is the way a virus is transmitted from one person to another.

Vaccination is the administration of a vaccine to help the immune system develop immunity from a disease. Vaccination is the most effective method of preventing infectious diseases. Models are most often run with ordinary differential equations (which are deterministic), but can also be used with a stochastic (random) framework.

Models try to predict how a disease spreads, the total number of infected, or the duration of an epidemic, and to estimate various epidemiological parameters such as reproductive number. A disease's main characteristics are as follows:

– transmission rate;

– healing rate;

– type of transmission;

– virus dynamics;

– influence on the organism;

– immunity.

The general structure of an epidemic model is shown in Figure 24.1.

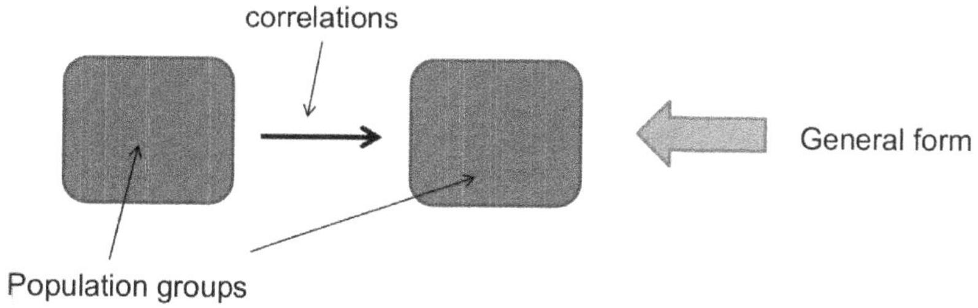

Figure 24.1. *General form of an epidemic model*

– *Susceptible*: this is symbolized by S. This class includes people in the population who are healthy but can become infected.

– *Exposed people in the latent period (Exposed)*: this is symbolized by E. This class includes vulnerable people who are infected but are still not able to transmit the disease during a period which is characterized as latent.

– *Infected*: this is symbolized by I. This class includes people who are infected with a disease and are carriers of it during a period designated as an infection period.

– *Immunized (Removed)*: this is symbolized by R. This class includes people who have either been cured, become immune or have died. For a stable population, no deaths from disease and so this class is for people who have recovered and acquired immunity (Thieme 2003).

24.3. Vaccination models analysis

24.4. SEIVR model

The SEIVR model using differential equations considers the following populations: susceptible (S); exposed without showing symptoms (E); actively infected (I); regressive (R); that is, the cured and the dead, and vaccinated (V).

In this model, we will need to make two biological assumptions. In the first, we assume that people who get vaccinated are selected by people who have not been exposed to the virus or have not been immunized against it. In the second, we assume that for individuals belonging to the vaccinated compartment, the vaccine may not be fully protective (vaccine failure). In this case, we will assume that vaccinated individuals become infected when exposed to the virus.

The model representation is given in Figure 24.2 with N(t) = S(t) + E(t) + I(t) + V(t) + R(t).

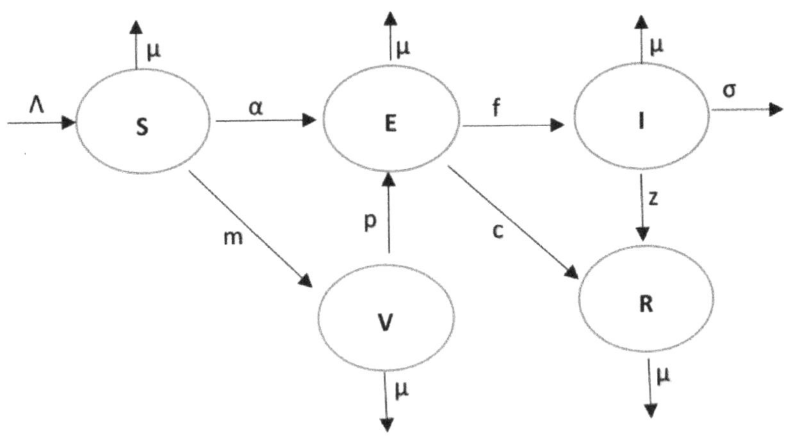

Figure 24.2. *Model representation of SEIVR*

So, the equations that describe the epidemic model are as follows (Binuyo et al. 2014; Shadabfar et al. 2021; Mahata et al. 2022):

$$\frac{dS}{dt} = \Lambda - (\alpha E + m + \mu) S$$

$$\frac{dE}{dt} = \alpha SE + pVE - (fI + c + \mu)E$$

$$\frac{dI}{dt} = fEI - (z + \mu + \sigma)I$$

$$\frac{dV}{dt} = mS - (pE + \mu)V$$

$$\frac{dR}{dt} = zI + cE - \mu R$$

with $S(0) = S_0, E(0) = E_0, I(0) = I_0, V(0) = V_0, R(0) = R_0$. Also S(t), E(t), I(t), V(t), R(t) are considered as continues functions for t > 0. The parameters for the models are as follows:

- population (N);
- awareness rate (Λ);
- transition rate from sensitive individuals to exposed individuals (α);
- vaccination rate (m);
- rate at which the exposed persons become infected (f);
- disease exposure rate for vaccinated individuals (p);
- recovery rate of infected individuals (z);
- natural death rate (μ);
- recovery rate of exposed individuals (c);
- mortality related to disease (σ).

People who have been exposed to the virus but have no symptoms are increasing with a fast rate in the first days and then show a decreasing rate course. The patient population shows a similar trend.

The vulnerable individuals are drastically reduced within the first five days, while in contrast, the recoveries are increasing at a small but steady rate.

The people who have been vaccinated initially show a small increase and then decrease at a very slow pace (Figure 24.3).

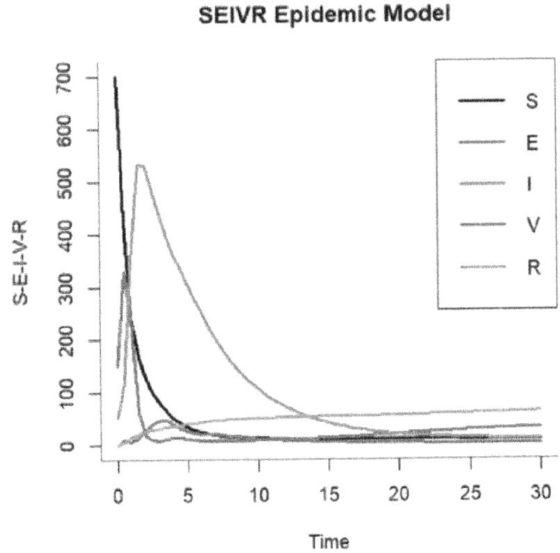

Figure 24.3. *SEIVR epidemic model graph. For a color version of this figure, see www.iste.co.uk/dimotikalis/data5.zip*

24.5. SIRV model

The SIRV model includes the compartments of the susceptible (S), the infected (I), the repatriates (R), that is, those who have recovered from the infection or deaths, and the vaccinated (V).

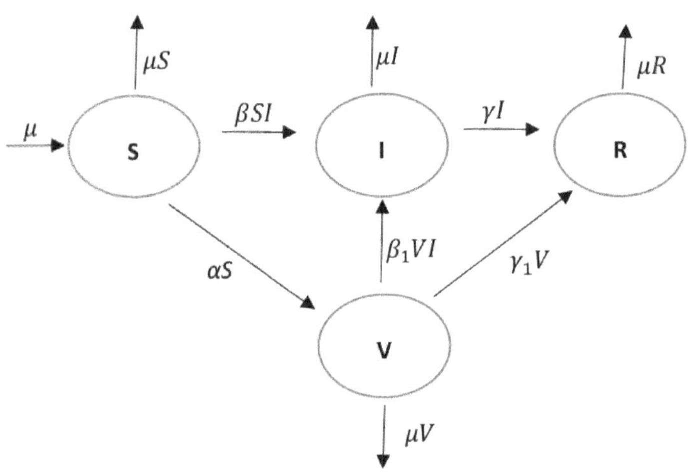

Figure 24.4. *Model representation of SIRV*

Atoms in group V are different from those in both S and R. During vaccination, the immune system will create antibodies against the disease because the vaccine doses are taken during this process. However, it may not be at a fully protective level. There will need to be some fixed amount of time in between doses to complete the vaccination process by achieving one sufficient level of antibodies to protect the organism.

We assume that the birth rate and the death rate from natural causes are equal, and denoted as m. The transmission rate of the virus with those having the infection is transmitted to the susceptible, denoted by b. The infected heal/remove is at rate c. Recovered individuals are supposed to have immunity (so-called natural immunity) against the disease. We define α as the rate at which susceptible individuals are vaccinated. They will become immune through vaccines either during or after the end of the vaccination process. They will acquire immunity at an average rate γ_1 and they will be moved to the recovered section. The average time for the acquisition of immunity is $1/\gamma_1$.

We will not separate immunity from immunity acquired through vaccines, because the latter can last for a long time (Figure 24.4). The $\beta_1 < \beta$ because the vaccinated have either acquired partial immunity during the embolization process or they can recognize the features transmission and therefore avoid/reduce contacts with infected persons.

So, the equations that describe the epidemic model are given as (Liu et al. 2008):

$$\frac{dS}{dt} = \mu - \mu S - \beta SI - \alpha S$$

$$\frac{dI}{dt} = \beta SI + \beta_1 VI - \gamma I - \mu I$$

$$\frac{dR}{dt} = \gamma_1 V + \gamma I - \mu R$$

$$\frac{dV}{dt} = \alpha S - \beta_1 VI - \gamma_1 V - \mu V$$

with $S(0) = S_0, E(0) = E_0, I(0) = I_0, V(0) = V_0, R(0) = R_0$. Also, $\alpha > 0$ and $\mu, \beta, \beta_1, \gamma, \gamma_1 > 0$.

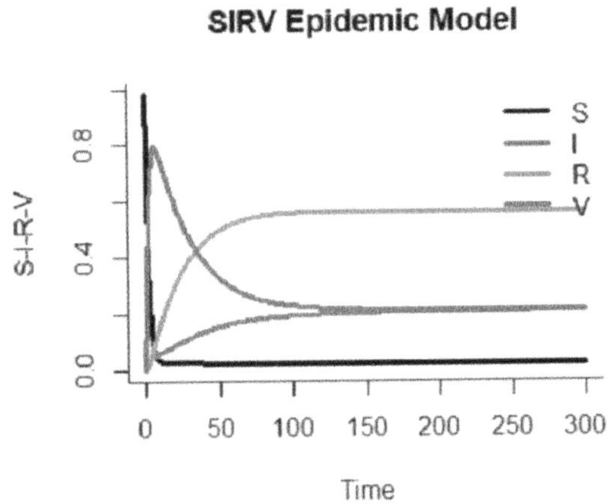

Figure 24.5. *SIVR epidemic model graph. For a color version of this figure, see www.iste.co.uk/dimotikalis/data5.zip*

We note in the above graph that both infected and recovered individuals are increasing and gradually starting to stabilize after the first 100 days. The vulnerable population dramatically decreases from the very first days. Finally, we note that the inoculated, after rising sharply, begin to decline until they also stabilize after 100 days (Figure 24.5).

24.6. Conclusions

To understand how an epidemic spreads, it becomes necessary to analyze and test epidemiological models. The mathematical epidemiological models can contribute to the reduction and fight the disease, thus helping decision-making in real time during an epidemic.

In this chapter, a series of epidemiological models were analyzed in order to control the spread of infectious diseases in a population. The analysis of SEIVR and SIRV, models that take vaccination into account, was done through simulations with the goal of investigation of vaccination effectiveness in the population. The results of this analysis showed us that as the number of susceptible individuals decreases, the number of recoveries increases. The population of exposed exhibits motility similar to that of infected, showing a slowdown in the population of the latter. The addition of the vaccinated led to a decrease in the number of infected as the number of vaccinated individuals increased.

24.7. References

Abbey, H. (1952). An examination of the Reed–Frost theory of epidemics. *Human Biology*, 24, 201–233.

Ackerman, E., Elveback, L.R., Fox, J.P. (1984). *Simulation of Infectious Disease Epidemics*. Charles C. Thomas, Springfield, IL.

Allen, L.J.S. and Allen, E.J. (2003). A comparison of three different stochastic population models with regard to persistence time. *Theoretical Population Biology*, 64, 439–449.

Binuyo, A.O., Odejide, S.A., Aregbesola, Y.S.O. (2014). Numerical study of a SEIVR epidemic model among infants with vaccination and temporary immune protection. *Journal of Applied and Computational Mathematics*, 3(1). doi: 10.4172/2168-9679.1000151.

Hikmah, H., Nisardi, M.R., Slim, S.M.S. (2023). Mathematical model of Covid-19 with quarantine and vaccination. *Jurnal Matematika, Statistika dan Komputasi*, 19(2), 266–285.

Liu, X., Takeuchi, Y., Iwami, S. (2008). SVIR epidemic models with vaccination strategies. *Journal of Theoretical Biology*, 253(1), 1–11.

Mahata, A., Paul, S., Mukherjee, S., Das, M., Roy, B. (2022). Dynamics of Caputo fractional order SEIRV epidemic model with optimal control and stability analysis. *International Journal of Applied and Computational Mathematics*, 8(1), 28.

Shadabfar, M., Mahsuli, M., Sioofy Khoojine, A., Hosseini, V.R. (2021). Time-variant reliability-based prediction of COVID-19 spread using extended SEIVR model and Monte Carlo sampling. *Results in Physics*, 26, 104364.

Thieme, H.R. (2003). *Mathematics in Population Biology*. Princeton University Press, Princeton.

List of Authors

Volodymyr ANISIMOV
Center for Design & Analysis
Amgen
London
UK

Alexandros APOSTOLAKIS
Department of Business
Administration and Tourism
Hellenic Mediterranean University
Heraklion
Crete
Greece

Ioanna ATSALAKI
Production & Management
Engineering
Technical University of Crete
Greece

George S. ATSALAKIS
Production & Management
Engineering
Technical University of Crete
Greece

Konstantinos BLAZAKIS
School of Electrical and Computer
Engineering
Technical University of Crete
Greece

Paolo BONFINI
Quantum Innovation Pc
Greece
and
Alma-Sistemi Srl
Guidonia
Italy

Frederico CAEIRO
NOVA School of Science and
Technology (NOVA FCT)
Caparica Campus
University of Lisbon
Portugal

Raffaella CALATI
Department of Psychology
University of Milano-Bicocca
Milan
Italy
and
Department of Adult Psychiatry
Nîmes University Hospital
France

Matthew CAMILLERI
Department of Statistics and Operations Research
Faculty of Science
University of Malta
Msida
Malta

Anastasia CHARALAMPI
Department of Social Policy
Panteion University of Social and Political Sciences
Athens
Greece

Franca CRIPPA
Department of Psychology
University of Milano-Bicocca
Milan
Italy

Kainaat DANYAL
Department of Psychology
Jamia Milla Islamia
Jamia Nagar
New Delhi
India

Yiannis DIMOTIKALIS
Department of Management Science and Technology
Hellenic Mediterranean University
Heraklion
Crete
Greece

Adelaide FIGUEIREDO
Faculdade de Economia (FEP)
Universidade do Porto
and
INESC TEC
Universidade do Porto
Portugal

Fernanda Otília FIGUEIREDO
Faculdade de Economia (FEP)
Universidade do Porto
and
Centro de Estatística e Aplicações (CEAUL)
Universidade de Lisboa
Portugal

Christos FLOROS
Department of Accounting and Finance
Hellenic Mediterranean University
Heraklion
Crete
Greece

M. Ivette GOMES
CEAUL, DEIO, FCUL
Universidade de Lisboa
Portugal

Giulia GOTTI
Department of Psychology
University of Milano-Bicocca
Milan
Italy

Erika GRAMMATICA
Department of Statistics and Quantitative Methods
University of Milano-Bicocca
Italy

Francesca GRESELIN
Department of Statistics and Quantitative Methods
University of Milano-Bicocca
Italy

Maria GRYDAKI
Department of Accounting and Finance
Hellenic Mediterranean University
Crete
Greece

Lígia HENRIQUES-RODRIGUES
School of Science and Technology (ECT-UE) and CIMA
Universidade de Évora
Portugal

Monique Borg INGUANEZ
Department of Statistics and Operations Research
Faculty of Science
University of Malta
Msida
Malta

Margarita IOANNIDOU
Hellenic Open University
Greece

Naved IQBAL
Department of Psychology
Jamia Milla Islamia
Jamia Nagar
New Delhi
India

Ioanna KALLIAMPAKOU
Department of Management Science and Technology
University of Patras
Greece

Gerasimos KALOGERATOS
Department of Management Science and Technology
University of Patras
Greece

Derya KARAGÖZ
Department of Statistics & Operations Research
Faculty of Science
University of Malta
Msida
Malta

Emmanuel KARAPIDAKIS
Institute of Energy, Environment and Climate Change
Hellenic Mediterranean University
Crete
Greece

Yiannis KATSIGIANNIS
Department of Electrical and Computer Engineering
Hellenic Mediterranean University
Crete
Greece

Adele H. MARSHALL
School of Mathematics and Physics
Mathematical Sciences Research Centre
Queen's University of Belfast
UK
and
Joint Research Centre in AI for Health and Wellness
Faculty of Business and IT
Ontario Tech University
Oshawa
Canada

George MATALLIOTAKIS
Hellenic Mediterranean University
Crete
Greece

Ayana MATEUS
NOVA School of Science and Technology (NOVA FCT)
Caparica Campus
University of Lisbon
Portugal

Aristea MAVROGIANNI
Department of Philosophy
Faculty of Letters
University of Crete
Greece

Catherine MICHALOPOULOU
Department of Social Policy
Panteion University of Social and Political Sciences
Athens
Greece

Hannah MITCHELL
School of Mathematics and Physics
Mathematical Sciences Research Centre
Queen's University of Belfast
UK

Wojciech NIEMIRO
Institute of Applied Mathematics and Mechanics
University of Warsaw
Poland

Marios NIKOLOGIANNIS
Institute of Energy, Environment and Climate Change
Hellenic Mediterranean University
Crete
Greece

Lucas OLIVER
University of Bath
UK

Neir Antunes PAES
Federal University of Paraíba
João Pessoa
Brazil

Ioannis PASSAS
Department of Business Administration and Tourism
Hellenic Mediterranean University
Heraklion
Crete
Greece

Elena ŘÍHOVÁ
Department of Quantitative Methods
ŠKODA Auto University
Czech Republic

Nikolaos SCHETAKIS
School of Production Engineering and Management
Technical University of Crete
and
Quantum Innovation Pc
Greece

Christos H. SKIADAS
Technical University of Crete
Chania
and
ISAST
Athens
Greece

Georgios STAVRAKAKIS
School of Electrical and Computer Engineering
Technical University of Crete
Greece

David SUDA
Department of Statistics and Operations Research
Faculty of Science
University of Malta
Msida
Malta

Kornélia SVAČINOVÁ
Department of Quantitative Methods
ŠKODA Auto University
Czech Republic

Leonidas THEODORAKOPOULOS
Department of Management Science and Technology
University of Patras
Greece

Alexandra THEODOROPOULOU
Department of Management Science and Technology
University of Patras
Greece

Grażyna TRZPIOT
Department of Demography and Business Statistics
University of Economics in Katowice
Poland

Moustapha Aminou TUKUR
Department of Statistics
Faculty of Science
Yildiz Technical University
Istanbul
Turkey

Eleni VASILAKI
Department of Primary Education
School of Education
University of Crete
Greece

D. VASILEIOU
Department of Statistics and Actuarial-Financial Mathematics
University of the Aegean
Samos
Greece

Nikos VENIANAKIS
Department of Physics
University of Crete
Greece

Dimitrios VORTELINOS
Department of Accounting and Finance
Hellenic Mediterranean University
Heraklion
Crete
Greece

Aggeliki YFANTI
Research Centre for Greek Society
Academy of Athens
Greece

Fotini ZAKKA
Department of Management Science and Technology
University of Patras
Greece

Marta ZALEWSKA
Department of Environmental Hazards Prevention, Allergology and Immunology
Medical University of Warsaw
Poland

Mariangela ZENGA
Department of Statistics and Quantitative Methods
University of Milano-Bicocca
and
Bicocca Applied Statistics Center
University of Milano-Bicocca
Italy

S. ZIMERAS
Department of Statistics and Actuarial-Financial Mathematics
University of the Aegean
Samos
Greece

Index

G, H

I, L

M, N

O, P

Q, R

S, T

U, V

W, X

Other titles from

ISTE

in

Innovation, Entrepreneurship and Management

2025

GRENIER Corinne, FRANKLIN-JOHNSON Elizabeth, CAJAIBA-SANTANA Giovany
Promoting a More Inclusive Society for Dependent or Disabled People: New Paradigms
(Health and Innovation – Volume 6)

CHABAUT Didier, EYNAUD Philippe, RAULET-CROSET Nathalie
Reinventing Territories through Solidarity
(Solidarity-based Management and Organizations – Volume 1)

GORIA Stéphane
Serious Games and Innovation Gains: Think Innovation through Games
(Innovation in Engineering and Technology – Volume 9)

KLESZCZOWSKI Julien, RAULET-CROSET Nathalie
Social Impact in Solidarity-based Organizations: Values and Assessment Practices
(Solidarity-based Management and Organizations – Volume 2)

2024

AÏT-EL-HADJ Smaïl
Environmental Transition and Technological Change
(Smart Innovation – Volume 43)

ALBERT-CROMARIAS Anne, ALBERTINI Thérèse, TERRAMORSI Patrice
Collective Dynamics and Territories: 9 Issues for Competitive, Innovative and Sustainable Territories
(Territorial Entrepreneurship and Innovation – Volume 3)

BRASSEUR Martine, BARTOLI Annie, CHABAUD Didier, GROUIEZ Pascal, ROUET Gilles
Inclusive Territories 2: Role of Institutions and Local Actors
(Territorial Entrepreneurship and Innovation Set – Volume 2)

COURIE-LEMEUR Aline
Innovation, Collective Intelligence and Resiliency in Healthcare Organizations
(Health and Innovation Set – Volume 4)

DARTIGUEPEYROU Carine, SALOFF-COSTE Michel
Futures in Action: Strategic Anticipations and Deployments in Organizations Facing the Future
(Innovation and Technology Set – Volume 19)

DELÉCOLLE Thierry, JACOB Florence, PRIM-ALLAZ Isabelle
New Frontiers of Customer Strategy: Managing Sustainable, Environmental and Ethical Transitions

DIMOTIKALIS Yannis, SKIADIS Christos H.
Data Analysis and Related Applications 3: Theory and Practice – New Approaches
(Big Data, Artificial Intelligence and Data Analysis Set – Volume 11)
Data Analysis and Related Applications 4: New Approaches
(Big Data, Artificial Intelligence and Data Analysis Set – Volume 12)

FLORA Luigi, GRENIER Corinne, PONISGNON Frédéric
Experience in Healthcare Innovation: Fad or New Paradigm?
(Health and Innovation – Volume 5)

MERLIN-BROGNIART Céline
Functional Economy: Economic Models, Challenges and Innovation Dynamics
(Smart Innovation – Volume 44)

PARMENTIER Guy
Organizational Creative Capabilities: Management Factors, Processes and Devices
(Organizational Creativity Set – Volume 1)

RUIZ Émilie
The Creative Capabilities of Open Organizations
(Organizational Creativity Set – Volume 2)

VERNIER Marie-France
Eco-Design and Ecological Transition: Questioning the Economic Model
(Smart Innovation Set – Volume 42)

2023

BOLLINGER Sophie
Management Control and Creativity: Challenges of Managing Innovation Processes
(Smart Innovation Set – Volume 41)

BOUVIER-PATRON Paul
Frugal Innovation and Innovative Creation
(Smart Innovation Set – Volume 40)

BRASSEUR Martine, BARTOLI Annie, CHABAUD Didier, GROUIEZ Pascal, ROUET Gilles
Inclusive Territories 1: Role of Enterprises and Organizations
(Territorial Entrepreneurship and Innovation Set – Volume 1)

CASADELLA Vanessa, UZUNIDIS Dimitri
Agri-Innovations and Development Challenges: Engineering, Value Chains and Socio-economic Models
(Innovation in Engineering and Technology Set – Volume 8)

DARTIGUEPEYROU Carine, SALOFF-COSTE Michel
Futures: The Great Turn
(Innovation and Technology Set – Volume 18)

PEYROUX Élisabeth, RAIMOND Christine, VIEL Vincent, LAVIE Émilie
Development and Territorial Restructuring in an Era of Global Change: Theories, Approaches and Future Research Perspectives

SAULAIS Pierre
Knowledge and Ideation: Inventive Knowledge Analysis for Ideation Stimulation
(Innovation and Technology Set – Volume 17)

2022

AOUINAÏT Camille
Open Innovation Strategies
(Smart Innovation Set – Volume 39)

BOUCHÉ Geneviève
Productive Economy, Contributory Economy: Governance Tools for the Third Millennium
(Innovation and Technology Set – Volume 15)

BRUYÈRE Christelle
Caring Management in Health Organizations: A Lever for Crisis Management
(Health and Innovation Set – Volume 3)

ENJOLRAS Manon
Innovation and Export: The Joint Challenge of the Small Company
(Smart Innovation Set – Volume 37)

FLEURY Sylvain, RICHIR Simon
Immersive Technologies to Accelerate Innovation: How Virtual and Augmented Reality Enables the Co-Creation of Concepts
(Smart Innovation Set – Volume 38)

HELLER David
Valuation of the Liability Structure by Real Options
(Modern Finance, Management Innovation and Economic Growth Set – Volume 5)

MATHIEU Valérie
A Customer-oriented Manager for B2B Services: Principles and Implementation

MORALES Lucía, DZEVER Sam, TAYLOR Robert
Asia-Europe Industrial Connectivity in Times of Crisis
(Innovation and Technology Set – Volume 16)

NOËL Florent, SCHMIDT Géraldine
Employability and Industrial Mutations: Between Individual Trajectories and Organizational Strategic Planning
(Technological Changes and Human Resources Set – Volume 4)

DE SAINT JULIEN Odile
The Innovation Ecosystem as a Source of Value Creation: A Value Creation Lever for Open Innovation
(Diverse and Global Perspectives on Value Creation Set – Volume 4)

SALOFF-COSTE Michel
Innovation Ecosystems: The Future of Civilizations and the Civilization of the Future
(Innovation and Technology Set – Volume 14)

SOULÉ Bastien, HALLÉ Julie, VIGNAL Bénédicte, BOUTROY Éric, NIER Olivier
Innovation in Sport: Innovation Trajectories and Process Optimization
(Smart Innovation Set – Volume 35)

VALLIER Estelle
Innovation in Clusters: Science–Industry Relationships in the Face of Forced Advancement
(Smart Innovation Set – Volume 36)

VAYRE Emilie
Digitalization of Work: New Spaces and New Working Times
(Technological Changes and Human Resources Set – Volume 5)

ZAFEIRIS Konstantinos N, SKIADIS Christos H, DIMOTIKALIS Yannis, KARAGRIGORIOU Alex, KARAGRIGORIOU-VONTA Christina
Data Analysis and Related Applications 1: Computational, Algorithmic and Applied Economic Data Analysis
(Big Data, Artificial Intelligence and Data Analysis Set – Volume 9)
Data Analysis and Related Applications 2: Multivariate, Health and Demographic Data Analysis
(Big Data, Artificial Intelligence and Data Analysis Set – Volume 10)

2021

ACH Yves-Alain, RMADI-SAÏD Sandra
Financial Information and Brand Value: Reflections, Challenges and Limitations

ARCADE Jacques
Strategic Engineering
(Innovation and Technology Set – Volume 11)

BÉRANGER Jérôme, RIZOULIÈRES Roland
The Digital Revolution in Health
(Health and Innovation Set – Volume 2)

BOBILLIER CHAUMON Marc-Eric
Digital Transformations in the Challenge of Activity and Work: Understanding and Supporting Technological Changes
(Technological Changes and Human Resources Set – Volume 3)

BUCLET Nicolas
Territorial Ecology and Socio-ecological Transition
(Smart Innovation Set – Volume 34)

DIMOTIKALIS Yannis, KARAGRIGORIOU Alex, PARPOULA Christina, SKIADIS Christos H
Applied Modeling Techniques and Data Analysis 1: Computational Data Analysis Methods and Tools
(Big Data, Artificial Intelligence and Data Analysis Set - Volume 7)
Applied Modeling Techniques and Data Analysis 2: Financial, Demographic, Stochastic and Statistical Models and Methods
(Big Data, Artificial Intelligence and Data Analysis Set – Volume 8)

DISPAS Christophe, KAYANAKIS Georges, SERVEL Nicolas, STRIUKOVA Ludmila
Innovation and Financial Markets
(Innovation between Risk and Reward Set – Volume 7)

GAUDIN Thierry, MAUREL Marie-Christine, POMEROL Jean-Charles
Chance, Calculation and Life

GASMI Nacer
Corporate Innovation Strategies: Corporate Social Responsibility and Shared Value Creation
(Smart Innovation Set – Volume 33)

GIORGINI Pierre
The Contributory Revolution
(Innovation and Technology Set – Volume 13)

GOGLIN Christian
Emotions and Values in Equity Crowdfunding Investment Choices 1: Transdisciplinary Theoretical Approach
Emotions and Values in Equity Crowdfunding Investment Choices 2: Modeling and Empirical Study

GRENIER Corinne, OIRY Ewan
Altering Frontiers: Organizational Innovations in Healthcare
(Health and Innovation Set – Volume 1)

GUERRIER Claudine
Security and Its Challenges in the 21st Century
(Innovation and Technology Set – Volume 12)

HELLER David
Performance of Valuation Methods in Financial Transactions (Modern Finance, Management Innovation and Economic Growth Set – Volume 4)

LEHMANN Paul-Jacques
Liberalism and Capitalism Today

LIMA Marcos
Entrepreneurship and Innovation Education: Frameworks and Tools (Smart Innovation Set – Volume 32)

MACHADO Carolina, DAVIM J. Paulo
Sustainable Management for Managers and Engineers

MEUNIER François-Xavier
Dual Innovation Systems: Concepts, Tools and Methods (Smart Innovation Set – Volume 31)

UZUNIDIS Dimitri, KASMI Fedoua, ADATTO Laurent
Innovation Economics, Engineering and Management Handbook 1: Main Themes
Innovation Economics, Engineering and Management Handbook 2: Special Themes

2020

ANDREOSSO-O'CALLAGHAN Bernadette, DZEVER Sam, JAUSSAUD Jacques, TAYLOR Robert
Sustainable Development and Energy Transition in Europe and Asia (Innovation and Technology Set – Volume 9)

BEN SLIMANE Sonia, M'HENNI Hatem
Entrepreneurship and Development: Realities and Future Prospects (Smart Innovation Set – Volume 30)

CHOUTEAU Marianne, FOREST Joëlle, NGUYEN Céline
Innovation for Society: The P.S.I. Approach (Smart Innovation Set – Volume 28)

CORON Clotilde
Quantifying Human Resources: Uses and Analysis
(Technological Changes and Human Resources Set – Volume 2)

CORON Clotilde, GILBERT Patrick
Technological Change
(Technological Changes and Human Resources Set – Volume 1)

CERDIN Jean-Luc, PERETTI Jean-Marie
The Success of Apprenticeships: Views of Stakeholders on Training and Learning (Human Resources Management Set – Volume 3)

DELCHET-COCHET Karen
Circular Economy: From Waste Reduction to Value Creation
(Economic Growth Set – Volume 2)

DIDAY Edwin, GUAN Rong, SAPORTA Gilbert, WANG Huiwen
Advances in Data Science
(Big Data, Artificial Intelligence and Data Analysis Set – Volume 4)

DOS SANTOS PAULINO Victor
Innovation Trends in the Space Industry
(Smart Innovation Set – Volume 25)

GUILHON Bernard
Venture Capital and the Financing of Innovation
(Innovation Between Risk and Reward Set – Volume 6)

JURCZENKO Emmanuel
Machine Learning for Asset Management: New Developments and Financial Applications

LATOUCHE Pascal
Open Innovation: Human Set-up
(Innovation and Technology Set – Volume 10)

MAKRIDES Andreas, KARAGRIGORIOU Alex, SKIADAS Christos H.
Data Analysis and Applications 3: Computational, Classification, Financial, Statistical and Stochastic Methods
(Big Data, Artificial Intelligence and Data Analysis Set – Volume 5)
Data Analysis and Applications 4: Financial Data Analysis and Methods
(Big Data, Artificial Intelligence and Data Analysis Set – Volume 6)

MASSOTTE Pierre, CORSI Patrick
Complex Decision-Making in Economy and Finance

MICHAUD Thomas
Science Fiction and Innovation Design
(Innovation in Engineering and Technology Set – Volume 6)

MONINO Jean-Louis
Data Control: Major Challenge for the Digital Society
(Smart Innovation Set – Volume 29)

MORLAT Clément
Sustainable Productive System: Eco-development versus Sustainable Development (Smart Innovation Set – Volume 26)

SAULAIS Pierre, ERMINE Jean-Louis
Knowledge Management in Innovative Companies 2: Understanding and Deploying a KM Plan within a Learning Organization
(Smart Innovation Set – Volume 27)

UZUNIDIS Dimitri
Systemic Innovation: Entrepreneurial Strategies and Market Dynamics

2019

AMENDOLA Mario, GAFFARD Jean-Luc
Disorder and Public Concern Around Globalization

BARBAROUX Pierre
Disruptive Technology and Defence Innovation Ecosystems
(Innovation in Engineering and Technology Set – Volume 5)

DOU Henri, JUILLET Alain, CLERC Philippe
Strategic Intelligence for the Future 1: A New Strategic and Operational Approach
Strategic Intelligence for the Future 2: A New Information Function Approach

FRIKHA Azza
Measurement in Marketing: Operationalization of Latent Constructs

FRIMOUSSE Soufyane
Innovation and Agility in the Digital Age
(Human Resources Management Set – Volume 2)

GAY Claudine, SZOSTAK Bérangère L.
Innovation and Creativity in SMEs: Challenges, Evolutions and Prospects
(Smart Innovation Set – Volume 21)

GORIA Stéphane, HUMBERT Pierre, ROUSSEL Benoît
Information, Knowledge and Agile Creativity
(Smart Innovation Set – Volume 22)

HELLER David
Investment Decision-making Using Optional Models
(Economic Growth Set – Volume 2)

HELLER David, DE CHADIRAC Sylvain, HALAOUI Lana, JOUVET Camille
The Emergence of Start-ups
(Economic Growth Set – Volume 1)

HÉRAUD Jean-Alain, KERR Fiona, BURGER-HELMCHEN Thierry
Creative Management of Complex Systems
(Smart Innovation Set – Volume 19)

LATOUCHE Pascal
Open Innovation: Corporate Incubator
(Innovation and Technology Set – Volume 7)

LEHMANN Paul-Jacques
The Future of the Euro Currency

LEIGNEL Jean-Louis, MENAGER Emmanuel, YABLONSKY Serge
Sustainable Enterprise Performance: A Comprehensive Evaluation Method

LIÈVRE Pascal, AUBRY Monique, GAREL Gilles
Management of Extreme Situations: From Polar Expeditions to Exploration-Oriented Organizations

MILLOT Michel
Embarrassment of Product Choices 2: Towards a Society of Well-being

N'GOALA Gilles, PEZ-PÉRARD Virginie, PRIM-ALLAZ Isabelle
Augmented Customer Strategy: CRM in the Digital Age

NIKOLOVA Blagovesta
The RRI Challenge: Responsibilization in a State of Tension with Market Regulation
(Innovation and Responsibility Set – Volume 3)

PELLEGRIN-BOUCHER Estelle, ROY Pierre
Innovation in the Cultural and Creative Industries
(Innovation and Technology Set – Volume 8)

PRIOLON Joël
Financial Markets for Commodities

QUINIOU Matthieu
Blockchain: The Advent of Disintermediation

RAVIX Joël-Thomas, DESCHAMPS Marc
Innovation and Industrial Policies
(Innovation between Risk and Reward Set – Volume 5)

ROGER Alain, VINOT Didier
Skills Management: New Applications, New Questions
(Human Resources Management Set – Volume 1)

SAULAIS Pierre, ERMINE Jean-Louis
Knowledge Management in Innovative Companies 1: Understanding and Deploying a KM Plan within a Learning Organization
(Smart Innovation Set – Volume 23)

SERVAJEAN-HILST Romaric
Co-innovation Dynamics: The Management of Client-Supplier Interactions for Open Innovation
(Smart Innovation Set – Volume 20)

SKIADAS Christos H., BOZEMAN James R.
Data Analysis and Applications 1: Clustering and Regression, Modeling-estimating, Forecasting and Data Mining
(Big Data, Artificial Intelligence and Data Analysis Set – Volume 2)
Data Analysis and Applications 2: Utilization of Results in Europe and Other Topics
(Big Data, Artificial Intelligence and Data Analysis Set – Volume 3)

VIGEZZI Michel
World Industrialization: Shared Inventions, Competitive Innovations and Social Dynamics
(Smart Innovation Set – Volume 24)

2018

BURKHARDT Kirsten
Private Equity Firms: Their Role in the Formation of Strategic Alliances

CALLENS Stéphane
Creative Globalization
(Smart Innovation Set – Volume 16)

CASADELLA Vanessa
Innovation Systems in Emerging Economies: MINT – Mexico, Indonesia, Nigeria, Turkey
(Smart Innovation Set – Volume 18)

CHOUTEAU Marianne, FOREST Joëlle, NGUYEN Céline
Science, Technology and Innovation Culture
(Innovation in Engineering and Technology Set – Volume 3)

CORLOSQUET-HABART Marine, JANSSEN Jacques
Big Data for Insurance Companies
(Big Data, Artificial Intelligence and Data Analysis Set – Volume 1)

CROS Françoise
Innovation and Society
(Smart Innovation Set – Volume 15)

DEBREF Romain
Environmental Innovation and Ecodesign: Certainties and Controversies
(Smart Innovation Set – Volume 17)

DOMINGUEZ Noémie
SME Internationalization Strategies: Innovation to Conquer New Markets

ERMINE Jean-Louis
Knowledge Management: The Creative Loop
(Innovation and Technology Set – Volume 5)

GAUDIN Thierry, LACROIX Dominique, MAUREL Marie-Christine, POMEROL, Jean-Charles
Life Sciences, Information Sciences

GILBERT Patrick, BOBADILLA Natalia, GASTALDI Lise, LE BOULAIRE Martine, LELEBINA Olga
Innovation, Research and Development Management

VAN HOOREBEKE Delphine
The Management of Living Beings or Emo-management

IBRAHIMI Mohammed
Mergers & Acquisitions: Theory, Strategy, Finance

LEMAÎTRE Denis
Training Engineers for Innovation

LÉVY Aldo, BEN BOUHENI Faten, AMMI Chantal
Financial Management: USGAAP and IFRS Standards
(Innovation and Technology Set – Volume 6)

LOISY Catherine, COULET Jean-Claude
Competence and Program-based Approach in Training: Tools for Developing Responsible Activities
Innovation and Responsibility Set – Volume 1)

MILLOT Michel
Embarrassment of Product Choices 1: How to Consume Differently

PANSERA Mario, OWEN Richard
Innovation and Development: The Politics at the Bottom of the Pyramid
(Innovation and Responsibility Set – Volume 2)

RICHEZ Yves
Corporate Talent Detection and Development

SACHETTI Philippe, ZUPPINGER Thibaud
New Technologies and Branding
(Innovation and Technology Set – Volume 4)

SAMIER Henri
Intuition, Creativity, Innovation

TEMPLE Ludovic, COMPAORÉ SAWADOGO Eveline M.F.W.
Innovation Processes in Agro-Ecological Transitions in Developing Countries
(Innovation in Engineering and Technology Set – Volume 2)

UZUNIDIS Dimitri
Collective Innovation Processes: Principles and Practices
(Innovation in Engineering and Technology Set – Volume 4)

2017

AÏT-EL-HADJ Smaïl
The Ongoing Technological System
(Smart Innovation Set – Volume 11)

D'ANDRIA Aude, GABARRET Inés
Building 21st Century Entrepreneurship
(Innovation and Technology Set – Volume 2)

BAUDRY Marc, DUMONT Béatrice
Patents: Prompting or Restricting Innovation?
(Smart Innovation Set – Volume 12)

BÉRARD Céline, TEYSSIER Christine
Risk Management: Lever for SME Development and Stakeholder Value Creation

CHALENÇON Ludivine
Location Strategies and Value Creation of International Mergers and Acquisitions

CHAUVEL Danièle, BORZILLO Stefano
The Innovative Company: An Ill-defined Object
(Innovation between Risk and Reward Set – Volume 1)

CORSI Patrick
Going Past Limits To Growth

DAIDJ Nabyla
Cooperation, Coopetition and Innovation
(Innovation and Technology Set – Volume 3)

FERNEZ-WALCH Sandrine
The Multiple Facets of Innovation Project Management
(Innovation between Risk and Reward Set – Volume 4)

FOREST Joëlle
Creative Rationality and Innovation
(Smart Innovation Set – Volume 14)

GUILHON Bernard
Innovation and Production Ecosystems
(Innovation between Risk and Reward Set – Volume 2)

HAMMOUDI Abdelhakim, DAIDJ Nabyla
Game Theory Approach to Managerial Strategies and Value Creation
(Diverse and Global Perspectives on Value Creation Set – Volume 3)

LALLEMENT Rémi
Intellectual Property and Innovation Protection: New Practices and New Policy Issues
(Innovation between Risk and Reward Set – Volume 3)

LAPERCHE Blandine
Enterprise Knowledge Capital
(Smart Innovation Set – Volume 13)

LEBERT Didier, EL YOUNSI Hafida
International Specialization Dynamics
(Smart Innovation Set – Volume 9)

MAESSCHALCK Marc
Reflexive Governance for Research and Innovative Knowledge
(Responsible Research and Innovation Set – Volume 6)

MASSOTTE Pierre
Ethics in Social Networking and Business 1: Theory, Practice and Current Recommendations
Ethics in Social Networking and Business 2: The Future and Changing Paradigms

MASSOTTE Pierre, CORSI Patrick
Smart Decisions in Complex Systems

MEDINA Mercedes, HERRERO Mónica, URGELLÉS Alicia
Current and Emerging Issues in the Audiovisual Industry
(Diverse and Global Perspectives on Value Creation Set – Volume 1)

MICHAUD Thomas
Innovation, Between Science and Science Fiction
(Smart Innovation Set – Volume 10)

PELLÉ Sophie
Business, Innovation and Responsibility
(Responsible Research and Innovation Set – Volume 7)

SAVIGNAC Emmanuelle
The Gamification of Work: The Use of Games in the Workplace

SUGAHARA Satoshi, DAIDJ Nabyla, USHIO Sumitaka
Value Creation in Management Accounting and Strategic Management: An Integrated Approach
(Diverse and Global Perspectives on Value Creation Set –Volume 2)

UZUNIDIS Dimitri, SAULAIS Pierre
Innovation Engines: Entrepreneurs and Enterprises in a Turbulent World
(Innovation in Engineering and Technology Set – Volume 1)

2016

BARBAROUX Pierre, ATTOUR Amel, SCHENK Eric
Knowledge Management and Innovation
(Smart Innovation Set – Volume 6)

BEN BOUHENI Faten, AMMI Chantal, LEVY Aldo
Banking Governance, Performance And Risk-Taking: Conventional Banks Vs Islamic Banks

BOUTILLIER Sophie, CARRÉ Denis, LEVRATTO Nadine
Entrepreneurial Ecosystems
(Smart Innovation Set – Volume 2)

BOUTILLIER Sophie, UZUNIDIS Dimitri
The Entrepreneur
(Smart Innovation Set – Volume 8)

BOUVARD Patricia, SUZANNE Hervé
Collective Intelligence Development in Business

GALLAUD Delphine, LAPERCHE Blandine
Circular Economy, Industrial Ecology and Short Supply Chains
(Smart Innovation Set – Volume 4)

GUERRIER Claudine
Security and Privacy in the Digital Era
(Innovation and Technology Set – Volume 1)

MEGHOUAR Hicham
Corporate Takeover Targets

MONINO Jean-Louis, SEDKAOUI Soraya
Big Data, Open Data and Data Development
(Smart Innovation Set – Volume 3)

MOREL Laure, LE ROUX Serge
Fab Labs: Innovative User
(Smart Innovation Set – Volume 5)

PICARD Fabienne, TANGUY Corinne
Innovations and Techno-ecological Transition
(Smart Innovation Set – Volume 7)

2015

CASADELLA Vanessa, LIU Zeting, DIMITRI Uzunidis
Innovation Capabilities and Economic Development in Open Economies
(Smart Innovation Set – Volume 1)

CORLOSQUET-HABART Marine, GEHIN William, JANSSEN Jaques, MANCA Raimondo
Asset and Liabilities Management for Banks and Insurance Companies

CORSI Patrick, MORIN Dominique
Sequencing Apple's DNA

CORSI Patrick, NEAU Erwan
Innovation Capability Maturity Model

FAIVRE-TAVIGNOT Bénédicte
Social Business and Base of the Pyramid

GODÉ Cécile
Team Coordination in Extreme Environments

MAILLARD Pierre
Competitive Quality and Innovation

MASSOTTE Pierre, CORSI Patrick
Operationalizing Sustainability

MASSOTTE Pierre, CORSI Patrick
Sustainability Calling

2014

DUBÉ Jean, LEGROS Diègo
Spatial Econometrics Using Microdata

LESCA Humbert, LESCA Nicolas
Strategic Decisions and Weak Signals

2013

HABART-CORLOSQUET Marine, JANSSEN Jacques, MANCA Raimondo
VaR Methodology for Non-Gaussian Finance

2012

POMEROL Jean-Charles
Decision-Making and Action

SZYLAR Christian
UCITS Handbook

2011

LESCA Nicolas
Environmental Scanning and Sustainable Development

LESCA Nicolas, LESCA Humbert
Weak Signals for Strategic Intelligence: Anticipation Tool for Managers

MERCIER-LAURENT Eunika
Innovation Ecosystems

2010

SZYLAR Christian
Risk Management under UCITS III/IV

2009

COHEN Corine
Business Intelligence

ZANINETTI Jean-Marc
Sustainable Development in the USA

2008

CORSI Patrick, DULIEU Mike
The Marketing of Technology Intensive Products and Services

DZEVER Sam, JAUSSAUD Jacques, ANDREOSSO Bernadette
Evolving Corporate Structures and Cultures in Asia: Impact of Globalization

2007

AMMI Chantal
Global Consumer Behavior

2006

BOUGHZALA Imed, ERMINE Jean-Louis
Trends in Enterprise Knowledge Management

CORSI Patrick, CHRISTOFOL Hervé, RICHIR Simon, SAMIER Henri
Innovation Engineering: the power of intangible networks

Printed and bound by CPI Group (UK) Ltd, Croydon, CR0 4YY
13/09/2026
14961012-0008